VOL. 2

# ARCHITECTURE
# NOW!

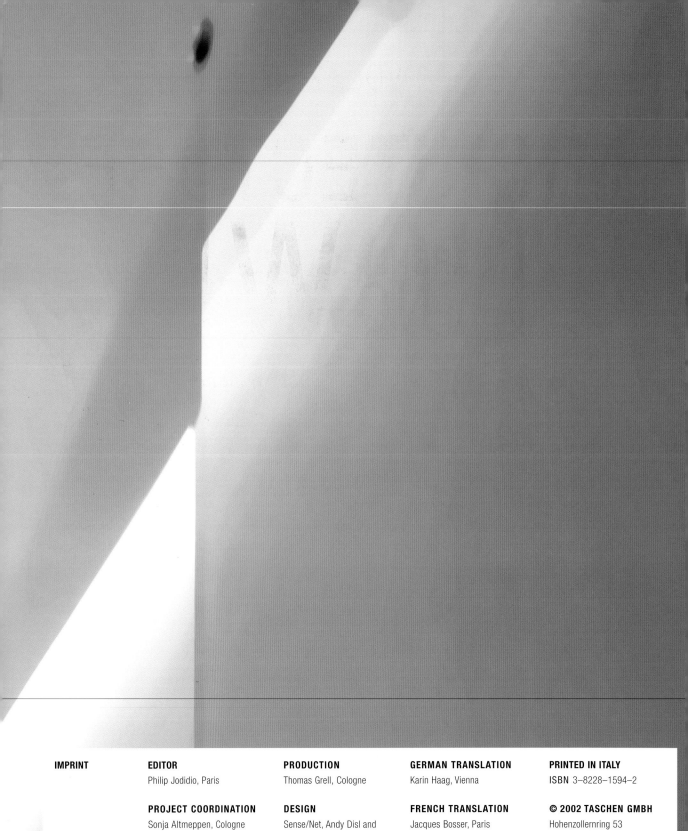

**IMPRINT**

**EDITOR**
Philip Jodidio, Paris

**PROJECT COORDINATION**
Sonja Altmeppen, Cologne

**PRODUCTION**
Thomas Grell, Cologne

**DESIGN**
Sense/Net, Andy Disl and
Birgit Reber, Cologne

**GERMAN TRANSLATION**
Karin Haag, Vienna

**FRENCH TRANSLATION**
Jacques Bosser, Paris

**PRINTED IN ITALY**
ISBN 3–8228–1594–2

**© 2002 TASCHEN GMBH**
Hohenzollernring 53
D – 50672 Köln
**www.taschen.com**

VOL. 2

# ARCHITECTURE NOW!

*Architektur heute / L'architecture d'aujourd'hui*
*Philip Jodidio*

**TASCHEN**

KÖLN LONDON LOS ANGELES MADRID PARIS TOKYO

# CONTENTS

# CONTENTS

# INTRODUCTION

## BACK TO THE FUTURE

The forms of architecture as we know it are deeply inscribed in human nature and anatomy. From the first inhabited caves, the need for protection from the elements or from adversaries dictated the existence of a door or a roof. The columns of Greek temples and the arborescent splendor of the Gothic trace their roots to the forests of a time before civilization. And if the anatomical nature of architecture were not evident in a thousand other places, it would suffice to view the dome and outstretched "arms" of Saint Peter's in Rome to understand that what is built flows forth from what we are. Nor are such references to the body limited to ancient architecture. Clearly, towers are amongst the most explicitly anatomical architectural forms. With the essential tasks of protection long since mastered, the symbolic value of architecture, as an expression of power for example, continues to seek its legitimacy in the most basic facts of human existence.

Although modern economic and urban development has privileged increasingly ephemeral architecture, the Vitruvian virtue of "solidity" has remained another of the deeply rooted premises of the builder's art. "Flexibility" is praised in many designs, but rarely do architects imagine that their vaunted work should be able to change with time. That is, they didn't imagine such a possibility until quite recently. Certain American architects like Frank O. Gehry or Peter Eisenman have made well-publicized attempts to break out of the mold of traditional architectural forms. Gehry has assumed a large measure of artistic freedom, aided by sophisticated computer software originally intended for the design of fighter aircraft. Buildings such as his Guggenheim-Bilbao cannot be said to fit easily into the anatomical models of the past. And though this particular structure is clad in titanium, its very solidity seems to dissolve into a complex orchestration of non-Euclidean curves.

The virtue of solidity in architecture is surely related at its origin to the need for protection. Once that goal was achieved, durability, in both real and symbolic terms, could be construed as a victory over time. And though columns may evoke the form of a tree, and a dome a human skull, stone architecture seems more closely related to the geology of nature than its biological reality. Adaptability, sensitivity to the environment, growth and rapid change are the hallmarks of the living world. Might it be that a paradigm shift is occurring in architecture, with its ephemeral or ecologically oriented sides coming to the fore? The American architect Neil Denari asks, "What constitutes the architectural world system? It could be asked, when related to the biological model, if architecture must now always be an open and dynamic system, rejecting completely the near equilibrium of the static or closed system? After all, if architecture has undergone radically positive conceptual transformations via the biological model of systems, will it ever, as a disciple, be able to refer to equilibrium or the fixed again? It will not, even if buildings *appear* otherwise."*

Even without reaching the radical conclusions of Neil Denari, it can certainly be argued that far-reaching changes are underway. What if Frank O. Gehry's free forms were just the first step in the liberation of architecture from its ancestral heritage? Not the *tabula rasa* of Gropius, but rather the beginning of a quest for a new architecture. Here, issues of function and cost necessarily would play a major role, but this new architecture exists for the most part only on computer screens and thus is not subjected to the same mundane constraints as its

* Neil M. Denari, *Gyroscopic Horizons*, Thames & Hudson, London, 1999.

steel and concrete cousins. Imagine new programs such as the so-called "genetic algorithms" that are capable of creating forms that the most inventive architects could not have conceived. Some brave souls imagine that architecture can exist as a discipline without ever leaving the screen, as an intellectual, formal, artistic exercise. Others are already taking the leap from truly computer driven design into the "real" world, and the forms of a new world are beginning to appear.

### BUILDING VIRTUAL REALITY

Neil Denari is one of a number of architects whose influence is considerable despite their having built a decidedly limited number of buildings. This is not in itself a new phenomenon. Architects such as Rem Koolhaas established their reputations long before having built through books for example, but it is the next generation, the students of Koolhaas as it were who are now taking architecture in new directions. Born in 1957, the Dutch architect Ben van Berkel (UN Studio) studied under Koolhaas at the AA in London and has been one of the pioneers in the exploration of built forms generated by computer assisted design. "I see an increasing tendency to investigate ways in which architecture might include more and more complexity in one comprehensive complexity," he says. "It looks more and more at organic systems; and the way in which, through the impact and effect of external forces, a generic model is differentiated. The model is perceived as a whole, but is at the same time very fragmented."

The Dutch have proven to be very open to the development of new archetypes both in virtual and in built forms. Lars Spuybroek, who was born in 1959 in Rotterdam, and Maurice Nio created NOX, a firm dedicated to the use of computers. Together with another colleague (Kas Oosterhuis), in 1997, they created one of the first truly innovative buildings of the computer era on the artificial island of Neeltje Jans, to the southwest of Rotterdam near the "Delta Project" seawalls. Spuybroek aptly describes this remarkable building as "A turbulent alloy of the hard and the weak, of human flesh, concrete and metal, interactive electronics and water. A complete fusion of body, environment and technology." "The design," he goes on to say, "was based on the metastable aggregation of architecture and information. The form itself is shaped by the fluid deformation of fourteen ellipses spaced out over a length of more than 65 meters. Inside the building, which has no horizontal floors and no external relation to the horizon, walking becomes akin to falling. The deformation of the object extends to the constant metamorphosis of the environment that responds interactively to the visitors to the water pavilion via a variety of sensors that register this constant reshaping of the human body called action."

California has been another of the sources of creativity in the search for new architectural paradigms. Greg Lynn, who is based in Venice, California, has worked on the concept of what he calls an "Embryological House." Sensitive to the need for the architect to be "practical" in his designs, he writes, "The Embryological House can be described as a strategy for the invention of domestic space that engages contemporary issues of brand identity and variation, customization and continuity, flexible manufacturing and assembly, and most importantly an unapologetic investment in the contemporary beauty and voluptuous aesthetics of undulating surfaces rendered vividly in iridescent and opalescent colors. The Embryological House employs a rigorous system of geometrical limits that liberate an exfoliation of endless variations. This provides a generic sensibility common to any Embryological House at the same time that no two houses are ever identical."

Some of Lynn's contemporaries do not see an acute need to be closely involved with the practical aspects of building. The most radical of these designers may be Marcos Novak, seen by many as the "pioneer of the architecture of virtuality." His concepts of "liquid architecture" or "transarchitecture" exist exclusively on computer screens, though his thinking clearly extends to the possibility of work that exists in the "real" world. "Cyberspace itself was never limited to virtual reality," he says, "but had more to do with our invention of a pervasive and inescapable information space completely enmeshed with culture." "We have moved," continues Novak, "from specialization of disciplines to multidisciplinarity, interdisciplinarity, and now transdisciplinarity." "In a more tangible sense," says the architect, "transarchitectures have to do with the full spectrum of what might be called new tectonics: algorithmic conception, rapid prototyping, robotic fabrication, interactive habitation, telepresence and telecommunications, nano- and giga- presence, and the link to and through virtuality, creating a new continuum of space: (local)physical-virtual-(non-local)physical." Marcos Novak's thinking opens horizons in architecture that more mundane designers may disdain, yet he is clearly representative of a new wave of design that will influence the profession for many years to come. "My work moves in two directions," he says: "from real space into virtual space, via immersion, and from virtual space to real space, via what I have termed 'eversion.' At the interface of the two, sensors create 'invisible architectures' that mediate the two into one another. I am currently working on a series of projects called 'allotopes,' building in Xenakis's 'polytopes,' and extending them through the use of virtual space, in performances that seek to reanimate powerful but neglected spaces. At the same time, I am using various kinds of numerical milling and rapid prototyping to explore physical forms that are derived from virtuality." An interesting aspect of Novak's work is its obvious relationship to contemporary art, a relationship that Frank O. Gehry may have inspired indirectly.

Half a world away, operating in a very different mode, the Japanese architect Makoto Sei Watanabe has just carried out "the world's first implementation of what we call PGA, Program Generated Architecture." His design for the Iidabashi Subway Station (Tokyo, Japan, 1999–2000) seeks to lay bare what he perceives as the hidden world of underground transport, in a tubular mesh that almost literally invades the subway station, designed with a system he calls "The Web Frame." The approach used here is related to that of the "genetic algorithms" cited above. "The Web Frame 'inherits' the DNA of the engineering framework," says Watanabe, "selecting, transforming and enhancing its features: an interweaving, entangling, expanding, pulsating Web, growing towards the light of day, a second species of subterranean tubule. The growth of the Web Frame," he concludes, "was facilitated by computer program for automated generation of code."

The quest for sophisticated computer generated forms that may closely mimic the adaptability of nature is sweeping through certain architectural circles, and yet, at its origin, a much simpler concept drives and transforms a far larger part of actual construction. Flexibility is the key word in what can only be perceived as a true sea-change in architecture. Terry Riley's exhibition "The Un-Private House" (Museum of Modern Art, 1999) called attention to a new generation of homes like Shigeru Ban's Curtain Wall House (Tokyo, 1995) that challenge the very precepts of residential design. Ban's more recent Naked House, is made up of a shed-like exterior with internal bedroom units that move on wheels into variable configurations. No longer do homes correspond to a set stereotype with a living room, dining room, kitchen and upstairs bedrooms. Life styles and indeed architecture itself have moved beyond this kind of rigidity, whether or not computer-driven forms are involved.

What is suggested here is that the computer is beginning to make possible the kind of true flexibility that escaped the construction techniques of an earlier time. The "data-driven pneumatic structure" presented by Kas Oosterhuis at the 2000 Venice Architecture Biennial (trans-ports) might be one of the first proofs of the viability of total computer design. "The most important feature of the trans-ports pavil-ion," says Oosterhuis, "is that architecture for the first time in its history is no longer fixed and static. Due to its full programmability of both form and information content the construct becomes a lean and flexible vehicle for a variety of usage."

**IMPROVING THE PAST**

However far-reaching the changes underway in the design of new buildings, it remains that existing architecture can often be rehabil-itated at much lower cost than what is required to rebuild on a given site. Depending on budgetary constraints, sophisticated methods and materials can obviously be used in such instances, but low-cost renovation is the more frequent solution. This was certainly the case in two rather ambitious art-related programs, one in the United States, the other in France. The first of these, Mass MoCA (North Adams, Massa-chusetts, 1988–1999) was the brainchild of none other than Thomas Krens, the Director of the Guggenheim, and client for Frank O. Gehry's Bilbao structure. Although a group of very high-profile architects were involved in the early phases of this project (Frank O. Gehry, Robert Ven-turi, Skidmore, Owings & Merrill), Simeon Bruner carried it out with intelligence and talent. With no less than 27 industrial buildings to choose from on the site and a limited $31.4 million budget, Bruner opted for an almost inevitable rough renovation. This is also the case in the cavernous Palais de Tokyo in Paris, a 1937 building on the banks of the Seine that has been converted into a contemporary art space. Archi-tects Lacaton & Vassal, a young couple from Bordeaux, stripped the 9,000 square meter space bare and dared to not even paint the walls or give more than a rough finish to the concrete floors.

Talented architects, including another young Parisian couple, Dominique Jakob and Brendan MacFarlane (Jakob & MacFarlane) are carrying out more ambitious renovations in a number of other locations. Authors of the Georges Restaurant in the Pompidou Center, they have been called on to redo the so-called "Metal 57" factory building owned by Renault in Boulogne-Billancourt, making it into a conference and exhibition center. They have chosen to create a new shell inside the existing 15,000 square meter factory structure, redefining its use while retaining the external form. In a very different style, Manolo Nuñez-Yanowsky, a former associate of Ricardo Bofill, took on the creation of the Teatre Lliure Fabià Puigserver in Barcelona, retaining an external aspect of the existing structure that may bring to mind the "post-modern" attitude of Nuñez in the years subsequent to his separation from Bofill's Taller team. And yet what Nuñez had to work with from the outset was a building erected for the 1929 International Exhibition, the Palau de l'Agricultura, a far cry from Mies van der Rohe's German Pavilion for the same Exhibition. Esthetically speaking, however, the existence of such projects calls attention to the continuing lack of any dominant style in contemporary architecture. Between the extravagant "data-driven forms" of a Marcus Novak and the concrete austerity of Tadao Ando's Pulitzer Museum in Saint-Louis, there is such a divide that almost any other sensibility can find its own niche of respectability.

If stripping old buildings naked and turning them into usable modern facilities is a fashionable activity in today's architectural world, so is dressing up structures so that they appear to be in today's style. With their Umbra World Headquarters (Toronto, Canada, 1998–1999) Kohn Shnier Architects, took on an "ugly and banal" concrete factory, wrapped it in identical vacuum-formed modules of green copolyester plastic shaped by a resin mold, and made it into a glamorous headquarters for the manufacturers of Karim Rashid's "Garbo" garbage can. Admittedly, this kind of intervention does have as much to do with fashion design as it does with more solid kinds of architecture, but with so many ugly old buildings available for a refit, renovation of all types looks like it will long be a mainstay of contemporary architecture.

## DOWN ON THE FARM

Ecological concerns are more and more significant in contemporary architecture, but it may be said that such interest is taking a more "mature" form than it did a few years ago. Then, architects who were interested in "green" design almost felt an obligation to make their buildings look strange just so that clients and visitors would get the point. "See, this building is ecologically correct," they seemed practically to scream out. In the case of the Institute for Forestry and Nature Research (Behnisch, Behnisch & Partner, Wageningen, The Netherlands, 1994–1998), the "client's brief was for a functional yet hospitable building in harmony with nature and the environment, versatile and ecologically sound." A determining factor in the design was also that the client was not willing to pay a premium in order to obtain ecologically sound design. It is increasingly being assumed that natural climate control systems and other "green" concepts are to be part of any new building, this especially in Northern Europe.

At a time when sophisticated designs and materials are frequently employed by the most famous architects, it is interesting to underline the existence of a radically different approach – that which seeks out affordable and attractive designs in some of the poorer parts of the world. In an unexpected location, the Swedish architects Heikkinen-Komonen have worked extensively in Guinea on just such modest projects. Their Kahere Eila Poultry Farming School (Kindia, Guinea, 1998–1999) was one of the winners of the 2001 Aga Khan Award, where it was cited as "a fine example of an elegantly humble yet modern architecture that successfully crosses the boundaries of local Guinean and Nordic traditions and, in the process, avoids mimicry." This 350 square meter structure was built for just $104,000 out of stabilized earth bricks made locally in a manual press.

Another innovative adventure in modest architecture was led by the late Samuel Mockbee, and based at Auburn University in Alabama. His Rural Studio called on students at the University to participate actively in the construction of decent housing and community buildings for the extremely poor local population, in particular in the town of Masons Bend. Built for only $20,000, the Masons Bend Community Center (Masons Bend, Alabama, United States, 1999–2000) was described by Mockbee as a "windshield chapel with mud walls that picks up on the community's vernacular forms and shapes." The reference to the unusual glazing material is due to the fact that the roof of the structure was made with eighty Chevy Caprice windshields obtained by one of the participants in the project for $120.

In both the case of the work in Guinea of Heikkinen-Komonen and in that of Samuel Mockbee's Rural Studio, local traditions and materials are respected, rather than attempting to impose an esthetic diktat in any sense. Although artistically inclined architects do often attempt to impose their own vision on clients, there may be other ways of judging quality in contemporary design. Sensitivity to place and a capacity to deal with very low budgets could be some of the criteria to be retained, as is often the case for the projects that receive the Aga Khan Award, for example.

## INVENTING NEW FORMS

Whether using computers or not, inventive architects continue to attempt to create new forms. One of the most surprising of these is the Spanish-born Zurich based architect-engineer Santiago Calatrava. His Quadracci Pavilion (Milwaukee Art Museum, Milwaukee, Wisconsin, 1994–2001), and the so-called "Burke Brise-Soleil," a reception hall shaded by a moveable sunscreen, has an astonishing bird-like form that some may judge excessive. This biomorphic structure corresponds well to the Museum's brief requiring a "new grand entrance, a point of orientation for visitors, and a redefinition of the museum's identity though the creation of a strong image." Frank O. Gehry, a master of unexpected forms, has recently created another surprising building in Berlin. The DG Bank (Berlin, Germany, 1995–2001), located on the Pariser Platz, is outwardly austere, but contains an astonishing conference facility within the atrium that Gehry likens to a horse's head. This freely undulating stainless-steel clad shape resembles one developed for the unbuilt residence of Peter Lewis, and also that of a large sculptural object the architect showed in the Los Angeles gallery of Larry Gagosian. Gehry has long had a fascination with forms inspired by the natural world, as his Fish Dance restaurant in Kobe (1984) testifies, or Rebecca's, a Mexican restaurant designed by Gehry (Venice, California, 1982–1985) that contains dangling crocodiles, fish lamps and an octopus chandelier.

Without feeling a need to go quite as far in the area of biomorphic references, architects such as Japan's Toyo Ito continue to create innovative buildings. His latest completed project, the Mediatheque in Sendai (1998–2001) calls on a fluidity of design and a transparency that bear some resemblance to the computer-driven shapes of Californian or Dutch architects. In fact, Ito does refer to "seaweed" in describing the thirteen structural white steel tubes that hold up the building and carry its technical conduits, undulating through the structure. If further proof were needed that the biological world is providing more inspiration today than the geometric rigidity of the Modernist era, the Japanese propensity to theorize about the creation of a kind of artificial nature provides it. Architects such as Itsuko Hasegawa have long held to this type of position.

Nor is the idea of freely designed forms by any means restricted to ambitious large-scale projects like Gehry's DG Bank or Ito's Mediatheque. The young team of Jakob + MacFarlane carried out the design of the Librairie Florence Loewy, (Paris, France, 2001) on computers, but the unexpected curving wooden bookshelves they installed in this modest space do not immediately bring to mind the cutting edge of architecture. Rather, such a project serves to emphasize the breadth of the movement towards new models that are approaching the flexibility of nature rather than the rigidity of Euclidean geometry.

## ARCHITECTURE = ART = ARCHITECTURE

Few architects have the means to truly envisage their profession as an art. Economic pressures most often get the better of esthetics even when the designer is intellectually capable of making something that is more than just a functional building. Tadao Ando's rigorous mastery of concrete is nearly legendary, but until now, his major works have all been in Japan. With the Fort Worth Museum of Contemporary Art nearing completion and The Pulitzer Foundation for the Arts recently inaugurated in Saint Louis, Ando can now claim to have extended the geographic reach of his artistry. Tadao Ando's work is far from the extravagant forms of a Marcos Novak. It is resolutely born of Euclidean geometry, and the Pulitzer Foundation is no exception. Two rectangular blocks in fact form the entire design. Despite this extreme simplicity the architect did have a disagreement with one artist participating in the project, Richard Serra. A major sculpture by Serra is situated outside the Foundation, and enclosed by concrete walls designed by Ando. Serra would have preferred not to have this architectural device enclose the complex curve of his work. It is interesting to note that this conflict comes at the point of intersection between one of the most "artistic" of architects, and one of the sculptors who ventures closest to architecture. A case of professional rivalry?

Serra most frequently uses Corten steel for his work, a material more common in shipbuilding than in architecture, and yet Rem Koolhaas chose precisely that type of steel for the gallery walls in his new Guggenheim Hermitage in Las Vegas. Rarely have "high" and "low" culture come into such close proximity. In the heart of one of the most outrageously "kitsch" of the Las Vegas casino-hotels, The Venetian, Thomas Krens, the Director of the Guggenheim, in association with the Hermitage of Saint Petersburg, dared to install not one but two spaces for ambitious temporary exhibitions. The Guggenheim Las Vegas, also designed by Koolhaas, features a much more free-wheeling design inaugurated with Frank O. Gehry's spectacular installation of the "The Art of the Motorcycle" show already seen in New York and Bilbao. Krens is of course known for stirring up the museum world, and his Guggenheim-Bilbao designed by Gehry was one of the most successful pieces of new architecture of the 1990s. If Krens has his way, another Gehry designed Guggenheim will rise not far from the site of the former World Trade Center in New York. It was Krens, too, who called on Jean Nouvel and Zaha Hadid to participate in a competition won by Hadid to design a new "kunsthall" type structure in Tokyo for the Guggenheim. Krens has found that architecture can, in and of itself, attract visitors, much as the original 1959 Frank Lloyd Wright building in New York has long drawn curious admirers of architecture as well as art lovers. For the Director of the Guggenheim, an installation like that of Frank O. Gehry for the " The Art of the Motorcycle" is "50% of the artistic value of the show." It is Richard Serra who says that the "difference between art and architecture is that art serves no purpose." Nonetheless, the artistic aspect of architecture encouraged by the success of such figures as Gehry continues to be a significant source of inventiveness.

It is rare that an artist, especially one of significance, like James Turrell creates a work that can readily be seen to cross the borders between art and architecture. And yet that is precisely what he is in the process of doing in the Arizona desert in a place called Roden Crater. Set about sixty kilometers from Flagstaff, Arizona, Roden Crater is in the midst of the fifty thousand hectares of land that the artist has acquired since 1977. Though the massive earthworks he has undertaken, displacing hundreds of thousands of cubic meters on the site, may bring to mind the scale of large civil engineering projects, he has set out to create an "observatory of celestial phenomena." Turrell explains his actions in terms that do call on architectural references: "I am interested in the fact that we are builders," he says, "we do make things and this is something of human nature to mark in some way. All artists do that, the fact that you make a statement in a place. We have things here like Paolo Soleri, making Arcosanti, or in architecture, Frank Lloyd Wright with Taliesin, or the Watts Towers by Simon Rodia in Los Angeles, these are examples of one person or artist's vision." Turrell is interested in the perception of light and Roden Crater must be interpreted not as a piece of contemporary architecture, but as a work of art. And yet the visionary quality of someone like Turrell does serve as an inspiration to the built environment. Architects like Steven Holl have called extensively on the effects of light and reflection that are not completely unrelated to the studies of Turrell.

Art work at the frontiers of architecture or architecture that approaches pure art are sources of potential confusion, but also of an enriching stimulation that is one of the significant trends in building design in the past twenty years. The fact that many great contemporary architects are called on to build museums by clients such as Tom Krens is a significant indication of their own proximity to the process of making art. Gehry has spoken clearly on this point, and others have followed in his footsteps, or enlarged on his thoughts.

## WHEN IS A HOUSE NOT A HOME?

Private homes have long been an area of predilection for the most creative architects. Their small scale and the often wealthy clients permit a degree of inventiveness that is often excluded in larger, more economically-driven work. The Spanish architect Alberto Campo Baeza has responded to the specific site of the De Blas House (Sevilla la Nueva, Madrid, Spain, 2000) with a typically minimalist solution for example. "A concrete box was built," he explains, "a platform upon which to sit. A transparent glass box, roofed by a delicate and light steel structure, painted in white, is placed upon this podium. One with the earth, the poured-in-place concrete box like a cave houses the program of a traditional house with a clear diagram of served spaces to the front and service spaces to the rear. The glass box is placed upon the platform, like a hut, is a Belvedere to which one rises from within the house. Below, the cave is a refuge. Above the hut, an urn, is a space from which to contemplate nature. This house attempts to be a literal translation of tectonic and stereotomic questions: a tectonic piece set upon a stereotomic box. A distillation of what is essential in architecture. Once again, 'more with less'." Though it was built half a world away, Waro Kishi's House in Kurakuen II (Nishinomiya, Hyogo, Japan, 2000–2001) is described by the architect in terms that are comparable: "I created two blocks of floating steel reinforced structure. On the left is the private room zone, while on the right are the public living and dining room areas, and both are joined by a sloping ramp. The roof of the topmost floor on the left side individual room block is made to appear as thin as possible,"

Campo Baeza and Kishi share a minimalist esthetic that has been a consistent factor in recent contemporary architecture all over the world. Sean Godsell, working in Australia, has also made use of a geometric vocabulary in his Carter/Tucker House, (Breamlea, Victoria, Australia, 1999–2000). This house is a three level twelve by six meter box embedded in a sand dune. Its fundamental external simplicity is made richer by a system of unexpected openings in the facade; a timber screen skin tilts open creating awnings on all three levels.

Just as minimalist solutions appear in varying forms all over the world, so too do more complex and colorful solutions such as that adapted by Ettore Sottsass for the Ernest Mourmans House (Birdhouse, Maastricht, The Netherlands, 1999–2001). Born in 1917, Sottsass is of course best known for his furniture design and his role in creating movements such as Memphis (1981). It might be uncharitable to say that the Birdhouse brings to mind precisely the esthetics of that period, but that is not to say that given forms of modernity are necessarily to be limited to very specific time-spans. Indeed, it would seem far healthier to not give in to the fashion consciousness that has often prevailed in architectural circles. The Birdhouse is certainly contemporary in its disposition and finish. It is probably its exuberant complexity that links it to a period now quite foreign to the younger generations of architects. There is a new complexity in contemporary architecture, which is that born of computer design. The design of Sottsass in some ways looks back to post-modernism, where theoretical references were made to the layout of Hadrian's Villa for example.

For many architects, the challenge of changing styles has been a significant factor. Some, like Richard Meier or Tadao Ando have steadfastly clung to a strict modernist vocabulary whose classicism in some sense puts them above the movements of fashion. Others, like Philip Johnson in his time, or more recently Arata Isozaki, move rapidly from one style to another according to circumstances. An interesting case is that of the Finnish architect Jyrki Tasa, born in 1944 and once a decidedly "post-modern" designer. His more recent Into House (Espoo, Finland, 1997–1998) manages the delicate transition from his past style to a more contemporary attitude that still bears the marks of imbalance and surprise that characterized his buildings previously. Private houses are in any case a domain of personal taste, both that of the architect and, of course, that of the client in many cases. Being "fashionable" is a relative notion that varies according to the viewer. Persons not well informed about architectural fashion may feel that a post-modern flavor is quite up to date. There is also an age factor that enters this equation of course.

## SHOPPING OR RELIGION?

In his recent *Harvard Design School Guide to Shopping* (Taschen, Cologne, 2001), Rem Koolhaas dares to draw an analogy between shopping and religion ("The Divine Economy"). "In an effort to reinvent the vehicles by which they reach their markets," writes Sze Tsung Leong, "churches are becoming more and more similar to shopping, both in their configurations and in their methods." In any case, sophisticated architecture is seen in both religious and marketing circles as being the key to reaching new audiences. Some of the most remarkable structures by the Japanese architect Tadao Ando are his temples and churches. The most recent one, (Komyo-ji Temple, Saijo, Ehime, Japan, 1999–2000), is defined as "a place of gathering" that also happens to draw on the origins of Japanese wooden temple architecture. The German architects Allmann Sattler Wappner also make use of a minimalist vocabulary in their Herz Jesu Kirche (Munich, Germany, 1996–2001) that does more to suggest religious function indirectly than to state it specifically. Again the notion of a place of gathering – that might also adequately describe shopping malls – is perfectly applicable to this church. In Germany, as in Japan, the subtlety of the architects is such that the faithful will find all of the signs they require to recognize places of worship, while others will not feel unduly subjected to a given doctrine.

Though religion is not meant to be subjected to fashion, it is precisely the ephemeral attraction of the briefly new that draws buyers into clothing boutiques. The Japanese designers Issey Miyake and Rei Kawakubo (Comme des Garçons) have long been at the forefront of boutique design, calling on top architects and getting personally involved in the "art direction" of their retail spaces. For his new flagship store in New York, Miyake called on none other than Frank O. Gehry to give the space on Hudson Street in Tribeca a contemporary feeling. Working with an associate on this project (Gordon Kipping), Gehry spins one of his trademark undulating metal sheets through the high-ceilinged warehouse-type space. This together with sophisticated uses of metal and glass provides a dramatic updating for this landmark cast iron building. Renovation is now seen as one of the primary areas of expression for contemporary architecture, and the Miyake Tribeca shop by Gehry and Kipping is proof that cutting edge fashion design, architecture and interior design can find a successful meeting point.

Rei Kawakubo, if anything, has been much more radical in her boutique designs than Miyake or indeed almost any of her other colleagues. After working with Future Systems for her New York and Tokyo shops, she called on Ab Rogers, the son of Richard Rogers of Pompidou Center fame to create a spectacular and very red space just opposite the Elysees Palace on the Faubourg Saint Honoré in Paris. As is the case in her other shops, though, it is Kawakubo herself who has the final decision on design, and she can duly be considered to be the actual "architect" of the spaces. There is in her work an active attempt at symbiosis between spaces, objects and clothing that goes to create a spirit, that which must be identified with the Comme des Garçons label. You don't buy religion when you enter her shops, but you do enter a kind of esthetic movement that covers all aspects of the environments she defines.

## THE BUTCHER, THE BAKER, THE CANDLESTICK MAKER

Although the ethereal research of a Marcos Novak may well point to the future of architecture, it remains obvious that for all but the most "artistic" designers, there is a necessity to build, and indeed to fit into programmatic requirements just to stay in business. And construction, when it goes beyond the scale of the private house, is most often intended for very pragmatic uses – a kind of "bread and butter" architecture that allows people to see movies, get on the train, go to court, a concert or a library, or even just to the office. Solving the problems inherent in any of these building types is the true measure of architectural excellence, in particular when endless budgets are not available. The German-based architects Bolles + Wilson recently completed the New Luxor Theatre (Rotterdam, Netherlands, 1998–2000) in the Kop van Zuid area. They had already carried out the design of the Quay Buildings (Kop van Zuid, Rotterdam, 1991–1996) in the same area, and the Luxor Theatre represents another step toward making this formerly almost abandoned dock area into a vibrant new city area. Set near the landing point of Ben van Berkel's spectacular Erasmus Bridge (1996), the Luxor offers a bright red sign to attract visitors from the city center. Though it cannot be said to be spectacularly inventive, the Luxor Theater is a key element in an ambitious urban renewal project – a useful project by any measure, in a city that has shown its taste for fine contemporary architecture.

Bringing good architecture to building types that have seen a decline is another laudable enterprise, especially when millions of ordinary travelers are involved in the process. This is certainly the case of Jean-Marie Duthilleul and his AREP, the construction arm of France's SNCF train network. Duthilleul has actively campaigned to make railroad stations more hospitable and modern, in conjunction with the substantial efforts that have been made in France to update the rail network itself with the TGV lines. The most recent extension of the TGV, from Lyon to the South of France, was the object of the construction of new rail lines and three new stations, in Valence, Avignon and Aix-en-Provence. Each of these stations is different and each brings a degree of modern comfort and sophistication to locations where voyagers no longer expected to be treated so well. The Valence Station (Valence, France, 1998–2001) is cantilevered over the tracks. Tilted forward towards the incoming trains, it has an unexpected sloping wooden floor, and a transparency that makes it an agreeable place to wait if necessary. Working on stations from Lille to Marseille, Duthilleul has almost single-handedly transformed the appearance of France's major railroad stations, and in a way looked back to the late nineteenth century when the spectacular glass and iron shed of the Gare Saint-Lazare for example inspired artists like Monet. Train travel at that time was seen as modern and forward-looking, an aspect which the combined arrival of the TGV and Duthilleul's stations has restored at the beginning of the 21st century.

Justice is another area where the arrival of quality contemporary architecture has played a significant role in a number of countries, including France and the United States. Richard Meier, with his Federal Building & United States Courthouse (Phoenix, Arizona, 1998–2000), brings something of his utopian whiteness to the judicial process. Cynics might note that the system itself could do with a bit of clarity and sense of purpose, but in a way, it is the architect who can remind all concerned of the lofty ideals of the judicial process. A 35 meter high glass atrium gives this building an openness that seeks too to obviate the security consciousness born of such tragedies as the 1995 bombing of the Alfred P. Murrah Federal Building in Oklahoma City, Oklahoma. Meier's orderly whiteness does seem particularly well-suited to structuring and defining the courthouse environment, to restoring dignity where excess and error seem to have been the key words of recent years.

Banking has long been seen as a stodgy profession, indeed the banker's propensity to choose classical, even funereal architecture to symbolize solidity and continuity is partially to blame for this image. The Hypo Alpe-Adria Center (Klagenfurt, Austria, 1998–2000) by Morphosis looks clearly in the opposite direction, giving more than anything else a sense of movement. "Its dynamic juxtaposition of volumes evokes shifting tectonic plates," say the architects, "yet it strives to establish nodes of stability within turbulence." Investors might indeed be pleased to sense the presence of such "nodes of stability" in what remains a very unexpected structure. Architecture here serves to redefine the public image and perhaps even the purpose of a profession acutely challenged by rapidly evolving international trends. Another very different example of the relationship between banking and architecture is offered by the new headquarters of the Bank of China (Pei Partnership, Beijing, China, 1997–2001). Here, a very dense program and the client's affirmed desire to project precisely the image of stability that the Austrian bank did not put such a premium on, have led to an almost diametrically opposed result. Though not particularly imaginative in its exterior appearance, the bank's 45-meter high, 3,000 square meter atrium gives the kind of spectacular public space that the architects' father, I. M. Pei, is well-known for. Architects cannot frequently alter the image their clients seek to project, but buildings as forward-looking at the Hypo Alpe-Adria Center or as massively reliable as the Bank of China in Beijing certainly play a role in the future perception of these institutions.

Office buildings, and in particular skyscrapers have long been the object of a certain ridicule because of their obviously phallic connotations. Jean Nouvel may be the first architect to take this image to its logical limits, as it were. His Torre Agbar (Barcelona, Spain, 2001) will be located just off the Diagonal boulevard, and does seem also to have a relationship to the client's water business (a fountain), but the upright, lozenge form is otherwise fairly explicit. With its sophisticated design, the Torre Agbar is certainly not to be considered as a joke, and it might be argued that by taking the phallic imagery seriously, Nouvel has succeeded in going beyond any potential criticism. Jean Nouvel is one of the most important contemporary architects and he is often fairly blunt about his ideas. One can almost imagine him saying, "Sure, its a blatant phallic symbol. So what?"

Many critics feel that enormous international competitions rarely live up to their expectations. The Bibliotheca Alexandrina (Snøhetta Architects, Alexandria, Egypt, 1995–2001) is the result of just such a competition, one that drew no less than 524 entries from 52 countries. Although it may also be true that few major libraries built in recent times have really lived up to their architectural expectations (for example the French National Library by Dominique Perrault), the work of Snøhetta in Alexandria would seem to be particularly heavy-going. Massive in every way, the building certainly gives the Egyptian city a new landmark, but does it really fulfill the kind of hopes that its Unesco backing and wide press coverage might have given rise to? Symbolically loaded from the outset, this library may have been destined to disappoint, no matter what the architects did.

Another category of facilities that often disappoints is the kind of concert hall-convention center that France has built in many of its provincial cities in recent years. Bernard Tschumi's Zenith (Rouen, France, 1999–2001) is actually a brilliant success, with its floating metallic double shell. Tschumi has influenced numerous students of architecture as Dean of the Columbia Graduate School of Architecture, but with structures such as the Zenith in Rouen, he is showing that his reputation is backed by a solid ability to conceive innovative solutions despite restricted budgets. Like Duthilleul's work on France's railway stations, the Rouen Zenith is a highly successful instance of quality architecture applied to use by the general public.

## BACK TO THE FUTURE

Buildings designed by architects who have a real esthetic sense are rare. Most cities are filled with inept imitations, economically handicapped reproductions of once grandiose ideas brought down to their lowest common denominator. As this overview makes plain, the theoretical cutting edge of architecture is even more at the periphery of public interest. Most buildings in the real world are still conceived in modes, and even in styles that might not have seemed unfamiliar to Ludwig Mies van der Rohe fifty years ago. And yet the idea of a new architecture based on models that have some relationship to the changing world of biology – an architecture that will come out of computer design, perhaps even genetic algorithms that spew forth shapes that no architect has ever imagined before – is advancing. Computers, as Frank O. Gehry has shown with his use of Dassault's Catia program, can also greatly facilitate the construction of highly complex forms. If such sculptural shapes are in the future of architecture, then they have to be more than an esthetic whim, even that of an aging diva of the profession. Adaptability, capacity to change with use and evolve with time – these are the underlying virtues of the new architecture, a living, breathing architecture for a new world.

exaktes System geometrischer Grenzen ein, die eine Entwicklung endloser Variationsmöglichkeiten bieten. Das verleiht allen diesen Häusern eine gattungsmäßige Sensibilität, während es gleichzeitig die Existenz zweier identischer Häuser ausschließt.«

Einige von Greg Lynns Zeitgenossen sehen keine dringende Notwendigkeit, sich eingehend mit den praktischen Aspekten des Bauens zu befassen. Der radikalste Vertreter dieser Richtung dürfte Marcos Novak sein, der von Vielen als »der Pionier der virtuellen Architektur« betrachtet wird. Seine Konzeptionen einer »fließenden Architektur« oder »Transarchitektur« existieren ausschließlich in virtuellen Sphären. Novak erklärt: »Der Cyberspace selbst war nie auf die virtuelle Realität beschränkt, sondern hatte mehr mit unserer Erfindung eines allgegenwärtigen und unentrinnbaren Informationsraums zu tun, der vollkommen eins ist mit Kultur. Wir haben uns von der Spezialisierung der Disziplinen zum Multi- oder Interdisziplinären und nun zum Transdisziplinären vorwärts bewegt. Im konkreteren Sinn haben Transarchitekturen mit dem vollen Spektrum dessen zu tun, was man die neue Tektonik nennen könnte: algorithmische Konzeption, Rapid Prototyping, Roboterfabrikation, interaktive Wohnstätten, Telepräsenz und Telekommunikation, Nano- und Giga-Präsenz sowie die Verknüpfung mit der und durch die Virtualität, wodurch ein neues Raumkontinuum geschaffen wird: (lokal)physikalisch-virtuell-(nicht-lokal)physikalisch.« Novaks Denken eröffnet der Architektur Horizonte, die profanere Gestalter gering schätzen mögen, doch zweifellos ist er repräsentativ für eine Architekturbewegung, die den Berufsstand auf viele Jahre hinaus beeinflussen wird. Novak weiter: »Meine Arbeit bewegt sich in zwei Richtungen: vom realen Raum zum virtuellen Raum, durch Immersion, und vom virtuellen Raum zum realen Raum durch etwas, das ich ›Eversion‹ (Umstülpung) nenne. An der Schnittstelle von diesen beiden wird mittels Sensoren eine ›unsichtbare Architektur‹ erzeugt, welche beide Pole miteinander verbindet. Zur Zeit arbeite ich an einer Serie von Projekten namens ›Allotopes‹. Hierbei gehe ich von den ›Polytopes‹ des Komponisten und Architekten Iannis Xenakis aus, die Elemente von Architektur und Video-Performance kombinieren, und erweitere sie durch den Einsatz virtueller Technologien, um in diesen Inszenierungen bestehende, aber vernachlässigte architektonische Räume zu reanimieren. Gleichzeitig arbeite ich mit unterschiedlichen Arten von numerischer Fräsung sowie Rapid Prototyping, um virtuell erzeugte physikalische Formen zu erforschen.«

Auf der anderen Seite der Erdkugel hat der japanische Architekt Makoto Sei Watanabe in einer ganz anderen Arbeitsweise soeben die erste so genannte »PGA« oder Program Generated Architecture implementiert. Mit seinem Entwurf für die U-Bahnstation Iidabashi in Tokio will Watanabe aufdecken, was er als die verborgene Welt des unterirdischen Transportsystems empfindet. Dazu hat er mittels eines Computerprogramms, des so genannten »Web Frame«, ein Netzwerk aus Röhren geplant, das beinahe den gesamten U-Bahnhof überzieht. Die dabei eingesetzte Methode ist mit den oben erwähnten »genetischen Algorithmen« verwandt. Watanabe erklärt dazu: »Das Web Frame ›übernimmt‹ die DNS der maschinentechnischen Rahmenkonstruktion, indem es deren Funktionsmerkmale aussiebt, umwandelt und verbessert. Daraus entsteht ein verflochtenes, expandierendes und pulsierendes unterirdisches Netzwerk, das sich zum Tageslicht hin entfaltet. Die Ausdehnung des Web Frame wurde durch ein Computerprogramm für automatische Programmierung ermöglicht.«

Das Streben nach ausgeklügelten, computergenerierten Formen, die in ihrer Anpassungsfähigkeit der Natur möglichst nahe kommen, ist in gewissen Architekturkreisen durchaus verbreitet. Und doch bestimmt an seinem Ursprung ein sehr viel simpleres Konzept einen wesentlich größeren Teil des aktuellen Baugeschehens. Flexibilität ist das Schlüsselwort für das, was man nur als den wahren großen Wandel in der

Architektur ausmachen kann. Die von Terry Riley konzipierte Ausstellung »The Un-Private House«, die 1999 im New Yorker Museum of Modern Art gezeigt wurde, lenkte die Aufmerksamkeit auf eine neue Generation von Wohnhäusern wie das von Shigeru Ban 1995 in Tokio gebaute Curtain Wall House, die sämtliche Regeln und Gebote der Wohnhausarchitektur in Frage stellen. Bans neueres Werk, Naked House, gleicht von außen einem Schuppen und besteht im Inneren aus Raumeinheiten, die sich mittels Räder verschieben und zu wechselnden Konstellationen anordnen lassen. Wohnhäuser entsprechen nicht länger der stereotypen Aufteilung in Wohnzimmer, Esszimmer, Küche im unteren und den Schlafzimmern im oberen Stock. Nicht nur die Lebensstile, sondern auch die Architektur selbst.

Durch den Einsatz der Computertechnik wird ein Ausmaß an Flexibilität möglich, das den Konstruktionstechniken früherer Zeiten verschlossen war. »trans-ports«, die von Kas Oosterhuis auf der Architekturbiennale 2000 in Venedig präsentierte »datenerzeugte pneumatische Konstruktion«, ist möglicherweise einer der ersten Beweise für die Entwicklungsfähigkeit des totalen Computerdesigns. Oosterhuis über den von ihm entworfenen Pavillon: »Der wichtigste Aspekt von ›trans-ports‹ besteht darin, dass hier Architektur zum ersten Mal in ihrer Geschichte nicht feststehend und statisch ist. Aufgrund der vollständigen Programmierbarkeit von sowohl Form als auch Informationsgehalt wird die Konstruktion zu einem sparsamen und wandelbaren Vehikel für eine Vielfalt von Anwendungsmöglichkeiten.«

## DIE VERGANGENHEIT VERBESSERN

Die Veränderungen in der Architektur neuer Gebäude mögen noch so weitreichend sein, das ändert nichts an der Tatsache, dass es oft sehr viel kostengünstiger ist, ein bestehendes Bauwerk zu sanieren, als ein neues zu errichten. Je nach Budget lassen sich in solchen Fällen natürlich ausgefeilte Methoden und hochwertige Materialien verwenden, häufiger wird jedoch die Lösung einer möglichst kostengünstigen Renovierung gewählt. So geschehen auch bei zwei recht ambitiösen Museumsprojekten in den Vereinigten Staaten und Frankreich. Ersteres, das Mass MoCA in North Adams, Massachusetts (1988–99), war die geistige Schöpfung von niemand anderem als Thomas Krens, dem heutigen Guggenheim-Direktor und Auftraggeber für Gehrys Bauwerk in Bilbao. Obwohl in der ersten Planungsphase eine Reihe hochkarätiger Architekten involviert war, wie Frank O. Gehry, Robert Venturi, Skidmore, Owings & Merrill, war es Simeon Bruner, der das Projekt mit Intelligenz und Talent ausführte. Bruner entschied sich für eine unvollkommene Renovierung. Das war auch die Strategie im zweiten Fall, dem Palais de Tokyo in Paris. Die Architekten Lacaton & Vassal versetzten die Ausstellungsfläche in ihren ursprünglichen Zustand, wobei sie es sogar wagten, die Wände ungestrichen zu lassen und die Betonböden lediglich grob zu glätten.

Dominique Jakob und Brendan MacFarlane aus Paris erhielten den Auftrag, das im Besitz von Renault befindliche »Métal 57« genannte Gebäude in Boulogne-Billancourt zu einem Kongress- und Ausstellungszentrum umzubauen. Der Entwurf der beiden Architekten sieht den Einbau einer neuen Schalenkonstruktion in den 15.000 m² messenden Industriebau vor, wodurch sie das Gebäude unter Beibehaltung der äußeren Form einem neuen Nutzen zuführen können. Auf ganz andere Art und Weise ging Manolo Nuñez-Yanowsky, ein früherer Mitarbeiter von Ricardo Bofill, bei der Gestaltung des Teatre Lliure Fabià Puigserver in Barcelona vor. Er behielt das äußere Erscheinungsbild der bestehenden Fassade bei. Nun hatte es der Architekt im Fall des Palau de l'Agricultura aber mit einem Bauwerk zu tun, das für die Weltausstellung von 1929 errichtet worden war. In ästhetischer Hinsicht weist die Existenz solcher Bauprojekte jedoch auf den bleibenden Mangel eines dominanten Stils in der Architektur unserer Tage hin. Zwischen den extravaganten »datengenerierten Formen« eines Marcos Novak und der nüchternen Betonarchitektur von Tadao Andos Pulitzer Museum in St. Louis liegt ein so himmelweiter Unterschied, dass sich darin für beinahe jede andere Stilrichtung eine eigene, respektable Nische finden lässt.

Ist es auf der einen Seite in der heutigen Architekturwelt modern geworden, alte Gebäude bis auf die Grundmauern zu entkleiden und in neue, funktionale Einrichtungen zu verwandeln, so ist es auf der anderen Seite ebenso angesagt, Bauten derart herauszuputzen, dass sie aussehen, als seien sie in heutigem Stil erbaut. Mit ihrem Entwurf für den Hauptsitz von Umbra World in Toronto (1998–99), umhüllten Kohn Shnier Architects ein »hässliches und banales« Gebäude, eine ehemalige Betonfabrik mit identisch vakuumgeformten Modulen aus grünem Copolyester-Kunststoff und verwandelten es in die spektakuläre Zentrale einer Einrichtungsfirma. Zugegeben, ein solcher Eingriff hat vielleicht mehr mit Modedesign als mit einer solideren Art von Architektur zu tun, aber bei so vielen hässlichen alten Gebäuden könnten Renovierungsprojekte aller Art auf lange Zeit eine der Hauptstützen der zeitgenössischen Architektur sein.

### ÖKO-ARCHITEKTUR

Ökologische Belange nehmen in der heutigen Architektur einen immer größeren Stellenwert ein. Inzwischen wird dieses Anliegen in einer »reiferen« Form umgesetzt als noch vor einigen Jahren. Damals fühlten sich Architekten, die sich für ökologisches Bauen interessierten, fast verpflichtet, ihren Gebäuden ein sonderbares Aussehen zu verleihen, damit Auftraggeber und Besucher auch ja verstanden, worum es ihnen ging. Im Fall des von Behnisch, Behnisch & Partner entworfenen Instituts für Forst- und Naturforschung im niederländischen Wageningen (1994–98) wünschte der Auftraggeber ein Gebäude, das funktional und doch einladend sein sollte. Es sollte sich harmonisch in die natürliche Umgebung einfügen, vielseitig und umweltfreundlich sein. Außerdem war der Auftraggeber nicht bereit, für die ökologisch korrekte Ausstattung einen Aufpreis zu zahlen. Heute wird in zunehmendem Maß vorausgesetzt, dass natürliche Klimaregelungssysteme und andere »grüne« Konzepte ein selbstverständlicher Teil jedes neuen Gebäudes sind, und zwar besonders in Nordeuropa.

In einer Zeit, in der die berühmtesten Architekten häufig ausgefeilte Gestaltungstechniken und Materialien einsetzen, lässt sich interessanterweise ein radikal anderes Konzept ausmachen – nämlich eines, das nach kostengünstigen und attraktiven Bauformen in ärmeren Regionen der Erde sucht. Die Architekten Mikko Heikkinen und Markku Komonen gehören mit ihrer Geflügelzuchtschule Kahere Eila in Guinea (1998–99) zu den Preisträgern des Aga Khan Award des Jahres 2001. In der Begründung wurde ihr Entwurf als ein hervorragendes Beispiel für eine elegant bescheidene und doch moderne Architektur gelobt, die sich erfolgreich über die Grenzen lokaler guineischer und nordischer Traditionen hinwegsetzt. Das Gebäude wurde für lediglich 104.000 Dollar gefertigt.

Ein anderes innovatives Unternehmen in Richtung kostengünstiger Architektur wurde von dem verstorbenen Samuel Mockbee geleitet und nahm seinen Anfang an der Auburn University in Alabama. Das von Mockbee gegründete Rural Studio lud Architekturstudenten der Universität ein, sich aktiv am Bau von Wohn- und Gemeindebauten für die äußerst arme Bevölkerungsschicht, insbesondere der Stadt Masons Bend, zu beteiligen. Mockbee beschrieb das für nur 20.000 Dollar erbaute Masons Bend Community Center in Masons Bend, Alabama (1999–2000), als »eine Kapelle aus Windschutzscheiben und Wänden aus Schlamm, die die ortsüblichen Bauformen aufgreift«. Sein Verweis auf das ungewöhnliche Baumaterial bezieht sich auf das Dach des Gebäudes, das aus 80 Chevy-Caprice-Windschutzscheiben hergestellt wurde.

Sowohl in den Arbeiten von Heikkinen und Komonen in Guinea als auch in Samuel Mockbees Rural Studio werden einheimische Traditionen und Materialien respektiert, ohne diese einem bestimmten ästhetischen Diktat zu unterwerfen. Obgleich künstlerisch ausgerichtete Architekten häufig versuchen, ihren Auftraggebern die jeweils eigene Vision aufzuzwingen, gibt es vielleicht auch andere Methoden der Qualitätsbeurteilung für zeitgenössisches Bauen. So könnte man etwa Sensibilität für die Umgebung und die Fähigkeit, mit äußerst geringen Budgets auszukommen, in den Kriterienkatalog aufnehmen.

### DIE ERFINDUNG NEUER GESTALTUNGSFORMEN

Ob mit oder ohne Einsatz von Computer führen schöpferische Architekten ihre Suche nach neuen Gestaltungsformen weiter. Einer der bemerkenswertesten Vertreter unter ihnen ist Santiago Calatrava. Sein Quadracci Pavillon für das Milwaukee Art Museum in Milwaukee, Wisconsin (1994–2001), hat eine Empfangshalle, die so genannte »Burke Brise-Soleil«, die von einer verschiebbaren Sonnenschutzblende abgeschirmt wird und eine ungewöhnliche, an einen Vogel erinnernde Form aufweist. Auch Frank O. Gehry, ein Meister der überraschenden Formen, hat kürzlich ein erstaunliches Bauwerk in Berlin realisiert. Die am Pariser Platz gelegene DG-Bank (1995–2001) wirkt von außen sachlich-nüchtern, enthält in ihrem Innenhof jedoch einen spektakulär geformten Bauteil für Konferenzräume, der Ähnlichkeit mit einem Pferdekopf hat. Diese frei schwingende, mit rostfreiem Stahl ummantelte Form gleicht sowohl jener, die Gehry für die bislang unrealisierte Villa von Peter Lewis entwickelt hat, als auch dem großen skulpturalen Objekt, das er in der Galerie von Larry Gagosian in Los Angeles präsentierte. Dass dieser Architekt schon lange von biomorphen Formen fasziniert ist, beweisen die von ihm gestalteten Restaurants Fish Dance in Kobe (1984) und Rebecca's in Venice (1982–85). Letzteres ist ausgestattet mit an der Decke hängenden Krokodilen, fischförmigen Lampen sowie einem krakenähnlichen Kronleuchter.

Auch ohne das Bedürfnis, die morphologischen Analogien auszureizen, versuchen Architekten wie der Japaner Toyo Ito, möglichst innovative Gebäude zu entwerfen. Sein zuletzt ausgeführtes Projekt, die Mediathek in Sendai (1998–2001) zeigt eine fließend gestalterische Transparenz, die eine gewisse Ähnlichkeit mit den computergenerierten Formen kalifornischer oder niederländischer Architekten hat. Tatsächlich verwendet Ito den Begriff »Meeresalgen« in der Beschreibung der 13 Röhren aus weißem Stahl, die wellenartig durch die Konstruktion verlaufen und das Gebäude sowie dessen technische Installationen tragen.

Das Konzept frei gestalteter Formen ist jedoch keineswegs auf ehrgeizige Großprojekte wie Gehrys DG-Bank oder Itos Mediathek beschränkt. Das junge Team von Jakob + MacFarlane führte die Gestaltung der Librairie Florence Loewy in Paris (2001) mittels Computer aus, doch die außergewöhnlichen, gekrümmten Bücherregale, die sie für diesen unspektakulären Raum entwarfen, erscheinen nicht sofort als architektonische Avantgarde. Eher ist ein solches Projekt dazu geeignet, die Bandbreite neuer Bauweisen zu verdeutlichen.

### ARCHITEKTUR ALS KUNST – KUNST ALS ARCHITEKTUR

Nur wenige Architekten können es sich wirklich erlauben, ihren Beruf als Kunst zu begreifen. Ökonomische Zwänge bekommen häufig die Oberhand über ästhetische Ansprüche, selbst wenn die Gestalter intellektuell im Stande sind, mehr als nur ein funktionales Gebäude zu entwerfen. Tadao Andos exakte Beherrschung des Baumaterials Beton ist fast legendär, doch seine bedeutendsten Bauten wurden, jedenfalls bis vor kurzem, alle in Japan realisiert. Nun, mit der bevorstehenden Fertigstellung des Modern Art Museum of Fort Worth und der gerade in St. Louis eröffneten Pulitzer Foundation for the Arts, kann Ando für sich beanspruchen, den geografischen Wirkungskreis seines Könnens ausgeweitet zu haben. Im Gegensatz zu den extravaganten Formen eines Marcos Novak beruht Andos Arbeit ganz entschieden auf den Prinzipien der euklidischen Geometrie. So auch die Pulitzer Foundation, deren gesamte Bauform im Grunde von zwei rechtwinkligen Blöcken gebildet wird. Obwohl dieser Entwurf extrem schlicht ist, hatte der Architekt Meinungsverschiedenheiten mit einem der an diesem Projekt teilnehmenden Künstler, nämlich Richard Serra. Außerhalb des Gebäudes wurde eine große Skulptur von Serra errichtet, umgeben von Betonwänden, die Ando gestaltet hat. Serra hätte es vorgezogen, die komplexen Kurvenlinien seiner Arbeit nicht von diesem architektonischen Einfall umschlossen zu sehen. Interessant ist, dass sich dieser Konflikt dort abgespielt hat, wo die Arbeit eines der »künstlerischsten« Architekten auf das Werk eines jener Bildhauer trifft, das eine größtmögliche Nähe zur Architektur wagt. Ein Fall von beruflicher Rivalität?

Serra verwendet in seinen Arbeiten meistens Corten-Stahl, ein Material das häufiger im Schiffsbau als in der Architektur eingesetzt wird. Auch Rem Koolhaas wählte genau diese Art Stahl für die Wände der Ausstellungsräume in der von ihm gestalteten neuen Dependance Guggenheim Eremitage in Las Vegas. Im Herzen der größten Casino-Kitsch-Architektur von Las Vegas, dem Venetian, hat es der Direktor der Guggenheim Museen Thomas Krens in Kooperation mit der St. Petersburger Eremitage gewagt, nicht nur einen, sondern zwei Säle für anspruchsvolle, zeitgenössische Ausstellungsprojekte einzurichten. Das ebenfalls von Koolhaas gestaltete Guggenheim Las Vegas zeichnet sich durch ein sehr viel zwangloseres Design aus. Es wurde mit der von Frank O. Gehry spektakulär eingerichteten Ausstellung »The Art of the Motorcycle« eröffnet, die zuvor bereits in New York und Bilbao zu sehen gewesen war. Krens hat den Ruf, die Kunstwelt aufzumischen, und das von ihm bei Gehry in Auftrag gegebene Guggenheim Museum Bilbao war eines der erfolgreichsten Beispiele neuer Architektur der 1990er Jahre. Wenn es nach Krens geht, wird eine weitere von Gehry entworfene Guggenheim Dependance unweit des ehemaligen World Trade Center in New York entstehen. Der Museumsdirektor war es auch, der Jean Nouvel und Zaha M. Hadid einlud, an einem Wettbewerb für den Entwurf eines neuen, »kunsthallenartigen« Gebäudes für das Guggenheim in Tokio teilzunehmen, den Hadid dann gewann. Krens hat erkannt, dass die Architektur an sich eine Attraktion darstellen kann, was auch das 1959 in New York von Frank Lloyd Wright gebaute Originalgebäude des Guggenheim Museums belegt. Richard Serra dagegen sagt, der Unterschied zwischen Kunst und Architektur liege darin, dass die Kunst nicht zweckgebunden sei. Dennoch bleibt der künstlerische Aspekt von Architektur, bestärkt vom Erfolg solcher Gestalter wie Gehry, eine wichtige Quelle für kreative architektonische Neuerungen.

Selten kommt es vor, dass ein Künstler, besonders ein so namhafter wie James Turrell, ein Werk ausführt, das sich ohne weiteres als gelungene Grenzüberschreitung zwischen Kunst und Architektur bezeichnen lässt. Genau das ist es jedoch, woran Turrell in der Wüste von Arizona an einem Ort namens Roden Crater arbeitet. Etwa 60 km von Flagstaff entfernt, liegt Roden Crater inmitten eines 50.000 ha umfassenden Geländes, das der Künstler 1977 zusammen mit dem Vulkan aufgekauft hat. Obwohl die umfangreichen Erdarbeiten, bei denen mehrere 100.000 m$^3$ Erde verschoben wurden, eher an ein bautechnisches Großprojekt der öffentlichen Hand denken lassen, hat sich der Künstler vorgenommen, ein »Observatorium für Himmelserscheinungen« zu schaffen. Turrell selbst erklärt sein Vorhaben denn auch mit architektonischem Bezug, wenn er sagt: »Was mich interessiert, ist die Tatsache, dass wir Künstler Erbauer sind. Wir stellen Dinge her. Das ist ein Teil der menschlichen Natur, der in irgendeiner Form hervorgehoben werden muss. Allen Künstlern ist eigen, dass sie mit ihren Werken eine

Aussage machen. Ich denke daran, was Paolo Soleri hier mit Arcosanti oder Frank Lloyd Wright mit Taliesin geschaffen haben, oder auch an die Watts Towers von Simon Rodia in Los Angeles. Das alles sind Beispiele für die Vision einer Person oder eines Künstlers.« Turrell ist besonders an der Wahrnehmung von Licht interessiert und Roden Crater sollte nicht als Beispiel zeitgenössischer Architektur, sondern als Kunstwerk interpretiert werden. Und dennoch dient die visionäre Qualität solcher Arbeiten auch als Inspiration für das bauliche Umfeld.

Kunstwerke an der Grenze zur Architektur beziehungsweise Architektur, die sich dem rein Künstlerischen annähert, führen potentiell zu Konfusion, aber auch zu einer bereichernden Stimulation, die einen der wichtigsten Trends im Baudesign der letzten 20 Jahre ausmacht. Die Tatsache, dass etliche hervorragende Architekten von Klienten wie Thomas Krens mit dem Bau von Museen beauftragt werden, ist ein bedeutsamer Indikator für deren eigene Nähe zum Prozess des Kunstschaffens.

### WANN IST EIN HAUS KEIN ZUHAUSE?

Private Wohnhäuser sind seit langem eins der bevorzugten Tätigkeitsfelder für die meisten kreativen Architekten. Ihre überschaubaren Dimensionen und die oft wohlhabenden Bauherren erlauben ein großes Maß an gestalterischer Freiheit. So hat zum Beispiel der spanische Architekt Alberto Campo Baeza bei seinem 2000 in Sevilla la Nueva, Madrid, erbauten Haus De Blas mit einer typisch minimalistischen Lösung auf den speziellen Standort reagiert. Campo Baeza dazu: »Zunächst wurde ein Betongehäuse gebaut, das die Plattform abgibt für das darauf gesetzte Gehäuse aus Glas, das wiederum von einer leichten, weiß gestrichenen Stahlkonstruktion überdacht ist. Wie in einer Höhle beherbergt ein in die Erde eingelassener und vor Ort gegossener Betonsockel den schematisch klaren Bauplan eines traditionellen Wohnhauses mit Neben- und Versorgungsräumen. Das auf diesem Podium ruhende Glasgehäuse ist eine Art Belvedere, in das man vom Inneren des Hauses aus aufsteigt. Während die darunter liegende Höhle ein Refugium darstellt, ist das Belvedere ein Raum, von dem aus sich die Natur ringsum betrachten lässt. Dieses Haus ist der Versuch einer Übertragung theoretischer Fragestellungen der Tektonik und der Stereotomie in die Praxis, indem ein tektonischer, also der Gestaltung dienender Teil auf ein stereotomisches Gehäuse platziert wurde. Daraus entsteht die Essenz dessen, was in der Architektur wichtig ist, wobei auch hier gilt: ›Weniger ist mehr‹.« Waro Kishi beschreibt sein Haus Kurakuen II im japanischen Nishinomiya, Hyogo (2000–01), mit ähnlichen Begriffen: »Ich entwarf zwei mit Stahlverstärkung konstruierte Blöcke. Im linken liegen die Privaträume, während sich im rechten die öffentlichen Bereiche mit Wohn- und Esszimmer befinden. Beide Bauteile sind durch eine Schrägrampe miteinander verbunden. Das Dach auf dem obersten Geschoss des linken Blocks ist so gestaltet, dass es so dünn wie möglich wirkt.« Campo Baeza und Kishi teilen eine minimalistische Ästhetik, die weltweit einen beständigen Faktor in der aktuellen Architektur bildet. Auch der in Australien tätige Architekt Sean Godsell hat im Entwurf des 2000 fertig gestellten Hauses Carter/Tucker in Breamlea, Victoria, eine geometrische Formensprache verwendet. Hierbei handelt es sich um einen 12 x 6 m messenden Bauteil, der in eine Sanddüne eingebaut wurde. Die elementare äußere Schlichtheit des Hauses erhält durch die Anordnung überraschender Öffnungen in der Fassade ein dekoratives Attribut, wobei eine auf allen drei Stockwerken angebrachte, nach oben klappbare Holzblende als Markise fungiert.

Genauso wie ein minimalistischer Ansatz auf der ganzen Welt in vielfältiger Form umgesetzt wird, treten auch allenthalben mehr komplexe und farbenfrohe Bauformen in Erscheinung, wie bei dem von Ettore Sottsass entworfenen Haus Ernest Mourmans, genannt Birdhouse, in Maastricht (1999–2001). Der 1917 geborene Sottsass ist vor allem als Möbeldesigner und Begründer des Designstudios Memphis bekannt geworden und es ließe sich kritisch anmerken, dass das Birdhouse genau die Ästhetik zu Beginn der 1980er Jahre in Erinnerung ruft. Aber das soll nicht heißen, dass man bestimmte Formen von Modernität auf spezifische Zeitspannen beschränken sollte. Das Birdhouse ist von seinem Entwurf und seiner Ausführung her zweifellos zeitgemäß und aktuell. Wahrscheinlich ist es seine ungeheure Komplexität, die es mit einer Periode in Zusammenhang bringt, die der heutigen Generation von Architekten einigermaßen fremd geworden ist.

Für viele Architekten ist die mit den sich wandelnden Stilen verbundene Herausforderung ein bedeutsamer Faktor ihrer Arbeit. Während sich manche, wie Richard Meier oder Tadao Ando, konsequent an eine streng modernistische Formensprache halten, deren Klassizismus sie gewissermaßen über den jeweiligen Modeströmungen stehen lässt, bewegen sich andere, wie Philip Johnson oder in jüngerer Zeit Arata Isozaki, je nach den Umständen rasch von einem Stil zum anderen. Ein in diesem Zusammenhang interessanter Fall ist der des 1944 geborenen finnischen Architekten Jyrki Tasa, einst ein entschiedener Vertreter des postmodernen Baudesigns. In seinem neueren Projekt, dem 1998 im finnischen Espoo fertig gestellten Haus Into, gelingt ihm der heikle Übergang von seinem vorherigen Baustil zu einer zeitgemäßeren Haltung. Es gibt jedoch immer noch jene Momente einer Unausgewogenheit und Überraschung, welche charakteristisch für seine früheren Gebäude waren. Privathäuser gehören in jedem Fall zur Domäne des persönlichen Geschmacks, und zwar sowohl dem des Architekten als natürlich dem des Auftraggebers. »Modernität« ist ein relativer Begriff, der von der subjektiven Betrachtungsweise abhängt. Menschen, die sich in architektonischen Modeströmungen nicht besonders gut auskennen, mögen eine postmoderne Stilrichtung für aktuell halten.

### SHOPPING ODER RELIGION?

In seinem neuesten *Harvard Design School Guide to Shopping* wagt Rem Koolhaas eine Analogie zwischen Einkaufen und Religion. In dem Kapitel »Divine Economy« (Die Göttliche Ökonomie) schreibt Sze Tsung Leong, dass die Kirchen in dem Bestreben, das Medium für ihre Märkte neu zu erfinden, sowohl in ihrer äußeren Gestalt als auch in ihren Methoden immer kommerzieller werden. In jedem Fall wird sowohl in religiösen als auch in marktstrategischen Kreisen eine anspruchsvolle Architektur als Schlüsselfaktor betrachtet, um neue Zielgruppen zu gewinnen. Zu den bemerkenswertesten Bauten des japanischen Architekten Tadao Ando gehören denn auch Tempel und Kirchen. Sein jüngstes Werk, der Komyo-ji Tempel in Saijo, Ehime (1999–2000) wird als ein »Versammlungsraum« definiert und stellt überdies eine Verbindung zu den Ursprüngen der japanischen Tempelarchitektur her. Die deutsche Architektengruppe Allmann Sattler Wappner verwendet in ihrer Herz Jesu Kirche in München (1996–2001) ebenfalls eine minimalistische Formensprache, mit der sie die religiöse Funktion des Gebäudes eher indirekt andeuten, statt sie explizit darzustellen. Sowohl in dem deutschen als auch dem japanischen Beispiel besteht die Finesse der Architekten darin, dass gläubige Menschen alle Symbole darin finden werden, um es als ein Gotteshaus zu erkennen.

Im Gegensatz zur Religion, wo modische Erwägungen keine Rolle spielen sollten, ist es gerade die kurzlebige Attraktion des Neuen, die Käufer in Modegeschäfte zieht. Die japanischen Designer Issey Miyake und Rei Kawakubo (Comme des Garçons) behaupten seit langem eine herausragende Stellung im Bereich des Ladendesigns, indem sie erstklassige Architekten heranziehen und sich auch persönlich an der Gestaltung ihrer Boutiquen beteiligen. Für seinen neuen Flagship Store in New York beauftragte Miyake keinen Geringeren als Frank O. Gehry. Gehry, der an diesem Projekt mit seinem Kollegen Gordon Kipping arbeitet, verwendet eines seiner Markenzeichen, wellenförmige Metallbleche, die sich durch den hohen, lagerhausähnlichen Raum winden. Dieses Element zusammen mit dem raffinierten Einsatz von Metall und

Glas verleiht dem Wahrzeichen aus Gusseisen einen spannenden modernen Akzent. Die Miyake-Boutique in Tribeca beweist, dass avant-gardistisches Modedesign, Architektur und Innenraumgestaltung eine gelungene Symbiose eingehen können.

Rei Kawakubo ist sogar wesentlich radikaler als Miyake oder irgendein anderer ihrer Kollegen. Nach ihrer Zusammenarbeit mit Future Systems bei der Gestaltung ihrer Geschäfte in New York und Tokio gab sie Ab Rogers, dem Sohn des für sein Centre Pompidou berühmten Richard Rogers, den Auftrag, einen spektakulären, roten Verkaufsraum auf der Pariser rue du Faubourg Saint-Honoré, genau gegenüber dem Élysée-Palast, zu entwerfen. Die endgültigen Entscheidungen trifft Rei Kawakubo selbst, weshalb es angemessen ist, sie als die eigentliche »Architektin« zu betrachten. Sie stellt eine Verbindung zwischen Räumen, Objekten und Kleidung her, um eine Atmosphäre zu kreieren, die man mit dem Comme-des-Garçons-Label identifizieren soll. Man erwirbt zwar keine Religion, wenn man Rei Kawakubos Geschäfte betritt, aber man nimmt an einer Art ästhetischer Ausrichtung teil, die sich auf alle Aspekte der von ihr definierten Umgebung erstreckt.

## FUNKTIONALE ARCHITEKTUR

Auch wenn die vergeistigten Arbeiten eines Marcos Novak für die Architektur durchaus zukunftweisend sein mögen, bleibt für alle Gestalter, mit Ausnahme der am stärksten »künstlerisch« geprägten, offensichtlich die Notwendigkeit bestehen, ihre Entwürfe zu realisieren und sich zudem den gegebenen programmatischen Anforderungen anzupassen, um im Geschäft zu bleiben. Denn meistens ist ein Bauprojekt, wenn es über die Dimensionen eines Privathauses hinausgeht, für sehr pragmatische Zwecke konzipiert. Daraus entsteht eine Art »Brot-erwerbsarchitektur«, die Menschen ermöglicht, Kinofilme zu sehen, einen Zug zu besteigen, ein Gericht aufzusuchen, ein Konzert oder eine Bücherei zu besuchen oder einfach nur in einem Büro zu arbeiten. Die Erfüllung der Anforderungen solcher Gebäudetypen ist der wahre Grad-messer für architektonische Qualität, insbesondere bei begrenztem Budget. Die in Deutschland lebenden Architekten Bolles + Wilson haben im Jahr 2000 das New Luxor Theatre im Rotterdamer Gebiet Kop van Zuid fertig gestellt, auf dem sie zuvor schon die Kaianlagen gestaltet haben (Kop van Zuid, 1991–96). Das Luxor Theatre ist ein weiterer Schritt zur Umwandlung der früheren Docks von Rotterdam in ein lebendi-ges, neues Stadtviertel. Obwohl man von dem Gebäude nicht behaupten kann, dass es sensationell innovativ ist, stellt es ein Schlüsselelement für dieses ehrgeizige Stadterneuerungsprojekt dar.

Gute Architektur an vernachlässigten Gebäuden umzusetzen ist ein weiteres lobenswertes Unternehmen, besonders wenn Millionen Reisender davon profitieren. Das ist mit Sicherheit der Fall bei Jean-Marie Duthilleul und seiner Baufirma AREP, einem Tochterunternehmen der französischen Eisenbahngesellschaft SNCF. Im Zusammenhang mit der Einführung der TGV-Züge hat sich Duthilleul aktiv dafür eingesetzt, auch die Bahnhöfe einladender und moderner zu gestalten. Für den jüngsten Ausbau der TGV-Verbindung von Lyon nach Südfrankreich wurden neue Gleiswege und drei neue Bahnhöfe gebaut: in Valence, Avignon und Aix-en-Provence. Jeder dieser Bahnhöfe ist anders gestaltet und jeder bringt ein gewisses Maß an modernem Komfort und Eleganz an diese Orte. So ist zum Beispiel der Bahnhof in Valence (1998–2001) eine über die Schienen hinausragende Freibaukonstruktion. Der zu den einfahrenden Zügen hin geneigte Bauteil verfügt über einen unge-wöhnlichen, schräg abfallenden Boden und eine Transparenz, die ihn bei eventuellen Wartezeiten zu einem angenehmen Aufenthaltsort macht. Mit seinen Renovierungsarbeiten an Bahnhöfen von Lille bis Marseille hat Duthilleul das Erscheinungsbild der wichtigsten französischen Bahnhöfe verändert. Es ist wie ein Rückblick auf das ausgehende 19. Jahrhundert, als etwa die grandiose Hülle aus Glas und Eisen des Gare

Saint-Lazare Künstler wie Claude Monet inspirierte. Damals wurde das Reisen mit der Eisenbahn als modern und fortschrittlich angesehen, ein Aspekt, den die Einführung des TGV in Kombination mit Duthilleuls Bahnhöfen zu Beginn des 21. Jahrhunderts zu neuem Leben erweckt hat.

Das Gerichtswesen ist ein weiterer Bereich, in dem eine hochwertige zeitgenössische Architektur eine bedeutende Stellung einnimmt, wie zum Beispiel in Frankreich und den Vereinigten Staaten. Richard Meier bringt mit seinem Entwurf für das Federal Building & United States Courthouse in Phoenix, Arizona (1998–2000), etwas von seiner visionären, lichterfüllten Reinheit in die Jurisdiktion ein. Ein 35 m hohes verglastes Atrium verleiht dem Gebäude eine Offenheit, die auch als Ausdruck des Bemühens zu verstehen ist, einem Sicherheitsdenken entgegenzuwirken, das auf Tragödien wie den Bombenanschlag 1995 auf das Alfred P. Murrah Federal Building in Oklahoma City zurückzuführen ist. Meiers wohl geordnete Helligkeit scheint besonders geeignet zur Strukturierung dieser Räumlichkeiten und zur Wiederherstellung einer Würde, die in den letzten Jahren von Überreaktion und Irrtum dominiert wurde.

Das Bankgewerbe betrachtete man lange Zeit als ein uninteressantes und von Behäbigkeit geprägtes Tätigkeitsfeld. Zweifellos ist die in den Chefetagen der Kreditinstitute herrschende Vorliebe für klassische, ja sogar niederdrückend-starre Bauformen, die Seriosität und Dauerhaftigkeit symbolisieren sollen, zum Teil für dieses Image verantwortlich. Die von Morphosis in Klagenfurt realisierte Bankzentrale, das Hypo Alpe-Adria-Zentrum (1998–2000), weist eindeutig in die entgegengesetzte Richtung, setzt sie doch vor allem auf Bewegung und Lebendigkeit. »Die dynamische Anordnung der Bauelemente evoziert das Bild tektonischer Verschiebungen«, erklären die Architekten, »wobei jedoch Knotenpunkte installiert sind, die innerhalb der Turbulenz für Stabilität sorgen.« Die Investoren sind wahrscheinlich erfreut, solche »Knotenpunkte der Stabilität« in einem Gebäude ausmachen zu können, das in seiner Gestaltungsweise überraschend und ungewöhnlich bleibt. Hier dient die Architektur dazu, das öffentliche Image und vielleicht sogar den Sinn und Zweck eines Berufsstandes, den der allzu schnelle Wandel internationaler Trends vor akute Herausforderungen stellt, neu zu definieren. Ein ganz anderes Beispiel für die Beziehung zwischen Bankgeschäft und Architektur bietet der neue, von Pei Partnership entworfene Hauptsitz der Bank of China in Beijing (1997–2001). In diesem Fall nämlich führten ein äußerst dicht gedrängter Bauplan sowie der explizite Wunsch des Bauherrn, dass sich in dem Gebäude gerade jenes Image von Stabilität ausdrücken sollte, auf das die österreichische Bank keinen großen Wert legte, zu einem fast diametral entgegengesetzten Resultat. Obgleich von der äußeren Erscheinung her nicht besonders originell, schafft das 45 m hohe und 3.000 m² umfassende Atriumhaus der Bank die spektakuläre Art von öffentlichem Raum, für die der Vater des Architekten, I. M. Pei, weithin bekannt ist. Architekten können nur selten das Image verändern, das ihre Auftraggeber vermitteln möchten, aber Bauwerke, die so zukunftweisend sind wie das Hypo Alpe-Adria-Zentrum oder so grundsolide wie die Bank of China in Beijing werden mit Sicherheit einen Einfluss darauf haben, wie diese Institutionen in Zukunft wahrgenommen werden.

Bürogebäude und insbesondere Wolkenkratzer sind seit längerem das Objekt eines gewissen Spotts, und zwar wegen ihrer offensichtlich phallischen Konnotationen. Jean Nouvel ist wahrscheinlich der erste Architekt, der dieses Bild gleichsam an seine logischen Grenzen führt. Die äußere Gestalt seiner 2001 in Barcelona errichteten Torre Agbar unweit des Boulevard Diagonal hat einerseits offensichtlich mit dem Geschäft des Auftraggebers zu tun – einer Wasserversorgungsgesellschaft. Andererseits ist seine hoch aufgerichtete, rautenförmige

Gestalt ziemlich eindeutig. Mit ihrem ausgeklügelten Design ist die Torre Agbar sicher keine Ironisierung. Man könnte sogar argumentieren, dass Nouvel, indem er die Assoziation mit dem Phallus ernst nimmt, jeder potentiellen Kritik den Boden entzieht.

Viele Kritiker sind der Ansicht, dass gigantische Architekturwettbewerbe nur selten den in sie gesetzten Erwartungen gerecht werden. Die von Snøhetta Architects im ägyptischen Alexandria realisierte Bibliotheca Alexandrina (1995–2001) ist das Ergebnis eines solchen Wettbewerbs, für den 524 Beiträge aus 52 Ländern eingereicht wurden. Auch wenn es zutreffen mag, dass nur wenige in jüngster Zeit erbaute Bibliotheken die in sie gesetzten hohen architektonischen Erwartungen zu erfüllen vermochten – wie etwa die französische Nationalbibliothek in Paris von Dominique Perrault – scheint das Snøhetta-Projekt in Alexandria besonders bedeutungsvoll. Das in jeder Hinsicht massive Bauwerk verleiht der ägyptischen Stadt mit Sicherheit ein neues Wahrzeichen. Aber erfüllt es wirklich all jene Hoffnungen, die durch die UNESCO-Unterstützung und die umfangreiche Medienberichterstattung geweckt wurden? Von Beginn an mit Symbolen überfrachtet, ist die allgemeine Enttäuschung über die Bibliothek möglicherweise vorprogrammiert, ganz gleich, was die Architekten geleistet haben.

Eine weitere Kategorie von Bauwerken, die häufig Anlass zur Enttäuschung gibt, ist die Art von Kultur- und Kongresszentren, wie sie während der letzten Jahre in vielen französischen Provinzstädten erbaut wurden. Bernard Tschumi dagegen ist mit seinem Zenith in Rouen (1999–2001) und dessen Doppelgehäuse aus fließendem Metall ein brillanter Wurf geglückt. Mit Gebäuden wie dem Zenith beweist er, dass sein Ruf auch durch das verlässliche Talent gerechtfertig ist, trotz begrenzter Budgets innovative Lösungen zu finden. Ebenso wie Duthilleuls Modernisierung französischer Bahnhöfe ist diese Veranstaltungshalle in Rouen ein ungemein gelungenes Beispiel für qualitativ hochwertige Architektur, die einer breiten Öffentlichkeit zugute kommt.

## ZURÜCK IN DIE ZUKUNFT

Gebäude, die von Architekten mit einem wirklichen Sinn für Ästhetik entworfen wurden, sind selten. In den meisten Städte werden unpassende Imitationen, billige Reproduktionen einstmals großartiger Ideen errichtet. Wie dieser Überblick über die zeitgenössische Architektur offenbart, ist ihre theoretische Vorreiterrolle sogar noch stärker an den Rand des öffentlichen Interesses gerückt. Und dennoch entwickelt sich die Idee einer neuen Form von Architektur, die ihre Modelle aus der wandlungsfähigen Welt der Biologie bezieht. Eine Architektur, die aus dem Computerdesign entstehen und vielleicht sogar als genetische Algorithmen, Formen hervorbringen wird, die sich kein Architekt je zuvor vorstellen konnte. Darüber hinaus können Computerprogramme, wie es Frank O. Gehry in seiner Anwendung von Dassaults Catia-Programm gezeigt hat, die Konstruktion höchst komplexer Bauformen außerordentlich erleichtern. Sollten solch skulpturale Formen jedoch die Zukunft der Architektur sein, dann müssen sie mehr darstellen als eine ästhetische Laune. Flexibilität und die Fähigkeit, sich funktionalen Notwendigkeiten und der Entwicklung der Zeit anzupassen, machen den grundlegenden Erfolg der neuen Architektur aus – einer lebendigen, atmenden Architektur für eine neue Welt.

# INTRODUCTION

## RETOUR VERS LE FUTUR

Les formes d'architecture que nous connaissons sont profondément inscrites dans la nature et l'anatomie humaine. Dès les premières cavernes habitées, le besoin de se protéger des éléments ou des ennemis a dicté l'existence d'une porte ou d'un toit. Les colonnes des temples grecs et la splendeur arborescente du style gothique prennent leurs racines dans les forêts d'avant la civilisation. Et si la nature anatomique de l'architecture n'était pas encore assez évidente dans des milliers d'autres exemples, il suffit de regarder la coupole et les « bras » déployés de Saint-Pierre de Rome pour comprendre que le construit vient de ce que nous sommes. Ces références au corps ne sont pas limitées à l'architecture ancienne. Il est clair, entre autres, que les tours appartiennent aux formes architecturales les plus explicitement anatomiques. La fonction de protection étant depuis longtemps maîtrisée, la valeur symbolique de l'architecture, comme expression du pouvoir par exemple, continue à chercher sa légitimité dans les réalités les plus basiques de l'existence de l'homme.

Bien que le développement économique et urbain privilégie de plus en plus l'architecture éphémère, la vertu vitruvienne de « solidité » reste l'une des prémisses les plus fortement enracinées de l'art du constructeur. Si la « flexibilité » de nombreux projets est appréciée, il est rare que les architectes pensent à l'évolution de leur œuvre avec le temps. En fait, ils n'imaginaient pas cette possibilité jusqu'à assez récemment. Certains praticiens américains comme Frank O. Gehry ou Peter Eisenman se sont livré à des tentatives largement médiatisées de rupture avec le moule des formes architecturales traditionnelles. Gehry assume dans une large mesure sa liberté artistique, aidé en cela par un logiciel sophistiqué conçu à l'origine pour le dessin des avions de chasse, et des réalisations comme le Guggenheim de Bilbao ne peuvent guère être rapprochées des modèles anatomiques du passé. Bien qu'il soit plaqué de titane, sa solidité semble se dissoudre dans une symphonie complexe de courbes non euclidiennes.

À l'origine, la vertu de solidité en architecture trouve certainement ses sources originales dans un besoin de protection. Une fois cet objectif atteint, la durabilité, en termes à la fois concrets et symboliques, peut être considérée comme une victoire sur le temps. Bien que la colonne évoque la forme d'un arbre, et le dôme un crâne humain, l'architecture de pierre semble plus étroitement liée à la géologie naturelle qu'à la réalité biologique. Adaptabilité, sensibilité à l'environnement, croissance et changements rapides sont les signes du vivant. Se pourrait-il que l'on assiste en architecture à la venue au premier plan d'un glissement paradigmatique marqué par certains aspects éphémères ou le souci de l'écologie ? L'architecte américain Neil Denari pose la question : « Qu'est-ce qui constitue le système architectural du monde ? On peut se demander, par rapport au modèle biologique, si l'architecture doit devenir maintenant un système ouvert et dynamique qui rejette complètement le quasi-équilibre d'un système statique ou fermé ? Après tout, si l'architecture a entrepris des transformations conceptuelles positives radicales via un modèle biologique de systèmes, pourra-t-elle, en tant que discipline, se référer de nouveau à un équilibre ou à quelque chose d'immuable ? Cela ne se fera pas, même si le construit *semble* différent. »*

Même sans arriver aux conclusions aussi radicales de Neil Denari, on peut s'attendre avec une quasi-certitude à ce que surviennent des changements importants. Et si les formes libres de Frank O. Gehry n'étaient que les premiers pas de la libération de l'architecture de son

* Neil M. Denari, *Gyroscopic Horizons*, Thames & Hudson, Londres, 1999

héritage ancestral ? Pas la *tabula rasa* de Gropius, mais plutôt le début de la quête d'une nouvelle architecture. Les enjeux de fonction et de coût joueront nécessairement un rôle majeur, mais cette nouvelle architecture existe pour sa plus grande partie uniquement sur les écrans d'ordinateurs et n'est donc pas soumise aux mêmes contraintes bassement matérielles que leurs cousines d'acier et de béton. Imaginons de nouveaux logiciels, comme les « algorithmes génétiques », capables de créer des formes que les plus inventifs des architectes n'auraient pu rêver. Certains téméraires imaginent que l'architecture peut exister en tant que discipline sans jamais quitter l'écran, sorte d'exercice intellectuel, formel et artistique. D'autres ont déjà fait le saut du numérique au « réel », et les formes d'un monde nouveau commencent à apparaître.

## CONSTRUIRE LE VIRTUEL

Neil Denari fait partie de ces quelques architectes dont l'influence est considérable, même s'ils n'ont que très peu construit. Ce n'est pas en soi un phénomène nouveau. Des créateurs comme Rem Koolhaas ont établi leur réputation par leurs écrits, longtemps avant d'avoir édifié quoi que ce soit, mais c'est la génération suivante, celle des étudiants de Koolhaas entre autres, qui entraîne désormais l'architecture vers de nouvelles directions. Né en 1957, l'architecte néerlandais Ben van Berkel (UN Studio) a étudié auprès de Koolhaas à l'Architectural Association de Londres avant de devenir l'un des pionniers de l'exploration des formes construites conçues à l'aide de l'ordinateur. « J'observe une tendance croissante à rechercher des manières dont l'architecture pourrait introduire de plus en plus de complexité dans une complexité globale », dit-il. « Cette tendance s'oriente de plus en plus vers les systèmes organiques, et la façon dont, par l'impact et l'effet de forces externes, un modèle générique se différencie. Le modèle est perçu comme un tout, tout en restant dans le même temps très fragmenté. »

Les Néerlandais se montrent très ouverts aux développements de nouveaux archétypes formels à la fois virtuels et réels. Lars Spuybroek, né en 1959 à Rotterdam, et Maurice Nio ont créé NOX, agence qui se consacre au travail sur ordinateur. En 1997, Kas Oosterhuis et un autre confrère ont créé l'un des premiers bâtiments réellement novateurs de l'ère de l'informatique sur l'île artificielle de Neeltje Jans, au sud-ouest de Rotterdam, non loin des digues du projet Delta. Spuybroek décrit habilement cette remarquable construction comme « un alliage turbulent du résistant et du faible, de la chair humaine, du béton et du métal, de l'électronique interactive et de l'eau. Une fusion intégrale de corps, d'environnement et de technologie. » « Le projet », poursuit-il, « était basé sur l'agrégation métastable d'architecture et d'information. La forme elle-même étant générée par la déformation fluide de quatorze ellipses espacées sur plus de 65 m de long. À l'intérieur du bâtiment, sans sols horizontaux ni relation externe avec l'horizon, marcher devient presque tomber. La déformation de l'objet s'étend à la métamorphose permanente de l'environnement qui répond de manière interactive aux visiteurs de ce pavillon d'eau par le biais de toute une panoplie de capteurs qui enregistrent cette remise en forme constante du corps humain que l'on appelle action. »

La Californie représente une autre des sources de créativité en quête de nouveaux paradigmes architecturaux. Greg Lynn, basé à Venice, a travaillé sur le concept de ce qu'il nomme une « Maison embryologique. » Sensible au besoin de l'architecte d'être « pratique » dans ses projets, il explique : « La Maison embryologique peut être décrite comme une stratégie pour l'invention de l'espace domestique qui affronte des enjeux contemporains d'identité de marque et de variation, de « customisation » et de continuité, de fabrication flexible et d'assemblage et, plus important encore, d'un investissement non apologétique dans la beauté contemporaine et l'esthétique voluptueuse de surfaces ondulées animées par des couleurs iridescentes et opalescentes. La Maison embryologique fait appel à un système rigoureux de limites géométriques qui libèrent une exfoliation de variations infinies. Ceci apporte une sensibilité générique commune à toute Maison embryologique alors que dans le même temps deux maisons ne seront jamais identiques. »

Certains contemporains de Lynn n'éprouvent pas le besoin aigu de s'impliquer d'aussi près dans les aspects pratiques de la construction. Le plus radical de ces concepteurs est peut-être Marcos Novak, que beaucoup considèrent comme « le pionnier de l'architecture de la virtualité ». Ses concepts d'« architecture liquide » ou de « transarchitecture » existent exclusivement sur écran d'ordinateur, bien que sa pensée élabore à l'évidence un travail qui pourrait exister dans le monde « réel ». « Le cyberespace lui-même n'a jamais été limité à la réalité virtuelle », poursuit-il, « mais est plus en rapport avec notre invention d'un espace d'information pénétrant auquel on ne peut échapper, complètement lié à la culture. Nous nous sommes déplacés de la spécialisation des disciplines à la multidisciplinarité, à l'interdisciplinarité, et aujourd'hui à la transdisciplinarité. » « De façon plus tangible », précise-t-il, « les transarchitectures traitent du spectre entier de ce que l'on pourrait appeler une nouvelle tectonique : conception algorithmique, prototypage rapide, réalisation robotique, habitation interactive, téléprésence et télécommunications, nano- et gigaprésence, et le lien à la virtualité et à travers elle, pour créer un nouveau continuum spatial : physique (local) – virtuel (non local) – physique. » La pensée de Marcos Novak ouvre à l'architecture des horizons que des concepteurs plus pragmatiques peuvent dédaigner, mais il est clairement représentatif d'une nouvelle vague qui influencera la profession pour de nombreuses années à venir. « Mon travail s'oriente dans deux directions », dit-il, « de l'espace réel à l'espace virtuel, via l'immersion, et de l'espace virtuel vers l'espace réel, via ce que j'ai appelé ‹ l'éversion ›. À l'interface entre les deux, des capteurs créent des ‹ architectures invisibles › qui réalisent le rapprochement des deux l'un dans l'autre. Je travaille actuellement à une série de projets appelés ‹ allotopes ›, à l'intégration de ‹ polytopes › de Xenakis, et à leur extension par l'utilisation de l'espace virtuel dans des performances qui cherchent à réanimer des espaces puissants mais négligés. En même temps, j'utilise différentes sortes de foulage numérique et de prototypage rapide pour explorer des formes physiques dérivées de la virtualité. » Un intéressant aspect du travail de cet architecte est une relation évidente à l'art contemporain, que Frank O. Gehry a pu indirectement inspirer.

Non loin, mais sur un mode très différent, l'architecte japonais Makoto Sei Watanabé vient d'aboutir à la « première mise en œuvre au monde de ce que nous appelons la PGA, l'architecture générée par programme informatique ». Son projet pour la station de métro Idabashi (Tokyo, Japon, 1999–2000) cherche à mettre à nu ce qu'il perçoit du monde caché des transports souterrains, au moyen d'un maillage tubulaire conçu à l'aide d'un système appelé « The Web Frame », une ossature en réseau, qui envahit littéralement la station. L'approche utilisée ici est celle des algorithmes génétiques cités plus haut. Le « Web Frame » hérite « de l'ADN de l'ossature d'ingénierie », précise Watanabé, « sélectionnant, transformant et améliorant ses caractéristiques d'entrelacement, d'enchevêtrement, d'expansion, de vibration : un réseau qui s'oriente vers la lumière du jour, une seconde espèce de tubulure souterraine. La croissance du ‹ Web Frame ›», conclut-il, « a été facilitée par un programme d'ordinateur de génération automatique de codes. »

La quête de formes sophistiquées générées par ordinateur qui, à l'occasion, imitent de très près l'adaptabilité de la nature se répand dans certains cercles architecturaux, bien que ce soit à l'origine un concept beaucoup plus simple qui anime et transforme le secteur nette-

ment plus important de la construction « réelle ». La flexibilité est le mot-clé de ce que l'on est bien obligé de percevoir comme un changement massif en architecture. L'exposition de Terry Riley « The Un-Private House » (Museum of Modern Art, New York, 1999) a attiré l'attention
sur une nouvelle génération de maisons comme la Curtain Wall House de Shigeru Ban (Tokyo, 1995) qui défie les préceptes même de la
conception résidentielle. Plus récente encore, la Maison nue de Ban vue de l'extérieur est une sorte de shed qui contient des unités-chambres
déplaçables sur roulettes selon diverses configurations. Les maisons ne reprennent donc plus le prototype figé du séjour, salle à manger,
cuisine et chambres à l'étage. Les styles de vie et l'architecture elle-même ont dépassé ce type de rigidité, que des formes générées par
ordinateur soient en jeu ou non.

On peut imaginer que l'ordinateur commence à permettre un mode authentique de flexibilité qui avait échappé aux techniques de
construction du passé. La « structure pneumatique pilotée par données » présentée par Kas Oosterhuis à la Biennale d'architecture de Venise
en 2000 (trans-ports) pourrait être l'une des premières preuves de la viabilité de la conception globale par ordinateur. « La plus importante
caractéristique du pavillon trans-ports », dit Oosterhuis, « est que pour la première fois dans l'histoire l'architecture n'est plus fixe ni statique.
Par la programmabilité complète de sa forme et de son contenu d'information le bâti devient un véhicule souple et flexible qui s'ouvre à une
multiplicité d'usages. »

## AMÉLIORER LE PASSÉ

Aussi importants puissent être les changements actuellement en cours dans la conception de nouveaux bâtiments, il reste que la
réhabilitation de l'existant peut se mener à bien moindre coût qu'une reconstruction à neuf sur le même terrain. En fonction du budget, des
méthodes et des matériaux sophistiqués pourraient être utilisés dans ce cas, mais la rénovation économique est la solution la plus fréquemment retenue. C'est ce qui s'est passé dans deux programmes assez ambitieux liés à l'art, l'un aux États-Unis, l'autre en France. Le premier,
le Mass MoCA (North Adams, Massachusetts, 1988–99) est né de l'imagination de Thomas Krens, le directeur du Guggenheim qui a com-
mandé à Frank O. Gehry le musée de Bilbao. Si quelques architectes de haute notoriété avaient été contactés lors des premières phases de ce
projet (Frank O. Gehry, Robert Venturi, Skidmore, Owings & Merrill), c'est Simeon Bruner qui l'a mené à bien avec talent et intelligence. Face à
pas moins de 27 bâtiments industriels et avec un budget limité à 31,4 millions de dollars, Bruner a opté pour une rénovation assez brutale,
presque inévitable. Tel a également été le cas du caverneux Palais de Tokyo, bâtiment édifié en 1937 au bord de la Seine à Paris et reconverti
en espace d'art contemporain. Les architectes Lacaton & Vassal, un jeune couple de Bordeaux, ont mis à nu ses 9 000 m$^2$ et n'ont pas même
hésité à laisser les murs sans peinture ou à donner une finition plus que brute aux sols de béton.

Des architectes talentueux, dont un autre jeune couple parisien, Dominique Jakob et Brendan MacFarlane (Jakob & MacFarlane), ont
mené à bien des rénovations plus ambitieuses dans un certain nombre de lieux. Auteurs du restaurant Georges du Centre Pompidou, ils ont
été appelés pour transformer l'usine Métal 57 de Renault à Boulogne-Billancourt, en centre de conférences et d'expositions. Ils ont choisi de
créer une coquille à l'intérieur de la structure existante de 15 000 m$^2$, afin de redéfinir son utilisation tout en conservant sa forme externe.
Dans un style très différent un ancien associé de Ricardo Bofill, Manolo Nuñez-Yanowsky, chargé de la création du Teatre Lliure Fabià Puigserver à Barcelone, rappelle son postmodernisme des années qui ont suivi son départ du Taller. Il a conservé l'aspect extérieur de la structure

existante, le Palau d'Agricultura élevé pour l'Exposition internationale de 1929, qui n'a pas le moindre rapport avec le pavillon de Mies van der Rohe réalisé à la même occasion. Sur le plan esthétique, l'existence de tels projets souligne l'absence persistante de tout style dominant en architecture contemporaine. Entre les « formes computérisées » extravagantes de Marcus Novak et l'austérité toute de béton du Pulitzer Museum de Tadao Ando à Saint-Louis, l'écart est tel que presque n'importe quelle sensibilité peut trouver une petite niche de respectabilité.

Si dénuder de vieux bâtiments et les transformer en équipements utilisables et modernes est une activité à la mode dans l'architecture actuelle, rhabiller des bâtiments pour les faire paraître plus contemporains l'est également. Pour l'Umbra World Headquarters (Toronto, Canada, 1998–99) Kohn Shnier Architects ont investi une usine en béton « moche et banale » qu'ils ont enveloppée de modules en copolyester moulés sous vide dans un moule en résine pour en faire le siège sophistiqué des fabricants de la poubelle « Garbo » de Karim Rashid. On peut penser que ce type d'intervention doit autant à la mode du design qu'à des approches plus solides de l'architecture, mais si l'on considère le nombre de bâtiments laids qui auraient bien besoin d'être rajeunis, la rénovation a toutes les chances de devenir un axe important de l'architecture contemporaine.

## RETOUR À LA FERME

Les préoccupations écologiques jouent un rôle de plus en plus significatif en architecture contemporaine, mais il semble que cet intérêt prenne des formes plus matures qu'il y a quelques années. À cette époque, les architectes intéressés par l'approche « verte » se sentaient presque obligés de donner à leurs projets une apparence étrange afin que clients et visiteurs comprennent clairement leur propos. « Vous voyez, c'est un immeuble écologiquement correct », proclamaient-ils. Dans le cas de l'Institut de recherche sur la forêt et la nature (Behnisch, Behnisch & Partner, Wageningen, Pays-Bas, 1994–98), le « brief du client portait sur une construction fonctionnelle mais accueillante en harmonie avec la nature et l'environnement, polyvalente et écologique ». Un des facteurs déterminants était également que le commanditaire ne voulait pas payer de supplément pour une solution écologique. On pense de plus en plus, en particulier en Europe du Nord, que les systèmes naturels de contrôle de la climatisation et autres concepts verts doivent être dorénavant intégrés à toutes les constructions nouvelles.

À une époque où concepts et matériaux sophistiqués sont fréquemment employés par les architectes les plus célèbres, il est intéressant de souligner l'existence d'une approche radicalement différente qui propose des projets séduisants et économiquement abordables dans certains des pays les plus pauvres du monde. Dans un lieu inattendu, en Guinée, les architectes suédois Heikkinen-Komonen ont beaucoup œuvré à ce type de projets modestes. Leur école d'aviculture Kahere Eila (Kindia, Guinée, 1998–99) a remporté l'un des prix Aga Khan 2001 en tant que « bel exemple d'architecture d'une modestie élégante et néanmoins moderne qui croise avec succès les traditions locales guinéennes et nordiques, tout en évitant l'imitation ». Cette structure de 350 m$^2$ a été construite pour à peine 104 000 dollars en briques de terre stabilisée fabriquée localement sur une presse manuelle.

Autre exploration innovante dans ce domaine de l'architecture modeste : l'expérience menée par Samuel Mockbee, aujourd'hui disparu, à partir de sa base d'Auburn University, en Alabama. Son Rural Studio fait participer des étudiants de l'université à la construction de logements et de bâtiments communautaires décents destinés à une population locale extrêmement pauvre, en particulier dans la ville de Masons

Bend. Édifié pour juste 20 000 dollars, le Masons Bend Community Center (Masons Bend, Alabama, États-Unis, 1999–2000) est décrit par Mockbee comme « une chapelle en pare-brise à murs de boue, qui s'inspire des formes vernaculaire de la communauté ». La référence à ce vitrage peu courant en architecture vient de ce que le toit se compose de 80 pare-brises de Chevy Caprice obtenus par l'un des participants pour 120 dollars.

Chez Heikkinen-Komonen comme chez Mockbee, les traditions et les matériaux locaux sont respectés, loin de toute tentative d'imposition de diktats esthétiques. Bien que les architectes de sensibilité artistique s'efforcent souvent d'imposer leur propre vision à leurs clients, il existe peut-être d'autres façons de juger de la qualité de l'architecture contemporaine. La sensibilité au lieu et la capacité à s'adapter à des budgets faibles pourraient être un critère, comme c'est souvent le cas dans les projets distingués par le prix Aga Khan, par exemple.

### INVENTER DE NOUVELLES FORMES

Qu'ils se servent d'ordinateurs ou non, les architectes inventifs poursuivent leur recherche de formes nouvelles. L'un des plus surprenants est certainement l'architecte-ingénieur d'origine espagnole établi à Zurich, Santiago Calatrava. Son Quadracci Pavilion (Milwaukee Art Museum, Milwaukee, Wisconsin, 1994–2001) et son « Brise-Soleil Burke », un hall de réception protégé du soleil par un écran mobile, évoque une forme d'oiseau que certains peuvent juger excessive. Cette structure zoomorphique correspond pourtant bien à l'attente du musée qui voulait « une entrée prestigieuse, un point d'orientation des visiteurs et une redéfinition de l'identité du musée par la création d'une image forte ». Frank O. Gehry, maître ès-formes inattendues, a récemment créé une autre surprise à Berlin. Le siège de la DG Bank sur Pariser Platz (Berlin, Allemagne, 1995–2001) semble bien austère vu de l'extérieur mais contient une étonnante salle de conférence logée dans l'atrium, que l'architecte compare à une tête de cheval. Cette forme libre toute en courbes et habillée d'acier inoxydable évoque le projet de la maison non construite de Peter Lewis, ainsi qu'un grand objet-sculpture présenté par Gehry dans la galerie de Larry Gagosian à Los Angeles. Gehry est depuis longtemps fasciné par les formes inspirées du monde naturel, comme dans son Fish Restaurant à Kobé (1984), ou le Rebecca's, restaurant mexicain dessiné pour Venice (Californie 1982–85) peuplé de crocodiles suspendus, de lampes-poissons et d'un lustre-pieuvre.

Sans aller tout à fait aussi loin dans le champ des références biomorphiques, des architectes comme le Japonais Toyo Ito poursuivent leurs recherches novatrices. Son dernier projet achevé, la médiathèque de Sendaï (1998–2001) témoigne d'une fluidité de conception et d'une transparence non sans ressemblance avec les formes « informatisées » d'architectes californiens ou néerlandais. En fait, Ito se réfère aux « algues » pour décrire les 13 tubes d'acier structurel qui constituent l'ossature, intègrent ses réseaux techniques et ondulent à travers toute la structure. S'il fallait une preuve supplémentaire de ce que l'univers de la vie inspire davantage que la rigidité géométrique moderniste, la propension japonaise à théoriser sur la création d'une sorte de nature artificielle le prouve. Des architectes comme Itsuko Hasegawa défendent depuis longtemps ce type de position.

L'idée de formes libres ne se réduit en aucun cas à des projets ambitieux à grande échelle comme la DG Bank de Gehry ou la médiathèque d'Ito. La jeune équipe que forment Jakob+MacFarlane a conçu la Librairie Florence Loewy (Paris, France, 2001) sur ordinateur, mais les curieuses étagères incurvées en bois de ce modeste espace n'évoquent pas à première vue une approche avant-gardiste. Un tel projet sert davantage à illustrer l'ampleur du mouvement en faveur de modèles proches de la flexibilité de la nature plutôt que de la rigidité de la géométrie euclidienne.

## ARCHITECTURE = ART = ARCHITECTURE

Peu d'architectes ont réellement les moyens d'envisager leur profession comme un art. Les pressions économiques ont le plus souvent raison de l'esthétique, même lorsque le créateur est intellectuellement capable de réaliser une œuvre qui soit davantage qu'un simple bâtiment fonctionnel. La rigoureuse maîtrise du béton dont fait preuve Tadao Ando est quasi légendaire, mais jusqu'à présent, ses principales réalisations se trouvaient toutes au Japon. Avec le Fort Worth Museum of Contemporary Art, bientôt achevé, et The Pulitzer Foundation for the Arts récemment inaugurée à Saint Louis, il peut aujourd'hui prétendre avoir su étendre le champ géographique de ses interventions dans le domaine artistique. Les formes extravagantes d'un Novak ne sont pas pour lui. Son œuvre s'appuie résolument sur la géométrie euclidienne, et la Pulitzer Foundation n'y fait pas exception. Malgré l'extrême simplicité de ce projet, l'architecte a rencontré quelques difficultés avec l'un des artistes participant au projet, Richard Serra. Une importante sculpture de ce dernier est implantée à l'extérieur de la Fondation, mais encerclée de murs de béton dessinés par Ando. Serra aurait préféré que la courbe complexe de son œuvre ne se retrouve pas ainsi enfermée. Il est intéressant de noter que ce conflit s'est déclenché à l'occasion de la rencontre entre l'un des architectes les plus « artistiques » et l'un des sculpteurs qui frôle le plus près l'architecture. Rivalité professionnelle ?

Serra utilise très fréquemment l'acier Corten, matériau plus courant en construction navale qu'en architecture, et pourtant c'est précisément le type d'acier choisi par Rem Koolhaas pour les murs de la galerie du nouveau Guggenheim Hermitage à Las Vegas. Rarement la « haute » culture et la culture « populaire » n'ont été aussi proches. Au cœur de l'un des hôtels-casinos les plus outrageusement kitsch de Las Vegas, The Venetian, Thomas Krens, directeur du Guggenheim, en association avec le musée de l'Ermitage de Saint-Pétersbourg, n'a pas hésité à installer non pas un mais deux espaces muséaux pour accueillir d'importantes expositions temporaires. Le Guggenheim Las Vegas, également conçu par Koolhaas, affiche une conception plus libre, inaugurée par la spectaculaire installation signée Frank O. Gehry de « L'art de la moto », déjà vue à New York et Bilbao. Krens est connu pour aimer bousculer le monde des musées et son Guggenheim-Bilbao dessiné par Gehry est l'une des créations architecturales les plus réussies des années 1990. Un autre Guggenheim de Gehry devrait s'élever non loin du site de l'ancien World Trade Center à New York. C'est également Krens qui a fait appel à Jean Nouvel et à Zaha Hadid pour participer au concours (remporté par Hadid) pour la création d'une structure type Kunsthalle, à Tokyo, toujours pour le Guggenheim. Il a découvert que l'architecture pouvait attirer à elle seule des visiteurs, un peu comme le musée de New York dessiné par Frank Lloyd Wright attire depuis 1959 autant d'admirateurs de l'architecture que d'amateurs d'art. Pour lui, une installation comme celle de Gehry pour « L'Art de la moto » représente « 50 % de la valeur artistique de l'exposition ». Richard Serra, pour sa part, tient à préciser que « la différence entre l'art et l'architecture est que l'art n'est au bénéfice d'aucun but ». Néanmoins, l'aspect artistique de l'architecture encouragé par le succès de personnalités telles que Gehry reste une source significative d'inventivité.

Il est rare qu'un artiste, en particulier de l'importance de James Turrell, crée une œuvre qui franchisse aussi allègrement les frontières entre art et architecture. C'est précisément ce qu'il est en train de faire dans le désert de l'Arizona en un lieu nommé Roden Crater. À environ soixante kilomètres de Flagstaff, cet ancien cratère se trouve au centre d'un terrain de cinquante mille hectares acheté par l'artiste en 1977. Par des travaux de terrassement gigantesques qui ont déplacé des centaines de milliers de mètres cubes de terre – du niveau des plus grands projets de génie civil – il a réussi à créer un «observatoire des phénomènes célestes». L'artiste explique son action en termes qui s'appuient sur des références architecturales : «Je m'intéresse au fait que nous sommes des constructeurs», dit-il, «nous faisons des choses et c'est ce qui caractérise d'une certaine façon la nature humaine. Nous avons ici des choses comme Arcosanti, construit par Paolo Soleri, le Taliesin de Frank Lloyd Wright ou les Watts Towers de Simon Rodia à Los Angeles, exemples de la vision d'une personne ou d'un artiste.» Turrell s'intéresse à la perception de la lumière et Roden Crater doit s'interpréter non comme une réalisation d'architecture contemporaine, mais comme une œuvre d'art. Sa qualité visionnaire peut inspirer notre environnement construit. Des architectes comme Steven Holl travaillent beaucoup sur les effets de la lumière et de la réflexion, non sans lien avec les recherches de Turrell.

L'art qui œuvre aux frontières de l'architecture ou l'architecture qui se rapproche de l'art pur sont des sources potentielles de confusion mais aussi de stimulation enrichissante. Tous deux représentent l'une des tendances significatives de la conception du bâti de ces vingt dernières années. Le fait que de nombreux grands architectes d'aujourd'hui soient appelés pour édifier des musées par des clients comme Tom Krens manifeste d'ailleurs leur proximité du processus de l'élaboration artistique. Gehry s'est clairement exprimé sur ce point, et d'autres se sont engagés sur ses pas ou ont élargi sa réflexion.

### MAISON OU FOYER ?

Les résidences privées ont longtemps été le terrain de prédilection des plus créatifs des architectes. Leurs petites dimensions et la richesse fréquente de leurs commanditaires autorisent un degré d'inventivité souvent exclu pour des réalisations plus vastes, davantage soumises à des impératifs économiques. Pour donner un exemple, l'architecte espagnol Alberto Campo Baeza a répondu à la spécificité du site de la maison De Blas (Sevilla de la Nueva, Madrid, Espagne, 2000) par une solution typiquement minimaliste. «On a construit une boîte de béton», explique-t-il, «une plate-forme sur laquelle se poser. Une boîte transparente, au toit formé d'une structure délicate et légère en acier peint en blanc, est disposée sur ce socle. Ne faisant qu'un avec le sol, la boîte en béton coulé sur place fonctionne comme une caverne et accueille le programme d'une maison traditionnelle selon un plan clair et précis, espaces servis à l'avant et des espaces serveurs à l'arrière. La boîte de verre est posée sur cette plate-forme un peu comme un belvédère auquel on accède de l'intérieur. En dessous, la caverne est un refuge. Au-dessus, la hutte – une urne – est un espace d'où l'on peut contempler la nature. Cette maison se veut une translation littérale de problématique de tectonique et de stéréotomie : une pièce tectonique posée sur une boîte stéréotomique. Un condensé de ce qui est l'essentiel de l'architecture. Une fois encore, faire «plus avec moins.» Bien que construite à l'autre bout du monde, la maison édifiée par Waro Kishi à Kurakuen II (Nishinoamiya, Hyogo, Japon, 2000–2001) est décrite par l'architecte en termes comparables : «J'ai créé deux blocs structurels en acier flottant renforcé. À gauche, se trouve la zone privée et à droite les zones de séjour et de repas, les deux étant reliées par une rampe inclinée. Le toit du dernier niveau à gauche de la pièce individuelle est réalisé de façon à apparaître aussi mince que possible. »

Campo Baeza et Kishi partagent une esthétique minimaliste qui se trouve être l'un des facteurs constants de la récente architecture contemporaine, où que ce soit dans le monde. Sean Godsell, qui travaille en Australie, a également fait appel à un vocabulaire géométrique pour sa Carter/Tucker House (Breamlea, Victoria, Australie, 1999–2000), boîte de 12 x 6 m sur trois niveaux, engoncée dans une dune de sable. Sa simplicité externe fondamentale est enrichie d'un système de curieuses ouvertures en façade. Une peau-écran de bois bascule pour s'ouvrir et former des auvents sur trois côtés.

Pour de nombreux architectes, le défi des changements de style a pu représenter un facteur important. Certains, comme Richard Meier ou Tadao Ando s'en tiennent fermement à un strict vocabulaire moderniste dont le classicisme les place en quelque sorte au-dessus des modes. D'autres, comme Philip Johnson en son temps, ou plus récemment Arata Isozaki, passent rapidement d'un style à un autre selon les circonstances. Un cas intéressant dans ce domaine est celui de l'architecte finlandais Jyrki Tasa, né en 1944, postmoderniste jadis sans réserve. Sa récente Maison Into (Espoo, Finlande, 1997–98) réussit la délicate transition entre son style passé et une attitude plus contemporaine qui porte néanmoins encore la marque du déséquilibre et de la surprise qui caractérisaient ses précédentes réalisations. Les résidences privées relèvent en tout état de cause du goût personnel, celui de l'architecte et, bien sûr, celui du client dans de nombreux cas. Être «à la mode» est une notion relative qui varie en fonction du spectateur. Des gens peu informés de la mode architecturale peuvent encore penser que le postmodernisme est assez «tendance». Dans cette équation entre aussi, bien entendu, un facteur d'âge.

### SHOPPING OU RELIGION ?

Dans son récent *Harvard Design School Guide to Shopping* (Taschen, Cologne, 2001), Rem Koolhaas n'hésite pas à tracer une analogie entre le shopping et la religion («Divine Economy» (L'économie divine). «Dans un effort de réinvention des moyens par lesquels elles touchent leur marché», écrit Sze Tsung Leon, «les églises deviennent de plus en plus semblables au shopping, à la fois dans leur configuration et leurs méthodes.» En tout cas, une architecture sophistiquée s'observe dans les cercles à la fois de la religion et du marketing. Elle serait le moyen-clé de toucher une nouvelle clientèle. Certaines des plus remarquables réalisations de l'architecte japonais Tadao Ando sont ses temples et ses églises. Le plus récent, le temple Komyo-ji (Saïjo, Ehimé, Japon, 1999–2000) se définit comme un «lieu de rassemblement» qui s'inspire des origines de l'architecture des temples de bois nippons. Les architectes allemands Allmann Sattler Wappner font également appel à un vocabulaire minimaliste dans leur église du Cœur-de-Jésus (Munich, Allemagne, 1996–2001) qui évoque davantage et indirectement la fonction religieuse qu'il ne la désigne spécifiquement. Là encore, la notion de lieu de réunion, qui pourrait également s'appliquer aux centres commerciaux, s'applique parfaitement à cette construction. En Allemagne, comme au Japon, la subtilité des architectes est telle que les fidèles y trouveront les signes attendus pour reconnaître leur lieu de prière, tandis que d'autres ne se sentiront pas soumis pour autant à une doctrine religieuse donnée.

Ici religion ne signifie pas qu'il faille se soumettre à la mode, c'est précisément l'attraction éphémère du neuf qui attire les acheteurs dans les magasins de vêtements. Les stylistes japonais Issey Miyake et Rei Kawabuko (Comme des Garçons) ont longtemps été à l'avant-garde de la conception de boutiques. S'ils font appel à des architectes réputés, ils s'impliquent personnellement dans la direction artistique de leur espace de vente. Pour son nouveau «vaisseau amiral» de New York, Miyake s'est adressé à nul autre que Frank O. Gehry pour faire de l'espace qu'il venait d'acquérir à Hudson Street à Tribeca un lieu réellement contemporain. Travaillant sur ce projet avec un associé, Gordon Kipping, Gehry a implanté l'une de ses grandes ondulations de métal typiques de son style à travers l'ancien entrepôt à hauts plafonds. Cette intrusion et le recours à des utilisations sophistiquées du verre et du métal ont transformé de manière spectaculaire cet immeuble ancien classé à structure de fonte. La rénovation semble maintenant l'un des lieux d'expression favoris de l'architecture contemporaine et le magasin Miyake Tribeca de Gehring et Kipping prouve que la mode, l'architecture et l'architecture intérieure d'avant-garde peuvent se conjuguer avec succès.

Rei Kawabuko est beaucoup plus radicale encore que Miyake ou presque tous ses confrères. Après avoir travaillé avec Future Systems pour ses boutiques de New York et de Tokyo, elle a fait appel à Ab Rogers, fils de Richard Rogers, coauteur du Centre Pompidou, pour créer un espace spectaculaire intégralement rouge rue du Faubourg Saint-Honoré, à quelques pas du palais de l'Élysée à Paris. Comme dans ses autres magasins, c'est elle qui a eu le dernier mot sur toutes les décisions de conception et elle peut donc en être à juste titre considérée comme le véritable « architecte ». On remarque dans son travail la recherche d'une symbiose active entre l'espace, les objets, les vêtements qui illustre et nourrit l'esprit du label « Comme des Garçons ». Entrer dans un de ses magasins, c'est un peu comme entrer en religion, c'est rejoindre une sorte de mouvement esthétique qui recouvre tous les aspects des environnements qu'elle imagine.

## LE BOUCHER, LE BOULANGER ET LE FABRICANT DE CHANDELLES

Si les recherches éthérées d'un Marcos Novak nous montrent peut-être le futur de l'architecture, il reste évident pour tous, si ce n'est pour les plus « artistiques » des praticiens, qu'il est nécessaire à un moment donné de construire et de se plier aux contraintes programmatiques si l'on veut continuer à travailler. La construction, quand elle dépasse les besoins d'une résidence privée, est le plus souvent entreprise pour répondre à des usages très précis, une sorte d'architecture « alimentaire » qui permette à chacun d'aller voir des films, de prendre le train, d'assister à un concert, de lire dans une bibliothèque ou même tout simplement de travailler à son bureau. Résoudre les problèmes inhérents à ce type de bâtiments est en fait la mesure de l'excellence architecturale, en particulier lorsque le budget de réalisation est limité. Les architectes Bolles + Wilson, installés en Allemagne, ont récemment achevé le Nouveau Luxor Theater (Rotterdam, Pays-Bas, 1998–2000) dans le quartier de Kop van Zuid. Ils avaient déjà mené à bien le chantier des Quay Buildings (Kop van Zuid, Rotterdam, 1991–96) non loin de là et le Luxor Theater représente une autre étape de la transformation de cette zone portuaire abandonnée en un quartier neuf et animé. Non loin du spectaculaire Pont Erasme (1996) de Ben van Berkel, le Luxor est un signal rouge vif qui attire les visiteurs venus du centre de la ville. Bien qu'elle ne soit pas d'une inventivité spectaculaire, cette salle constitue l'élément clé d'un projet ambitieux de rénovation urbaine dans une ville qui a déjà fait amplement preuve de son goût pour l'architecture contemporaine de qualité.

Insuffler la « bonne » architecture dans des typologies de bâtiments longtemps restées en déclin est une entreprise tout aussi louable, en particulier lorsque le projet concerne des millions de voyageurs chaque jour. C'est certainement le cas de Jean-Marie Duthilleul et de l'agence AREP, le bras armé de la construction des gares de la SNCF. Duthilleul s'est dépensé depuis des années pour réaliser des gares de chemin de fer plus hospitalières et plus modernes, dans le cadre des investissements considérables engagés pour la rénovation du réseau ferré lui-même et créer de nouvelles lignes de T. G. V. La plus récente ligne à grande vitesse entre Lyon et le Midi méditerranéen a demandé la construction d'une nouvelle ligne et de nouvelles gares à Valence, Avignon et Aix. Chacune d'entre elles est différente et offre aux voyageurs qui n'espéraient pas être aussi bien traités un réel degré de modernité et de sophistication dans le confort. La gare de Valence (1998–2001) se projette en porte-à-faux au-dessus des voies. Inclinée vers les trains qui la pénètrent, elle est caractérisée par un étonnant sol en bois incliné et une transparence qui rend l'attente éventuelle agréable. En œuvrant sur de nombreuses gares de Lille à Marseille, Duthilleul a presque à lui seul transformé l'aspect de la plupart des grandes gares françaises, et d'une manière qui regarde vers le XIX$^e$ siècle lorsque les immenses verrières de la gare Saint-Lazare, par exemple, inspiraient des artistes comme Monet. Le voyage en train était considéré à l'époque comme moderne et même futuriste, attitude que l'arrivée combinée des nouvelles lignes T. G. V. et gares de Duthilleul a remis au goût du jour en ce début de XXI$^e$ siècle.

La justice est un autre domaine où l'irruption de l'architecture contemporaine a joué un rôle important dans un certain nombre de pays dont la France et les États-Unis. Richard Meier et son Federal Building and United States Courthouse (Phoenix, Arizona, 1998–2000) ont symboliquement enrichi le processus judiciaire d'une pureté moderniste utopique. Les cyniques peuvent dire que la justice pourrait avoir besoin d'un peu plus de clarté et de nécessité, mais d'une certaine manière, l'architecte n'est-il pas le mieux placé pour rappeler les idéaux élevés de la justice ? Un atrium en verre de 35 m de haut donne au bâtiment une ouverture qui cherche à obvier au sentiment d'insécurité issu de tragédies comme l'attentat d'Oklahoma City contre un bâtiment fédéral. La blancheur et l'ordre de Meier semblent particulièrement bien adaptés à la structuration et à la définition d'un environnement de tribunal, et à la restauration d'une dignité face aux excès et aux erreurs des années récentes.

La banque est longtemps restée une profession un peu fermée, et la propension des banquiers à choisir une architecture classique, voire funéraire pour symboliser la solidité et la continuité est en partie responsable de cette image. Le Hypo Alpe-Adria Center (Klagenfurt, Autriche, 1998–2000) de Morphosis regarde clairement dans l'autre direction, et donne avant tout un sens de mouvement. « La juxtaposition dynamique de volumes évoque le glissement de plaques tectoniques », explique l'architecte, « et pourtant elle s'efforce d'établir des nœuds de stabilité au milieu de cette turbulence. » Les investisseurs ont dû être assez contents de sentir la présence de ces « nœuds » dans cet ensemble plutôt curieux. L'architecture sert ici à redéfinir l'image publique voire même les buts d'une profession profondément remise en cause par l'évolution économique internationale. Un autre exemple très différent des relations entre la banque et l'architecture nous est offert par le nouveau siège de la Banque de Chine (Pei Partnership, Pékin, Chine, 1997–2001). Un programme très dense et le désir affirmé du client de projeter précisément cette image de stabilité qui n'intéressait pas la banque autrichienne ont conduit à un résultat presque diamétralement opposé. Bien que pas particulièrement imaginatif dans son aspect extérieur, l'atrium de 45 m de haut et de 3 000 m$^2$ décline le type d'espace public spectaculaire qui a rendu si célèbre le père des deux praticiens. Les architectes n'ont pas souvent l'occasion de modifier l'image que leurs clients cherchent à projeter, mais les bâtiments aussi futuristes que l'Hypo Alpe-Adria Center ou aussi massivement rassurant que la Banque de Chine joueront certainement un rôle dans la perception future de ces institutions.

Les connotations phalliques évidentes des immeubles de bureaux, et en particulier des gratte-ciel, sont depuis longtemps l'objet de certaines moqueries. Jean Nouvel est peut-être le premier architecte à pousser cette image dans ses limites logiques. Sa Torre Agbar (Barcelone, Espagne, 2001) qui se dressera à proximité de l'avenue Diagonal semble avoir un lien (la fontaine) avec l'activité principale du client (la société des eaux de la capitale catalane), mais sa forme dressée provoque d'autres rapprochements assez explicites. Sa conception sophistiquée ne permet pas de la considérer comme une plaisanterie et l'on pourrait avancer qu'en s'attaquant sérieusement à la forme phallique, Nouvel va au-delà des critiques potentielles. Un des plus importants architectes actuels, souvent assez elliptique sur ses intentions, on peut très bien l'imaginer répondre: « Bien sûr, c'est un symbole phallique évident. Et alors? »

De nombreux critiques pensent que les grands concours internationaux s'élèvent rarement au niveau des attentes qu'ils suscitent. La Biblioteca Alexandrina (Snøhetta Architects, Alexandrie, Égypte, 1997–2001) est le résultat de l'un de ces concours qui a attiré pas moins de 524 participants de 52 pays. Bien qu'il soit vrai que quelques grandes bibliothèques publiques récentes aient répondu aux espoirs que l'on mettait en elles (par exemple la Bibliothèque Nationale de France, de Dominique Perrault), le travail de Snøhetta à Alexandrie semble particulièrement lourd. Massif à tous égards, le bâtiment fournit certainement au grand port égyptien un nouveau monument, mais répond-il vraiment aux objectifs de l'UNESCO et aux innombrables articles de la presse internationale qu'il avait suscités à l'origine? Symbole trop fort, cette bibliothèque était peut-être destinée à décevoir quelle que soit la qualité du travail de ses architectes.

Une autre catégorie d'équipements souvent décevante est le type de centre de congrès-salle de concert que la France édifie dans ses régions depuis quelques années. Le Zénith de Bernard Tschumi (Rouen, France, 1999–2001) et sa double coquille métallique flottante représente en fait un brillant succès. À travers ses fonctions de Doyen de l'École supérieure d'architecture de Columbia University, l'architecte a influencé de nombreux étudiants en architecture, mais à travers une réalisation comme le Zénith il montre que sa réputation s'appuie sur une solide capacité à imaginer des solutions novatrices même contraint par un budget limité. Comme pour les gares de Duthilleul, le Zénith rouennais est un exemple réussi d'architecture de qualité appliquée aux besoins du plus grand public.

## RETOUR VERS LE FUTUR

Les bâtiments conçus par des architectes doués d'un véritable sens esthétique sont rares. La plupart des villes sont remplies d'imitations ineptes, de reproductions sans moyen, d'idées naguère grandioses rabaissées à leur plus petit commun dénominateur. Comme ce survol le montre, l'avant-garde théorique de l'architecture est toujours davantage repoussée vers la périphérie de ce qui intéresse le public. La plupart des constructions édifiées dans le monde réel sont toujours conçues d'une façon, dans un style même, qui n'auraient pas paru étrange à Ludwig Mies van der Rohe il y a plus de cinquante ans. Et cependant, l'idée d'une nouvelle architecture appuyée sur des modèles en relation avec l'univers évolutif de la biologie – une architecture issue de la conception assistée par ordinateur, peut-être même par des algorithmes génétiques qui explorent et révèlent des formes qu'aucun architecte n'avait jamais imaginées – se fraye son chemin. L'ordinateur, comme Frank O. Gehry l'a montré avec le logiciel Dassault, CATIA, peut aussi grandement faciliter l'élaboration de formes de haute complexité. Si ces formes sculpturales doivent trouver leur place dans le futur de l'architecture, elles doivent néanmoins devenir plus qu'un caprice esthétique, même signées d'une diva vieillissante de la profession. L'adaptabilité, la capacité au changement en fonction de l'usage et de la marche du temps, sont les vertus sous-jacentes de la nouvelle architecture, une architecture vivante, une architecture qui respire, pour édifier un monde.

# ALLMANN SATTLER WAPPNER

Allmann Sattler Wappner Architekten
Bothmerstrasse 14
80634 Munich
Germany

Tel: + 49 89 165 615
Fax: + 49 89 169 263
e-mail: info@allmannsattlerwappner.de

*Herz Jesu Kirche*

**MARKUS ALLMANN** was born in 1959 in Ludwigshafen. He studied at the Technological University in Munich from which he received a diploma in 1986. The following year he created the firm of Allmann Sattler in Munich. **AMANDUS SATTLER** was born in 1957 in Marktredwitz and also studied at the Technological University in Munich, like **LUDWIG WAPPNER**, he received his diploma there in 1985 and the firm of Allmann Sattler Wappner was created in 1993. Their work includes the Flöha School Complex and sports facilities (Flöha/Sachsen, 1992–1996); the Wertstoffhof in Munich (1995–1997); the Feix House (Bad Wörishofen, 1996–1998); and the Münchner Tor Office Building (Munich, 1999–2002). In describing their philosophy, the architects ask, "How can a building be popular in the original sense of the word, without the necessity of being opportunistic. The development of an architectural position is worthless," they say, "without the ability to integrate it into society."

**MARKUS ALLMANN**, geboren 1959 in Ludwigshafen, schloss 1986 sein Studium an der Technischen Universität in München ab. Im folgenden Jahr gründete er die Firma Allmann Sattler in München. Auch **AMANDUS SATTLER**, geboren 1957 in Marktredwitz, und **LUDWIG WAPPNER** studierten an der Technischen Universität in München, wo sie 1985 ihre Diplome erwarben. Die drei Architekten gründeten 1993 die gemeinsame Firma Allmann Sattler Wappner. Zu ihren Bauten zählen der Flöha Schulkomplex sowie die Sportanlagen im sächsischen Flöha (1992–96), der Wertstoffhof in München (1995–97), das Haus Feix in Bad Wörishofen (1996–98) und das Bürogebäude Münchner Tor in München (1999–2002). Ihre Philosophie umreißen die Gestalter, indem sie fragen: »Wie kann ein Gebäude im ursprünglichen Sinn des Wortes populär sein, ohne opportunistisch sein zu müssen?« Und sie führen aus: »Die Entwicklung einer architektonischen Position ist wertlos ohne die Fähigkeit, sie in die Gesellschaft zu integrieren.«

**MARKUS ALLMANN**, né à Ludwigshafen en 1959, étudie à l'Université de Technologie de Munich dont il sort diplômé en 1986. L'année suivante, il crée l'agence Allmann Sattler à Munich. **AMANDUS SATTLER** (diplômé en 1985) est né à Marktredwitz en 1957 et a suivi les mêmes études que **LUDWIG WAPPNER**. L'agence Allmann Sattler Wappner est fondée en 1993. Parmi leurs réalisations : complexe scolaire et équipements sportifs de Flöha (Flöha, Saxe, Allemagne, 1992–96) ; Wertstoffhof à Munich (1995–97) ; Maison Feix (Bad Wörishofen, 1996–98) et immeuble de bureau Münchner Tor (Munich, 1999–2002). « Comment un bâtiment peut-il être populaire au sens original du terme, en évitant l'opportunisme ? Le développement d'une posture architecturale est sans valeur, si elle ne peut s'intégrer à la société » expliquent les architectes interrogés sur leur philosophie.

# HERZ JESU KIRCHE

*Munich, Germany, 1996–2001*

*Client: Katholische Pfarrkirchenstiftung Herz Jesu, Munich. Floor area: Ground floor Church: 999 m². Gallery: 120 m². Ground floor Sacristy: 211 m². Basement: 245 m². Steeple: 22 m². Cost: DM 28,000,000. Artists: Glass entrance door: Alexander Beleschenko. Curtain behind the Altar: Lutzenberger & Lutzenberger. Five Wounds: M+M. 14 Stations of the Cross: Matthias Wähner*

The problem of creating religious architecture in a time when traditions have gone by the wayside is rarely dealt with in a convincing manner. Some architects like Tadao Ando, Mario Botta or Alvaro Siza have come up with brilliant solutions that respect liturgical requirements without ceding to an historicist interpretation. The **HERZ JESU KIRCHE**, set in a residential suburb of Munich, was built by the architects Allmann Sattler Wappner subsequent to a competition organized by the Archbishop of Munich. Their entry, selected over one hundred-fifty others, employs a modernist vocabulary in a sixteen-meter high cubic glass structure. Light, frequently present in Catholic churches as a symbolic element, here plays a central role. A stylized cross that could be a geometric decor graces the pale maple interior wall behind the altar. Other reminiscences of more ancient architecture, from the bluish glass near the entrance to the opening walls that recall opened arms, convincingly bridge the gap between past and present. A structural purity is obtained by concentrating the necessary mechanical facilities in the basement of this DM 28 million church.

Das Problem der Gestaltung von Sakralbauten in einer Zeit, in der religiöse Traditionen ihren Stellenwert weitgehend verloren haben, wird selten auf überzeugende Weise gelöst. Wobei einige Architekten, wie Tadao Ando, Mario Botta oder Alvaro Siza, diese Aufgabe hervorragend gemeistert haben, indem sie die liturgischen Anforderungen respektierten, ohne in eine historisierende Interpretation auszuweichen. Die in einer Wohngegend von München gelegene **HERZ JESU KIRCHE** wurde von den Architekten Allmann Sattler Wappner in Folge eines vom Münchner Erzbischof veranstalteten Wettbewerbs erbaut. Ihr Entwurf, der vor 157 anderen als Sieger nominiert wurde, überträgt eine modernistische Formensprache in eine 16 m hohe kubische Glaskonstruktion. Das Licht, in katholischen Kirchen häufig als symbolisches Element eingesetzt, spielt auch hier eine zentrale Rolle. Die hinter dem Altar liegende Trennmauer aus hellem Ahorn schmückt ein stilisiertes Kreuz, bei dem es sich ebenso gut um ein geometrisches Dekor handeln könnte. Es gibt hier aber auch Anklänge an ältere Architekturformen wie das bläuliche Glas im Eingangsbereich oder die durchbrochenen Wände, die in ihrer Anordnung an die Geste geöffneter Arme erinnern, die auf überzeugende Weise die Kluft zwischen Vergangenheit und Gegenwart überbrücken. Durch die Verlegung der erforderlichen technischen Anlagen ins Untergeschoss wurde in dieser für 28 Millionen Mark erbauten Kirche ein hohes Maß an baulich-stilistischer Reinheit erzielt.

Le problème de la création d'une architecture religieuse à une époque où les traditions s'estompent est rarement traité de manière convaincante. Certains architectes comme Tadao Ando, Mario Botta ou Alvaro Siza ont néanmoins proposé de brillantes solutions qui respectent les exigences liturgiques sans céder à une interprétation historiciste. **L'ÉGLISE DU CŒUR DE JÉSUS**, située dans une banlieue résidentielle de Munich, a été construite par les architectes Allmann Sattler Wappner à la suite d'un concours organisé par l'archevêché de Munich. Leur projet, sélectionné parmi plus de 150, utilise un vocabulaire moderniste appliqué à une structure cubique en verre de 16 m de haut. Souvent présente dans les églises catholiques pour sa symbolique, la lumière joue ici un rôle central. Une croix stylisée, qui pourrait être un décor géométrique, orne le mur intérieur derrière l'autel, habillé d'érable clair. D'autres évocations d'architectures plus anciennes, comme le verre teinté de bleu près de l'entrée dont les murs font penser à des bras ouverts, réduisent le fossé entre les traditions passées et le présent de façon convaincante. Le sentiment de pureté de la structure est en partie obtenu par le rassemblement des équipements techniques dans le sous-sol de cette église qui a coûté 28 millions de DM.

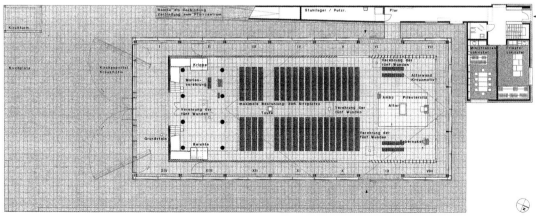

*Grundriss des Erdgeschosses mit dem Altar auf der rechten Seite. Die drei Außenansichten zeigen das große Eingangstor aus Glas.*

*Ci-dessus, plan du niveau supérieur, l'autel à droite. Les trois vues extérieures montrent les énormes portes de verre pivotantes.*

The outer glass shell encases
the freestanding pale maple interior
walls of the Church. To the right,
below, three sections of the building
show the relationship of the main
structure and the sacristy to the
bell tower.

Die frei stehenden Kirchenwände aus
hellem Ahorn sind mit einer äußeren
Hülle aus Glas umgeben. Die drei Teil-
ansichten (rechts unten) verdeutlichen
die Relation zwischen dem Haupt-
gebäude mit der Sakristei und dem
abgesetzten Glockenturm.

L'enveloppe de verre extérieure
enchâsse les murs intérieurs de
l'église habillés d'érable clair. À
droite, en bas, trois coupes montrent
la relation entre la partie principale,
la sacristie et le clocher.

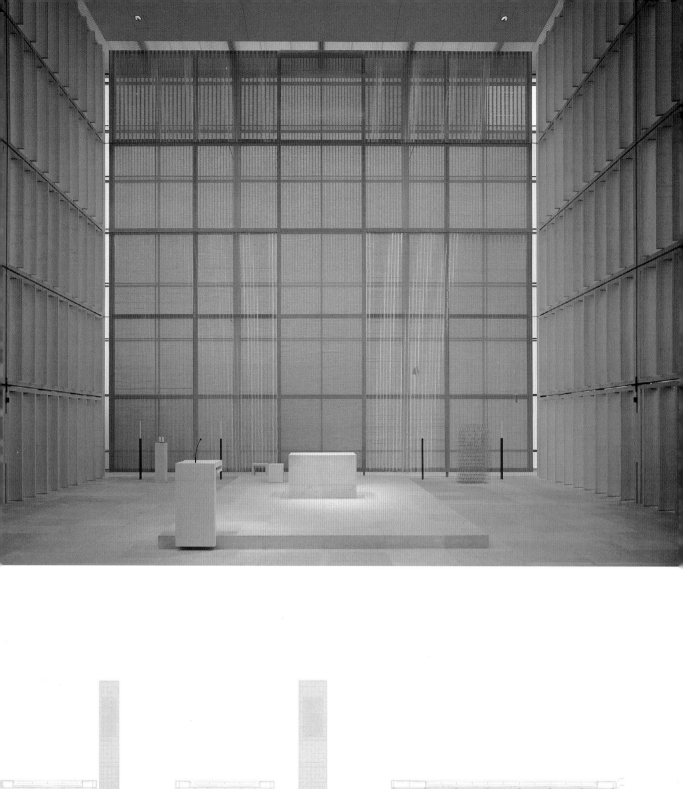

Layered golden metal mesh creates
the impression of a cross above the
altar, whose lighting was carefully
studied. To the right, a view with the
pivoting glass entrance doors open.

Ein schichtweise aufgebautes golde-
nes Metallgewebe evoziert die Vorstellung eines Kreuzes über dem
Altar, dessen Beleuchtung sorgfältig
ausgearbeitet wurde. Ansicht mit
den geöffneten Glasflügeln des Ein-
gangstors (rechts).

Un réseau de fil métallique doré crée
l'impression d'une croix au dessus de
l'autel, dont l'éclairage a été étudié
avec soin. À droite, une vue des
portes de verre pivotantes de l'entrée
en position ouverte.

# TADAO ANDO

*Tadao Ando Architect & Associates*
*5–23, Toyosaki 2-Chome, Kita-ku*
*Osaka 531*
*Japan*

*Tel: + 81 6 6375 1148*

*Komyo-ji Temple* ▶

Born in Osaka in 1941, **TADAO ANDO** was self-educated as an architect, largely through his travels in the United States, Europe and Africa (1962–1969). He founded Tadao Ando Architect & Associates in Osaka in 1969. He has received the Alvar Aalto Medal, Finnish Association of Architects (1985); Medaille d'or, French Academy of Architecture (1989); the 1992 Carlsberg Prize and the 1995 Pritzker Prize. He has taught at Yale (1987); Columbia (1988) and at Harvard (1990). Notable buildings include: Rokko Housing, Kobe (1981–1993); Church on the Water, Hokkaido (1988); Japan Pavilion Expo '92, Seville, Spain (1992); Forest of Tombs Museum, Kumamoto (1992); and the Suntory Museum, Osaka (1994). Recent work includes the Awaji Yumebutai, Awajishima, Hyogo, Japan (1997–2000); the Modern Art Museum of Fort Worth, Fort Worth, Texas, United States (1999–2002); and The Pulitzer Foundation for the Arts, Saint-Louis, Missouri, 1999–2001. He recently won the competition to design the new Pinault Foundation on the Ile Seguin, Paris, France.

**TADAO ANDO**, geboren 1941 in Osaka, erlernte den Beruf des Architekten als Autodidakt, vorwiegend auf seinen Reisen durch Nordamerika, Europa und Afrika (1962–69). 1969 gründete er das Büro Tadao Ando Architect & Associates in Osaka. Er wurde mit der Alvar-Aalto-Medaille des Finnischen Architektenverbands (1985), der Medaille d'or der Académie Francaise d'Architecture (1989), dem Carlsberg Preis (1992) und dem Pritzker Prize (1995) ausgezeichnet. Ando lehrte an den Universitäten Yale (1987), Columbia (1988) und Harvard (1990). Seine bekanntesten Bauten sind: die Rokko Wohnanlage in Kobe, Japan (1981–93), die Kirche auf dem Wasser in Hokkaido (1988), der Japanische Pavillon für die Expo '92 in Sevilla, das Forest of Tombs Museum in Kumamoto, Japan (1992) und das Suntory Museum in Osaka (1994). Zu seinen jüngsten Projekten zählen der Komplex Yumebutai in Awajishima, Hyogo (1997–2000), das Modern Art Museum of Fort Worth, Texas (1999–2002) und die Pulitzer Foundation for the Arts in St. Louis, Missouri (1999–2001). Kürzlich gewann Ando den Wettbewerb für den Entwurf der neuen Fondation Pinault auf der Île Seguin in Paris.

Né à Osaka en 1941, **TADAO ANDO** est un architecte autodidacte formé en grande partie par ses voyages aux États-Unis, en Europe et en Afrique (1962–69). Il fonde Tadao Ando Architects & Associates à Osaka en 1969. Titulaire de la Médaille Alvar Aalto de l'Association finlandaise des architectes (1985), de la Médaille d'or 1989 de l'Académie d'Architecture (Paris), du Prix Carlsberg (1992) et du Pritzker Prize (1995). Il a enseigné à Yale (1987), Columbia (1988) et Harvard (1990). Parmi ses réalisations les plus notables : immeuble de logements Rokko, Kobé (1981–83) ; église sur l'eau, Hokkaido (1988) ; pavillon japonais pour Expo '92, Séville, Espagne (1992) ; Musée de la forêt des tombes, Kumamoto (1992) ; Musée Suntory, Osaka (1994). Parmi ses réalisations récentes : le projet Awajishima (Awajishima, Hyogo, Japon, 1997–2000) ; le Modern Art Museum de Fort Worth (Fort Worth, Texas, 1999–2002) et The Pulitzer Foundation for the Arts (Saint Louis, Missouri, 1999–2001). Il a récemment remporté le concours pour la construction de la Fondation Pinault (Île Seguin, Boulogne-Billancourt, France).

# KOMYO-JI TEMPLE

*Saijo, Ehime, Japan, 1999–2000*

*Planning: January 1998 – March 1999. Site area: 3,222 m².*
*Building area: 1,227 m². Total floor area: 1,287 m².*

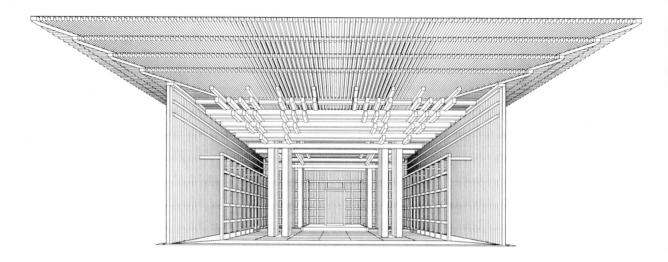

Set on a 3,222 square meter site in the Inland Sea city of Saijo, this structure has a total floor area of 1,287 square meters. Intended as the reconstruction of an existing 250-year-old temple, **KOMYO-JI** was to be "a place where people would come to gather together." Although the design does not specifically adhere to religious tradition, its wooden forms are not entirely alien to temple architecture either. The architect insisted that his design, consisting of three layers of interlocking beams supported by sixteen columns in four groups, should represent something of a return to the founding principles of wooden temple structures. Open lattice walls allow ample daylight to penetrate into the main sanctuary hall, and, as is often the case in Tadao Ando's architecture, light from the surrounding reflecting pool adds a variety and liveliness to the otherwise inanimate forms. Ando is of course better known for his use of concrete than for wood, but as he did in the Japanese Pavilion for Expo '92 in Seville or in other later buildings such as the Museum Of Wood, (Mikata-Gun, Hyogo, 1994), he shows a mastery of this traditional Japanese building material that contributes to a renewal of its esthetic and structural usefulness in architecture.

Das in der Stadt Saijo am Japanischen Binnenmeer Setonaikai errichtete Bauwerk liegt auf einem 3.222 m² umfassenden Gelände und bietet eine Nutzfläche von 1.287 m². Als Rekonstruktion eines existierenden, 250 Jahre alten Tempels war **KOMYO-JI** als Ort geplant, an dem Menschen zusammenkommen können. Obgleich sich der Entwurf nicht besonders an religiöse Traditionen hält, sind seine hölzernen Formen der klassischen Tempelarchitektur durchaus nicht fremd. Der Bau ist aus drei Schichten ineinander greifender Balken konstruiert, welche durch 16 Säulen à vier Gruppen gestützt werden, und soll nach Aussage des Architekten so etwas wie eine Rückkehr zu den ursprünglichen Konstruktionsprinzipien von Holztempelbauten darstellen. Gitterförmig durchbrochene Trennwände sorgen für eine ausreichende Belichtung des großen Sanktuariums, und – wie häufig in Tadao Andos Architektur – lockern die Lichtreflexionen des umlaufenden Wasserbeckens die eher statischen Formen auf und lassen diese lebendig erscheinen. Ando ist zwar eher für die Verwendung von Beton als für den Einsatz von Holz bekannt, aber wie schon in seinem Japanischen Pavillon für die Expo '92 in Sevilla und in jüngeren Gebäuden wie dem 1994 fertig gestellten Holzmuseum in Mikata-Gun, Hyogo, beweist er auch hier großes Können im Umgang mit diesem traditionellen japanischen Baumaterial, wodurch er zu einer Erneuerung der ästhetischen und bautechnischen Verwendungsmöglichkeiten von Holz in der Architektur beiträgt.

Érigé sur un terrain de 3 222 m² dans la ville de Saïjo, en bordure de la mer intérieure, cet édifice occupe une surface totale au sol de 1 287 m². Reconstruction d'un temple vieux de 250 ans, **KOMYO-JI** se veut « un lieu où les gens viennent se réunir ». Bien que le dessin n'évoque pas de tradition religieuse spécifique, les formes ne sont pas totalement étrangères à l'architecture des temples nippons. L'architecte précise que le projet – quatre niveaux de poutres imbriquées soutenues par seize colonnes groupées par quatre – représente une sorte de retour aux principes structurels des temples en bois. Des parois à claire-voie permettent à une généreuse lumière naturelle de pénétrer jusqu'à la salle principale du sanctuaire et, comme souvent le cas chez Ando, les reflets de la lumière du bassin environnant animent des formes par ailleurs statiques. L'architecte est plus connu pour son travail sur le béton que sur le bois même s'il a réalisé, entre autres, dans ce matériau le pavillon japonais pour Expo '92 à Séville ou le Musée du bois (Mikata-Gun, Hyogo, 1994). Mais il fait ici preuve d'une grande maîtrise de ce matériau de construction traditionnel au Japon et contribue à un renouveau de son esthétique et de son utilisation structurelle en architecture.

*Interior and exterior views together with the drawing of the interior shown above illustrate how the architect has created a link between traditional Japanese wooden temple architecture and his own contemporary point of view.*

*Die Interieurskizze (oben) sowie Außen- und Innenansicht zeigen wie der Architekt die Verbindung von traditioneller japanischer Holztempelarchitektur mit seiner eigenen zeitgenössischen Interpretation hergestellt hat.*

*Les vues intérieures et extérieures et le dessin de l'intérieur, ci-dessus, illustrent la manière dont l'architecte a su créer un lien entre l'architecture traditionnelle des temples japonais et sa vision contemporaine.*

Although permission was given to
the architect to demolish the existing
main gate and bell tower of the
temple, he chose to conserve both,
and set the new structure on a
spring-fed pond.

Obwohl der Architekt die Erlaubnis
hatte, das bestehende Haupteingangs-
tor und den Glockenturm des Tempels
abzureißen, beschloss er, beides
zu erhalten und verlegte die neue
Konstruktion auf einen von einer
Quelle gespeisten Teich.

Bien que l'architecte ait été autorisé
à démolir le portail principal et le
campanile du temple, il a choisi de
conserver ces deux éléments et
d'implanter la nouvelle construction
sur un bassin alimenté par une
source.

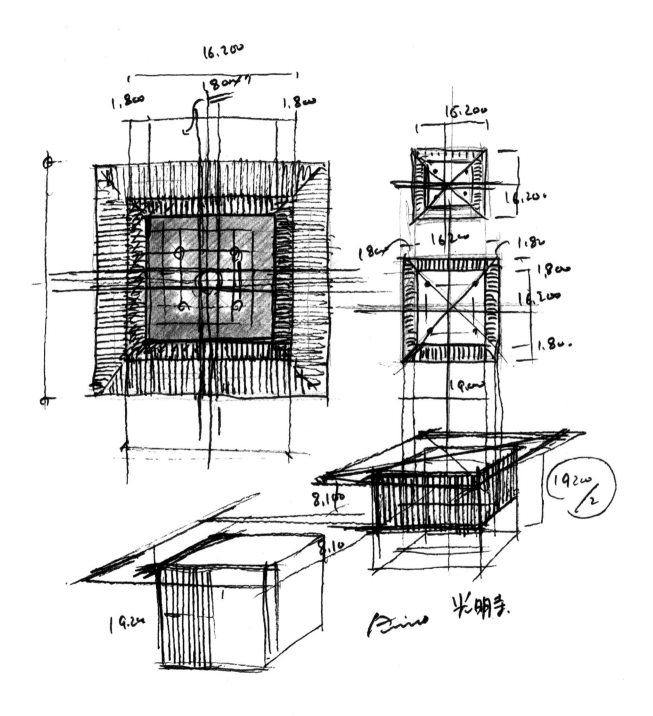

Sketches by Tadao Ando and the view to the left highlight his predilection for rigorous geometric designs. A flat top replaces the more traditional steeply sloped roof of Buddhist temples.

Tadao Andos Skizzen und die Ansicht links belegen die Vorliebe des Architekten für eine streng geometrische Gestaltung. Ein flaches Dach ersetzt die traditionellerweise stark abgeschrägte Überdachung buddhistischer Tempel.

Les croquis de Tadao Ando et la vue de gauche soulignent sa prédilection pour une organisation géométrique rigoureuse. Un toit plat remplace le toit traditionnel à forte pente des temples bouddhistes

# THE PULITZER FOUNDATION
# FOR THE ARTS

*St. Louis, Missouri, United States, 1997–2000*

*Construction: November 1997 – September 2000. Site area: 3,920 m².
Building area: 1,040 m². Total floor area: 2,380 m².*

Surrounded by a certain amount of secrecy, the design and construction of this new private foundation museum were exceedingly simple in their conception. On a 3,920 square meter site in the revitalized Grand Center district of St. Louis, laid out as two rectangular boxes both 7.3 meters wide, but with slightly different lengths: 65.27 meters and 65.88 meters. The total floor area of the Foundation is 2,380 square meters. The taller of the two volumes (there is a 3.66 meter differential) contains the double-height main gallery, and the almost austere concrete design is enlivened by a central reflecting pool. Tadao Ando himself calls the design, his first completed public building in the United States, "an uncompromising box." In describing his reaction to the American context, the architect recalls that he was influenced by the work of both Ludwig Mies van der Rohe and Louis Kahn. Indeed, there is a Miesian simplicity in this design, and a recollection of the kind of simple volumetric repetition seen in Kahn's Kimbell Museum for example. The Foundation is destined to the display of contemporary art from the collection of Emily Rauh Pulitzer and her late husband Joseph Pulitzer, Jr, with large commissioned works by Richard Serra and Ellsworth Kelly holding prominent positions, conferring an almost permanent aspect to the displays in the architect's mind.

Entwurf und Konstruktion dieses neuen Museums der Privatstiftung sind, ungeachtet der Tatsache, dass ein Geheimnis daraus gemacht wurde, überaus schlicht in ihrer Konzeption. Das auf einem 3.920 m² großen Grundstück im wiederbelebten Stadtteil Grand Center in St. Louis angelegte Bauwerk besteht aus zwei rechtwinkligen Teilen, die beide jeweils 7,3 m breit sind, aber leicht unterschiedliche Längen aufweisen: nämlich 65,27 und 65,88 m. Die Gesamtnutzfläche des Stiftungsgebäudes beträgt 2.380 m². Der um 3,66 m höhere von beiden Baukörpern beherbergt den Hauptausstellungssaal mit einer doppelten Raumhöhe, und sein beinahe strenges Beton-design wird von einem zentral gelegenen reflektierenden Wasserbecken belebt. Tadao Ando selbst bezeichnet den Entwurf dieses ersten von ihm in den Vereinigten Staaten realisierten öffentlichen Bauwerks als »eine kompromisslose Gebäudebox«. Auf die Frage, was an dem amerikanischen Umfeld ihn beeinflusst habe, nennt der Architekt die Arbeiten von Ludwig Mies van der Rohe und Louis Kahn. Und tatsächlich enthält seine Gestaltung sowohl eine Reminiszenz an die Schlichtheit eines Mies van der Rohe als auch an eine volumetrische Formwiederholung, wie sie Kahn beispielsweise in seinem Kimbell Museum eingesetzt hat. Die Stiftung ist für die Präsentation der modernen Kunst aus der Sammlung von Emily Rauh Pulitzer und ihrem verstorbenen Mann, Joseph Pulitzer, Jr., vorgesehen. Durch die herausragende Positionierung der großformatigen Auftragsarbeiten von Richard Serra und Ellsworth Kelly hatte der Architekt die Absicht, der Ausstellung einen beständigen Charakter zu verleihen.

Entourées d'un certain secret, la conception et la construction de ce nouveau musée édifié par une fondation privée n'en sont pas moins d'esprit extrêmement simple. Deux boîtes rectangulaires de 7,3 m de large chacune mais de longueur légèrement différente (65,27 m et 65,88 m) se dressent sur un terrain de 3 920 m² dans le quartier en rénovation de Grand Center à St. Louis. La surface totale au sol de la fondation est de 2 380 m². Le plus haut des deux volumes (3,66 m de plus que l'autre) contient la galerie principale à double hauteur. L'austérité provoquée par la présence du béton est tempérée par un bassin central réfléchissant. Tadao Ando qualifie son premier bâtiment public réalisé aux États-Unis, de « boîte sans compromis ». Pour expliquer sa réaction au contexte américain, il précise avoir été influencé par Mies van der Rohe et Louis Kahn. On retrouve en effet en l'occurrence la simplicité miesienne et le rappel du principe de répétition volumétrique mis en œuvre dans le Kimbell Museum de Kahn, par exemple. La Fondation a pour but l'exposition d'œuvres d'art contemporain de la collection d'Emily Rauh Pulitzer et de son mari disparu, Joseph Pulitzer Jr. De grandes œuvres commandées à Richard Serra et Ellsworth Kelly y occupent une place éminente, ce qui confère à l'exposition, dans l'esprit de l'architecte, un caractère quasi permanent.

Despite Tadao Ando's frequent use of concrete and a geometric vocabulary, the Pulitzer Foundation is unusually strict and rigorous. The reflecting pond, a frequent device in Ando's architecture, separates the two main rectangular volumes.

Selbst für einen Entwurf von Tadao Ando, der für die Verwendung von Beton und seine geometrische Formensprache bekannt ist, wirkt das Gebäude der Pulitzer Foundation ungewöhnlich nüchtern und streng. Das spiegelnde Wasserbecken, ein häufig wiederkehrendes Gestaltungsmittel in seiner Architektur, trennt die beiden rechteckigen Bauteile voneinander.

Même si Tadao Ando fait souvent appel au béton et à un vocabulaire géométrique, la Pulitzer Foundation semble particulièrement stricte et rigoureuse. Le bassin réfléchissant, fréquent dans l'architecture de Ando, sépare les deux principaux volumes rectangulaires.

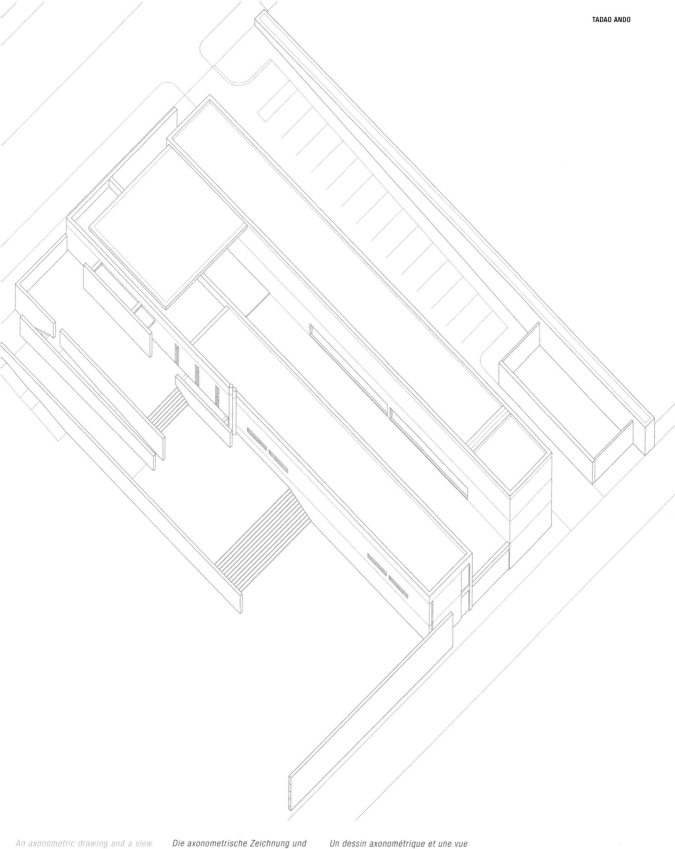

An axonometric drawing and a view towards the pond highlight the rectilinear severity of the Foundation – a scheme intended to put emphasis on the works of art.

Die axonometrische Zeichnung und die Ansicht mit Blick auf den Teich betonen die geradlinige Strenge des Stiftungsgebäudes – ein Gestaltungskonzept, das die Kunstwerke hervorheben soll.

Un dessin axonométrique et une vue vers le bassin soulignent la sévérité rectiligne de la Fondation, voulue pour mettre en valeur les œuvres d'art.

Although Tadao Ando's design may bring to mind a Miesian quality, his use of light and an alternation of opacity and transparency are very much in his own style.

Tadao Andos Entwurf mag an Mies van der Rohe erinnern, der Einsatz von Licht und der Wechsel von opaken und transparenten Elementen sind hingegen eindeutige Merkmale des persönlichen Stils dieses Architekten.

Même si la conception de Ando peut rappeler certains éléments miesiens, son utilisation de la lumière et l'alternance entre l'opacité et la transparence n'appartiennent qu'à lui.

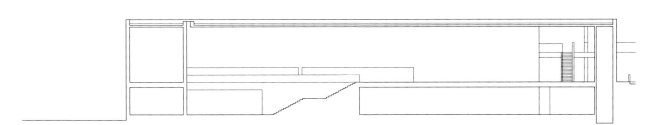

# ASYMPTOTE

*Asymptote Architecture*
*561 Broadway, #5A*
*New York, NY 10012*
*United States*

*Tel: + 1 212 343 7333*
*Fax: + 1 212 343 7099*
*e-mail: info@asymptote.net*
*Web: www.asymptote-architecture.com/*

*Hydra-Pier* ▶

**LISE ANN COUTURE** was born in Montreal in 1959. She received her Bachelor of Architecture degree from Carlton University, Canada, and her Master of Architecture degree from Yale. She has been a Design Critic in the Master of Architecture program at Parsons School of Design, New York. **HANI RASHID** received his degree as Master of Architecture from the Cranbrook Academy of Art, Bloomfield Hills, Michigan. They created **ASYMPTOTE** in 1987. Projects include their 1988 prize-winning commission for the Los Angeles West Coast Gateway 1988; a commissioned housing project for Brig, Switzerland; and their participation in the 1993 competition for an Art Center in Tours, France (1993). Other work by Asymptote includes a theater festival structure built in Denmark in 1997, a virtual trading floor for the New York Stock Exchange, and the Guggenheim Virtual Museum, an ongoing multimedia project aiming to create an on-line museum. In 2001, Asymptote participated in competitions for the Daimler-Chrysler and Mercedes-Benz Museums in Stuttgart, an expansion of the Queen's Museum, and the Eyebeam Center in New York.

**LISE ANN COUTURE**, geboren 1959 in Montreal, erwarb ihren Bachelor of Architecture an der Carleton University in Kanada und ihren Master of Architecture an der Yale University. Anschließend war sie im Rahmen des Master-of-Architecture-Programms als Designkritikerin an der Parsons School of Design in New York tätig. **HANI RASHID** machte seinen Master of Architecture an der Cranbrook Academy of Art in Bloomfield Hills, Michigan. Zusammen gründeten sie 1987 die Firma **ASYMPTOTE**. Zu ihren Projekten gehören der preisgekrönte Entwurf für den Los Angeles West Coast Gateway (1988), die Ausarbeitung eines Wohnhausprojekts in Brig in der Schweiz und ihr Wettbewerbsbeitrag für ein Kunstzentrum im französischen Tours (1993). Außerdem zählen zu ihren Projekten: ein Bau für das Theaterfestival 1997 im dänischen Århus, ein virtuelles Börsenparkett für die New Yorker Börse sowie das Guggenheim Virtual Museum, ein fortlaufendes Multimediaprojekt mit dem Ziel, ein Online-Museum zu installieren. 2001 beteiligten sich Couture und Rashid an den Wettbewerben für das Mercedes-Benz-Museum in Stuttgart, den Erweiterungsbau des Queen's Museum of Art und das Eyebeam Center, beide in New York.

**LISE ANN COUTURE**, née à Montréal en 1959, est B. Arch. De Carlton University, Canada, et M. Arch de Yale University. Elle a été critique de projets pour le programme du Master of Architecture de la Parsons School of Design, New York. **HANI RASHID** est M. Arch de la Cranbrook Academy of Art, Bloomfield Hills, Michigan. Ensemble, ils ont fondé **ASYMPTOTE** en 1987. Parmi leurs projets : le West Coast Gateway couronné d'un prix, une commande de logements pour Brig, Suisse ; la participation au concours pour un Centre d'art à Tours, France (1993), un théâtre pour un festival au Danemark en 1997, une salle de marchés virtuelle pour la Bourse de New York, et le Guggenheim Virtual Museum, projet multimedia en cours qui vise à la création d'un musée en ligne. En 2001, Asymptote a participé aux concours pour les musées Daimler-Chrysler et Mercedes-Benz à Stuttgart, une extension du Queen's Museum et le Eyebeam Center, tous deux à New York.

# HYDRA-PIER

*Haarlemmermeer, The Netherlands, 2002*

*Area: 1,750 m² (approx). Client: Municipality of Haarlemmermeer, Arnold Huijsmans, Rik Bolderheij.
Cost: withheld at request of the client.*

Haarlemmermeer, the area in which Schiphol airport is located, is host to the Floriade 2002 World Horticultural Exhibition. The exhibition brings together nations from around the globe to present in pavilions throughout the site. Following an international competition, Asymptote was commissioned to design the main municipal pavilion, whose purpose is to promote the host city of Haarlemmermeer as a vital and growing urban environment. **HYDRA-PIER** is a covered landscape on the shore of the Haarlemmermeer Bos, an entrance bridge between the two water-walls. It is also an enclosed multimedia exhibition space surrounded by a large deck that projects onto the lake. The architecture of the pavilion itself consists of two inclined, liquid-covered metallic planes deformed to incorporate an interior volume and an exterior pool. Continual pumping circulates water over the aluminum surfaces, and the controlled flow of water fuses with the winglike structure to create reflective, glistening, seemingly fluid surfaces.

Haarlemmermeer, die südlich von Haarlem gelegene Großgemeinde, in der sich auch der Flughafen Schiphol befindet, ist Gastgeber der internationalen Garten-bauausstellung Floriade 2002. In den zahlreichen Pavillons zeigen Nationen aus aller Welt ihre gartenbaulichen Erzeugnisse. Im Anschluss an einen internationalen Wett-bewerb erhielt Asymptote den Auftrag zur Gestaltung des gemeindeeigenen Hauptpavillons, der Haarlemmermeer als eine lebendige und wirtschaftlich aufstrebende urbane Region präsentieren soll. Ihr **HYDRA-PIER** genannter Entwurf ist eine überdachte Landschaft am Rand des vor 20 Jahren angelegten Walds Haarlemmermeer Bos und sieht eine Zugangsbrücke zwischen den beiden »Wasserwänden« vor. Er enthält außerdem einen multimedialen Ausstellungsraum, der von einer großen, bis auf den See hinausragenden Plattform umgeben ist. Die Architektur des Pavillons selbst besteht aus zwei schräg abfallenden und mit Flüssigkeit bedeckten Metallflächen, die so verformt wurden, dass sie einen Innenraum und einen Außenpool ergeben. Mittels einer Pumpvorrichtung zirkuliert kontinuierlich Wasser über die Aluminiumoberflächen und dieses strömende Wasser verbindet sich mit dem flügelartigen Baukörper zu einer Komposition spiegelnder, glitzernder, scheinbar flüssiger Oberflächen.

Haarlemmermeer, la zone dans laquelle se trouve l'aéroport de Schiphol, est l'hôte de Floriade 2002, une exposition florale universelle, qui réunit des nations du monde entier, présentes sous forme de pavillons. C'est à la suite d'un concours international qu'Asymptote a reçu commande du principal pavillon de la municipalité, dont l'objectif est de promouvoir la ville-hôte de Haarlemmermeer à travers son environnement urbain et la dynamique de son expansion. **HYDRA-PIER** est un paysage couvert sur la rive du Haarlemmermeer Bos, pont d'entrée entre deux murs d'eau. C'est également un espace clos pour expositions multimédias, entouré d'un vaste pont-terrasse qui se projette sur le lac. L'architecture du pavillon lui-même consiste en deux plans métalliques inclinés, couverts d'eau, qui contiennent un volume intérieur et un bassin extérieur. Un système de pompage permanent permet de faire circuler l'eau sur les plans d'aluminium. Ce flux liquide contrôlé et la forme en aile de la structure créent des surfaces réfléchissantes et brillantes qui paraissent fluides.

*With few built works to their credit, Asymptote nevertheless have a signature style seen here in the powerful upward thrust of this building, located near Schiphol Airport.*

*Obgleich Asymptote nur wenige realisierte Bauten vorzuweisen hat, verfügt das Architektenduo über eine typische Handschrift, die sich auch aus dem kraftvollen Aufwärtsschwung des hier abgebildeten Gebäudes nahe dem Flughafen Schiphol ablesen lässt.*

*Bien que peu de leurs créations aient été édifiées, Asymptote possède néanmoins un style reconnaissable ici dans la puissante poussée ascendante de ce bâtiment situé près de l'aéroport Schiphol.*

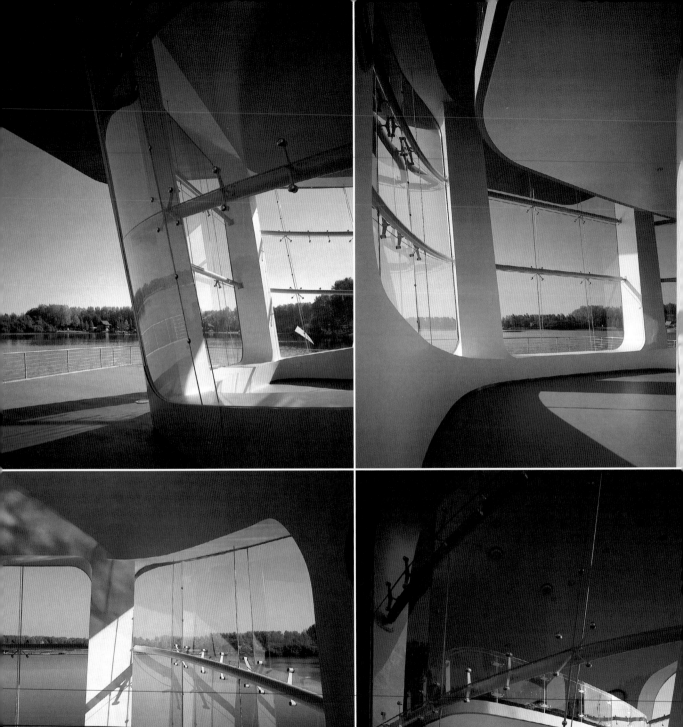

The surrounding presence of water and the wilfull alternation of opaque and transparent surfaces characterize the non-linear computer generated shapes of the Pavilion.

Das umgebende Wasser und die alternierende Anordnung opaker und transparenter Oberflächen charakterisieren die nichtlinearen computergenerierten Formen des Pavillons.

La présence de l'eau aux alentours et l'alternance de surfaces opaques et transparentes caractérisent les formes non linéaires du pavillon créées par ordinateur.

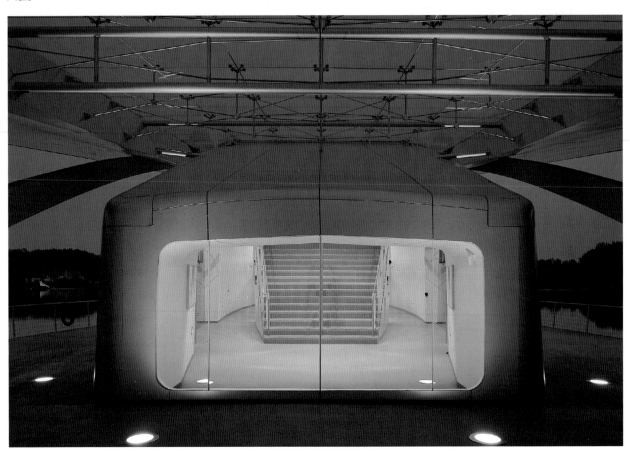

The eery spacecraft like feeling of
the structure in these night views
confirms the up-to-date esthetics of
Asymptote, architects who are just
as comfortable with virtual buildings
as they are with real ones.

In dem unheimlichen, raumschiffarti-
gen Eindruck, den die Konstruktion
in diesen nächtlichen Ansichten vermittelt, drückt sich die zeitgemäße
Ästhetik der Asymptote-Architekten
aus, die sich mit virtuellen Bauten
ebenso wohl fühlen wie mit realen.

L'inquiétante impression d'engin
spatial se dégageant de ces vues de
nuit confirme l'esthétique moderne
d'Asymptote, architectes qui se
sentent à l'aise aussi bien avec les
constructions virtuelles que les
réelles.

# SHIGERU BAN

*Shigeru Ban, Architects*
*5-2-4 Matubara Ban Bldg. 1Fl*
*Setagaya-ku, Tokyo*
*Japan*

*Tel: + 81 3 3324 6760*
*Fax: + 81 3 3324 6789*
*e-mail: SBA@tokyo.email.ne.jp*

*Naked House*

Born in 1957 in Tokyo, **SHIGERU BAN** studied at the Southern California Institute of Architecture (SciArc) from 1977 to 1980. He attended the Cooper Union School of Architecture, where he studied under John Hejduk (1980–1982). He worked in the office of Arata Isozaki (1982–1983) before founding his own firm in Tokyo in 1985. His work includes numerous exhibition designs (Alvar Aalto show at the Axis Gallery, Tokyo, 1986). His buildings include the Odawara Pavilion, Kanagawa, 1990; the Paper Gallery, Tokyo, 1994; the Paper House, Lake Yamanaka, 1994–95; and the Paper Church, Takatori, Hyogo, 1995. He has also designed ephemeral structures such as his Paper Refugee Shelter made with plastic sheets and paper tubes for the United Nations High Commissioner for Refugees (UNHCR). He designed the Japanese Pavilion at Expo 2000 in Hanover. Current work includes a small museum of Canal History in Pouilly-en-Auxois, France and housing in Beijing, China.

**SHIGERU BAN**, geboren 1957 in Tokio, studierte von 1977 bis 1980 am Southern California Institute of Architecture (SCI-Arc) und von 1980 bis 1982 bei John Hejduk an der Cooper Union School of Architecture in New York. Von 1982 bis 1983 arbeitete er im Büro von Arata Isozaki und gründete 1985 seine eigene Firma in Tokio. Shigeru Ban gestaltete zahlreiche Ausstellungen, so die 1986 in der Axis Gallery in Tokio gezeigte Alvar Aalto-Ausstellung. Zu seinen Bauten gehören der Odawara Pavillon in Kanagawa (1990), die Paper Gallery in Tokio (1994), das Paper House am Yamanaka-See (1994–95) und die Paper Church in Takatori, Hyogo (1995), alle in Japan. Shigeru Ban hat auch Behelfsbauten entworfen wie sein für den Hohen Flüchtlingskommissar der Vereinten Nationen (UNHCR) aus Plastikfolie und Pappröhren gebauter Paper Refugee Shelter. Für die Expo 2000 plante er den Japanischen Pavillon. Zu seinen jüngsten Projekten zählen ein kleines Museum für die Geschichte des Kanals im französischen Pouilly-en-Auxois und eine Wohnsiedlung in Peking.

Né en 1957 à Tokyo, **SHIGERU BAN** étudie au Southern California Institute of Architecture (SCI-Arc) de 1977 à 1980, puis à la Cooper Union School of Architecture où il suit l'enseignement de John Hejduk (1980–82). Il travaille auprès d'Arata Isozaki (1982–83) avant de fonder son agence à Tokyo en 1985. Il a conçu de nombreuses expositions (dont une sur Alvar Aalto, Axis Gallery, Tokyo, 1986). Parmi ses réalisations architecturales : le Pavillon Odawara (Kanagava, 1990) ; la Paper Gallery (Tokyo, 1997) ; la Maison de papier (Lac Yamanaka, 1994–95) ; l'Église de papier (Takatori, Hyogo, 1995). Il conçoit également des structures éphémères comme un « abri en papier pour réfugiés » en feuilles de plastique et tubes de papier pour le Haut Commissariat aux Réfugiés (HCRNU). Il a dessiné le pavillon japonais à Expo 2000, Hanovre. Parmi ses réalisations récentes figurent un petit musée sur l'histoire du canal de Bourgogne à Pouilly-en-Auxois, et des logements à Pékin.

# NAKED HOUSE

*Kawagoe, Saitama, Japan, 1999–2000*

*Site area: 516 m². Building area: 183 m². Total floor area: 138 m².
Structure: wood; 1 story.*

Shigeru Ban has attempted on numerous occasions to redefine the limits of architecture, in particular in his own Case Study Houses, such as the Wall-less House (Karuizawa, Nagano, Japan, 1997). In the **NAKED HOUSE** (Case Study House Number 10), located in an agricultural district about twenty kilometers north of Tokyo, he has created a shed-like design with moveable bedroom units that can be rolled into any location, even outside the limits of the house itself. Inspiring himself from local materials and agricultural architecture, he employed white extruded polyethylene – a packing material for fruits – in the skin of the shed, which resembles a greenhouse to some extent. Thirty-four arched trusses form the essential shape of the building. Inside, the actual "bedrooms" are made of brown paper honeycomb panels set on wooden frames, the whole on wheels, each unit measuring a modest six square meters. Bathroom, kitchen and laundry areas are in fixed locations separated from the rest of the house by high white curtains.

Shigeru Ban hat bereits in mehreren seiner Arbeiten versucht, die Grenzen von Architektur neu zu definieren, insbesondere in seinen Case Study Houses, zu dem beispielsweise das Wall-less House in Karuizawa, Nagano (1997), gehört. Das als Case Study House Number 10 geplante **NAKED HOUSE** liegt in einem landwirtschaftlich genutzten Gebiet circa 20 km nördlich von Tokio und wirkt von außen wie eine kleine Lagerhalle. Inspiriert von lokalen Baumaterialien und ländlicher Architektur verwendete Ban für die Außenhülle weiß gespritztes Polyethylen. Da dieser Kunststoff normalerweise zur Verpackung von Früchten dient, kann man eine gewisse Ähnlichkeit mit einem Gewächshaus nicht von der Hand weisen. Die Grundform des Gebäudes wird von 34 bogenförmigen Tragbalken gebildet. Seine Raumeinheiten lassen sich in jede beliebige Position verschieben, sogar über die Grenzen des Hauses selbst hinaus. Die im Inneren vorhandenen »Zimmer« bestehen aus wabenartig durchbrochenen und in Holzrahmen gespannten Tafeln aus braunem Papier. Das Ganze ist auf Rädern montiert, wobei jede Einheit bescheidene 6 m² misst. Badezimmer, Küche und Wirtschaftsraum/Waschküche sind in unverschiebbaren Bereichen untergebracht, die vom Rest des Hauses durch hohe, weiße Vorhänge abgetrennt sind.

Shigeru Ban a tenté à de nombreuses reprises de redéfinir les limites de l'architecture, en particulier dans ses Case Study Houses personnelles dont la « Maison sans mur » (Karuizawa, Nagano, Japon, 1997). Dans la **« MAISON NUE »** (Case Study House n° 10), construite dans une zone agricole à 30 km environ de Tokyo), il a créé une sorte de shed abritant des unités de chambres mobiles sur roulettes qui peuvent être déplacées dans n'importe quelle partie de la maison, voire au dehors. Inspiré par les matériaux locaux et l'architecture rurale, il s'est servi d'un polyéthylène extrudé, que l'on utilise pour emballer les fruits, pour tendre d'une peau l'intérieur du shed qui fait ainsi un peu penser à une serre. Trente-quatre poutres en arc donnent à la structure sa forme. À l'intérieur, les « chambres » sur roulettes sont en panneaux de papier d'emballage en nids d'abeilles fixés sur une structure en bois, chaque unité mesurant 6 m² à peine. La salle de bains, la cuisine et la buanderie sont fixes, séparées du reste de la maison par de grands rideaux blancs.

*The long walls of the rectangular structure are made of corrugated plastic and textile membranes. The open interior permits numerous configurations.*

*Die langen Wände des rechteckigen Hauses bestehen aus gewelltem Kunststoff und Textilfolie. Die offene Innenarchitektur bietet vielfältige Gestaltungsmöglichkeiten.*

*Les longs murs de la construction rectangulaire sont en plastique ondulé et membrane textile. L'intérieur à plan ouvert se prête à de nombreuses configurations.*

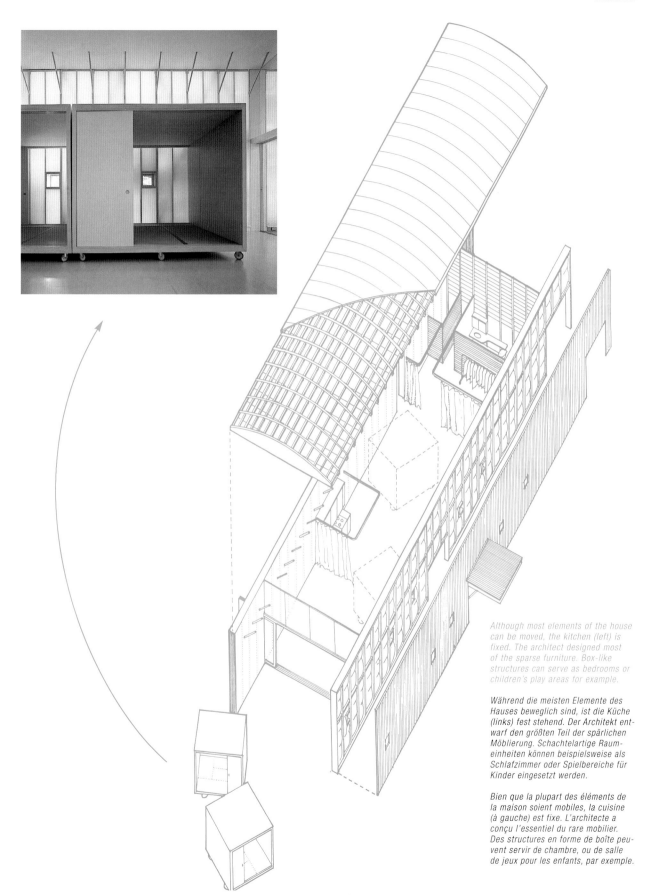

Although most elements of the house can be moved, the kitchen (left) is fixed. The architect designed most of the sparse furniture. Box-like structures can serve as bedrooms or children's play areas for example.

Während die meisten Elemente des Hauses beweglich sind, ist die Küche (links) fest stehend. Der Architekt entwarf den größten Teil der spärlichen Möblierung. Schachtelartige Raumeinheiten können beispielsweise als Schlafzimmer oder Spielbereiche für Kinder eingesetzt werden.

Bien que la plupart des éléments de la maison soient mobiles, la cuisine (à gauche) est fixe. L'architecte a conçu l'essentiel du rare mobilier. Des structures en forme de boîte peuvent servir de chambre, ou de salle de jeux pour les enfants, par exemple.

# BEHNISCH, BEHNISCH & PARTNER

Behnisch, Behnisch & Partner
Christophstr. 6
70178 Stuttgart
Germany

Tel: + 49 711 607 720
Fax: + 49 711 607 7299
e-mail: buero@behnisch.com

Born in 1922 in Dresden, **GÜNTER BEHNISCH** grew up in Dresden and in Chemnitz. He studied architecture from 1947 to 1951 at the Technical University of Stuttgart (Dipl.-Ing.) before setting up his own practice in 1952. In 1966 he created the firm of Behnisch & Partner, and from 1967 to 1987, he was a Professor for Design, Industrial Buildings and Planning, and Director of the Institute for Building Standardization at the Technical University, Darmstadt. In 1989, he established a city office in Stuttgart, which has now become Behnisch, Behnisch & Partner. **STEFAN BEHNISCH** was born in 1957 in Stuttgart. He studied philosophy at the Philosophische Hochschule der Jesuiten, Munich (1976–1979), economics at the Ludwig Maximilians University, Munich; and architecture at the University of Karlsruhe (1979–1987). He worked at Stephen Woolley & Associates (Venice, CA, 1984–1985), and has been a Principal Partner at Behnisch, Behnisch & Partner since 1992. He has been involved in numerous workshops and conferences on sustainable and green buildings since 1997. Born 1959 in Neuhausen, **GÜNTHER SCHALLER**, studied in architecture at the Technical College of Stuttgart (Dipl.-Ing. FH) and the University of Stuttgart (Dipl.-Ing.) from 1982 to 1991, when he joined the office Behnisch & Partner. Project Architect and Project Partner for the New Administration Building of the Landesgirokasse, in Stuttgart, he has been a Partner in Behnisch, Behnisch & Partner since 1997.

**GÜNTER BEHNISCH**, geboren 1922 in Dresden, wuchs in Dresden und Chemnitz auf. Von 1947 bis 1951 studierte er Architektur an der Technischen Universität in Stuttgart, wo er sein Ingenieurdiplom erwarb und machte sich 1952 mit einem eigenen Architekturbüro selbständig. 1966 gründete er die Firma Behnisch & Partner und von 1967 bis 1987 war er Professor für Entwerfen, Industriebauten und Baugestaltung sowie Direktor des Instituts für Baunormung an der TH Darmstadt. 1989 eröffnete Günter Behnisch ein Innenstadtbüro in Stuttgart, das heutige Behnisch, Behnisch & Partner. **STEFAN BEHNISCH** wurde 1957 in Stuttgart geboren. Er studierte Philosophie an der Philosophischen Hochschule der Jesuiten in München (1976–79), Wirtschaftswissenschaft an der Ludwig Maximilians Universität in München und Architektur an der Universität Karlsruhe (1979–87). Von 1984 bis 1985 arbeitete er bei Stephen Woolley & Associates in Venice, Kalifornien, und ist seit 1992 einer der Partner der Firma Behnisch, Behnisch & Partner. Seit 1997 war er auf zahlreichen Workshops und Konferenzen zum Thema nachhaltiges und ökologisches Bauen tätig. **GÜNTHER SCHALLER**, 1959 in Neuhausen geboren, studierte von 1982 bis 1991 Architektur an der Fachhochschule für Technik (Diplom 1987) und an der Technischen Universität in Stuttgart (Diplom 1991). Anschließend trat er in das Büro Behnisch & Partner ein. Er war Projektarchitekt und Projektpartner für das Dienstleistungsgebäude Am Bollwerk der Landesgirokasse in Stuttgart und ist seit 1997 Partner im Büro Behnisch, Behnisch & Partner.

Né en 1922 à Dresde, **GÜNTER BEHNISH** a grandi dans cette ville et à Chemnitz. Il étudie l'architecture de 1947 à 1951 à l'Université technique de Stuttgart (Dipl.-Ing.), et crée son agence en 1952. En 1966, il fonde Behnisch & Partner et, de 1967 à 1987, est professeur de design de bâtiments industriels et de programmation ainsi que directeur de l'Institut de standardisation de la construction à l'Université technique de Darmstadt. En 1989, il transfère son agence à Stuttgart, qui prend le nom de Behnisch, Behnisch & Partner. **STEFAN BEHNISCH** est né en 1957 à Stuttgart. Il étudie la philosophie à la Philosophische Hochschule der Jesuiten (Munich, 1976–79), l'économie à l'Université Ludwig Maximilian (Munich) et l'architecture à l'Université de Karlsruhe (1979–87). Il a travaillé chez Stephen Woolley & Associates (Venice, Californie, 1984–85) et est associé principal depuis 1992 de l'agence créée par son père. Il a participé à de nombreux colloques et conférences sur les immeubles verts et durables depuis 1997. Né en 1959 à Neuhausen, **GÜNTHER SCHALLER** a étudié l'architecture au Collège Technique de Stuttgart (Dipl.-Ing. FH) et à l'Université de Stuttgart (Dipl.-Ing.) de 1982 à 1991, date de son arrivée chez Behnisch & Partner. Architecte de projet et responsable de celui du nouvel immeuble administratif de la Landesgirokasse à Stuttgart, il est associé de l'agence depuis 1997.

# INSTITUTE FOR FORESTRY AND NATURE RESEARCH

*Wageningen, The Netherlands, 1994–1998*

*Client: Rijksgebouwdienst Direktie Ost. Competition: 1993. Planning and construction: 1994–1998.*
*Costs: DM 25,600,000. Gross Area: 11,800 m². Volume: 70,000 m³.*

Set to the north of Wageningen near other similar facilities, this structure was intended from the first to be "in harmony with nature and the environment, versatile and ecologically sound." Selected as a result of a 1993 invited competition, the project of Behnisch, Behnisch & Partner has a total floor area of 11,800 square meters and cost 25.6 million DM to build. The budget was set despite the ecological constraints on the basis that such goals can be attained without greatly increasing costs. Using a standard horticultural glazing system similar to that found in Dutch greenhouses for the internal garden areas, the actual office or laboratory spaces are conceived like more normal buildings within the overall glazed structure. Concrete slab ceilings in the offices and other devices are used to avoid air conditioning except in the laboratory areas of the structure. Local wood is used for doors, windows and office floors. A great deal of attention was paid to the choice of environmentally friendly materials, down to the chlorine-free plastic tubing used for the wiring. The natural climate control systems chosen do lead to seasonal or daily variations in temperature, but such relatively minor inconveniences have been readily accepted by the client and the users of the building. Though the esthetics of the Institute have been in good part determined by budgetary and environmental concerns, the overall result is pleasant and efficient.

Das Institut für Forst- und Naturwissenschaft im Norden von Wageningen liegt in der Nachbarschaft ähnlicher Einrichtungen und war von Anfang an so geplant, dass es im Einklang mit der Natur und der Umgebung, vielseitig und umweltfreundlich ist. Der 1993 als Sieger aus einem Wettbewerb hervorgegangene Entwurf von Behnisch, Behnisch & Partner sieht eine Gesamtnutzfläche von 11.800 m² vor und seine Realisierung kostete 25,6 Millionen Mark. Dieses Budget wurde unter der Voraussetzung festgesetzt, dass die ökologischen Auflagen ohne Mehrkosten erfüllt werden. Die innen gelegenen Gartenflächen wurden mit einem Glasbaukonstruktion überdacht, wie sie allgemein für den Gartenbau und speziell für holländische Gewächshäuser verwendet wird. Die eigentlichen Büro- und Laborbereiche sind als eher konventionelle Gebäude innerhalb der gläsernen Gesamtkonstruktion angelegt. Um auf eine Klimaanlage außerhalb der Labors verzichten zu können, sind die Decken der Büros und anderer Nutzräume aus Betonplatten gefertigt, während Türen, Fenster und Fußböden aus heimischem Holz bestehen. Bis zu den chlorfreien Plastikrohrleitungen für die Verkabelung wurden die umweltfreundlichen Baumaterialien mit großer Sorgfalt ausgewählt. Zwar führen die natürlichen Klimaregelungen zu saisonalen, manchmal täglich auftretenden Temperaturschwankungen, aber solch relativ harmlose Unannehmlichkeiten werden sowohl vom Bauherrn als auch von den Benutzern des Gebäudes bereitwillig hingenommen. Obgleich die bauliche Ästhetik des Institutsgebäudes zum großen Teil von finanziellen und ökologischen Anforderungen diktiert wurde, ist das Gesamtergebnis gefällig und funktionstüchtig.

Implantée au nord de Wageningen non loin d'institutions similaires, cette construction a été voulue dès l'origine « en harmonie avec la nature et l'environnement, flexible et écologiquement correcte ». Sélectionné lors d'un concours sur invitation organisé en 1993, le projet de Behnisch, Behnisch & Partner se développe sur une surface au sol totale de 11 800 m² et représente un budget de construction de 25,6 millions de DM. Les bureaux et laboratoires sont conçus comme des bâtiments classiques à l'intérieur d'une structure globale en verre qui fait appel à un système de vitrage standard utilisé en horticulture ou dans les serres des jardins d'hiver néerlandais. Les plafonds en dalles de béton ou autres matériaux permettent d'éviter le conditionnement mécanique de l'air dans les bureaux, néanmoins adopté pour les zones de laboratoire. Portes, fenêtres et sols des bureaux sont fabriqués dans un bois de la région. Une attention soutenue a été portée au choix de matériaux écologiques, dont des tubes en plastique sans chlore pour le câblage électrique. Les systèmes de contrôle de la climatisation naturelle n'évitent pas les variations saisonnières et quotidiennes de température, mais ces inconvénients relativement mineurs étaient acceptés d'avance par le client et les utilisateurs du bâtiment. Bien que l'esthétique de l'Institut ait été en grande partie déterminée par des soucis environnementaux et budgétaires, le résultat final de l'ensemble est agréable et efficace.

*Built on a former cornfield, whose earth was depleted by intensive farming, the Institute has a lively appearance despite rigorous adherence to environmental rules.*

*Das auf dem durch intensiven Ackerbau völlig ausgelaugten Boden eines ehemaligen Kornfelds errichtete Institutsgebäude vermittelt trotz der strengen Einhaltung von Umweltschutzauflagen einen lebendigen Eindruck.*

*Édifié sur un ancien champ de blé dont la terre avait été épuisée par une culture intensive, l'Institut présente une architecture animée bien qu'il se conforme en tous points à des principes stricts d'écologie.*

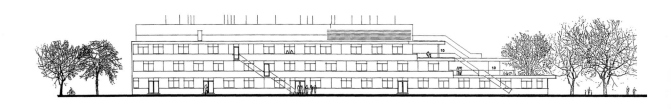

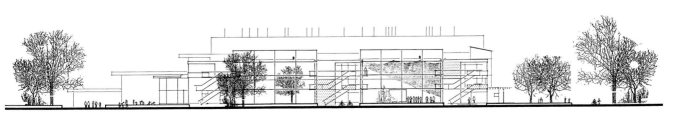

Two internal gardens serve as a "thermal buffer" allowing a large proportion of the office walls to be made of glass. Evaporating water from the gardens helps to cool the building, where research and the practical implications of ecological methods are closely related.

Die zwei Innengärten dienen als »Wärmepuffer« und ermöglichen, einen Großteil der Bürowände aus Glas zu errichten. Das Verdunstungswasser der Gärten trägt zur Kühlung des Gebäudes bei, in dem die Erforschung und praktische Anwendung ökologischer Techniken Hand in Hand gehen.

Deux jardins intérieurs servent de « tampon thermique », ce qui a permis de traiter en vitrage une grande partie des murs des bureaux. L'eau qui s'évapore des jardins contribue à rafraîchir ce bâtiment consacré à la recherche et aux implications pratiques des méthodes écologiques.

# BOHLIN CYWINSKI JACKSON

*Bohlin Cywinski Jackson*
*Wilkes-Barre Philadelphia Pittsburgh Seattle Berkeley*
*1932 First Avenue*
*Suite 916*
*Seattle, Washington 98101*
*United States*

*Tel: + 1 206 256 0862*
*Fax: + 1 206 256 0864*
*Web: www.bcj.com*

**BOHLIN CYWINSKI JACKSON**, founded in 1965, has offices in Wilkes-Barre, Pittsburgh, Philadelphia, Seattle and Berkeley. **PETER BOHLIN**, founding Design Principal, holds a Bachelor's Degree in Architecture from Rensselaer Polytechnic Institute, and a Master's Degree in Architecture from Cranbrook Academy of Art. **BERNARD J. CYWINSKI** serves as Design Principal for many of the firm's important commissions and collaborator in the great range of the firm's work, from corporate and civic buildings to academic and cultural facilities. He received Bachelor of Arts and Master of Architecture degrees from Columbia University. **JON C. JACKSON** received Bachelor of Science and Bachelor of Architecture degrees from Rensselaer Polytechnic Institute in 1973 and 1974. Significant work includes: Forest House (West Cornwall, Connecticut, 1975); Residential Compound for Bill and Melinda Gates (Medina, Washington, 1997, joint venture with James Cutler); Fishery Sciences Building, School of Aquatic and Fishery Sciences, University of Washington (1999, Seattle, Washington); Headquarters for Pixar Animation Studios (2001, Emeryville, California); Prototype and Flagship stores for Apple Computer (2002 and later, various Locations in the United States); Liberty Bell Center Independence National Historical Park (2003, Philadelphia, Pennsylvania).

Die 1965 gegründete Architekturfirma **BOHLIN CYWINSKI JACKSON** hat Niederlassungen in Wilkes-Barre, Pittsburgh, Philadelphia, Seattle und Berkeley. **PETER BOHLIN**, Gründer und Planungschef, erwarb seinen Bachelor of Architecture am Rensselaer Polytechnic Institute und seinen Master of Architecture an der Cranbrook Academy of Art. **BERNARD J. CYWINSKI** fungiert ebenfalls als Planungschef für viele der Großaufträge, die von Firmen- und Amtsgebäuden bis zu Universitätsinstituten und kulturellen Einrichtungen reichen. Er machte seinen Bachelor of Arts und seinen Master of Architecture an der Columbia University. **JON C. JACKSON** erwarb 1973 seinen Bachelor of Science und 1974 den Bachelor of Architecture am Rensselaer Polytechnic Institute. Zu ihren wichtigsten Bauten zählen: das Forest House in West Cornwall, Connecticut (1975), den in Zusammenarbeit mit James Cutler realisierten Wohnkomplex für Bill und Melinda Gates in Medina, Washington (1997), das Fishery Sciences Building der School of Aquatic and Fishery Sciences an der University of Washington in Seattle (1999), die Zentrale der Pixar Animation Studios im kalifornischen Emeryville (2001), Prototyp und Flagship-Stores für Apple Computer (2002 und in den folgenden Jahren weitere Geschäfte an verschiedenen Standorten in den USA) sowie der Liberty Bell Center Independence National Historical Park in Philadelphia, Pennsylvania, der 2003 fertig gestellt sein soll.

L'agence **BOHLIN CYWINSKI JACKSON**, fondée en 1965, possède des bureaux à Wilkes-Barre, Pittsburgh, Philadelphie, Seattle et Berkeley. **PETER BOHLIN**, directeur et fondateur est B. Arch. de la Cranbrook Academy of Art. **BERNARD J. CYWINSKI**, B. A. et M. Arch. de Columbia University, est responsable de la conception de nombreux projets importants de l'agence qui intervient dans le vaste domaine des bâtiments officiels, sièges sociaux, équipements universitaires et culturels. **JON C. JACKSON** est B. Sc. et B. Arch du Rensselaer Polytechnic Institute en 1973–74. Principales réalisations : Forest House (West Cornwall, Connecticut, 1975) ; résidence de Bill et Melinda Gates (Medina, Washington, 1997, en association avec James Cutler) ; Fishery Sciences Building, École des sciences de l'eau et de la pêche, University of Washington (Seattle, Washington, 1999) ; siège de Pixmar Animation Studios (Emeryville, Californie, 2000) ; magasin prototype et magasin principal de Apple Computer (divers lieux aux U.S.A., 2002) ; Liberty Bell Center Independence National Historical Park (Philadelphie, Pennsylvanie, 2003).

# GOSLINE HOUSE

*Seattle, Washington, United States, 2000*

*Area: 190 m². Structure: concrete and wood frame*

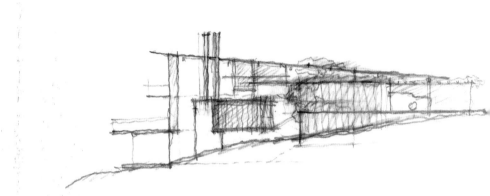

*The transparency and lightness of the house are evident in these images, showing the relationship of a design sketch to the completed facade (below). Ample glazed surfaces emphasize the view.*

*Diese Bilder spiegeln die Transparenz und Leichtigkeit des Hauses wider, ebenso wie das Verhältnis einer der Entwurfszeichnungen zur fertigen Fassade (unten). Die großflächigen Verglasungen zeigen, wie viel Wert auf den Ausblick gelegt wurde.*

*La transparence et la légèreté de la maison apparaissent dans ces images qui montrent un croquis de conception de la façade et celle-ci achevée (ci-dessous). De vastes surfaces vitrées mettent la vue en valeur.*

*Interiors emphasize the structural simplicity of the house and its inherent modesty – a fact that does not prohibit the residence from having a spectacular openness toward its environment. Wood surfaces give a warmth that might otherwise be lacking in this residence.*

*Die Innenräume heben die bauliche Schlichtheit und Bescheidenheit des Hauses hervor – ein Aspekt, der keinesfalls im Widerspruch zu seiner spektakulären Einbindung in die Umgebung steht. Oberflächen aus Holz verleihen den Räumen die nötige Wärme.*

*L'aménagement intérieur tire le meilleur profit de la simplicité structurelle de maison et de sa modestie intrinsèque, ce qui ne lui empêche pas de s'ouvrir de manière spectaculaire sur son environnement. Des surfaces habillées de bois apportent à l'ensemble une chaleur qui, sans elles, aurait pu manquer.*

The small, 190 square-meter **GOSLINE HOUSE** for a retired couple stretches along a narrow sloping site with views of an arboretum and the Cascade Mountains. The building is positioned to preserve a Madrona tree and large Deodar Cedar. The owners, encouraged an architecture that reveals the nature and assembly of its basic building materials, including common wood framing, plywood, polycarbonate sheets, concrete, steel and glass. The open layout includes a second-floor master bedroom that overlooks the living room, two offices that can double as guestrooms, and details such as a mail-sorting nook shielded by a small sliding barn door. The modest house reveals the particular nature of its site, its owners and its materials. Exterior materials are fiber-cement siding with exposed fasteners, metal roof, exposed fir beams, polycarbonate glazing, and Ipé wood decking. Interior materials include maple plywood wall panels, integrally colored concrete floors, exposed fir framing, gypsum wall board, and maple cabinets.

Das 190 m² große **GOSLINE HAUS** wurde für ein Paar im Ruhestand gebaut. Es liegt auf einem schmalen Hanggrundstück mit Blick auf einen Baumgarten und die Cascade Mountains. Der Standort wurde so gewählt, dass ein Madrona-Baum und eine ausladende Deodarazeder erhalten werden konnten. Die Eigentümer wünschten sich eine Architektur, die die Beschaffenheit der ausgewählten Baumaterialien wie Holzrahmen, Sperrholz, Polycarbonatplatten, Beton, Stahl und Glas erkennen lässt. Der offen angelegte Grundriss enthält ein Hauptschlafzimmer, das den Blick auf den Wohnraum freigibt, zwei Arbeitszimmer, die auch als Gästezimmer genutzt werden können, und so raffinierte Details wie die kleine, von einer Schiebetür abgetrennte Nische zum Sortieren der Post. In diesem einfachen Wohnhaus spiegelt sich der besondere Charakter seiner Lage, seiner Eigentümer sowie der verwendeten Materialien wider. Die Außenverkleidung besteht aus Faserzement mit sichtbaren Halterungen für die Seitenwandung, einer Metallüberdachung, frei liegenden Tannenbalken, Polycarbonatverglasung und Überdachungen aus Ipéholz. Zur Innenraumausstattung gehören Wandpaneele aus Ahornsperrholz, farbige Betonböden, freiliegendes Tannenholzgebälk, Gipsplatten und Einbauschränke aus Ahorn.

La petite **MAISON GOSLINE** de 190 m² construite pour un couple de retraités se développe sur une étroite parcelle inclinée qui donne sur un arboretum et les Cascade Mountains. Elle a été implantée de façon à éviter d'abattre un arbre de Madrona et un grand cèdre. Les propriétaires ont voulu une architecture qui révèle la nature et la mise en œuvre des matériaux de construction simples utilisés, dont une ossature en bois classique, du contre-plaqué, des feuilles de polycarbonate, du béton, de l'acier et du verre. Le plan ouvert comprend à l'étage une chambre principale qui domine le séjour, deux bureaux transformables en chambres d'amis et des détails comme un petit local de courrier protégé par une porte de bar. Les matériaux extérieurs sont un placage en fibrociment à fixations apparentes, un toit métallique, des poutres de pin apparentes, des panneaux transparents en polycarbonate et une terrasse en Ipé. On trouve à l'intérieur des lambris en contre-plaqué d'érable, des sols en béton coloré dans la masse, l'ossature en pin apparente, des panneaux de placoplâtre et des meubles en érable.

# BOLLES + WILSON

*Architekturbüro Bolles + Wilson*
*Alter Steinweg 17*
*48143 Münster*
*Germany*

*Tel: + 49 251 482 720*
*Fax: + 49 251 482 7224*
*e-mail: info@bolles-wilson.com*

**PETER WILSON** was born in Melbourne, in 1950. He studied at the University of Melbourne (1968–1970), and at the Architectural Association in London (1972–1974). **JULIA BOLLES WILSON** was born in 1948 in Münster, and studied at the University of Karlsruhe (1968–1976) and at the A. A. in London (1978–1979) while Wilson was Unit Master (1978–1988). They formed the Wilson Partnership in London in 1980, and Architekturbüro Bolles + Wilson in 1987. The office moved in 1988 to Münster. Their projects include a "Garden folly" at the International Garden and Greenery Exposition 1990 in Osaka. Peter Wilson built the Suzuki House (1993), Tokyo. Other recent projects include the WLV Office Building in Münster, Germany (1991–1996); the Kop van Zuid Quay Buildings in Rotterdam (1991–1996), the Volksbank Borken Headquarters, Borken, Germany (1997–2000); and the TGZ II Laboratory in Halle-Wittenberg, Germany (1999–2000).

**PETER WILSON**, geboren 1950 in Melbourne, studierte von 1968 bis 1970 an der University of Melbourne und von 1972 bis 1974 an der Architectural Association (AA) in London. **JULIA BOLLES WILSON** wurde 1948 in Münster geboren und studierte von 1968 bis 1976 an der Universität Karlsruhe und von 1978 bis 1979 an der AA, während Peter Wilson dort Unit Master war (1978–88). 1980 gründeten beide in London die Wilson Partnership und 1987 das Architekturbüro Bolles + Wilson, das sie 1988 nach Münster verlegten. Zu ihren Projekten zählen ein Garden Folly (Lusthaus) für die International Garden and Greenery Exposition in Osaka 1990 und das von Peter Wilson entworfene Suzuki House in Tokio (1993). Zu ihren neueren Bauten gehören außerdem das Bürogebäude der WLV in Münster (1991–96), die Kaianlagen Kop van Zuid in Rotterdam (1991–96), die Zentrale der Volksbank Borken in Borken (1997–2000) und das Labor TGZ II in Halle-Wittenberg (1999–2000).

**PETER WILSON**, né à Melbourne en 1950, a étudié à l'Université de cette ville (1968–70) et à l'Architectural Association de Londres (1972–74). **JULIA BOLLES WILSON**, née en 1948 à Münster a étudié à l'Université de Karlsruhe (1968–76) et à l'A. A. de Londres (1978–79) quand Wilson y était Unit Master (1978–88). Ils ont créé l'agence Wilson Partnership à Londres en 1980 et l'Architekturbüro Bolles + Wilson en 1987, installé à Münster en 1988. Parmi leurs projets, une «Folie de jardin» pour la International Garden and Greenery Exposition 1990 à Osaka. Peter Wilson a édifié la Suzuki House (Tokyo, 1993). D'autres projets récents comprennent l'immeuble de bureaux WLV (Münster, Allemagne, 1991–96); les Quay Buildings de Kop van Zuid à Rotterdam (1991–96); le siège de la Volksbank (Borken, Allemagne, 1997–2000); le laboratoire TGZ II (Halle-Wittenberg, Allemagne, 1999–2000).

ZAAL
MAAS
FOYER
BAR 4 ↗

# NEW LUXOR THEATRE

*Rotterdam, The Netherlands, 1998–2000*

*Client: Luxor Theatre Rotterdam. Gross floor area: 15,592 m² (theatre), 719 m² (Leipzig Restaurant).*
*Number of seats: 1,500. Stage size: 42 meters wide x 21 meters deep.*

Set near the landfall of Ben van Berkel's spectacular Erasmus Bridge in the Kop van Zuid area of Rotterdam, the **NEW LUXOR THEATRE** is an essential piece in the redevelopment of this former dockland area. Although office buildings have now been built in the still rather desolate area, aside from the nearby Hotel New York, there was no center of nighttime activity. The 1,500 seat New Luxor Theater thus truly announces the creation of a new area of the city. Selected as a result of a 1996 invited competition, the project of Bolles + Wilson won over the entries of Herman Hertzberger or Rem Koolhaas. The tomato-red spiral wrapping facades of the structure are readily visible from a distance, and the movement of the building gives the impression that there is an overall continuity between this unexpected exterior and the inside of the theatre. A 36-meter high tower announces the name Luxor in bold letters and large panel displays prominently indicate current features at the theatre. One unusual aspect of the site and the building was that 18-meter trucks had to be able to accede to the upper level stage. Taking into account the optimal turning radius of these large vehicles, the architects decided to use the roof of the truck ramp as a promenade through the building. The site of the theater is quite close to the architects' own Quay Buildings (Kop van Zuid, Rotterdam, 1991–96).

Das **NEW LUXOR THEATRE** liegt nahe der spektakulären Erasmus-Brücke von Ben van Berkel und den ebenfalls von Bolles + Wilson gestalteten Kaianlagen (1991–96). Es bildet ein signifikantes Teilstück in der Erneuerung und Modernisierung dieses ehemaligen Dockgeländes im Rotterdamer Bezirk Kop van Zuid. Obwohl inzwischen auch Bürogebäude in dem nach wie vor ziemlich trostlosen Gebiet errichtet wurden, gab es dort, abgesehen vom nahe gelegenen Hotel New York, bislang keinerlei Nachtleben. Somit markiert das 1.500 Plätze fassende Theater tatsächlich die Entstehung eines neuen Stadtviertels. Der von Bolles + Wilson für einen 1996 ausgeschriebenen Wettbewerb eingereichte Entwurf gewann vor den Modellen von Herman Hertzberger und Rem Koolhaas. Die tomatenrote, spiralförmig umlaufende Fassade ist auch aus der Ferne gut sichtbar und die dynamische Gestaltung des Gebäudes vermittelt den Eindruck einer engen Verbindung zwischen dem ungewöhnlichen Äußeren mit dem Inneren des Theaters. Der Name »Luxor« prangt in riesigen Leuchtbuchstaben auf dem 36 m hohen Turm und große Anzeigetafeln weisen auf aktuelle Veranstaltungen hin. Zu den ungewöhnlichen Merkmalen von Bauplatz und Gebäude gehörte die Bedingung, dass für 18 m lange Lastwagen eine Zufahrt auf die Bühnenebene im Obergeschoss ermöglicht werden musste. Angesichts des Wendekreises dieser Fahrzeuge beschlossen die Architekten, das Dach der Anlieferungsrampe für die Besucher zu einer Flaniermeile durch das Gebäude zu machen.

Non loin du spectaculaire pont Érasme de Ben van Berkel dans le quartier de Kop van Zuid à Rotterdam, cette nouvelle salle de spectacle est un élément essentiel de la rénovation de ces anciens docks. Bien que des immeubles de bureaux aient été édifiés, rien n'avait été prévu, en dehors de l'Hotel New York, pour les activités nocturnes dans ce quartier assez vide. Les 1 500 places du **NOUVEAU THÉÂTRE LUXOR** amorcent ainsi la création d'un nouveau quartier urbain. Sélectionné en 1996 à l'issue d'un concours sur invitation organisé en 1996, le projet de Bolles + Wilson a été retenu face à ceux d'Herman Hertzberger et de Rem Koolhaas. La façade à spirale rouge tomate de la structure est visible de loin et le mouvement inhérent au bâtiment donne l'impression d'une continuité d'ensemble entre le surprenant extérieur et l'intérieur. Une tour de 36 m de haut proclame le nom de Luxor en lettres majuscules et de grands panneaux affichent de manière très visible le programme des salles. Une des caractéristiques inhabituelles du site et du terrain est de permettre l'accès de camions de 18 m de long à la scène située au niveau supérieur. Prenant en compte le rayon de braquage de ces grands véhicules, les architectes ont décidé de faire du toit de la rampe d'accès une promenade intérieure au bâtiment. Le Luxor est assez proche des Quay Buildings réalisés par les mêmes architectes (Kop van Zuid, Rotterdam, 1991–96).

*The red coloring and large-scale signs of the Theatre make it visible from central Rotterdam. Its morphology gives it a very different appearance depending on the angle from which it is viewed.*

*Durch den roten Außenanstrich und den riesigen Schriftzug ist das Theater von der Rotterdamer Innenstadt aus gut zu sehen. Die Form des Gebäudes variiert je nach Blickwinkel des Betrachters.*

*La coloration rouge et les énormes enseignes du Théâtre le rendent visible du centre même de Rotterdam. Une morphologie complexe lui permet de présenter un visage différent selon l'angle d'observation.*

The unexpected openings in the structure and its combination of rectilinear and curving elements make for a lively design that does not specifically evoke traditional theatre architecture.

Die überraschenden Öffnungen in der Fassade sowie die Kombination geradliniger und gebogener Elemente tragen zu einer lebendigen Gesamtwirkung des Entwurfs bei, die nicht unbedingt an traditionelle Theaterarchitektur erinnert.

Des ouvertures inattendues et la combinaison d'éléments rectilignes et curvilignes contribuent à animer l'ensemble, sans évoquer spécifiquement une architecture traditionnelle de théâtre.

The extensive use of red is carried through to the entrance foyer and the interior of the theatre itself. The projecting red steel angle (above) contains a truck turning point on the lower level and a terrace above.

Die großflächige Verwendung roter Farbe setzt sich in der Eingangshalle und im Theaterinneren fort. Der vorspringende Winkel aus rotem Stahl (oben) dient als Wendemarke für LKWs und auf der darüber liegenden Ebene als Terrasse.

L'utilisation extensive de la couleur rouge se retrouve dans le hall d'entrée et à l'intérieur même du théâtre. La structure triangulaire rouge surmontée d'une terrasse et en projection au-dessus de l'eau (ci-dessus) correspond à un virage de la rampe d'accès des camions.

# BRUNER/COTT & ASSOCIATES, INC.

*Bruner/Cott & Associates, Inc.*
*130 Prospect St.*
*Cambridge, Massachusetts 02139*
*United States*

*Tel: + 1 617 492 8400*
*Fax: + 1 617 876 4002*
*e-mail: contact@brunercott.com*
*Web: www.brunercott.com*

*Mass MoCA* ▸

**SIMEON BRUNER** received an undergraduate degree in Biology from Brandeis University (1963) and a Master of Architecture from Yale (1969). He is specialized in the adaptive reuse of 19th and early 20th century buildings. His partner **LELAND COTT** received his Bachelor of Architecture degree from the Pratt Institute (1966) and a Master of Architecture in Urban Design at Harvard (1970). He has been active in the design and planning of university and large-scale public and private housing structures. According to the architects, Bruner/Cott's design philosophy embodies contextuality in its most comprehensive sense; design that is energized by the surrounding urban fabric and the historic, economic and social factors that characterize each project.

**SIMEON BRUNER** machte 1963 den Undergraduate-Abschluss in Biologie an der Brandeis University und erwarb 1969 seinen Master of Architecture an der Yale University. Er ist spezialisiert auf die adaptive Umgestaltung von Gebäuden aus dem 19. und frühen 20. Jahrhundert. Sein Partner **LELAND COTT** erwarb 1966 den Bachelor of Architecture am Pratt Institute und 1970 den Master of Architecture in Urban Design in Harvard. Cotts Spezialgebiet sind Großprojekte wie Universitätsgebäude, öffentliche Bauten oder private Wohnanlagen. Laut eigener Aussage haben Bruner und Cott eine im umfassenden Sinn kontextuelle Gestaltungsphilosophie. Ihr Ziel ist eine Architektur, die durch die städtebauliche Umgebung und die jedes Bauprojekt kennzeichnenden historischen, ökonomischen und sozialen Faktoren mit Leben erfüllt wird.

**SIMEON BRUNER** est diplômé de biologie de Brandeis University (1963) et M. Arch. de Yale (1969). Il est spécialisé dans la réadaptation d'immeubles des XIXe et XXe siècles. Son associé **LELAND COTT** est B. Arch. du Pratt Institute (1966) et M. Arch en urbanisme de Harvard (1970). Il a beaucoup œuvré dans la conception et la planification d'universités et de grands programmes de logements publics ou privés. Selon les architectes, la philosophie de conception de Bruner/Cott incarne la contextualité dans son sens le plus global ; conception qui tire son énergie du tissu urbain environnant et des facteurs historiques, économiques et sociaux qui peuvent caractériser chaque projet.

# MASS MOCA

*North Adams, Massachusetts, United States, 1988–1999*

*Site area: 72,500 m². Phase one area: 9,300 m² (galleries, two theaters, cafe, outdoor cinema etc.), 5,600 m² (boutiques).
Phase two area: 18,600 m². Phase one budget: $ 31.4 million.*

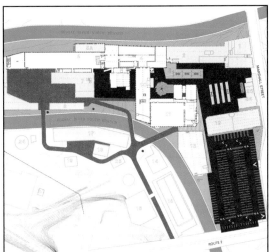

It was in 1988 that Thomas Krens, now Director of the Guggenheim and at the time Director of the Williams College Museum of Art, had the idea to transform an abandoned industrial site in North Adams, Massachusetts, into an innovative center for contemporary art. The six-hectare site, with structures built between 1862 and 1890 to house a textile firm, had been abandoned since 1985 when its last occupant, the Sprague Electric Company, went bankrupt. The 1988 competition for reuse of the site resulted in the selection of a prestigious group of architects: Frank O. Gehry, Robert Venturi, Skidmore, Owings & Merrill and Simeon Bruner. Bruner, a specialist in the renovation of industrial buildings, stuck with the task while his better known colleagues moved on to other assignments. With a total of twenty-seven buildings to chose from and a budget limited to $31.4 million, Bruner had his work cut out for him. Only the first phase of the project has been completed, with an accent having been placed on the buildings that were in the worst condition at the outset. An entrance deep within the complex, which unfortunately is not in real proximity to the center of North Adams, is intended to bring people to visit the site, large parts of which still remain off limits. The current fashion for roughly rehabilitated buildings, visible in a more polished form in the Chelsea area of Manhattan or even in the new Palais de Tokyo in Paris, may well have originated in North Adams.

Thomas Krens, der heutige Direktor des Guggenheim Museums und damalige Direktor des Williams College Museum of Art, hatte 1988 die Idee, ein aufgelassenes Industriegelände in North Adams, Massachusetts, in ein innovatives Zentrum für zeitgenössische Kunst zu verwandeln. Das sechs Hektar große Areal mit Gebäuden, die zwischen 1862 und 1890 für eine Textilfirma gebaut worden waren, stand seit 1985 leer, als der letzte Eigentümer, die Sprague Electric Company, Konkurs gemacht hatte. Als Ergebnis des 1988 ausgeschriebenen Wettbewerbs wurde eine Gruppe renommierter Architekten mit der Revitalisierung des Geländes beauftragt: Frank O. Gehry, Robert Venturi, Skidmore, Owings & Merrill und Simeon Bruner. Letztendlich blieb nur Bruner, ein Spezialist für die Umgestaltung von Industriegebäuden, bei der Aufgabe, während sich seine bekannteren Kollegen anderen Auftragsarbeiten zuwandten. Mit einer Gesamtzahl von 27 Gebäuden und einem auf 31,4 Millionen Dollar begrenzten Budget, hatte Bruner fortan mehr als genug zu tun. Bislang wurde lediglich die erste Phase des Projekts abgeschlossen, wobei der Schwerpunkt auf Bauten lag, die schon zu Beginn in einem besonders schlechten Zustand waren. Ein Eingang, der sich bis ins Innere des Komplexes erstreckt, aber leider nicht in der Nähe des Stadtzentrums von North Adams liegt, soll die Besucher auf das zum großen Teil immer noch unzugängliche Gelände führen. Es ist gut möglich, dass die aktuelle Vorliebe für einen ungeschliffenen Stil in der Wiederinstandsetzung alter Gebäude, die in etwas verfeinerter Form derzeit im New Yorker Stadtteil Chelsea und sogar im neuen Palais de Tokyo in Paris sichtbar wird, ihren Ursprung in North Adams hat.

C'est en 1988 que Thomas Krens, aujourd'hui directeur du Guggenheim, et alors du Williams College Museum of Art, eut l'idée de transformer un site industriel de North Adams en centre d'art contemporain novateur. Le terrain de six hectares et ses bâtiments édifiés de 1862 à 1890 pour une entreprise textile, était abandonné depuis 1985, date de la faillite de son dernier occupant, la Sprague Electric Company. Le concours de 1988 pour la réutilisation du site a mobilisé de prestigieux architectes : Frank O. Gehry, Robert Venturi, Skidmore, Owings & Merrill, Simeon Bruner. Bruner, spécialiste de la rénovation des bâtiments industriels, s'est mis à la tâche tandis que ses collègues plus célèbres partaient vers d'autres commandes. Avec vingt-sept bâtiments et un budget de 31,4 millions de dollars, il avait fort à faire et seule la première phase du projet, consacrée aux constructions en plus mauvais état, a été achevée. Une entrée profondément engoncée dans le complexe – malheureusement sans proximité immédiate avec le centre de North Adams – est supposée inciter à visiter le site, dont de grandes parties sont encore condamnées. L'origine de la mode actuelle de la réhabilitation de bâtiments industriels anciens, qui se manifeste sous une forme plus policée dans le quartier de Chelsea à Manhattan ou dans les nouveaux aménagements du Palais de Tokyo à Paris, se trouve peut-être à North Adams.

*Above left, site plan. Above right, the factory complex in 1980 prior to conversion. Right, Clocktower and entrance court.*

*Lageplan (oben links) und Ansicht des Fabrikkomplexes 1980 vor dem Umbau (oben rechts). Uhrturm und Eingangshof (rechts).*

*Ci-dessus à gauche, plan du terrain. À droite, le complexe industriel en 1980, avant sa reconversion. À droite, clocher, et cour d'entrée.*

The restoration intentionally preserved the colors and textures of the old structures (left). Remaining steel defines space in an exterior courtyard (above).

Bei der Renovierung wurden Farben und Oberflächenstruktur der alten Gebäude bewusst erhalten (links). Die alte Stahlkonstruktion markiert den Raum in einem Außenhof (oben).

La restauration a volontairement préservé les couleurs et les textures des anciens bâtiments (à gauche). Des vestiges d'éléments en acier définissent l'espace dans une cour extérieure (en haut).

A work by Joseph Beuys, "Blitzschlag mit Lichtschein auf Hirsch", a piece the artist began working on in 1958.

Eine Arbeit von Joseph Beuys, »Blitzschlag mit Lichtschein auf Hirsch«, die vom Künstler 1958 begonnen wurde.

Une œuvre de Joseph Beuys, Blitzschlag mit Lichtschein auf Hirsch, laquelle l'artiste avait commencé à travailler en 1958.

A combination of new trusses and an existing brick wall define a new two-story gallery space in Mass MoCA (left). Above, Bruner/Cott pioneered a trend in the reuse of industrial spaces for contemporary art now confirmed in the Chelsea area of New York.

Die Kombination der neuen Stützträgern mit der ursprünglichen Ziegelsteinwand kennzeichnen einen neuen zweigeschossigen Ausstellungsraum im Mass MoCA (links). Bruner/Cott waren Wegbereiter für den Trend, Industriegebäude für Ausstellungen zeitgenössischer Kunst zu nutzen, der sich heute im New Yorker Stadtteil Chelsea manifestiert (oben).

Une combinaison de poutres neuves et d'un mur de briques existant définit un nouvel espace de galerie sur deux niveaux (à gauche). En haut : Bruner/Cott sont les pionniers du mouvement de réutilisation des espaces industriels pour l'art contemporain, dont la rénovation du quartier de Chelsea à New York est un exemple récent.

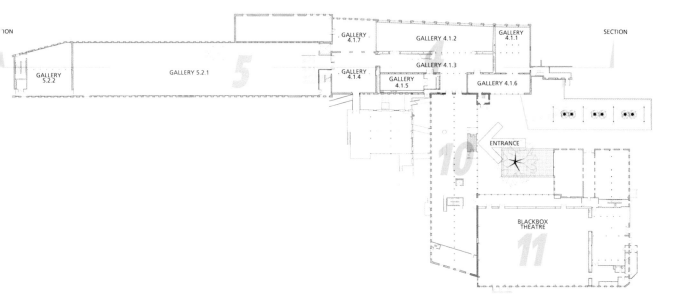

A new three-story space with north light coming through the tops of existing windows (left). Below a one hundred meter long gallery with a Robert Rauschenberg installation. Above, the ground floor plan of Phase one.

Ein neuer dreigeschossiger Raum, der durch die bestehende Fensterreihe oben Licht von Norden erhält (links). Ein hundert Meter langer Ausstellungsraum (unten) mit einer Installation von Robert Rauschenberg. Grundriss des Erdgeschosses von »Phase one« (oben).

Un nouvel espace sur trois niveaux, orienté au nord, bénéficie d'un éclairage naturel dispensé par la partie haute des fenêtres existantes (à gauche). En bas, une galerie de 100 m de long et une installation de Robert Rauschenberg. En haut, plan au sol de Phase un.

# SANTIAGO CALATRAVA

*Calatrava Valls Eurl*
*Obere Zaüne 14*
*8000 Zürich*
*Switzerland*

*Tel: + 41 14 25 28 87*
*Fax: + 41 14 22 56 00*

Born in Valencia in 1951, **SANTIAGO CALATRAVA** studied art and architecture at the Escuela Técnica Superior de Arquitectura in Valencia (1969–1974) and engineering at the ETH in Zurich (doctorate in Technical Science, 1981). He opened his own architecture and civil engineering practice the same year. His built work includes Gallery and Heritage Square, BCE Place, Toronto, 1987, the Bach de Roda Bridge, Barcelona, 1985–1987, the Torre de Montjuic, Barcelona, 1989–1992, the Kuwait Pavilion at Expo '92, Seville, and the Alamillo Bridge for the same exhibition, as well as the Lyon Satolas TGV Station, 1989–1994. He completed the Oriente Station in Lisbon in 1998. He was a finalist in the competition for the Reichstag in Berlin, and he recently completed the Valencia City of Science and Planetarium, (Valencia, Spain, 1996–2000); the Sondica Airport (Bilbao, Spain, 1990–1999); and a bridge in Orléans (1996–2000). He is currently working on the Oakland Diocese Cathedral in California.

**SANTIAGO CALATRAVA**, geboren 1951 in Valencia, studierte von 1969 bis 1974 an der dortigen Escuela Técnica Superior de Arquitectura Kunst und Architektur sowie Ingenieurbau an der Eidgenössischen Technischen Hochschule (ETH) in Zürich, wo er 1981 promovierte. Im selben Jahr gründete er sein eigenes Büro für Architektur und Bauingenieurwesen. Zu Calatravas Bauten gehören der Gallery and Heritage Square, die BCE Place in Toronto (1987), die Bach-de-Roda-Brücke (1985–87) und die Torre de Montjuic (1989–92) in Barcelona, der Kuwait-Pavillon und die Alamillo-Brücke für die Expo '92 in Sevilla sowie der TGV-Bahnhof Lyon-Satolas (1989–94). 1998 vollendete er den Oriente-Bahnhof in Lissabon. Calatravas Entwurf für den Reichstag in Berlin kam in die Endauswahl. Zu seinen jüngsten Projekten zählen das Opernhaus City of Science sowie das Planetarium in Valencia (1996–2000), der Flughafen Sondika in Bilbao (1990–99) und eine Brücke in Orléans (1996–2000). Derzeit arbeitet er an der Kathedrale der Diözese Oakland in Kalifornien.

Né à Valence en 1951, **SANTIAGO CALATRAVA** étudie l'art et l'architecture à l'Escuela Técnica Superior de Arquitectura de Valence (1969–74) et l'ingénierie à l'ETH de Zurich. Docteur en science des techniques en 1981, il ouvre sa propre agence d'architecture et d'ingénierie civile la même année. Parmi ses réalisations : Gallery and Heritage Square, BCE Place, Toronto, 1987 ; le pont Bach de Roda (Barcelone, 1985–87) ; la Torre de Montjuic (Barcelone, 1989–92) ; le Pavillon du Koweït à Expo '92 ; le pont de l'Alamillo (Séville) ; la gare de T. G. V. de Lyon-Saint-Exupéry (1989–94) ; la gare de l'Orient (Lisbonne, 1998). Il a été finaliste du concours du Reichstag à Berlin, et a récemment achevé la Cité des Sciences et le Planetarium de Valence (Valence, Espagne, 1996–2000) ; l'aéroport de Sondica (Bilbao, Espagne, 1990–2000) ; le pont de l'Europe à Orléans (1996–99). Il travaille actuellement à un projet de cathédrale pour Oakland en Californie.

# MILWAUKEE ART MUSEUM

*Quadracci Pavilion, Milwaukee, Wisconsin, United States, 1994–2001*

*Client: Milwaukee Art Museum. Floor area: 13,222 m². Gallery space: 1,106 m².*
*Height of Reception Hall: 27.45 meters. Cost: $75.1 million.*

The **MILWAUKEE ART MUSEUM** was housed in a 1957 structure designed by Eero Saarinen as a War Memorial overlooking Lake Michigan. The architect David Kahler added a large slab structure to the Museum in 1975. In 1994, the Trustees of the Milwaukee Art Museum considered a total of seventy-seven architects for a "new grand entrance, a point of orientation for visitors, and a redefinition of the museum's identity though the creation of a strong image." Santiago Calatrava won the competition with his proposal for a twenty-seven meter high glass and steel reception hall shaded by a moveable sunscreen (now baptized the "Burke Brise-Soleil"). Included in the design are 7,500 square meters of new space, with some 1,500 square meters set aside for temporary exhibitions. Although Calatrava generally denies specific biomorphic inspiration in his work, the Quadracci Pavilion has a decidedly bird-like quality to it, especially when the "wings" of the Brise Soleil are open. Calatrava is also responsible for the Reiman Bridge, a suspended pedestrian link between downtown and the lakefront. Public gardens for the complex were designed by the noted landscape architect Dan Kiley.

Das **MILWAUKEE ART MUSEUM** war in einem 1957 von Eero Saarinen als Kriegsdenkmal entworfenen Gebäude mit Blick über den Michigansee untergebracht. Der Architekt David Kahler fügte dem Museum 1975 einen ausladenden, mit Platten ummantelten Baukörper hinzu. 1994 lud das Museumskuratorium insgesamt 77 Architekten ein, ihre Vorschläge für einen neuen Eingangsbereich einzureichen. Er sollte von der Gestaltung her imposant sein, als Orientierungspunkt für die Besucher dienen und durch ein starkes Erscheinungsbild die Identität des Museums neu definieren. Santiago Calatrava gewann diesen Wettbewerb mit seinem Entwurf einer 27 m hohen Eingangshalle aus Glas und Stahl, ausgestattet mit einer beweglichen Sonnenschutzblende, die inzwischen den Namen »Burke Brise-Soleil« erhalten hat. In dem neuen Gebäudeteil ist eine zusätzliche Raumfläche von insgesamt 7.500 m² entstanden, von denen 1.500 m² für Sonderausstellungen reserviert sind. Obwohl Calatrava normalerweise bestreitet, dass seine Arbeit von bestimmten biomorphologischen Vorbildern inspiriert ist, hat der Quadracci Pavilion zweifellos Ähnlichkeit mit einem Vogel – besonders, wenn die »Flügel« der Sonnenblende geöffnet sind. Auch für die Reiman-Hängebrücke, die für Fußgänger eine Verbindung zwischen Stadtzentrum und Seeufer herstellt, ist Calatrava verantwortlich. Der öffentliche Park, in dem der Gebäudekomplex liegt, wurde von dem bekannten Landschaftsarchitekten Dan Kiley gestaltet.

Le **MILWAUKEE ART MUSEUM** était installé depuis 1957 au bord du lac Michigan dans un bâtiment conçu à l'origine par Eero Saarinen pour un Mémorial de guerre. L'architecte David Kahler y avait ajouté une construction en dalle en 1975. En 1994, ses administrateurs ont organisé un concours auquel ont participé 77 architectes sur le thème d'une « nouvelle entrée principale, qui serve de point d'orientation pour les visiteurs et contribue à redéfinir l'identité du musée par la création d'une image forte ». Santiago Calatrava a remporté la compétition grâce à une proposition de hall de réception en verre et acier de 27 m de haut, protégé par un brise-soleil mobile, aujourd'hui baptisé « Brise-Soleil Burke ». Ce volume contient 7 500 m² d'espaces nouveaux dont 1 500 réservés aux expositions temporaires. Bien que Calatrava réfute généralement toute source d'inspiration biomorphique, le Quadracci Pavillon fait indéniablement penser à un oiseau, en particulier lorsque les « ailes » du brise-soleil sont déployées. L'architecte est également l'auteur du Reiman Bridge, passerelle piétonnière suspendue entre le centre et la rive du lac. Les jardins publics qui entourent ce complexe ont été dessinés par le célèbre architecte paysager David Kiley.

*The most remarkable feature of the new Quadracci Pavilion is the so-called Burke Brise-Soleil, named after the donors John and Murph Burke. The 72 metal fins of the brise-soleil were made in Zaragoza, Spain.*

*Auffälligstes Merkmal des Quadracci Pavillon ist der nach den Stiftern John und Murph Burke genannte Burke Brise-Soleil. Die 72 Metallrippen dieser Sonnenschutzblende wurden im spanischen Saragossa hergestellt.*

*L'élément le plus remarquable du nouveau Quadracci Pavillon est le « Brise-Soleil Burke » ainsi nommé en hommage aux mécènes John et Murph Burke. Ses 72 ailettes de métal de ce brise-soleil ont été fabriquées à Saragosse, Espagne.*

In this view, looking south, the low gallery structure is in the foreground, the reception hall with the brise-soleil in the middle, and the pedestrian bridge (also designed by Calatrava) that spans gardens by Dan Kiley is on the right.

Diese Ansicht mit Blick nach Süden zeigt den ebenerdigen Ausstellungsraum im Vordergrund, die Eingangshalle mit dem Brise-Soleil in der Mitte und rechts die – ebenfalls von Calatrava entworfene – Fußgängerbrücke, die den von Dan Kiley gestalteten Park überspannt.

Vue vers le sud : au premier plan, la galerie inférieure ; au centre, le hall de réception et le brise-soleil ; à droite la passerelle piétonnière (également conçue par Calatrava) qui franchit les jardins de Dan Kiley.

A succession of curved concrete arches with skylights between them form the "gallerias" above. On the right-hand page, the reception hall.

Eine Abfolge von Betongewölben mit Oberlichtern in den Zwischenräumen bilden die »Gallerias« im Obergeschoss (oben). Die Eingangshalle (rechts).

En haut, une succession d'arches de béton incurvées reliées par des verrières forme les « gallerias ». Page de droite : le hall de réception.

Calatrava's architecture, although reminiscent of anthropomorphic forms here brings to mind his Lyon Satolas TGV Station (Lyon, France, 1989–1994) in a lighter, more sophisticated mode.

Trotz des biomorphologischen Bezugs erinnert Calatravas Entwurf an seinen TGV-Bahnhof Lyon-Satolas (1989–94), wenn auch in einer leichteren und eleganteren Ausführung.

Souvent de caractère anthropomorphique, l'architecture de Calatrava, rappelle ici sa gare de T. G. V. de Lyon-Saint-Exupéry (Lyon, France, 1989–94), dans un mode plus léger et plus sophistiqué.

# ALBERTO CAMPO BAEZA

*Alberto Campo Baeza*
*Arquitecto*
*Almirante, 9*
*28004 Madrid*
*Spain*

*Tel/Fax: + 34 91 521 7061*
*e-mail: campobaeza@retemail.es*

*Belvedere*

Born in Cadiz, **ALBERTO CAMPO BAEZA** studied in Madrid where he obtained his Ph.D. in 1982. He has taught in Madrid, at the ETH in Zurich (1989–1990), at Cornell University, and at the University of Pennsylvania (1986 and 1999). His work includes the Fene Town Hall (1980); S. Fermin Public School, Madrid (1985); Public Library, Orihuela (1992) and a Public School, Cadiz (1992), the BIT Center in Inca, Mallorca (1995–1998) as well as a number of private houses. Current work includes the headquarters for "La Caja General de Ahorros" in Granada, and a house for Tom Ford of Gucci in Santa Fe, New Mexico.

Der im spanischen Cádiz geborene **ALBERTO CAMPO BAEZA** studierte in Madrid, wo er 1982 promovierte. Seither lehrte er an der Universität Madrid, der Eidgenössischen Technischen Hochschule (ETH) in Zürich (1989–90), der Cornell University in Ithaca, New York und an der University of Pennsylvania in Philadelphia (1986 und 1999). Zu seinen Bauten gehören das Rathaus in Fene (1980), die Schule S. Fermin in Madrid (1985), die Stadtbücherei in Orihuela (1992) und eine weitere Schule in Cádiz (1992), alle in Spanien, ferner das BIT-Zentrum in Inca, Mallorca (1995–98) sowie eine Reihe von Privathäusern. Zu seinen neuesten Projekten zählen die Zentrale von La Caja General de Ahorros in Granada und ein Wohnhaus für Tom Ford von Gucci in Santa Fe, New Mexico.

Né à Cadix (Espagne), **ALBERTO CAMPO BAEZA** étudie l'architecture à Madrid (diplômé en 1971, docteur en 1982). Il a enseigné à Madrid, à l'ETH (Zurich, 1989–90), à Cornell University, et à l'University of Pennsylvania (1986 et 1999). Parmi ses interventions : hôtel de ville de Fene (1980) ; école publique San Firmin (Madrid, 1985) ; bibliothèque publique (Orihuela, 1992) ; un collège (Cadix, 1992) ; le centre BIT à Inca, Majorque (1995–98) ainsi qu'un certain nombre de résidences privées. Ses projets actuels comprennent le siège de La Caja General de Ahorros à Grenade, et une maison pour Tom Ford (Gucci) à Santa Fe (Nouveau-Mexique).

# BELVEDERE

*De Blas House, Sevilla la Nueva, Madrid, Spain, 2000*

*Client: Francisco de Blas. Total area: 243 m² (concrete box),
90 m² (metallic structure), 40,5 m² (glass box).*

Set on a hill southeast of Madrid facing north, towards the mountains, this house is set on a site-poured reinforced rough concrete box 9 by 27 meters in size. A transparent glass box 4.5 by 9 meters and 2.26 meters high, set on the concrete platform is topped with a white 6 by 15-meter steel structure. Set into the earth, the concrete box "houses the program of a traditional house with a clear diagram of served spaces to the front and service spaces to the rear." The architect views the glass box as a **BELVEDERE**, a place from which to contemplate nature. Summing up his thinking on this residence, Alberto Campo Baeza writes that it is a "tectonic piece set upon a stereotomic box, a distillation of what is essential in architecture" … once again, he concludes, he has sought to accomplish "more with less." This house follows the powerfully minimalist Center for Innovative Technologies BIT, (Inca, Majorca, Spain, 1997–1998) whose spare triangular design called Campo-Baeza to the attention of international architectural circles.

Das auf einem Hügel südöstlich von Madrid gelegene und nach Norden zu den Bergen hin ausgerichtete Haus wurde auf einen 9 x 27 m messenden, vor Ort gegossenen, unbearbeiteten Betonsockel gesetzt. Auf dieser Plattform ruht ein 4,5 x 9 m großer und 2,26 m hoher Glaskörper, der mit einer 6 x 15 m messenden Stahlkonstruktion überdacht ist. Der in die Erde eingelassene Betonsockel enthält den schematisch klar gegliederten Bauplan eines traditionellen Wohnhauses mit Neben- und Versorgungsräumen. Der Architekt betrachtet das Glasgehäuse als eine Art **BELVEDERE**, einen Ort für die kontemplative Betrachtung der Natur. Alberto Campo Baeza schreibt dazu, dass »die tektonische Form, die auf ein stereotomisches Gehäuse gesetzt wurde, die Quintessenz dessen sei, was Architektur ausmache«, und unterstreicht sein Bemühen, die »Weniger-ist-mehr-Devise« umzusetzen. Dieses Haus steht in der Tradition des stark minimalistisch ausgerichteten Center for Innovative Technologies BIT in Inca, Mallorca (1997–98), dessen sparsames, dreieckiges Campo-Baeza-Design den Architekten in internationalen Architekturkreisen bekannt machte.

Située sur une colline au sud-ouest de Madrid, orientée vers le nord et les montagnes, cette maison est constituée d'un caisson en béton armé de 9 x 27 m sur laquelle vient se poser une boîte transparente en verre de 4,5 x 9 m par 2,6 de haut, surmontée d'une structure métallique de 6 x 15 m. En partie pris dans le sol, le caisson de béton « abrite le programme d'une maison traditionnelle et bénéficie d'un plan clair » espaces servis à l'avant/espace servants à l'arrière. L'architecte a conçu la boîte de verre comme un **BELVÉDÈRE** d'où on peut contempler la nature. Pour résumer sa réflexion sur cette résidence, Alberto Campo Baeza la décrit comme « une pièce technique posée sur une boîte stéréotomique, une distillation de l'essentiel de l'architecture ». Il conclut, une fois de plus, qu'il a cherché à accomplir « plus avec moins ». Chronologiquement, cette maison suit le puissant et minimaliste Center for Innovative Technologies BIT (Inca, Majorque, Espagne, 1997–98) dont le plan triangulaire rigoureux a attiré l'attention des cercles internationaux sur l'architecte.

*With typical rigorous minimalism, Alberto Campo Baeza sets a steel and glass pavilion on top of a rectangular concrete "cave-like" house. The house sits on the crest of a hill in the rather barren environs of Madrid.*

*Mit der für ihn typischen minimalistischen Strenge setzt Alberto Campo Baeza einen Stahl- und Glaspavillon auf ein rechteckiges »höhlenartiges« Betongehäuse. Das Haus liegt auf einem Bergkamm im eher kargen Umland von Madrid.*

*Adepte d'un minimalisme rigoureux et typique, Alberto Campo Baeza a délicatement déposé un pavillon de verre et d'acier sur le toit d'une maison « caverne » en béton. Celle-ci est implantée au sommet d'une colline dans les environs assez dénudés de Madrid.*

Tending toward the purity of Mies
or even more recent designs like
the Wall-less House of Shigeru Ban,
Campo Baeza contrasts the rough
earth-bound solidity of the concrete
base with the ethereal lightness of
the glass box.

Inspiriert vom Purismus eines Mies
van der Rohe oder sogar von jüngeren
Entwürfen wie Shigeru Bans Haus
ohne Wände setzt der Architekt die
raue, erdverbundene Massivität des
Betonsockels gegen die ätherische
Leichtigkeit des Glasgehäuses.

Tendant à la pureté d'un Mies ou
de réalisations plus récentes comme
la Wall-less House de Shigeru Ban,
Campo Baeza a créé un puissant
contraste entre la base en béton
massive et brute et la boîte de verre
légère et éthérée.

# COOP HIMMELB(L)AU

Coop Himmelb(l)au
Wolf D. Prix, Helmut Swiczinsky
Zelinkagasse 2/4
1010 Wien
Austria

Tel: + 43 1 535 55 35
Fax: + 43 1 535 55 39
e-mail: communication@coop-himmelblau.at
Web: www.coop-himmelblau.at

*Confluence Museur*

**WOLF PRIX** and **HELMUT SWICZINSKY** founded Coop Himmelb(l)au in 1968 in Vienna, Austria. In 1988, they opened a second office in Los Angeles. Wolf Prix was born in 1942 in Vienna, and educated at the Technische Universität, Vienna, the Southern California Institute of Architecture (SCI-Arc), and the Architectural Association (AA), London. He has been a Professor of the Masterclass of Architecture at the University of Applied Arts, Vienna, and an Adjunct Professor at SCI-Arc. Helmut Swiczinsky, born in 1944 in Poznań, Poland, was raised in Vienna and educated at the Technische Universität, Vienna, and at the AA, London. Completed projects of the group include the Rooftop Remodeling in Vienna, masterplan for Mélun-Sénart, France; and the East pavilion of the Groninger Museum, Groningen, The Netherlands, 1990–94. They also remodeled the Austrian Pavilion in the Giardini, Venice, Italy. Recent work includes the Museum of Health, Dresden, the Academy of Fine Arts, Munich, the UFA Cinema Center (Dresden, Germany, 1997–98) and the SEG Apartment Tower, Vienna.

**WOLF PRIX** und **HELMUT SWICZINSKY** gründeten Coop Himmelb(l)au 1968 in Wien. 1988 eröffneten sie ein zweites Büro in Los Angeles. Der 1942 in Wien geborene Wolf Prix studierte an der Technischen Universität Wien, am Southern California Institute of Architecture (SCI-Arc) und an der Architectural Association (AA) in London. Er ist Professor der Meisterklasse für Architektur an der Universität für Angewandte Kunst in Wien und außerordentlicher Professor am SCI-Arc. Helmut Swiczinsky wurde 1944 in Posen (heute Poznań, Polen) geboren, wuchs in Wien auf und studierte an der dortigen TU sowie an der AA in London. Zu den realisierten Projekten der Gruppe gehören ein Dachausbau in Wien, der Masterplan für Mélun-Sénart in Frankreich und der Ostpavillon des Groninger Museums im niederländischen Groningen (1990–94). Außerdem führten Prix und Swiczinsky den Umbau des Österreichischen Pavillons in den Giardini in Venedig aus. Zu ihren neueren Projekten zählen ein Erweiterungsbau für das Deutsche Hygiene Museum und das UFA-Multiplexkino (1997–98), beide in Dresden, die Erweiterung der Akademie der Bildenden Künste in München sowie das SEG-Wohnhochhaus in Wien.

**WOLF PRIX** et **HELMUT SWICZINSKY** fondent Coop Himmelb(l)au à Vienne en 1968, et ouvrent une seconde agence à Los Angeles en 1988. Wolf Prix est né à Vienne en 1942 et a étudié à la Technische Universität de Vienne, au Southern California Institute of Architecture (SCI-Arc) et à l'Architectural Association de Londres (AA). Il a été professeur de la Masterclass d'Architecture à l'Université des Arts appliqués de Vienne et professeur-adjoint à SCI-Arc. Helmut Swiczinsky est né en 1944 à Poznań, Pologne, mais a grandi à Vienne et a fait ses études à la Technische Universität de cette ville ainsi qu'à l'AA de Londres. Parmi leurs projets réalisés : l'aménagement d'un toit-penthouse à Vienne ; le plan directeur de Melun-Sénart, France ; le pavillon Est du musée de Groningue (Pays-Bas, 1990–94). Ils ont également remodelé le Pavillon autrichien des Giardini (Venise). Récemment, ils ont réalisé le Musée de la Santé, à Dresde, l'Académie des Beaux-Arts de Munich, le complexe de salles de cinéma UFA (Dresde, Allemagne, 1997–98), et la tour d'appartements SEG (Vienne).

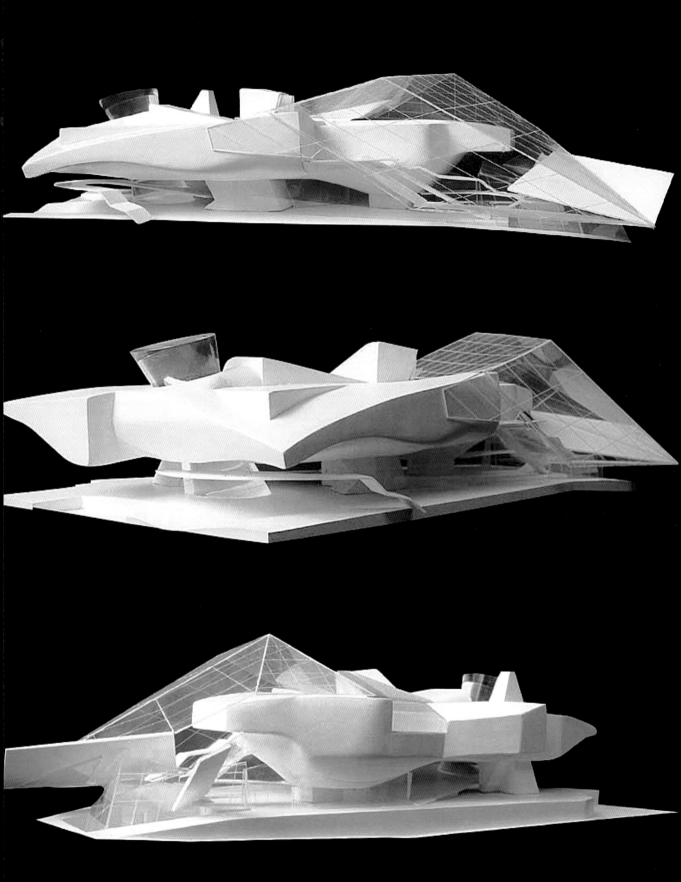

# CONFLUENCE MUSEUM

*Lyon, France, 2001–2005*

*Client: Conseil Général du Rhone. Budget: 61 million euros (2001 estimate).*
*Total floor area: 20,000 m². Expected visitors: 500,000 per year.*

Baptized the "Crystal Cloud of Knowledge" by the winning Austrian architects, this twenty thousand square meter facility, sponsored by the Conseil Général du Rhone and the City of Lyon is scheduled to open in 2005 and will have a 61 million euros budget. The museum is intended as the centerpiece of the redevelopment of a former industrial site set at the confluence of the city's two rivers. The amorphous, cloud-like exhibition structure is meant to give the impression that it is floating over an angled glass base. With a predicted flow of some five hundred thousand visitors a year, the museum is meant to be an "urban leisure space" according to the architects who were selected over Peter Eisenman, Steven Holl and François Seigneur. The most spectacular gesture within the structure appears to be the so-called "Double Cone," an interior patio tilted at a 23.5° angle like the Earth itself, and lined with a spiral staircase. Coop Himmelblau, in descriptive texts for their project, seek to obviate the question of style, preferring to claim that their design is an exercise in "simultaneity" and the result of a "profound negotiation of differences." Equally unclear is the actual function of the institution, which is apparently intended to take on not only cultural but also scientific issues.

Die von den Architekten Wolf Prix und Helmut Swiczinsky »Kristallwolke des Wissens« getaufte Anlage umfasst 20.000 m². Ihr mit 61 Millionen Euros budgetierter Bau wird vom Conseil Général du Rhône und der Stadtverwaltung von Lyon finanziell unterstützt; seine Eröffnung ist für das Jahr 2005 geplant. Konzipiert als Herzstück der Revitalisierung eines ehemaligen, am Zusammenfluss von Rhône und Saône liegenden Industriegeländes, soll das amorphe, wolkenartige Ausstellungsgebäude den Eindruck vermitteln, als schwebe es über einem winkelförmigen Glasfundament. Nach Aussage der Architekten, die den Wettbewerb vor Peter Eisenman, Steven Holl und François Seigneur gewannen, ist das Museum als »urbaner Freizeitraum« gedacht, die jährliche Besucherzahl wird auf circa 500.000 geschätzt. Spektakulärstes Merkmal dieser Anlage ist der so genannte »Doppelkegel«, ein offener Innenhof mit einer Wendeltreppe, der wie unsere Erde einen Neigungsgrad von 23,5 Prozent aufweist. In ihren Projektbeschreibungen umgehen die Planer von Coop Himmelb(l)au die Frage nach dem Stil mit dem Hinweis, dass ihre Gestaltungsweise eine Übung in »Simultanität« und das Resultat einer intensiven Auseinandersetzung mit verschiedenen Faktoren darstelle. Ähnlich vage bleibt die eigentliche Funktion der Institution, die anscheinend nicht nur kulturelle, sondern auch wissenschaftliche Aufgaben wahrnehmen soll.

Ce projet d'équipement culturel de 20 000 m², financé à raison de 61 millions d'euros par le Conseil général du Rhône et la ville de Lyon, a été baptisé « Nuage de cristal de la connaissance » par les architectes autrichiens qui ont remporté son concours. Il devrait ouvrir en 2005. Élément phare de la rénovation d'une ancienne zone d'activités au confluent du Rhône et de la Saône, sa structure d'exposition amorphe qui évoque un nuage devrait sembler flotter au-dessus de son angleux socle de verre. Espérant 500 000 visiteurs par an, le musée sera « un espace de loisirs urbains », selon les architectes choisis de préférence à Peter Eisenman, Steven Holl ou François Seigneur. Le geste le plus spectaculaire devrait être le « double-cône », patio intérieur incliné à 23°5' comme le globe terrestre, entouré d'un escalier en spirale. Coop Himmelb(l)au dans sa présentation écrite du projet, cherche à dépasser le problème du style, préférant affirmer que ce projet est un exercice de « simultanéité » et le résultat « d'une profonde négociation de différences ». La fonction réelle de cette nouvelle institution, qui répond à des préoccupations à la fois culturelles et scientifiques, n'est guère plus lumineuse.

An aerial view of the site, where the Rhone and Saone Rivers come together. The confluence of these rivers is intended as the symbolic theme of the architecture, as a place where ideas can be explained, and exchanged.

Eine Luftaufnahme des Geländes, an dem Rhône und Saône zusammen-fließen (links). Das Aufeinandertreffen dieser Flüsse soll als Symbol gelten für die Architektur eines Ortes, an dem Ideen erläutert und ausgetauscht werden können.

Vue aérienne du site au point de rencontre du Rhône et de la Saône. Cette confluence est le thème symbo-lique de l'architecture du projet, lieu d'échange et d'approfondissement d'idées.

# NEIL M. DENARI

Neil M. Denari Associates Inc.
11906 Lawler
Los Angeles, California 90066
United States

Tel: + 1 310 390 2968
Fax: + 1 310 390 2918
e-mail: nmda@denariarchitects.com

*LA Eyeworks Store*

**NEIL M. DENARI** received a Bachelor of Architecture in 1980 from the University of Houston, and a Master of Architecture degree from Harvard in 1982, where he also studied art theory and the philosophy of science. He then spent six months working as an intern for Aerospatiale, the French aviation and space company. Neil Denari worked in New York from 1983 to 1988 as a Senior Designer at James Stewart Polshek & Partners before teaching at Columbia's Graduate School of Architecture and Planning. Denari moved to Los Angeles in 1988 and taught at the Southern California Institute of Architecture (SCI-Arc). In 1997, he was named the third Director of SCI-Arc. In 1996, he completed the construction of a small, experimental space at Gallery Ma in Tokyo. His other work though highly influential has remained in its rather seductive virtual work. The Eyeworks project published here is to be built in Los Angeles.

**NEIL M. DENARI** erwarb 1980 den Bachelor of Architecture an der University of Houston und 1982 den Master of Architecture in Harvard, wo er außerdem Kunsttheorie und Wissenschaftsphilosophie studierte. Anschließend arbeitete er ein halbes Jahr als Praktikant bei dem französischen Flugzeug- und Raumfahrtunternehmen Aerospatiale. Von 1983 bis 1988 war Denari in New York als Planungsleiter bei James Stewart Polshek & Partners tätig und lehrte an der Graduate School of Architecture and Planning der Columbia University. 1988 zog er nach Los Angeles und lehrte am Southern California Institute of Architecture (SCI-Arc), wo er 1997 zum dritten Direktor ernannt wurde. 1996 führte er die Konstruktion eines kleinen, experimentellen Raums in der Galerie Ma in Tokio aus. Während seine anderen Arbeiten, obgleich sehr einflussreich und interessant, virtuelle Konstrukte blieben, soll das hier vorgestellte Eyeworks-Projekt in Los Angeles realisiert werden.

**NEIL M. DENARI** est B. Arch de l'Université de Houston (1980) et M. Arch de Harvard (1982), où il a également étudié la théorie de l'art et la philosophie des sciences. Il travaille ensuite pendant six mois à l'Aérospatiale en France. Il est senior designer chez James Stewart Polshek & Partners à New York (1983–88) avant d'enseigner à la Graduate School of Architecture and Planning de Columbia University. Il s'installe à Los Angeles en 1988 et enseigne au Southern California Institute of Architecture (SCI-Arc) dont il sera le troisième directeur en 1997. En 1996, il achève la construction d'un petit espace expérimental pour la Galerie Ma à Tokyo. Ses recherches dans le domaine du virtuel exercent une grande influence. Le projet Eyeworks présenté ici devrait être réalisé à Los Angeles.

# LA EYEWORKS STORE

*Los Angeles, California, United States, 2001–2002*

*Client: LA Eyeworks. Floor area: 100 m². Location: Beverly Boulevard.*

This store has a floor area of about one hundred square meters. The client, an eyeglass dealer, asked "that the design of the store resist not the ephemerality of fashion, but rather resist the fashion of architecture without recourse to minimalism or lack of expression." The architect uses a continuous suspended "gaseous blue" surface that serves as a "perforated ceiling plane, window display, bench, shelving unit, and sales counter." Furniture elements on wheels were also designed by Denari, and a wall of vacuum-formed panels designed by Jim Isermann fills the west wall of the store. As the architect says, "The piece acts as a thick two-dimensional vertical surface where the repetitive pattern of the panels forms a graphic field against which the rest of the store may be experienced." The transparency of the design is evident in computer perspectives that are typical of Denari's signature style. The idea of a "continuous suspended surface" also seems to be very much a recurring one in his work, carrying through from exterior to interior in designs such as that for his Multisection Office Block (Los Angeles, California, 1998).

Das Geschäft verfügt über eine Verkaufsfläche von circa 100 m². Wie vom Auftraggeber, einem Brillenhändler, gefordert, sollte die Gestaltung des Ladens die modischen Trends der Architektur überdauern, ohne sich in Minimalismus oder Ausdrucksschwäche zu flüchten. Der Architekt verwendet hier eine durchgehende Hängekonstruktion mit einer »gasartig blauen« Oberfläche, die gleichzeitig als perforierte Deckenbespannung, Schaufensterauslage, Sitzbank, Regalsystem und Verkaufstheke dient. Darüber hinaus entwarf Denari Einrichtungselemente auf Rädern, während von Jim Isermann gestaltete vakuumgeformte Paneele die westliche Wand ausfüllen. Dazu der Architekt: »Dieses Element fungiert als eine breite, zweidimensional-vertikale Fläche, auf der das sich wiederholende Muster der Paneele ein grafisches Feld bildet, vor dessen Hintergrund der Geschäftsraum wahrgenommen wird.« Die Transparenz des Designs wird in Computerperspektiven sichtbar, die Denaris Stil kennzeichnen. Auch die Idee einer durchgehenden Hängekonstruktion scheint ein immer wiederkehrendes Gestaltungselement zu sein, mit dem er in seinen Entwürfen einen Übergang von Innen nach Außen schafft, wie zum Beispiel bei seinem Multisection Office Block in Los Angeles (1998).

Pour ce magasin de 100 m² au sol, le client opticien avait demandé que « le projet sache résister non au caractère éphémère de la mode, mais plutôt à celui de la mode architecturale, et évite de recourir au minimalisme ou à l'absence d'expressivité ». Les architectes ont utilisé une surface continue « bleu gazeux » en suspension qui fait fonction de « plan de plafond perforé, présentoir de vitrine, banquette, étagère de rangement et comptoir de vente ». Les éléments de mobilier montés sur roulettes ont également été dessinés par Denari. Un mur de panneaux formés sous vide dû à Jim Isermann occupe le mur ouest du magasin. Comme le précise l'architecte : « La pièce joue à la manière d'une surface verticale épaisse bidimensionnelle dans laquelle le motif répétitif des panneaux forme un champ graphique sur le fond duquel le reste du magasin se découvre. » La qualité de transparence du projet ressort dans les perspectives en images de synthèse typiques du style de Denari. L'idée d'une « surface continue suspendue » semble également être récurrente dans son travail. Elle peut même aller de l'extérieur vers l'intérieur comme c'est le cas dans son Multisection Office Block (Los Angeles, Californie, 1998).

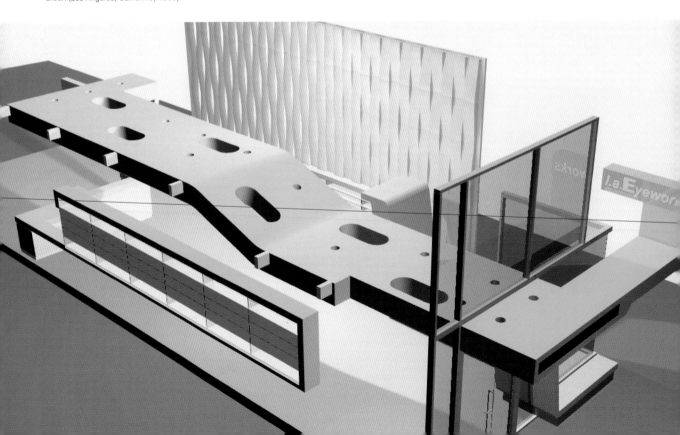

"By merging the functional demand with the formal ambitions of continuity, architecture and eyeglasses fuse as a coordinated design," according to the architect.

Nach Aussage des Architekten »gelangen Architektur und Verkaufsware Brille zu einem ausgewogenen Design, wenn die funktionalen Anforderungen mit dem formalen Streben nach Kontinuität verschmelzen«.

« Fusionnant les attentes fonctionnelles et les ambitions formelles de continuité, l'architecture et la lunetterie se fondent en un projet coordonné » a déclaré l'architecte.

# SUN MICROSYSTEMS CONCEPT PROJECTS

*2001*

*Clients: Sun Microsystems, Enterprise IG. Floor area: 334 m² (Trade Show Structure).*
*Structure: fiberglass panels and aluminum columns.*

Neil Denari was called on by the brand strategists Enterprise IG New York and the computer firm **SUN MICROSYSTEMS** "to design concepts for a new world rebranding campaign where architecture and space will play a vital role in developing a new corporate identity." He responded with two projects, the first of which is a Trade Show Structure set out on a 18.3 meter square form made of embossed fiberglass panels attached to aluminum columns designed for displaying Sun MicroSystems' network products. The second is a Work Space Design intended for existing offices located in Palo Alto, California. These are "concepts for individual and group work areas with new workstation prototypes and large graphical interface surfaces." In these modules, four people can work separately or together in an interconnected arrangement of identical workstations.

Neil Denari erhielt von den Markenstrategen Enterprise IG New York und der Computerfirma **SUN MICROSYSTEMS** den Auftrag, Konzepte für eine neue, weltweite Brandingkampagne zu entwerfen, bei der Architektur und Raumgestaltung eine wichtige Rolle in der Entwicklung einer neuen Corporate Identity spielen sollten. Denaris stellte zwei Projekte vor: Zunächst einen Messestand, eine Konstruktion, die auf einem Quadrat von 18,3 m Durchmesser angeordnet ist. Dieses Quadrat besteht aus geprägten Fiberglasplatten, die an Aluminiumsäulen fixiert sind, welche gleichzeitig zur Präsentation der Netzwerkprodukte von Sun Microsystems dienen. Das zweite Projekt namens Work Space Design ist für bestehende Büros im kalifornischen Palo Alto gedacht. Hierbei handelt es sich um Entwürfe für Arbeitsbereiche, die von Einzelpersonen oder Gruppen genutzt werden können, ausgestattet mit neuen Workstation-Prototypen und großzügigen übersichtlichen Verbindungsflächen. In diesen Modulen können vier Personen individuell oder im Team an miteinander verbundenen identischen Workstations arbeiten.

Neil Denari a été appelé par les stratèges en image de marque d'Enterprise IG New York et la firme d'informatique **SUN MICROSYSTEMS** « afin de trouver des concepts pour une campagne de modernisation de l'image de marque dans laquelle l'architecture et l'espace joueront un rôle vital en faveur du développement d'une nouvelle identité institutionnelle ». Sa réponse s'est présentée sous la forme de deux projets. Le premier est une structure de présentation commerciale posée sur un socle de 18,3 m et faite de panneaux de fibre de verre travaillés en relief fixés à des colonnes d'aluminium conçues pour la présentation des produits de réseau Sun Micro-Systems. Le second est un espace de travail étudié pour des bureaux existants à Palo Alto, en Californie. Il propose des « concepts pour individus ou groupes de travail intégrant de nouveaux prototypes de postes de travail et de vastes surfaces d'interface graphique ». Quatre personnes peuvent travailler séparément ou ensemble dans ces modules qui bénéficient d'une implantation interconnectée de postes de travail identiques.

For the Trade Show Structure shown here, the architect says, "The space allows a free flow of movement for which Sun can display its new network solutions."

Der Architekt über die hier gezeigte »Trade Show Structure« (Messestand): »Der Raum erlaubt ein freies Fliessen der Bewegung, in dem Sun seine neuen Netzwerklösungen präsentieren kann.«

Pour cette structure d'exposition, l'architecte précise : « L'espace permet la libre circulation de mouvements pour lesquels Sun peut présenter ses nouvelles solutions en réseau. »

In this Work Space Design for offices
of the firm in Palo Alto, NMDA uses
typical curving surfaces and furniture
on wheels to emphasize the mobility
and flexibility of the installation.

In diesem Arbeitsplatz-Design für
Büros der Firma in Palo Alto verwen-
det der Architekt geschwungene
Oberflächen und Möbel auf Rädern,
um Flexibilität und Mobilität der
Module zu betonen.

Dans cet espace de travail pour les
bureaux de l'entreprise à Palo Alto,
NMDA a fait appel à des surfaces
incurvées caractéristiques de son
style et à des meubles sur roulettes
qui confirment la mobilité et la flexibilité de l'installation.

# DILLER + SCOFIDIO

*Diller + Scofidio*
*36 Cooper Square*
*New York, NY 10003*
*United States*

*Tel: + 1 212 260 7971*
*Fax: + 1 212 260 7924*
*e-mail: disco@dillerscofidio.com*

**ELIZABETH DILLER** is Professor of Architecture at Princeton University and **RICARDO SCOFIDIO** is Professor of Architecture at The Cooper Union in New York. According to their own description, "Diller + Scofidio is a collaborative, interdisciplinary studio involved in architecture, the visual arts and the performing arts. The team is primarily involved in thematically-driven experimental works that take the form of architectural commissions, temporary installations and permanent site-specific installations, multi-media theater, electronic media, and print." Their work includes "Slither," 100 units of social housing in Gifu, Japan, and "Moving Target," a collaborative dance work with Charleroi/Danse Belgium. Installations by Diller + Scofidio have been seen at the Cartier Foundation in Paris (Master/Slave, 1999), the Museum of Modern Art in New York, or the Musée de la Mode in Paris. Recently, they completed The Brasserie Restaurant (Seagram Building, New York, 1998–2000), the Blur Building, (Expo '02, Yverdon-les-Bains, Switzerland, 1998–2002), and were selected as architects for the Institute of Contemporary Art in Boston.

**ELIZABETH DILLER** ist als Professorin für Architektur an der Princeton University und **RICARDO SCOFIDIO** als Professor an der Cooper Union School of Architecture in New York tätig. Ihrer eigenen Beschreibung zufolge ist »Diller + Scofidio ein interdisziplinäres Gemeinschaftsprojekt, das sich mit Architektur, bildender und darstellender Kunst beschäftigt. Das Team führt hauptsächlich experimentelle Arbeiten durch, die sich auf der Grundlage von Architektur, Installation, Multimediaveranstaltung, elektronischen Medien und Druckgrafik mit bestimmten Themen auseinander setzen.« Zu ihren Projekten zählen Slither, 100 Einheiten des sozialen Wohnungsbaus in Gifu, Japan, und Moving Target, eine Tanztheaterproduktion in Zusammenarbeit mit der belgischen Tanzgruppe Charleroi/Danses. Installationen von Diller + Scofidio wurden in der Fondation Cartier in Paris (Master/Slave, 1999), im Museum of Modern Art in New York und im Musée de la Mode in Paris gezeigt. Zu ihren jüngsten Projekten gehören das Restaurant The Brasserie im Seagram Building in New York (1998–2000) und das Blur Building für die Expo '02 im schweizerischen Yverdon-les-Bains (1998–2002). Ferner wurden Diller + Scofidio als Architekten für das Institute of Contemporary Art in Boston ernannt.

**ELIZABETH DILLER** est professeur d'architecture à Princeton, et **RICARDO SCOFIDIO** à Cooper Union, New York. Leur présentation indique : « Diller + Scofidio est une agence interdisciplinaire coopérative qui se consacre à l'architecture, aux arts plastiques et aux arts du spectacle. L'équipe travaille essentiellement sur des recherches thématiques expérimentales qui peuvent prendre la forme de commandes architecturales, d'installations temporaires, d'installations permanentes sur un site, de théâtres multimédia, d'œuvres sur médias électroniques et imprimées. » Parmi leurs projets récents : Slither, 100 logements sociaux (Gifu, Japon) ; Moving Target, une œuvre chorégraphique en collaboration avec Charleroi/Dance (Belgique). Leurs installations ont été présentées à la Fondation Cartier à Paris (Master/Slave, 1999), au Museum of Modern Art de New York et au Musée de la mode à Paris. Récemment, ils ont achevé The Brasserie Restaurant (Seagram Building, New York, 1998–2000) ; le Blur Building (Expo '02, Yverdon-les-Bains, Suisse, 1998–2002) et ont été sélectionnés en tant qu'architectes pour L'Institute of Contemporary Art de Boston.

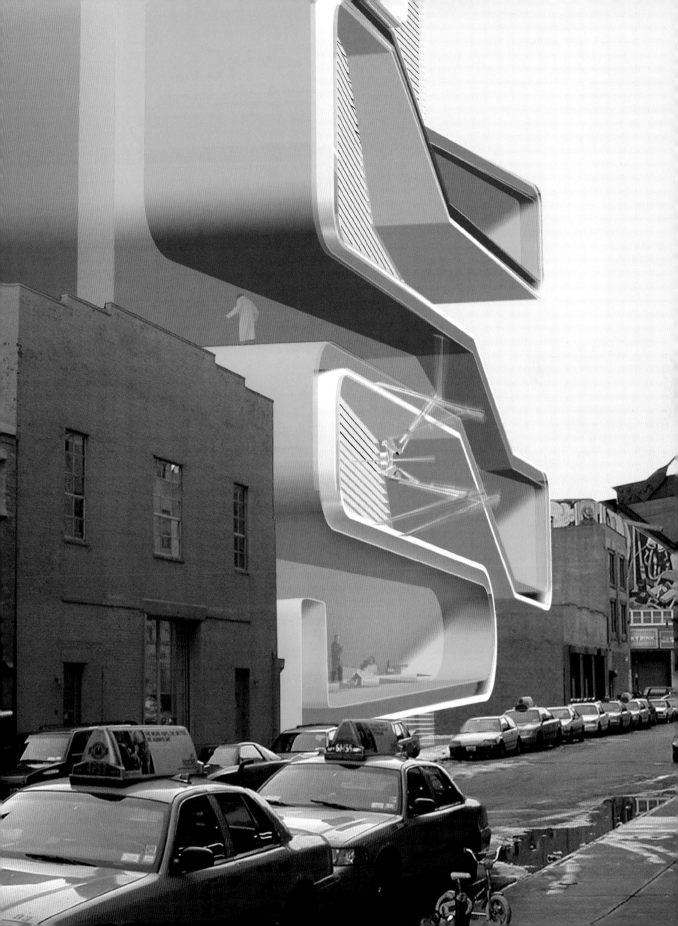

# EYEBEAM INSTITUTE

*New York, New York, United States, 2001–2006*

*Location: 540–548 West 21st Street. Estimated cost: $40 million.*
*Site area: 1,400 m². Floor area: 8,400m ² (approx.).*

*Diller + Scofidio won the international competition to design the new Eyebeam Institute building against a field including the best known contemporary architects on March 21, 2002.*

*Diller + Scofidio gewannen am 21. März 2002 den Wettbewerb zum Bau des neuen Eyebeam Institutsgebäudes. Zu ihren Konkurrenten zählten die bekanntesten Architekten der Gegenwart.*

*Diller + Scofidio ont remporté le concours international pour la conception du nouveau bâtiment de l'Eyebeam Institute contre une sélection des plus célèbres agences d'architecture le 21 mars 2002.*

Although the rise of Chelsea as the heart of the New York art world may have been delayed by the attacks of September 11, 2001, a movement from renovation of existing spaces to the construction of new art-related buildings was already well underway. A most significant example of that trend is the facility planned for the **EYE-BEAM INSTITUTE** at 540 West 21st Street. Called a "blue and white wave of a building" by *The New York Times*, the project submitted to the design competition by Diller + Scofidio is intended as a "pliable ribbon that locates production (atelier) to one side and presentation (museum/theater) to the other. Whether called a "wave" or an "undulating ribbon," the metal and reinforced concrete backbone of the twelve story building, intended for the production and exhibition of technologically-based art, serves as the conduit for the necessary technical infrastructure (wiring, heating, plumbing etc). Strict light control and sound isolation are provided for the exhibition spaces, whereas the production areas require steady natural and artificial light sources. The exuberant use of color (blue) on a large scale is a departure from the more usual reticence of contemporary architects to make such use of an extended palette in their designs.

Auch wenn sich der Aufstieg des Stadtteils Chelsea zum Mittelpunkt der New Yorker Kunstwelt durch die Anschläge vom 11. September 2001 verzögert hat, so waren die vorausgegangenen Bautätigkeiten für künstlerische Zwecke – von der Renovierung bestehender Räume bis zur Errichtung neuer Gebäude – bereits gut im Gang. Eins der signifikantesten Beispiele für diesen Trend ist der für das **EYEBEAM INSTITUTE** geplante Bau an der 540 West 21st Street. Von der *New York Times* als »blau-weiße Welle eines Gebäudes« bezeichnet ist der Wettbewerbsentwurf von Diller & Scofidio als »geschmeidiges Band« gestaltet, in dem Produktion (Atelier) auf der einen und Präsentation (Museum/Theater) auf der anderen Seite vorgesehen sind. Ob nun »Welle« oder »geschmeidiges Band«, das aus Metall und Stahlbeton bestehende Rückgrat des zwölfstöckigen Gebäudes wurde für die Produktion und Ausstellung technologisch orientierter Kunst konzipiert und dient als Rohrschacht für die technische Infrastruktur wie Strom- und Rohrleitungen, Heizung etc. Während die Produktionsbereiche eine gleichmäßige Versorgung mit natürlichem und künstlichem Licht erfordern, sind für die Ausstellungsräume eine präzise Lichtsteuerung sowie eine Schallisolierung vorgesehen. Der großzügige Einsatz von (blauer) Farbe auf großen Flächen bedeutet eine Abkehr von der unter den meisten heutigen Architekten üblichen Zurückhaltung bei der Farbwahl für ihre Entwürfe.

Les conséquences du 11 septembre 2001 influeront peut-être sur le mouvement de rénovation et de construction d'immeubles conçus pour des activités artistiques dans le quartier de Chelsea, à New York, cœur du marché de l'art contemporain américain. Un exemple significatif de cette tendance n'en reste pas moins le **EYEBEAM INSTITUTE**, 540 West 21st Street. Qualifié d'«immeuble-vague blanche et bleue» par le *New York Times*, ce projet de Diller + Scofidio, lauréat du concours, est un «ruban souple qui affecte un côté du volume à la production (atelier) et l'autre à la présentation (musée/théâtre)». «Vague» ou «ruban ondulé» l'ossature en métal et béton armé de cet immeuble de 12 niveaux sert de conduit pour les infrastructures techniques nécessaires (électricité, chauffage, plomberie, etc.). Les espaces d'exposition bénéficient d'un éclairage contrôlé et d'une isolation phonique, les zones de production de sources d'éclairage naturel et artificiel. Le recours exubérant et massif à la couleur bleue surprend, par rapport au peu de goût que montrent en général les architectes contemporains pour des palettes aussi vives.

Eyebeam is specialized in the production and exhibition of work by artists exploring "new media in video, film, moving image art, DVD production, installation, 2D/3D digital imaging, net art and sound and performance art forms."

Das Eyebeam Institute ist spezialisiert auf Produktion und Ausstellung der Arbeiten von Künstlern, die mit neuen Medien in verschiedenen Kunstformen experimentieren: Video, Film, DVD, Installationen, 2D/3D Digitalbilder, Netzkunst sowie Sounddesign und Performance.

Eyebeam est spécialisé dans la production et l'exposition d'œuvres d'artistes qui explorent « les nouveaux médias en vidéo, film, animation, production de DVD, installations, images numériques 2D/3D, art de l'internet et performances artistiques. »

# WINKA DUBBELDAM

*Winka Dubbeldam*
*Archi-Tectonics*
*111 Mercer Street, 2nd Floor*
*New York, NY 10012*
*United States*

*Tel: + 1 212 226 0303*
*Fax: + 1 212 219 3106*
*e-mail: winka@archi-tectonics.com*

*Maashaven Towers*

**WINKA DUBBELDAM** received a diploma from the Rotterdam Academy of Architecture in 1990, moved to New York in 1991 and received a Masters degree from Columbia where she worked in the Advanced Architectural Design program, in 1992. She worked with Steven Holl (1990), Bernard Tschumi (1992) and Peter Eisenman (1992–1994) before founding Archi-Tectonics in 1994. In her work and her teaching at Columbia she has been interested in the architectural implications of forces such as zoning, the stock market or migration patterns. She designed the Aida Hair Salon in New York. She has been working on an 11 story apartment building on Greenwich Street in New York and has declared that "The computer should be a tool for studying the forces operating within cities. Software-driven investigations," she says, "do not interest me."

**WINKA DUBBELDAM** erwarb 1990 ihr Diplom an der Akademie für Architektur in Rotterdam, zog 1991 nach New York und machte 1992 den Master-Abschluss an der Columbia University, wo sie im Advanced Architectural Design Program tätig war. Sie arbeitete bei Steven Holl (1990), Bernard Tschumi (1992) und Peter Eisenman (1992–94), bevor sie 1994 das Büro Archi-Tectonics gründete. Sowohl in ihrer praktischen Arbeit als auch in ihrer Lehrtätigkeit an der Columbia University hat sie sich mit den architektonischen Implikationen von Wirkungsfaktoren wie Flächennutzung, Aktienmarkt oder Zuzugsmodellen beschäftigt. Sie entwarf den Aida Hair Salon in New York und arbeitete an einem elfstöckigen Apartmentgebäude in Greenwich Street in New York. Von ihr stammt die Aussage: »Der Computer sollte ein Werkzeug sein, um die Kräfte zu studieren, die innerhalb von Städten wirksam werden. Eine Forschung, die nur auf Computerprogrammen basiert, interessiert mich nicht.«

**WINKA DUBBELDAM**, diplômée de l'Académie d'architecture de Rotterdam en 1990, s'installe à New York en 1991, et participe à l'Advanced Architectural Design Program en 1992 à Columbia University dont elle est M. Arch. Elle travaille auprès de Steven Holl (1990), Bernard Tschumi (1992) et Peter Eisenman (1992–94) avant de fonder Archi-Tectonics en 1994. Dans son travail et son enseignement à Columbia, elle s'intéresse aux implications architecturales d'influence comme celles du zoning, des marchés financiers, ou des flux migratoires. Elle a conçu le Aida Hair Salon à New York et un immeuble d'appartements de onze étages sur Greenwich Street, New York. Pour elle « l'ordinateur devrait être un outil d'étude des forces qui opèrent à l'intérieur des villes. Les recherches par logiciel ne m'intéressent pas. »

# MAASHAVEN TOWERS

*Rotterdam, The Netherlands, 1999*

*Total Area: 32,400 m². Structure: 3 towers of 30 stories concrete structure with glass/aluminum curtain wall.
Grain silo: concrete base structure with steel panel housing units on top. Parking lot area: 12,150 m².
Cost: $6,480,000 (estimated construction costs).*

The renovation of a concrete grain silo built in the 1930s located on a pier of the Maashaven harbor was the starting point for this project. Residential units made with a modern modular steel panel wall system are inserted into the existing building, as well as facilities such tennis courts, a running track and a fitness club in a courtyard. Aside from this renovation the project calls for the construction of three thirty-story towers that the architect has chosen to dramatically cantilever out over the pier. As she says, "Their modulation is reactive to the river current and sun position. The concrete base of the towers, together with the infra-structural elements, provide stability. The apartments are split-level with double height rooms, and sliding glass facades. The folded glass skin of the towers reflects the water surface and the city center across the river." Spectacular computer graphics are certainly a part of the appeal of this project in its unbuilt state.

Ausgangspunkt für dieses Projekt war die Renovierung eines Getreidesilos aus Beton, der in den 1930er Jahren auf einem Pier des Rotterdamer Hafens Maashaven erbaut worden war. Im Zuge der Revitalisierung sollen Wohnungen, die aus Stahlplattenwänden bausteinartig zusammengesetzt sind, in das bestehende Gebäude eingefügt und durch Freizeitanlagen wie Tennisplätze, eine Laufbahn und einen Fitnessclub im Hof ergänzt werden. Darüber hinaus sieht das Projekt die Errichtung dreier 30-stöckiger Türme vor, die nach den Plänen der Architektin sehr weit über den Pier hinauskragen sollen. Winka Dubbeldam über die Türme: »Ihr Erscheinungsbild passt sich der Strömung des Flusses und dem Stand der Sonne an. Der Betonsockel der Türme sowie die Bauelemente für die Infrastruktur verleihen dem Ganzen Stabilität. Die auf unterschiedlichen Ebenen angeordneten Wohnungen haben eine doppelte Raumhöhe und ihre Fassaden bestehen aus gläsernen Schiebewänden. In der gläsernen Ummantelung der Türme spiegeln sich Wasseroberfläche und die Silhouette der am gegenüberliegenden Flussufer gelegenen Innenstadt.« Die spektakulären Computergrafiken tragen sicherlich zum Reiz dieses Projekts im derzeitigen Planungsstadium bei.

Ce projet est parti de la rénovation d'un silo à grain en béton des années 1930, situé sur une jetée du port de Maashaven. Les unités d'habitation fabriquées grâce à un système de panneaux muraux modulaires en acier ont été insérées dans le bâtiment existant ainsi que certains équipements comme des terrains de tennis, une piste d'athlétisme et un club de remise en forme dans une cour. En dehors de cette rénovation, le projet comprend la construction de trois tours de 30 niveaux que l'architecte a choisi d'implanter en un spectaculaire porte-à-faux au-dessus de la jetée : « Leur modénature réagit au courant du fleuve et à la position du soleil. Leur base en béton, ainsi que certains éléments d'infrastructure apportent la stabilité nécessaire. Les appartements à niveaux décalés comportent des pièces double hauteur et des façades de verre coulissantes. La peau de verre des tours reflète la surface de l'eau et le centre de la ville de l'autre côté du fleuve. » Les impressionnantes images de synthèse participent certainement à la séduction de ce projet non encore réalisé.

The three thirty-story towers cantilevered out towards Maashaven harbor are visible at the top of both of these computer drawings representing the as yet unbuilt project.

Die drei über den Hafen auskragenden 30-stöckigen Türme sind im oberen Teil der Computerzeichnungen erkennbar, die das bisher unrealisierte Projekt vorstellen.

Les trois tours de 30 étages en porte-à-faux au dessus du port de Maashaven figurent dans la partie haute de ces deux tracés numériques qui représentent le projet non encore construit.

# GREENWICH STREET PROJECT

*New York, New York, United States, 2000–2002*

*Client: Take One LLC. Location: Soho, New York City. Floor area: 6,000 m².*

This is a renovation project for a former six-story warehouse, with a four-story penthouse being added on top. Adjacent to the original brick building, a new eleven-story residential building is being built. The total project has a floor area of 6,000 square meters. The architect seeks to "re-interpret" New York City building codes that favor horizontal planes by inserting a "diagonal surface that bifurcates the facade plane." The former warehouse building allows for an open loft plan that will also be the leitmotif of the new building. Terraces with views towards the Hudson River are provided in the former warehouse. Retail spaces and an art gallery are integrated into the ground floor near the lobby, in an effort to "ease the transition of the former industrial area into an integrated residential neighborhood."

Bei dem Projekt handelt es sich um die Renovierung eines ehemals sechsgeschossigen Lagergebäudes, auf dessen Dach ein vierstöckiges Penthouse gesetzt wird. An das ursprüngliche Backsteingebäude angrenzend wird außerdem ein neues elfstöckiges Wohnhaus gebaut. Der gesamte Komplex bietet eine Nutzfläche von 6.000 m². Die Architektin strebt in ihrem Entwurf eine »Neuinterpretation« der horizontale Flächen favorisierenden New Yorker Bauvorschriften an, indem sie eine diagonale Oberfläche einsetzt, durch die eine gabelförmige Teilung der Fassadenfläche entsteht. Das ehemalige Lagerhaus erlaubt offene Lofts, die auch in der grundsätzlichen Gestaltung des neuen Gebäudes wiederkehren. Im alten Bauteil werden Terrassenwohnungen mit Blick über den Hudson River angelegt und im Erdgeschoss, nahe der Eingangshalle, sollen Geschäfte und eine Kunstgalerie entstehen, die den Übergang dieses ehemaligen Industriegebiets in eine integrierte Wohngegend erleichtern.

Il s'agit de la rénovation d'un ancien entrepôt de six niveaux, sur lequel a été greffé un penthouse de quatre niveaux. Un immeuble d'appartements de onze niveaux est en cours de construction à côté du bâtiment d'origine en brique. L'architecte a cherché à « réinterpréter » la réglementation new-yorkaise de l'urbanisme en faveur des plans horizontaux par l'insertion d'une « surface diagonale qui divise en deux le plan de la façade ». L'ancien entrepôt a permis de créer des volumes à plan ouvert – principe également repris dans le nouvel immeuble – ainsi que des terrasses donnant sur l'Hudson. Surfaces commerciales et galerie d'art occupent le rez-de-chaussée, près du hall d'entrée, afin de « faciliter la transition entre l'ancienne zone industrielle et un quartier résidentiel intégré ».

*The existing brick structure is clearly visible in these images as well as the added eleven story residential building. The four-story penthouse running across the top of the older building integrates the two elements into a unexpected design.*

*Diese Bildern zeigen sowohl das bestehende Backsteingebäude wie auch das elfstöckige Wohnhaus, das angebaut werden soll. Das viergeschossige Penthouse auf dem älteren Teil verbindet beide Baukörper zu einem ungewöhnlichen Design.*

*La construction en briques existante comme l'immeuble résidentiel de onze étages sont clairement visibles sur ces images. Le penthouse de quatre niveaux au sommet du bâtiment ancien intègre les deux éléments de façon surprenante.*

*The penthouse spaces offer an open view onto lower Manhattan, while an entrance area for the new part of the building (above) gives a similar sense of transparency.*

*Die Räume im Penthouse bieten einen freien Ausblick auf Lower Manhattan und auch der Eingangsbereich im neuen Gebäudeteil (oben) vermittelt ein Gefühl von Transparenz.*

*Les espaces du penthouse donnent sur le bas de Manhattan. La zone d'entrée de la partie neuve du bâtiment (en haut) offre un sentiment similaire de transparence.*

MAIN FLOOR PLAN
1 – Art Gallery
2 – Office Space
3 – Retail
4 – Entry

SIXTH FLOOR PLAN
5 – Loft Space
6 – Kitchenette
7 – Bath
8 – Elevator Stair Core
9 – Balcony

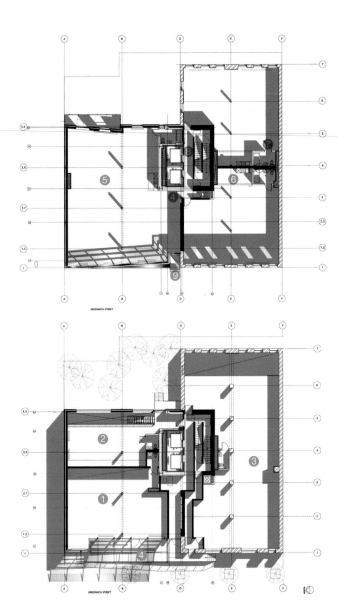

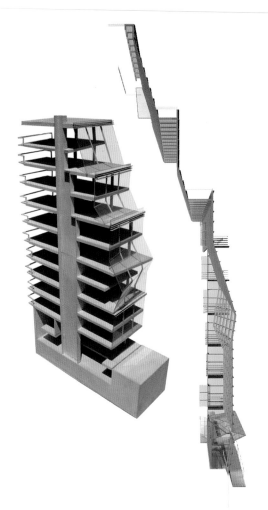

NYC Setback

Setback Interpreted

Setback Variation

Infelction 1

Infelction 2

The complex setbacks of the new facade give a variety that plays against the regularity of the older brick structure.

Die komplexen Zurückstufungen der neuen Fassade bieten eine reizvolle Abwechslung gegenüber der Regelmäßigkeit der älteren Backstein-fassade.

Les retraits complexes de la nouvelle façade créent une animation à l'opposé de la sévère régularité de l'ancienne structure de brique.

# JEAN-MARIE DUTHILLEUL

*AREP*
*163 bis, Avenue de Clichy*
*Impasse Chalabre*
*75017 Paris*
*France*

*Tel : + 33 1 56 33 05 95*
*Fax: + 33 1 56 33 04 16*

Born in 1952, **JEAN-MARIE DUTHILLEUL** is a graduate of the prestigious École Polytechnique and a registered architect (DPLG). He has been the Head Architect of the French National Railroads (SNCF) since 1986. His firms, the Agence des Gares, created in 1988, and AREP, created in 1997, are subsidiaries of the SNCF but have branched out well beyond the construction and renovation of French railway stations to build in several other countries, including China (Xizhimen Station, Beijing, 2000–2005; Shanghai South Station, Shanghai). He has been instrumental in redefining the appearance of French railway stations and has indeed has a broad influence in returning them to some degree of civility and brightness. He has renovated facilities such as the Gare du Nord in Paris (1998–2002) and built numerous new stations, such as the Lille-Europe TGV Station (Lille, 1988–1994) or the Roissy TGV Station (1991–1994, with Paul Andreu). The Agence des Gares and AREP respectively employ 60 and 200 people.

**JEAN-MARIE DUTHILLEUL**, geboren 1952, ist Absolvent der renommierten École Polytechnique und staatlich geprüfter Architekt (DPLG). Seit 1986 ist er Chefarchitekt der französischen Bahn (SNCF). Seine beiden Firmen, die 1988 gegründete Agence des Gares und die 1997 gegründete AREP, sind Tochtergesellschaften der SNCF. Sie haben jedoch ihre Tätigkeit weit über die Konstruktion und Renovierung französischer Bahnhöfe hinaus ausgeweitet und sind mit Bauprojekten in mehreren anderen Ländern aktiv, wie etwa mit den Bahnhöfen Xizhimen in Beijing (2000–05) und dem Südbahnhof in Shanghai. Duthilleul hat wesentlich dazu beigetragen, das Erscheinungsbild der französischen Bahnhöfe neu zu definieren und ihnen ein gewisses Maß an Gefälligkeit und Glanz zurückzugeben. Er modernisierte Bahnhöfe, wie den Gare du Nord in Paris (1998–2002) und baute zahlreiche neue Bahnhöfe, wie den TGV-Bahnhof Lille-Europe in Lille (1988–94), oder zusammen mit Paul Andreu den TGV-Bahnhof in Roissy (1991–94). Die Agence des Gares und AREP beschäftigen insgesamt 260 Mitarbeiter.

Né en 1952, **JEAN-MARIE DUTHILLEUL** est diplômé de la prestigieuse École Polytechnique et architecte DPLG. Il est architecte en chef de la SNCF depuis 1986. Ses agences, l'Agence des Gares, créée en 1988, et l'AREP en 1997, sont des filiales de la SNCF mais ont développé leurs activités au-delà de la construction ou de la rénovation des gares françaises dans plusieurs autres pays dont la Chine (gare de Xizhimen, Pékin, 2000–05 ; gare Sud de Shanghai). Duthilleul a joué un rôle essentiel dans le redéfinition de l'aspect des gares en France en leur apportant davantage de civilité et de visibilité. Il a rénové des installations comme la Gare du Nord à Paris (1998–2002) et édifié de nombreuses gares comme celle de Lille-Europe (Lille, 1988–94) ou la gare T. G. V. de Roissy (1991–94, avec Paul Andreu). L'Agence des Gares et l'Arep emploient respectivement 60 et 200 collaborateurs.

# AIX-EN-PROVENCE TGV RAILROAD STATION

*Aix-en-Provence, France, 1998–2001*

Client: SNCF (French national railways). Cost: $3.5 billion (for entire TGV Mediterranean line).
Speed: Channel Tunnel to Marseille in 3 hours 29 minutes (306 km/h, record set on May 28, 2001).

The southernmost of the three new railroad stations designed by Jean-Marie Duthilleul and Etienne Tricaut on the TGV Mediterranean line, the Aix-en-Provence Station is set on the Arbois plateau near the Montagne Sainte-Victoire and the Étoile Mountain range. It is near the RD9 highway running between Aix-en-Provence and Marignane. The highway was enlarged and deviated so as to be a prolongation of the platforms and better serve the station. A vast undulating concourse protects the service and platform areas from the sun and recalls the shape of the Montagne Sainte-Victoire. As in Valence and Avignon, long rows of trees run parallel to the tracks and mark the presence of the station in the landscape. The prospect of future urban development in the vicinity of the station has been taken into account. The skins covering the interior volumes are never completely opaque, allowing light to penetrate and travelers to view the countryside.

Der Bahnhof Aix ist der am weitesten südlich gelegene der drei neuen, von Jean-Marie Duthilleul und Etienne Tricaut entworfenen Bahnhöfe an der TGV-Mittelmeerstrecke. Er liegt auf der Hochebene von Arbois nahe der Montagne Sainte-Victoire und dem Gebirgszug Étoile sowie der RD9, die zwischen Aix-en-Provence und Marignane verläuft. Zur besseren Anbindung des Bahnhofs wurde die Autobahn um einen Zubringer erweitert. Eine ausladend geschwungene Bahnhofshalle, deren Form an die Montagne Sainte-Victoire erinnert, schützt die Serviceeinrichtungen und Bahnsteige vor der Sonne. Ebenso wie in Valence und Avignon wurden parallel zu den Gleisen lange Baumreihen gepflanzt, welche die Einbindung des Bahnhofs in die Landschaft unterstreichen. Auch die Aussicht auf eine zukünftige Stadtentwicklung in der Umgebung des Bahnhofs hat der Architekt einkalkuliert. Die Hüllen der inneren Baukörper sind an keiner Stelle ganz opak, sodass Tageslicht ins Innere fällt und gleichzeitig den Reisenden der Ausblick auf die ländliche Umgebung erhalten bleibt.

La plus méridionale des trois gares construites par Jean-Marie Duthilleul et Étienne Tricaut sur la nouvelle ligne du T. G. V.-Méditerranée, celle d'Aix est implantée sur le plateau d'Arbois, près de la montagne Sainte-Victoire et de la chaîne de l'Étoile, en bordure de la route départementale Aix-Marignane élargie et déviée pour améliorer sa desserte. Le vaste hall en forme de vague qui protège du soleil les zones techniques et les quais évoque le profil de la célèbre montagne Sainte-Victoire. Comme à Valence et Avignon, de longs alignements d'arbres courent parallèlement aux voies pour marquer la présence de la gare dans le paysage. Le développement urbain prévu dans le voisinage a été pris en compte. Les peaux qui habillent les volumes intérieurs ne sont jamais totalement opaques, ce qui permet à la lumière naturelle de les éclairer et aux voyageurs d'apercevoir le paysage.

*The undulating roof and facade of the Aix-en-Provence TGV Station are intended to recall local topography and to allow the ample Mediterranean light to filter into the station hall.*

*Geschwungenes Dach und Fassade des TGV-Bahnhofs nehmen die örtliche Topographie auf und lassen das helle mediterrane Licht in der Bahnhofshalle einfallen.*

*Le toit à ondulations et la façade de la gare T. G. V. d'Aix évoquent la topographie locale et permettent de filtrer la puissante lumière méditerranéenne qui éclaire le hall de la gare.*

Despite its rectilinear layout, the station's curving roof is a specific reference to the neighboring Montagne Sainte-Victoire often painted by Cézanne.

Trotz seines geradlinigen Entwurfs stellt das geschwungene Bahnhofsdach eine besondere Referenz an den benachbarten Berg Sainte-Victoire dar, der häufig von Cézanne gemalt wurde.

Au-dessus d'un plan au sol rectiligne, le toit en courbe de la gare est une référence volontaire à la proche Montagne Sainte-Victoire, souvent peinte par Cézanne.

Duthilleul has campaigned actively to introduce more generous spaces into France's railway stations and to give them a transparency vis-à-vis their environment. He makes interesting use here of wooden columns supporting the canopy above the tracks.

Duthilleul hat sich bei der Planung französischer Bahnhöfe besonders um eine großzügigere Raumgestaltung und eine stärkere Transparenz gegenüber ihrer Umgebung bemüht. Hier ein interessantes Beispiel für die Verwendung hölzerner Säulen als Stützpfeiler für die Überdachung der Gleisanlagen.

Duthilleul a beaucoup agi pour doter les nouvelles gares françaises d'espaces plus généreux et leur donner une certaine transparence vis-à-vis de leur environnement. Il fait ici un usage intéressant des colonnes en bois qui soutiennent les auvents au-dessus des voies.

# AVIGNON TGV RAILROAD STATION

*Avignon, France, 1998–2001*

*Client: SNCF (French national railways). Number of passengers: 23 million per year on the TGV Mediterranean line.
Number of trains: 168 on the TGV Mediterranean line.*

Located two kilometers from the historic Papal Palace of Avignon, the station is nonetheless set clearly outside the city's walled perimeter. Because of the topography of the site, the tracks arrive some seven meters above ground level. A long glass screen shelters passengers from the frequent Mistral winds on the northern platform. A form described by the architects as "an upturned stone hull" pierced with tall openings provides shelter from the sun opposite the Durance River, giving the 360 meter long station a slightly introverted aspect. The long, covered southern platform provides spectacular brightly-lit interior space, and emphasizes the architects' desire to render any stay in the station a pleasant one. A long, generously planted avenue links the station to the city itself, setting the tone for future urban development in this direction. Although greenery and pleasant views are amply provided for, the station does seem to be rather more distant from the town than might have been hoped.

Zwei Kilometer vom historischen Papstpalast entfernt befindet sich der Bahnhof ziemlich weit außerhalb der mittelalterlichen Stadtmauern. Die topographische Beschaffenheit des Geländes erfordert, dass die Gleise um etwa 7 m erhöht geführt werden. Auf dem nördlichen Bahnsteig schützt eine lange Glaswand die Passagiere vor dem häufig auftretenden Mistral. Ein von den Architekten als »umgedrehte Steinschale« bezeichneter Baukörper, der mit großen Schlitzen versehen ist, schützt den am Fluss Durance liegenden, 360 m langen Bau vor der Sonne und verleiht ihm ein leicht introvertiertes Aussehen. Der lang gestreckte, überdachte Bahnsteig im Süden hat einen spektakulären, lichtdurchfluteten Innenraum und unterstreicht das Anliegen der Architekten, den Aufenthalt im Bahnhof möglichst angenehm zu gestalten. Auch wenn die breite, großzügig bepflanzte Allee, die den Bahnhof mit der Stadt verbindet, stilbildend für die zukünftigen städtebaulichen Planungen sein mag, scheint der Bahnhof doch weiter von der Stadt entfernt zu liegen, als mancher sich wünschte.

À 2 km seulement du palais des Papes d'Avignon, cette gare se trouve néanmoins nettement à l'extérieur des murailles de la cité. La topographie explique que les voies se trouvent à quelque 7 m au-dessus du niveau du sol. Sur le quai nord, un long écran de verre protège les passagers du mistral fréquent dans cette région. Une forme que les architectes décrivent comme » un crâne de pierre retourné « percé de minces ouvertures hautes abrite du soleil et donne à cette gare de 360 m de long un aspect légèrement introverti. Le long quai sud, couvert, offre un espace intérieur étonnamment lumineux et met en valeur le désir de l'architecte de faire de l'arrêt dans cette gare un moment agréable. Une longue avenue généreusement plantée relie la gare au centre et donne le ton du futur développement de la ville dans cette direction. Bien que la végétation et les belles perspectives soient nombreuses, la gare semble plus distante de la ville que l'on aurait pu l'espérer.

*With the frequent "mistral" winds that blow in this region, and the very hot sun, the architects decided to give this station the appearance of a closed shell.*

*Wegen der in dieser Region häufigen Mistralwinde und der heißen Sonne gaben die Architekten diesem Bahnhof das Aussehen einer geschlossenen Muschelschale.*

*Pour se protéger du mistral, qui souffle dans cette région, et de l'ensoleillement élevé, les architectes ont choisi de donner à cette gare l'apparence d'une coquille fermée.*

The station hall stretches for 360 meters or the equivalent of two TGV trains without their locomotives. Although bright light enters the main hall, visitors are not subjected to direct sun in the white almost "unreal" environment.

Die Bahnhofshalle erstreckt sich über 360 m, was der Länge von zwei hintereinander stehenden TGV-Zügen ohne Lokomotiven entspricht. Obgleich helles Tageslicht in die Eingangshalle strömt, sind Fahrgäste und Besucher in diesem weißen, beinahe unwirklichen Ambiente keiner direkten Sonneneinstrahlung ausgesetzt.

Le hall de gare s'étend sur 360 m, l'équivalent de deux T. G. V. sans leur locomotive. Bien que le hall principal soit très éclairé, les visiteurs ne sont pas soumis au soleil direct malgré un environnement blanc, presque « irréel ».

JEAN-MARIE DUTHILLEUL

# VALENCE TGV RAILROAD STATION
*Valence, France, 1998–2001*

*Client: SNCF (French national railways). Structural materials: steel, wood, glass.
Length of station: 300 meters.*

The northernmost of the new TGV Mediterranean stations, the Valence facility can be considered the most architecturally spectacular of the three designs by Duthilleul and Tricaut. More technologically oriented in its esthetics than its cousins in Aix-en-Provence and Avignon, the structural volume, set up on red steel angled columns, gives a dynamic impression well-suited to the rapidity of the TGV trains. Set opposite the Vercors Mountain range between Romans and Valence, the station is at the intersection of the RN 532 highway and the Grenoble–Valence regional train line. A suspended, inclined volume hangs over the actual tracks, here set at eight meters below grade for reasons of the topography in the approach to the station. The sloping interior of the actual station area is graced with a wooden floor, and an open, luminous design. Local trains (TER) and buses can be accessed from the facility. Here as in the other stations, careful attention has been given to access and to landscape design. Not a truly urban facility, the Valence TGV Station is rather a transport node that may well attract future city development, a fact that the design clearly takes into account.

Als nördlichster der neuen Bahnhöfe an der TGV-Mittelmeerstrecke lässt sich der Bahnhof Valence in architektonischer Hinsicht als spektakulärster der drei Entwürfe von Duthilleul und Tricaut betrachten. In seiner Ästhetik mehr technisch orientiert als seine Pendants in Aix und Avignon, vermittelt das auf schrägen Säulen aus rotem Stahl ruhende Bauwerk einen dynamischen Eindruck, der gut zu den TGV-Hochgeschwindigkeitszügen passt. Der Bahnhof liegt gegenüber dem sich zwischen Romans und Valence hinziehenden Gebirgszug Vercors, dort, wo sich die RN 532 und die Regionalbahnlinie Grenoble–Valence kreuzen. Eine geneigte Hängekonstruktion überdacht die Gleisanlagen, welche hier aus topographischen Gründen um 8 m abgesenkt wurden. Das Innere des eigentlichen Bahnhofsbereichs ist offen und hell beleuchtet und wurde mit einem schräg abfallenden Holzboden ausgestattet. Der Bahnhof bietet Umsteigemöglichkeiten zu Nahverkehrszügen und Bussen. Wie bei den anderen Bahnhöfen auch wurde den Zufahrtswegen und der Landschaftsgestaltung besondere Aufmerksamkeit gezollt. Wenn auch kein wirklich urbaner Bau, sondern eher ein Verkehrsknotenpunkt, könnte der TGV-Bahnhof Valence durchaus zum Motor für eine zukünftige Stadtentwicklung werden – ein Umstand, dem der Entwurf eindeutig Rechnung trägt.

La plus septentrionale des nouvelles gares du T.G.V. Méditerranée, celle de Valence peut être considérée comme la plus spectaculaire des trois réalisées par Duthilleul et Tricaut. D'esthétique plus technologique que ses cousines d'Aix et d'Avignon, sa structure, montée sur colonnes inclinées en acier rouge, donne une impression de dynamisme qui fait écho à la vitesse du T.G.V. Face à la montagne du Vercors, entre Romans et Valence, elle est implantée à l'intersection de la nationale N 532 et de la ligne de trains régionaux Grenoble–Valence. Un volume incliné est suspendu au-dessus des voies qui se trouvent à cet endroit à 8 m en dessous du niveau naturel pour des raisons topographiques. L'intérieur en pente bénéficie d'un plan ouvert et lumineux ainsi que d'un sol en bois. Les lignes de trains (TER) et de bus régionaux lui sont reliées. Ici, comme dans les autres nouvelles gares de la ligne, un soin particulier a été apporté à l'accessibilité et aux aménagements du paysage. Hors de la ville, la gare de Valence est plus une plate-forme d'échanges de moyens de transports qui attirera sans doute un futur développement urbain, déjà pris en compte.

*Because of intersecting transport lines and local topography, the TGV tracks enter the Valence station eight meters below ground level, and the station hall is cantilevered over the tracks.*

*Aufgrund sich überschneidender Verkehrswege und der lokalen Topographie wurden die in den Bahnhof Valence hineinführenden TGV-Gleise um 8 m abgesenkt. Die Bahnhofshalle ragt über die Gleisanlagen hinaus.*

*Du fait de l'intersection avec les lignes régionales et de la topographie, les voies du T.G.V. pénètrent dans la gare à 8 m au-dessous du niveau du sol, et le hall se retrouve en porte-à-faux au-dessus des voies.*

The 200 meter long station hall is
set at an angle with a 3 % grade vis-
à-vis the tracks. Transparency and
light are, here as in other stations
designed by Duthilleul, omnipresent.

Die 200 m lange Bahnhofshalle
wurde mit einem Neigungswinkel
von drei Prozent gegenüber den
Gleisanlagen errichtet. Transparenz
und Licht sind hier – ebenso wie in
anderen Bahnhofsentwürfen von
Duthilleul – allgegenwärtig.

Le hall de la gare, de 200 m de long,
est incliné à 3 % par rapport aux
voies. Transparence et lumière naturelle sont omniprésentes, comme
dans les autres gares conçues par
Duthilleul.

# FRANK O. GEHRY

*Frank O. Gehry Associates, Inc.*
*1520-B Cloverfield Boulevard*
*Santa Monica, California 90404*
*United States*

*Tel: + 1 310 828 6088*
*Fax: + 1 310 828 2098*

Born in Toronto, Canada in 1929, **FRANK O. GEHRY** studied at the University of Southern California, Los Angeles (1949–51), and at Harvard (1956–1957). Principal of Frank O. Gehry and Associates, Inc., Los Angeles, since 1962, he received the 1989 Pritzker Prize. Some of his notable projects are the Loyola Law School, Los Angeles (1981–1984); the Norton Residence, Venice, California (1983); California Aerospace Museum, Los Angeles (1982–1984); Schnabel Residence, Brentwood (1989); Festival Disney, Marne-la-Vallée, France (1989–1992); Guggenheim Museum, Bilbao Spain (1991–1997); Experience Music Project (Seattle, Washington, 1996–2000); and the as yet unbuilt Guggenheim Museum (New York, 1998–). Gordon Kipping, his associate for the Tribeca Issey Miyake boutique published here, received a degree in engineering from the University of Toronto in 1989, and a Master of Architecture from SciArc in 1995. Kipping worked in the office of Philip Johnson, Greg Lynn, Pei Cobb Freed & Partners, and created his own firm G Tects, LLC in 2001.

**FRANK O. GEHRY**, geboren 1929 in Toronto, studierte von 1949 bis 1951 an der University of Southern California (USC) in Los Angeles und von 1956 bis 1957 in Harvard. Seit 1962 ist er Leiter von Frank O. Gehry and Associates, Inc. in Los Angeles. 1989 erhielt er den Pritzker Prize. Zu seinen bekanntesten Bauten zählen die Loyola Law School in Los Angeles (1981–84), das Haus Norton in Venice (1983), das California Aerospace Museum in Los Angeles (1982–84), das Haus Schnabel in Brentwood (1989), das Festival Disney im französischen Marne-la-Vallée (1989–92), das Guggenheim Museum in Bilbao (1991–97) und das Experience Music Project in Seattle, Washington (1996–2000). Sein 1998 entworfener Bau für das Guggenheim Museum in New York blieb bislang unrealisiert. Gordon Kipping, Gehrys Partner bei der hier vorgestellten Tribeca Issey Miyake Boutique, schloss 1989 sein Ingenieurstudium an der Universität von Toronto ab und erwarb 1995 den Master of Architecture am Southern California Institute of Architecture (SCI-Arc). Kipping arbeitete in den Büros von Philip Johnson, Greg Lynn, Pei Cobb Freed & Partners und gründete 2001 seine eigene Firma, G Tects, LLC.

Né à Toronto, Canada, en 1929, **FRANK O. GEHRY** étudie à l'University of Southern California, Los Angeles (1949–51), puis à Harvard (1956–57). Directeur de l'agence Frank O. Gehry and Associates, Inc., Los Angeles depuis 1962, il reçoit en 1989 le prix Pritzker. Parmi ses projets les plus remarqués : la Loyola Law School, Los Angeles (1981–84) ; la Norton Residence, Venice, Californie (1983) ; le California Aerospace Museum, Los Angeles (1982–84) ; la Schnabel Residence, Brentwood (1989) ; Festival Disney, Marne-la-Vallée, France (1989–92) ; le Guggenheim Museum, Bilbao, Espagne (1991–97) ; Experience Music Project, Seattle, Washington (1996–2000) et le Guggenheim Museum de New York (depuis 1998) qui reste à construire. Son associé dans le projet du magasin Issey Miyake à Tribeca, Gordon Kipping, est diplômé en ingénierie de l'Université de Toronto en 1989, et M. Arch du SCI-Arc en 1995. Il a travaillé dans les agences de Philip Johnson, Greg Lynn, Pei Cobb Freed & Partners et a créé sa propre agence, G Tects, en 2001.

# DG BANK

*Berlin, Germany, 1995–2001*

*Client: Hines Grundstücksentwicklung GmbH and DG Immobilien Management GmbH. Area: 20,000 m².*
*Location: Pariser Platz 3. Materials: steel, limestone, glass, alabaster, sheet metal.*

This ten-story office building with a conference center and a residential component has a floor area of 20,000 square meters. Set at Pariser Platz Number 3, not far from the famous Brandenburg Gate in Berlin, the **DG BANK** seems to blend harmoniously into the rigorous design codes that have stultified the reconstruction of the German capital. In fact, the exterior appearance of the building also corresponds to a dense office and apartment program, but the architect has managed within this envelope to create an unexpected atrium. By far the most astonishing feature of the building is the conference facility within the atrium that Gehry likens to a horse's head. This freely undulating stainless-steel clad shape resembles one developed for the unbuilt residence of Peter Lewis, and also that of a large sculptural object the architect showed in the Los Angeles gallery of Larry Gagosian. The conference center was modeled with CATIA, the software originally developed by Dassault for fighter plane design, and used both by Gehry in Bilbao and by Richard Serra for his "Torqued Ellipse" sculptures. Two by four meter, 4mm thick metal panels cover the unusual space, executed by contractors more used to shipbuilding than to architecture. A curved glass vault that highlights the very unusual nature of the conference room's volume covers the wood-paneled atrium.

Das Bürogebäude hat zusammen mit einem Konferenzzentrum und einem Wohntrakt eine Nutzfläche von 20.000 m². Die unweit vom Brandenburger Tor, am Pariser Platz 3 liegende **DG BANK** scheint sich harmonisch in die strengen Bauvorschriften einzufügen, die den Wiederaufbau der deutschen Hauptstadt so in Misskredit gebracht haben. Aber auch wenn die äußere Erscheinung des Bauwerkes einem gewöhnlichen Büro- und Wohnungsbauplan entspricht, ist es dem Architekten gelungen, innerhalb dieser Hülle ein überraschend unkonventionelles Atrium zu gestalten. Das mit Abstand außergewöhnlichste Merkmal des Gebäudes ist das im Atrium eingerichtete Konferenzgebäude, dem Gehry Ähnlichkeit mit einem Pferdekopf verliehen hat. Diese frei schwingende, mit rostfreiem Stahl ummantelte Form gleicht sowohl jener, die Gehry für die bislang unrealisierte Villa von Peter Lewis entwickelt hat, als auch einem großen skulpturalen Objekt, das er in der Galerie von Larry Gagosian in Los Angeles ausstellte. Die Gestaltung dieses Bauteils wurde mit der Software CATIA ausgeführt, einem Computerprogramm, das ursprünglich von Dassault für die Konstruktion von Jagdbombern entwickelt worden war und sowohl von Gehry in Bilbao als auch von Richard Serra für seine »Torqued Ellipse«-Skulpturen eingesetzt wurde. 2 x 4 m große und 4 mm dicke Metallplatten überdachen dieses ungewöhnliche Gebilde, das von Firmen konstruiert wurde, die bislang eher mit Schiffsbau als mit Architektur zu tun hatten. Das gesamte holzgetäfelte Atrium wird von einer Glaskuppel überdacht, die den äußerst unkonventionellen Charakter des Konferenztrakts noch hervorhebt.

Cet immeuble de bureaux de dix niveaux qui comprend également un centre de conférences et quelques appartements mesure 20 000 m² de surface utile. 3 Pariser Platz, non loin de la célèbre porte de Brandebourg, la **DG BANK** semble se jouer harmonieusement des contraintes urbanistiques rigoureuses qui ont présidé à la reconstruction de la capitale allemande. En fait, son aspect extérieur correspond aussi à un programme particulièrement lourd, ce qui n'a pas empêché l'architecte de créer dans cette enveloppe un atrium inattendu. Le plus étonnant élément est la salle de conférences qu'il a insérée dans cet atrium et qu'il compare à une tête de cheval. Cette forme libre et mouvementée, habillée d'acier inoxydable, fait penser à ce qu'il avait imaginé pour la résidence de Peter Lewis (non réalisée) ou à l'énorme objet-sculpture présentée à Los Angeles dans la galerie de Larry Gagosian. Le centre de conférences a été créé à l'aide du Logiciel CATIA développé par Dassault Électronique pour la conception d'avions, et déjà utilisé par Gehry à Bilbao ou Richard Serra pour ses « Torqued Ellipses ». D'épais panneaux de métal de 2 x 4 m et 4 mm d'épaisseur recouvrent ce curieux espace, réalisé par des entreprises plus spécialisées en construction navale qu'en architecture. La voûte en verre incurvé qui souligne l'originalité du volume de la salle de conférences, éclaire ce vaste atrium aux murs lambrissés de bois.

The exterior of the building is hardly typical of Frank O. Gehry, but accords with the rigorous "mineral" aspect of the guidelines set out by Berlin's urban authorities.

Die äußere Erscheinung des Gebäudes ist eher untypisch für Gehry, entspricht jedoch den strengen Bauvorschriften des Berliner Stadtbauamtes.

L'extérieur du bâtiment n'est pas typique du style de Frank O. Gehry, mais respecte l'aspect rigoureux et « minéral » voulu par la réglementation urbanistique berlinoise.

It is within the building that Gehry's style is evident, particularly in the conference center area with its metal clad "horse head" design, and in the complex atrium skylights.

Gehrys Stil offenbart sich erst im Gebäudeinneren, besonders im Konferenzgebäude mit seiner einem Pferdekopf ähnelnden Metallverkleidung und in der Glaskuppel des Atriums.

C'est à l'intérieur que le style de Gehry s'impose, en particulier dans la salle de conférences en « tête de cheval » à habillage métallique, et les complexes verrières de l'atrium.

# TRIBECA ISSEY MIYAKE

*New York, New York, United States, 2000–2001*

*Client: Issey Miyake. Area: 1,400 m².*
*Project Artists: Alejandro Gehry (murals), Neville Brody (graphic design).*

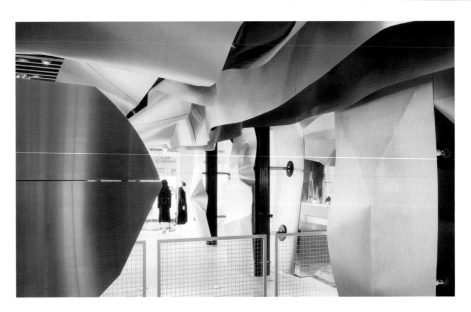

The Japanese designer Issey Miyake has a long history of calling on artists and architects in collaborative efforts. His Tokyo headquarters, designed by the brother of Tadao Ando, are a first indication of his interest in arts other than his own. In New York, at 119 Hudson Street, just blocks from the site of the former World Trade Center, Miyake opened his flagship store in October 2001. In a landmark cast iron building, Gehry signs what he describes as an "intervention" – an undulating strip of metal that indubitably carries his signature style. The rest of the architectural design was carried out by Gehry's protégé, the young architect Gordon Kipping. Seeking to open the high-ceilinged Tribeca space of the boutique to the advanced designs of Issey Miyake, Kipping creates a resolutely modern space without denying the industrial character of the existing building, leaving for example its cast iron elements visible. Murals executed by Alejandro Gehry, the son of the architect, and a visual identity devised by Neville Brody, former Art Director of *The Face* magazine, give Tribeca Issey Miyake all the makings of a space destined to animate and enliven its entire area, which suffered considerably in the wake of the events of September 11, 2001.

Der japanische Modedesigner Issey Miyake ist seit langem für seine Zusammenarbeit mit Künstlern und Architekten bekannt. Ein erstes Beispiel für sein Interesse an anderen als den eigenen Künsten zeigt sich in seinem Hauptsitz in Tokio, den er von Tadao Andos Bruder entwerfen ließ. Im Oktober 2001 eröffnete Miyake seinen New Yorker Flagship Store in Tribeca, 119 Hudson Street, nur wenige Straßen vom ehemaligen World Trade Center entfernt. Für die Fassade des historischen Gusseisenbaus entwarf Gehry ein geschwungenes Metallband, das unzweifelhaft seine Handschrift trägt und das er als »Intervention« bezeichnet. Die weitere architektonische Gestaltung wurde von Gehrys Protegé, dem jungen Architekten Gordon Kipping, ausgeführt. Im Bemühen, die hochwandigen Räume der Boutique für die avantgardistische Designermode von Issey Miyake zu öffnen, entwarf Kipping ein entschieden modernes Interieur. Er leugnete dabei keineswegs den industriellen Charakter des bestehenden Gebäudes und so blieben beispielsweise dessen gusseiserne Bauelemente sichtbar. Von Alejandro Gehry, dem Sohn des Architekten, ausgeführte Wandgemälde und eine von Neville Brody, dem früheren Artdirector der Zeitschrift *The Face*, gestaltete visuelle Corporte Identity erfüllen alle Voraussetzungen, damit die Räume von Tribeca Issey Miyake eine animierende und belebende Wirkung auf ihre gesamte Umgebung ausstrahlen, die beträchtlich unter den Folgen des 11. September 2001 gelitten hat.

Le styliste japonais Issey Miyake collabore depuis longtemps avec des artistes et des architectes. Son siège social de Tokyo, dessiné par le frère de Tadao Ando est une première indication de son intérêt pour des arts autres que le sien. Dans le quartier de Tribeca à New York, 119 Hudson Street, non loin de l'ancien World Trade Center, Miyake a ouvert en octobre 2001 son « vaisseau amiral » américain. Dans un immeuble historique à ossature de fonte, Gehry signe ici ce qu'il décrit comme une « intervention », une bande ondulée de métal fidèle à son style. Le reste des aménagements a été conçu par son protégé, Gordon Kipping. Pour adapter au mieux les volumes à hauts plafonds aux créations de Miyake, Kipping a créé un espace résolument moderne qui ne masque pas le caractère industriel de l'immeuble, par exemple en laissant des éléments de fonte visibles. Des peintures murales exécutées par Alejandro Gehry, fils de l'architecte, et une signalétique créée par Neville Brody, ancien directeur artistique du magazine britannique *The Face*, font de Tribeca Issey Miyake un espace qui devrait animer un quartier très touché par les événements du 11 septembre 2001.

*In a line of turn-of-the-century industrial type buildings along Hudson Street in lower Manhattan, the new Tribeca Issey Miyake stands apart as soon as visitors enter the main door (right), with its original cast-iron columns.*

*Die neue Tribeca Issey Miyake Boutique steht im Einklang mit dem industriellen Charakter der Anfang des letzten Jahrhunderts errichteten Gebäude in der Hudson Street von Lower Manhattan. Gleichzeitig hebt sich aber schon die Eingangstür mit den original gusseisernen Säulen (rechts) von der Umgebung ab.*

*Dans un bâtiment industriel de la fin du XIX° siècle qui s'élève sur Hudson Street dans le bas Manhattan, le nouveau Tribeca Issey Miyake, qui a conservé ses colonnes de fonte d'origine, se révèle dans toute son originalité dès que l'on en franchit le seuil (à droite).*

A glass box sets aside space for
clothes on the lower level (above).
To the right, the view from the main
entrance door on the ground floor,
with the original wooden beams contrasting with the undulating metal
forms by Frank O. Gehry.

Ein Glasgehäuse im Untergeschoss
bietet Raum für Kleidungsstücke
(oben). Blick von der Eingangstür ins
Erdgeschoss (rechts), in dem die
ursprünglichen Holzbalken mit den
geschwungenen Metallformen von
Frank O. Gehry kontrastieren.

Au niveau inférieur (en haut), une
boîte de verre permet de mettre en
valeur les vêtements. À droite, la vue
de la porte d'entrée principale au rez-
de-chaussée. La poutraison d'origine
en bois contraste avec les formes en
métal ondulé signées Gehry.

On the left, the main counter of the
boutique on the ground floor. Above,
the stairway leading to the lower
level.

Der Hauptverkaufstisch im Erdgeschoss (links). Die ins Untergeschoss führende Treppe (oben).

À gauche, le principal comptoir de
la boutique, au rez-de-chaussée.
En haut, l'escalier vers le sous-sol.

# SEAN GODSELL

*Sean Godsell Architects*
*8A Daly Street*
*South Yarra*
*Victoria 3141*
*Australia*

*Tel: + 61 3 9824 1444*
*Fax: + 61 3 9824 1477*
*e-mail: godsell@netspace.net.au*

*Carter/Tucker House*

SEAN GODSELL was born in Melbourne, Australia, in 1960. He graduated from the University of Melbourne in 1984 and worked from 1986 to 1988 in London with Sir Denys Lasdun. He created Godsell Associates Pty Ltd. Architects in 1994. After receiving a Masters of Architecture degree from RMIT University in 1999, he was a finalist in the Seppelt Contemporary Art Awards held by the Museum of Contemporary Art in Sydney for his work "Future Shack." He won the RAIA Award of Merit for new residential work for the Carter/Tucker House published here in 2000. He taught in the RMIT Department of Architecture from 1986 to 1997. His work has been shown in exhibitions in New York, Paris, London and Mendrisio, Switzerland.

**SEAN GODSELL**, geboren 1960 in Melbourne, schloss 1984 sein Studium an der Universität von Melbourne ab und arbeitete von 1986 bis 1988 bei Sir Denys Lasdun in London. 1994 gründete er Godsell Associates Pty Ltd. Architects. Nachdem er 1999 den Master of Architecture an der RMIT University erworben hatte, kam er mit seiner Arbeit »Future Shack« in die Endauswahl für die vom Museum of Contemporary Art in Sydney veranstaltete Verleihung der Seppelt Contemporary Art Awards. Für das hier vorgestellte Haus Carter/Tucker wurde Sean Godsell 2000 vom Royal Australian Institute of Architects mit dem RAIA Award of Merit für neue Wohnhausarchitektur ausgezeichnet. Von 1986 bis 1997 lehrte er an der Architekturabteilung der RMIT University. Seine Arbeit wurde in Ausstellungen in New York, London und Mendrisio, Schweiz, präsentiert.

**SEAN GODSELL** est né à Melbourne, Australie, en 1960. Diplômé de l'Université de Melbourne en 1984, il travaille à Londres de 1986 à 1988 pour Sir Denys Lasdun. Il crée Godsell Associates Pty Ltd. Architects en 1994. M. Arch de RMIT University en 1999, il est finaliste des Seppelt Contemporary Art Awards organisés par le Museum of Contemporary Art de Sydney pour son projet « Future Shack ». Il remporte le RAIA Award of Merit pour la Carter/Tucker House présentée ici. Il a enseigné au département d'architecture de RMITT de 1986 à 1997. Son travail a été exposé à New York, Paris, Londres et Mendriso, en Suisse.

# CARTER/TUCKER HOUSE

*Breamlea, Victoria, Australia, 1999–2000*

*Client: Earl Carter. Area: 210 m². Landscape architect: Sean Godsell.*
*Awards: 2000 RAIA Robin Boyd Award; AR + D Award, London; World Architecture Award, London.*

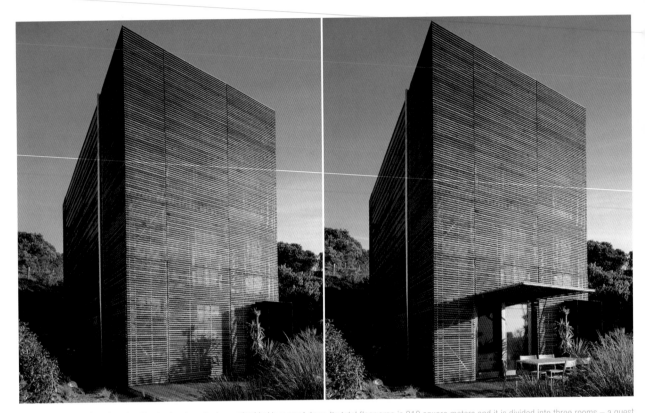

This house is a three level twelve by six meter box embedded in a sand dune. Its total floor area is 210 square meters and it is divided into three rooms – a guest area on the ground floor that can be divided in two by a sliding wall if necessary, a middle level with the owner's bedroom and a small sitting area, and the upper floor which is used for living and eating and as a daylight photographic studio as well. It is significant that Sean Godsell refers to the houses of Shigeru Ban in describing this residence, since he has adapted a similar sense of the open use of space. A timber screen skin tilts open creating awnings on all three levels. The opening of these screens simultaneously modifies the outward appearance of the house, and the perception of ceiling space from within. Conceived as a weekend house and not a permanent residence, set one hour from Melbourne, the **CARTER/TUCKER HOUSE** is approached by an uphill walk and is entered on the middle level "along a processional deck and through a ceremonial portal" according to the architect.

Das Haus besteht aus einem dreigeschossigen, 12 x 6 m messenden Baukörper und ist in eine Sanddüne eingebettet. Die Gesamtnutzfläche beträgt 210 m² und gliedert sich in drei Wohnbereiche: einen Raum für Gäste im Erdgeschoss, der sich bei Bedarf durch eine Schiebewand in zwei Räume teilen lässt, das Hauptschlafzimmer mit einem kleinen Wohnraum auf mittlerer Ebene und ein Obergeschoss mit Wohn- und Essbereich sowie einem Fotostudio für die Arbeit bei Tageslicht. Bezeichnenderweise bezieht sich Sean Godsell in der Beschreibung seines Entwurfs auf die Wohnhäuser von Shigeru Ban, da er hier eine ähnlich offene Raumgestaltung umgesetzt hat. Alle drei Stockwerke sind mit einer Holzblende umhüllt, die als Sonnenschutz dient. Klappt man sie auf, werden Öffnungen in der Fassade sichtbar, welche die äußere Erscheinung des Hauses verändern und sich auf die Wahrnehmung der Raumhöhe auswirken. Das eher als Wochenendhaus denn als Dauerwohnsitz geplante **HAUS CARTER/TUCKER** liegt eine Stunde Fahrtzeit von Melbourne entfernt. Man betritt es über einen ansteigenden Weg im mittleren Stockwerk, »über ein Promenadendeck und durch ein zeremoniell anmutendes Portal«, wie der Architekt sagt.

Cette maison est constituée par une boîte de 12 x 6 m, prise en partie dans une dune de sable. Sa surface totale de 210 m² se répartit en trois espaces : un pour les invités au rez-de-chaussée, qui est divisé en deux par une cloison coulissante, un niveau intermédiaire contenant la chambre du propriétaire et un petit salon, et le niveau supérieur consacré au séjour, aux repas et à un studio de photographie à éclairage naturel. Il est à noter que Sean Godsell se réfère à Shigeru Ban et fait preuve d'un sens similaire de liberté dans l'utilisation de l'espace. Une peau-écran en bois bascule pour créer des auvents de protection aux trois niveaux. Leur ouverture modifie à la fois l'apparence extérieure de la maison et la perception des plafonds, vus de l'intérieur. On accède à la **MAISON CARTER/TUCKER** à une heure de Melbourne par un chemin ascendant. L'entrée se fait au niveau intermédiaire « par une allée en caillebotis débouchant sur un portail cérémonieux ».

*In closed or open positions, the tilting wooden panels that cover the house alter its appearance and its internal lighting. When they are open, the panels also serve as awnings.*

*Je nach Position verändern die an der Fassade angebrachten Holzblenden die äußere Erscheinung und die Innenraumbelichtung des Hauses. Aufgeklappt dienen sie auch als Markisen.*

*En position fermée ou ouverte, les panneaux de bois basculants qui recouvrent la maison modifient son aspect et son éclairage intérieur. En position ouverte, ils servent également d'auvent.*

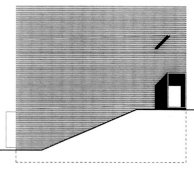

# NICHOLAS GRIMSHAW

*Nicholas Grimshaw and Partners*
*1 Conway Street*
*Fitzroy Square*
*London W1T 6LR*
*Great Britain*

*Tel: + 44 20 7291 4141*
*Fax: + 44 20 7291 4194*
*e-mail: ngp@ngrimshaw.co.uk*
*Web: www.ngrimshaw.co.uk*

A 1965 graduate of the Architectural Association, **NICHOLAS GRIMSHAW** was born in 1939 in London. He created his present firm, Nicholas Grimshaw and Partners Ltd. in 1980. His numerous factory structures include those built for Herman Miller in Bath (1976), BMW at Bracknell (1980), the furniture maker Vitra at Weil-am-Rhein, Germany (1981), and for *The Financial Times* in London in 1988. He also built houses associated with the Sainsbury Supermarket Development in Camden Town (1989), and the British Pavilion at the 1992 Universal Exhibition in Seville. One of his most visible works is the International Terminal of Waterloo Station, 1988–1993. Other work includes the Ludwig Erhard Haus (Berlin, Germany, 1996–1998); or the Health and Medical Sciences (EIHMS) building at the University of Surrey; and the RAC Regional Headquarters in Bristol.

**NICHOLAS GRIMSHAW**, geboren 1939 in London, schloss 1965 sein Studium an der Architectural Association (AA) in London ab. 1980 gründete er sein eigenes Büro, Nicholas Grimshaw and Partners Ltd. Zu seinen zahlreichen Werken gehören Industriebauten für die Firmen Herman Miller in Bath, England (1976), BMW in Bracknell (1980) und den Möbelhersteller Vitra in Weil am Rhein (1981) sowie das Gebäude der *Financial Times* in London (1988). Außerdem plante er Wohnhäuser für das Sainsbury Supermarket Development in Camden Town, London (1989) und entwarf den Britischen Pavillon für die Expo '92 in Sevilla. Eines seiner spektakulärsten Bauwerke ist der International Terminal im Londoner Bahnhof Waterloo (1988–93). Zu seinen neueren Bauten zählen das Ludwig Erhard Haus in Berlin (1996–98), das Gebäude für Gesundheit und Medizinwissenschaft (EIHMS) der Universität von Surrey sowie die RAC-Bezirkszentrale in Bristol.

Diplômé en 1965 de l'Architectural Association, **NICHOLAS GRIMSHAW** est né à Londres en 1939. Il crée son agence actuelle, Nicholas Grimshaw and Partners Ltd. en 1980. Il a conçu de nombreuses usines, dont celles d'Herman Miller à Bath (1976), de BMW à Bracknell (1980), du fabricant de meubles Vitra, à Weil am Rhein (1981, et l'imprimerie du *Financial Times*, à Londres (1988). Il a également construit des maisons dans le cadre du Sainsbury Supermarket Development, à Camden Town (1989), et le pavillon britannique d'Expo '92, à Séville (1992). L'une de ses réalisations les plus connues est le terminal international de la gare de Waterloo à Londres (1988–93). Parmi ses autres interventions : la Ludwig Erhard Haus (Berlin, Allemagne, 1995–98) ; le Health and Medical Sciences (EIHMS) de l'Université du Surrey ; le siège régional du Royal Automobile Club à Bristol (Grande-Bretagne).

# THE EDEN PROJECT

*St. Austell, Cornwall, England, 1998–2000*

*Total project cost: £ 80,350,000. Cost (building): £ 57,000,000.*
*Site area: 15 hectares. Project area: 23,000 m².*

This very unusual project is intended as a "showcase for global bio-diversity and human dependence upon plants." It is made up of 23,000 square meters of "linked, climate-controlled transparent capsules (biomes) set in a design landscape." The budget for the project, which makes use of the same consultants (Anthony Hunt Associates) who worked on Grimshaw's very successful Waterloo International Terminal, was £57 million. The domes in St. Austell are based on lightweight structures (lighter than the scaffolding used to erect them) with the highest possible volume vis-à-vis their surface. The cladding is made up of "optically clear air inflated foil (ETFE) pillows." This system allows the building to easily adapt itself to the topography of the former china clay pit in which it is set. The complex of geodesic domes of various sizes "gives the impression of a biomorphic organism." The **EDEN PROJECT** also looks like something akin to a mass of soap bubbles that have settled into the recessed site. With this project, Nicholas Grimshaw again demonstrates the adaptability of his style.

Dieses ungewöhnliche Projekt ist als »Schaukasten für die globale Bio-Vielfalt und die Abhängigkeit des Menschen von Pflanzen« gedacht. Es besteht aus einer 23.000 m² umfassenden Fläche »miteinander verbundener, klimatisierter, durchsichtiger Kapseln (Biome) in einer gestalteten Landschaft«. Das Budget für dieses Projekt, an dem – wie auch an Grimshaws äußerst gelungenem Waterloo International Terminal – Anthony Hunt Associates als Berater mitarbeiteten, betrug 57 Millionen Pfund. Die Kuppeln des Eden Projekts in St. Austell sind Leichtbaukonstruktionen (leichter als die Gerüste, die zu ihrem Aufbau nötig waren) mit dem höchstmöglichen Volumen im Verhältnis zu ihrer Oberfläche. Durchsichtige Luftkissen aus ETFE-Folie bilden die Umhüllung. Dieses System ermöglicht dem Gebäude, sich leichter an die topographische Beschaffenheit des Geländes, eine ehemalige Kaolingrube, anzupassen. Der gesamte Komplex aus verschieden großen Kuppeln erscheint wie ein biomorphologischer Organismus. Man könnte auch sagen: Das **EDEN PROJECT** sieht aus wie eine zusammenhängende Masse aus Seifenblasen, die sich in einer Bodenmulde niedergelassen haben. Nicholas Grimshaw demonstriert auch hier die Anpassungsfähigkeit seines Stils.

Ce projet très surprenant est une « vitrine de la biodiversité globale et de la dépendance de l'homme vis-à-vis des plantes ». Il consiste en 23 000 m² de « capsules transparentes interconnectées réagissant en fonction du climat (biomes) et implantées dans un paysage redessiné ». Le budget de l'opération qui a fait appel aux mêmes consultants (Anthony Hunt Associates) que le très réussi terminal international de Waterloo Station de Nicholas Grimshaw, s'est élevé à £57 millions. Les dômes de St. Austell reposent sur des structures ultra-légères (plus légères que les échafaudages qui ont permis de les monter) et recouvrent le plus grand volume possible par rapport à leur surface. Le bardage est constitué de « coussins en film plastique gonflé à l'air et optiquement clair (ETFE) », système qui permet au bâtiment de s'adapter de lui-même au site de l'ancienne carrière de kaolin dans lequel il se trouve. Cet ensemble de dômes géodésiques de tailles diverses « donne l'impression d'un organisme biomorphique ». L'**EDEN PROJECT** fait également penser à un agglomérat de bulles de savon qui se serait posé dans un creux de terrain. Nicholas Grimshaw démontre une fois de plus ici sa capacité à faire évoluer son style.

Set into a 60-meter deep china clay quarry pit, the geodesic domes of the Eden Project emerge from the Cornwall countryside.

Die in eine 60 m tiefe Kaolingrube gesetzten Kuppeln des Eden Project erheben sich unmittelbar aus der Landschaft von Cornwall.

Implantés dans une carrière d'argile de 60 m de profondeur, les dômes géodésiques de l'Eden Project pointent le nez dans le paysage de la Cornouaille.

The two large conservatories (biomes) are devoted respectively to flora of the humid tropics and to plants from the Mediterranean, southern Africa and the Southwestern United States.

Die beiden weitläufigen Gewächshäuser (Biome) wurden eingerichtet für Tropenpflanzen beziehungsweise für die Flora aus dem Mittelmeerraum, aus Südafrika und dem Südwesten der Vereinigten Staaten.

Les deux vastes serres (biomes) sont respectivement consacrées à la flore des tropiques et aux plantes de la Méditerranée, d'Afrique du Sud et du sud-ouest des États-Unis.

*The domes span up to 100 meters in a light steel structure requiring a glazing material lighter than glass – in this case a Teflon-like copolymer called ETFE, whose weight is only 1 % that of glass. A visitor center and restaurant complete the complex.*

*Die Kuppeln haben einen Durchmesser von bis zu 100 m und bestehen aus einer stählernen Leichtbaukonstruktion, deren Hülle – ein teflonartiges Kopolymer namens ETFE – nur ein Prozent des Gewichts von Glas hat. Ein Besucherzentrum und ein Restaurant vervollständigen den Komplex.*

*Les dômes de 100 m de diamètre sont composés d'une structure d'acier qui a exigé un matériau de couverture plus léger que le verre, en l'occurrence un copolymère de type Téflon, l'ETFE, dont le poids représente 1 % de celui du verre. Un centre d'accueil des visiteurs et un restaurant complètent les installations.*

# HEIKKINEN-KOMONEN

*Heikkinen-Komonen Architects*
*Kristianinkatu 11–13*
*00170 Helsinki*
*Finland*

*Tel: + 358 9 751 02 111*
*Fax: + 358 9 751 02 166*
*e-mail: ark@heikkinen-komonen.fi*
*Web: www.heikkinen-komonen.fi*

**MIKKO HEIKKINEN** was born in 1949 in Helsinki. He received his Master of Science in Architecture from Helsinki University of Technology in 1975. He created Heikkinen-Komonen-Tiiirikainen Architects in 1974, and Heikkinen-Komonen in 1978. He was a teacher at Helsinki University of Technology in 1977, 1978, 1987 and 1989, and a Visiting Critic at University College, Dublin, University of Virginia, Städelschule Frankfurt (1992) and Virginia Tech (1995). He has been the Chairman of the Board of the Finnish Foundation for the Visual Arts since 1999. **MARKKU KOMONEN** was born in 1945 in Helsinki. He received his Master of Science in Architecture from Helsinki University of Technology in 1974. He was Editor-in-chief of *Arkkitehti* Magazine from 1977 to 1980, and Director of the Exhibition Department at the Museum of Finnish Architecture (1978–1986). Komonen has been a Professor at Helsinki University of Technology since 1992. He was Chairman of the Board of the Free Art School in Helsinki from 1988 to 1995. Their work includes McDonald's Headquarters (Helsinki, 1995–1997); the European Film College (Ebeltoft, Denmark, 1990–1993); a Passenger Terminal at Rovaniemi Airport, 1989–1992; and the Finnish Embassy (Washington, D. C., 1994). More recently they have worked on Vuotalo Cultural Center (Helsinki, 2001), and the Extensioin of the Schönbühl Shopping Center (Lucerne, 2001).

**MIKKO HEIKKINEN**, geboren 1949 in Helsinki, erwarb 1975 seinen Master of Science in Architektur an der Technischen Universität in Helsinki. 1974 gründete er das Büro Heikkinen-Komonen-Tiiirikainen Architects und 1978 Heikkinen-Komonen. In den Jahren 1977 bis 1978, 1987 und 1989 lehrte er an der TU Helsinki und er war Gastkritiker am University College in Dublin, an der University of Virginia, der Städelschule in Frankfurt (1992) und der Virginia Tech (1995). Seit 1999 ist er Aufsichtsratsvorsitzender der finnischen Stiftung für Bildende Künste. **MARKKU KOMONEN**, geboren 1945 in Helsinki, erwarb 1974 den Master of Science in Architektur an der TU Helsinki. Von 1977 bis 1980 war er Chefredakteur der Architekturzeitschrift *Arkkitehti* und von 1978 bis 1986 Direktor der Ausstellungsabteilung am Museum für Finnische Architektur. Seit 1992 ist Komonen Professor an der TU Helsinki. Ferner war er von 1988 bis 1995 Aufsichtsratsvorsitzender der Free Art School in Helsinki. Zu den gemeinsam ausgeführten Bauprojekten gehören die Zentrale von McDonald's in Helsinki (1995–97), das European Film College im dänischen Ebeltoft (1990–93), ein Abfertigungsgebäude am Flughafen Rovaniemi (1989–92) und die Finnische Botschaft in Washington (1994). Zu ihren jüngsten Projekten zählen das Kulturzentrum Vuotalo in Helsinki (2001) und ein Erweiterungsbau für das Einkaufszentrum Schönbühl in Luzern (2001).

**MIKKO HEIKKINEN** naît en 1949 à Helsinki. M. Arch de l'Université de Technologie d'Helsinki en 1975, il crée Heikkinen-Komonen-Tiirikainen Architects en 1974 et Heikkinen-Komonen en 1978. Il enseigne à l'Université de Technologie d'Helsinki en 1977, 1978, 1987 et 1989, et sera critique invité à l'University College de Dublin, Irlande, à l'University of Virginia, la Städelschule de Francfort (1992), et Virginia Tech (1995). Il est président du conseil d'administration de la Fondation finnoise pour les arts visuels depuis 1999. **MARKKU KOMONEN** naît en 1945 à Helsinki. M. Arch. de l'Université de Technologie d'Helsinki en 1974, il est rédacteur en chef du magazine *Arkkitehti* de 1977 à 1980, puis directeur du département des expositions au Musée de l'architecture finlandaise (1978–86). Professeur à l'Université de Technologie d'Helsinki depuis 1992, il a été président du conseil d'administration de l'École libre des arts d'Helsinki de 1988 à 1995. Parmi leurs travaux : le siège de McDonald's (Helsinki, 1997) ; le Collège européen du film (Ebeltoft, Danemark, 1990–93) ; un terminal pour l'aéroport de Rovaniemi (1989–92) et l'Ambassade de Finlande (Washington D. C., 1994). Plus récemment, ils ont réalisé le Centre culturel Vuotalo (Helsinki, 2001), et l'extension du centre commercial de Schönbühl (Lucerne, Suisse, 2001).

# LUME MEDIA CENTER

*Helsinki, Finland, 1995–2000*

*Client: Varma-Sampo/Esko Viherlaiho. User: Helsinki University of Art and Design.*
*Total floor area: 11,400 m². Volume: 67,200 m³.*

Set in the historic section of Helsinki, the University of Art and Design occupies part of the premises of Arabia Ceramics. An element of a master plan for this industrial area, the **LUME MEDIA CENTER** contains four large, dark volumes intended to house a sound stage, two studios and an auditorium. Although these spaces are the most straightforward and least costly possible, added touches such as the draped metal mesh nets on the walls and ceilings of the auditorium introduce a note of the architect's careful design concept. The structure is in fact a cornerstone for the development of the "Design City Helsinki" project, with shops, restaurants, and an annex gallery of Helsinki's Museum of Art and Design nearby. With a total floor area of 11,400 square meters, the Lume Center is large and takes the form of a corrugated metal box linked via a glass corridor that becomes a bridge to old, existing structures on the site where the University of Art and Design uses some space. This light, luminous corridor is intended by the architects to contrast sharply with the "black box" atmosphere required for the Center's functional spaces.

Die im historischen Zentrum von Helsinki gelegene Universität für Kunst und Design nimmt einen Teil des Terrains der alt eingesessenen Keramikmanufaktur Arabia ein. Eine der im Bebauungsplan für dieses Industrieareal vorgesehenen Institutionen ist das **LUME MEDIA CENTER**, bestehend aus vier großen dunklen Baukörpern, in denen mehrere Tonstudios und ein Veranstaltungssaal untergebracht werden sollen. Obgleich diese Räumlichkeiten so unkompliziert und preisgünstig wie möglich gestaltet wurden, vermitteln zusätzliche Merkmale wie die Maschennetze aus Metall, die sich über Wände und Decken des Auditoriums ziehen, einen Eindruck von der Sorgfalt des Designkonzepts. Tatsächlich ist das Bauwerk ein Meilenstein im Stadtentwicklungsprojekt »Art and Design City Helsinki«, das Geschäfte, ein Restaurant und einen Erweiterungsbau des nahe gelegenen Museums für Kunst und Design vorsieht. Mit einer Gesamtnutzfläche von 11.400 m² ist das Lume Media Center eines der größten Einzelgebäude auf dem Areal. Es ist wie eine Schachtel aus Wellblech geformt. Die Glaspassage an einer der Fassaden fungiert als Brücke zu benachbarten, alten Fabrikbauten, in denen die Universität für Kunst und Design einige Räume bezogen hat. Dieser helle, lichtdurchflutete Durchgang wurde von den Architekten bewusst als starker Kontrast zu der in den funktionellen Räumen erforderlichen »Blackbox-Atmosphäre« konzipiert.

L'Université d'art et de design occupe une partie des installations de l'usine de céramique Arabia dans le quartier historique d'Helsinki. Un des éléments principaux du plan directeur d'aménagement de cette zone industrielle, le **LUME MEDIA CENTER** se compose de quatre importants volumes sombres qui abritent une scène de théâtre, deux studios et un auditorium. Bien que la conception soit des plus simples et des plus économiques, des détails comme les filets métalliques drapés aux murs et au plafond de l'auditorium prouvent à leur manière le soin apporté par les architectes à la réalisation. Ce projet est en fait la pierre angulaire du plan d'aménagement intitulé « Design City Helsinki » qui regroupera magasins, restaurants et une galerie annexe du Musée d'art et de design d'Helsinki voisin. Avec 11 4000 m² de surface totale, ce vaste centre se présente sous la forme d'une boîte en métal ondulé reliée par un corridor vitré qui se transforme en passerelle à des constructions existantes en partie utilisées par l'Université d'art et de design. Ce passage lumineux de construction légère contraste fortement avec l'atmosphère de « boîte noire » requise par les espaces fonctionnels.

*The old, renovated manufacturing structure and the new elements are integrated into a coherent whole. A certain roughness is implicit in both the old and new buildings.*

*Die alten, renovierten Fabrikgebäude und die neuen Bauten verschmelzen zu einem zusammenhängenden Ganzen. Beiden Elementen ist eine gewisse Robustheit eigen.*

*L'ancienne manufacture rénovée et les nouveaux éléments s'intègrent en un ensemble cohérent. Une certaine brutalité implicite réunit les anciens et les nouveaux bâtiments.*

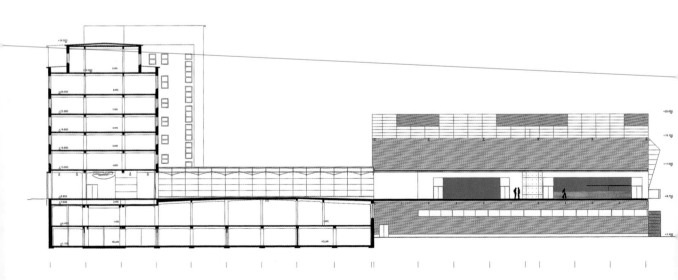

A section shows the relationship of the new and old buildings. Above, left, the "black-box" theater housed in the new addition. Ample but somewhat harsh spaces characterize the entire complex.

Der Querschnitt zeigt die Relation zwischen alten und neuen Gebäuden. Das im neuen Bauteil untergebrachte »Blackbox-Theater« (oben links). Großzügige, aber ein wenig hart wirkende Räume kennzeichnen den gesamten Komplex.

La coupe montre la relation entre les nouveaux et les anciens bâtiments. En haut, à gauche, la « boîte noire » – le théâtre – est implantée dans l'aile nouvelle. Le complexe se caractérise par l'ampleur de ses espaces assez bruts.

A curtain wall of glass next to a wide corridor alleviates the austerity of the building.

Die Vorhangwand aus Glas entlang eines breiten Ganges mildert die strenge Nüchternheit des Gebäudes.

Un mur-rideau de verre le long d'un large corridor allège l'austérité du bâtiment.

A dark palette of materials was chosen, heightening the impression of cavernous darkness that presides over much of the interior of the Lume Media Center.

Für die Innenarchitektur wurde eine Palette von dunklen Materialien ausgewählt. Diese verstärken den höhlenartigen Eindruck, den das Innere des Lume Media Center in großen Teilen vermittelt.

Une palette de matériaux sombres a été sélectionnée. Elle renforce l'impression caverneuse donnée par la plus grande partie de l'intérieur du Lume Media Center.

# KAHERE EILA POULTRY FARMING SCHOOL

*Kindia, Guinea, 1998–1999*

*Client: Centre Agricole Kahere, Bachir Diallo, Director. Area: 350 m². Cost: $104,000.*

Measuring just 350 square meters and having cost only $104,000, the **KAHERE EILA POULTRY FARMING SCHOOL** was a winner of the 2001 Aga Khan Award for Architecture. The architects, working with the Finn Eila Kivekäs (1931–1999) also have worked on a health care center, two village schools and the Villa Eila. The current project includes a classroom for twelve students, a student dormitory and a teacher's house grouped around a square courtyard. Construction was carried out with stabilized earth bricks made in a manual press. Double brick walls were erected in the school to provide thermodynamic insulation, and good airflow through the complex was a goal of the architects. As the Aga Khan Award citation has it, this building is "a fine example of an elegantly humble yet modern architecture that successfully crosses the boundaries of local Guinean and Nordic traditions and in the process, avoids mimicry."

Die gerade 350 m² große und für lediglich 104.000 Dollar erbaute **GEFLÜGELZUCHTSCHULE KAHERE** gewann 2001 den Aga Khan Award for Architecture. Die Architekten Heikkinen und Komonen haben – in Zusammenarbeit mit dem Finnen Eila Kivekäs (1931–99) im afrikanischen Guinea außerdem ein Gesundheitszentrum, zwei Dorfschulen und die Villa Eila realisiert. Zu dem hier vorgestellten Projekt gehören ein Klassenzimmer für zwölf Studenten, ein Wohntrakt für die Studenten sowie ein Wohnhaus für die Lehrer, gruppiert um einen quadratischen Hof. Die einzelnen Gebäude bestehen aus stabilisierten, in einer Handpresse gefertigten Erdziegeln. Im Schulbereich wurden zum Zweck der thermodynamischen Isolierung doppelte Ziegelwände errichtet, außerdem sorgten die Architekten für eine angenehme Luftströmung innerhalb der gesamten Anlage. Wie es in der Begründung für die Verleihung des Aga Khan Award hieß, handelt es sich bei diesem Gebäude um »ein hervorragendes Beispiel für eine elegant bescheidene und doch moderne Architektur, die die Grenzen lokaler guineischer und nordischer Traditionen gekonnt überschreitet, ohne ein oberflächliches Nachahmen zu riskieren.«

Construite pour un budget de 104 000 dollars, cette **FERME-ÉCOLE KAHERE** de 350 m² a remporté le Prix d'architecture Aga Khan 2001. Les architectes ont par ailleurs réalisé à proximité, en collaboration avec le Finlandais Eila Kivekäs (1931–99), un dispensaire, deux écoles de village et la villa Eila. Le projet de Kindia comprend une salle de cours pour douze étudiants, un dortoir et la maison du professeur, regroupés autour d'une cour carrée. La construction est en briques de terre stabilisée fabriquées à la presse manuelle. Des murs en brique double ont été montés pour assurer l'isolation thermodynamique, et les architectes ont veillé à la circulation naturelle de l'air. Comme le précise le texte de présentation du prix Aga Khan, ce bâtiment est « un bel exemple d'architecture d'une modestie élégante et néanmoins moderne qui croise avec succès les traditions locales guinéennes et nordiques, tout en évitant l'imitation ».

*The intriguing aspect of this project is that the efforts of talented Western architects are used for a low-cost structure in a developing country.*

*Das Faszinierende an diesem Projekt ist, dass sich das Können talentierter westlicher Architekten an einem Bau manifestiert, der mit geringem Budget in einem Entwicklungsland realisiert wurde.*

*L'aspect intéressant de ce projet tient aussi aux efforts d'architectes occidentaux de talent de proposer une construction à faible coût pour un pays en développement.*

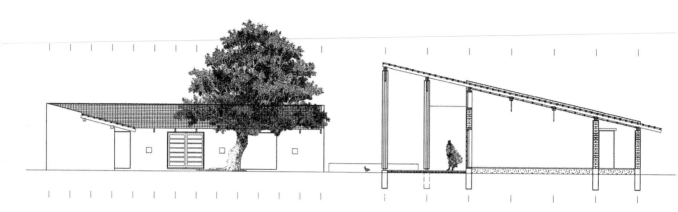

The shed-like structures take into account local materials and traditions while introducing a note of Western modernism.

*Die schuppenartigen Gebäude verbinden lokale Materialien und Traditionen mit den Merkmalen westlicher Modernität.*

*Les constructions en shed prennent en compte les matériaux locaux et les traditions, tout en introduisant une note de modernisme occidental.*

# JOHN HEJDUK

*1929–2000*

*Wall House 2*

**JOHN HEJDUK** was born in New York in 1929. He died in 2000. He studied at the Cooper Union (1947–1950), at the University of Cincinnati (1950–1952) and at Harvard (1952–1953). He worked in the office of I. M. Pei before setting up his own practice in New York in 1965. He was Dean of Architecture at the Cooper Union School beginning in 1975. His career was in a sense more devoted to the study and teaching of architecture than to construction since he built very few permanent structures. He did complete the Kreuzberg Tower and Wings, part of the IBA Social Housing project in Berlin in 1988. Hejduk often designed series of houses, including the so-called Wall Houses (1967–1973), of which more than 40 were designed, but only one (Wall House 2) built, after more than 30 years of hesitation. Hejduk had a considerable influence on the theory and development of architecture in the United States, assuming an almost mythical status during his lifetime.

**JOHN HEJDUK** wurde 1929 in New York geboren und starb 2000. Er studierte an der Cooper Union School for Architecture in New York (1947–50), an der University of Cincinnati (1950–52) und in Harvard (1952–53). Bevor er sich 1965 mit seinem eigenen Büro in New York selbständig machte, arbeitete er im Büro von I. M. Pei. Seit 1975 war er Dekan der Cooper Union School. Der Schwerpunkt seiner Karriere lag mehr auf dem Studium und dem Unterrichten von Architektur als auf dem konkreten Bauen und so realisierte er nur wenige Gebäude. Zu diesen gehört die 1988 im Rahmen des IBA-Sozialwohnungsbauprojekts fertig gestellte Wohnanlage mit Atelierturm in Berlin. Häufig hat John Hejduk Serien von Häusern geplant, wie die so genannten Wall Houses (1967–73), von denen er mehr als 40 entwarf. Aber nur eines, nämlich das hier vorgestellte Wall House 2, wurde nach mehr als 30-jährigem Zaudern schließlich gebaut. Dennoch hatte Hejduk einen beträchtlichen Einfluss auf Theorie und Entwicklung der Architektur in den Vereinigten Staaten, wo er bereits zu seinen Lebzeiten einen beinahe mythischen Status erlangte.

Né en 1929 à New York, **JOHN HEJDUK** est mort en 2000. Après des études à Cooper Union (1947–50), à l'Université de Cincinnati (1950–52), et Harvard (1952–53), il entre chez I. M. Pei avant de créer sa propre agence à New York en 1965. Il est doyen d'architecture de Cooper Union à partir de 1975. Sa carrière est d'une certaine façon davantage consacrée à l'étude et à l'enseignement de l'architecture qu'à la construction. Il a réalisé la Tour Kreuzberg, à Berlin, dans le cadre des projets de logements sociaux de l'IBA en 1988. Il a souvent conçu des séries de maisons, comme les Wall Houses (1967–73) dont plus de 40 ont été dessinées, mais une seule construite (Wall House 2) après plus de 30 ans d'hésitations. Il exerce une influence considérable sur la théorie et le développement de l'architecture aux États-Unis, au point d'avoir acquis un statut quasi mythique durant sa vie.

# WALL HOUSE 2
*Groningen, The Netherlands, 1973–2001*

*Client: Wilma Bouw, Groningen. Gross floor area: 265 m². Cost: $600,000.*

The Dutch architect and former chief planner of Groningen, Niek Verdonk, and the German Thomas Müller, a former student of John Hejduk, carried out the project. It was originally designed for Ed Bye, a colleague at the Cooper Union, and intended for construction in Ridgefield, Connecticut. Since this house was, unlike many other Hejduk projects, actually designed with the intention to build, it was a natural choice to constitute a sort of homage to the talent of Hejduk. Aside from being moved to The Netherlands, the project has also been increased 20% in size to satisfy local building codes. It has been said that the vertical organization of disparate, painterly objects in this context is a response to, or perhaps a contradiction of Le Corbusier's horizontal and rather colorless architectural object compositions, such as the Villa Savoye. As Hejduk wrote, "Life has to do with walls; we're continuously going in and out, back and forth, and through them." "A wall," he said, "is the quickest, the thinnest, the element we're always transgressing." The house cost $600,000 and was sold on the condition that it can be open to the public one month a year. In one month in 2001, some 12,000 people came to visit **WALL HOUSE 2**.

Der holländische Architekt und frühere leitende Stadtplaner von Groningen, Niek Verdonk, und der Deutsche Thomas Müller, ein ehemaliger Student von John Hejduk, waren die Ausführenden dieses Projekts. Ursprünglich hatte Hejduk das Haus für Ed Bye entworfen, einen Kollegen an der Cooper Union, und es sollte in Ridgefield, Connecticut errichtet werden. Anders als bei vielen von Hejduks Projekten plante man dieses Haus mit dem Vorsatz, es tatsächlich zu bauen. So lag es auf der Hand, seine Realisierung zu einer Art Hommage an den verstorbenen Architekten zu machen. Das Haus wurde nicht nur in die Niederlande verlegt, sondern auch um 20 Prozent vergrößert, um es den lokalen Bauvorschriften anzupassen. Die vertikale Anordnung disparater, mit einem Farbanstrich versehener Baukörper soll in diesem Kontext eine Replik auf – oder vielleicht auch ein Widerspruch zu – Le Corbusiers horizontalen und nicht sehr farbenfrohen architektonischen Kompositionen sein, wie etwa die Villa Savoye. Hejduk selbst schrieb dazu: »Das Leben hat mit Wänden zu tun. Wir gehen beständig zwischen ihnen hinein und hinaus, vorwärts und rückwärts und durch sie hindurch.« Und er sagte auch, eine Wand sei die schnellste und dünnste Grenze, die wir fortwährend überschreiten. Das Haus wurde für 600.000 Dollar mit der Auflage verkauft, es jedes Jahr einen Monat lang der Öffentlichkeit zugänglich zu machen. Im letzten Jahr kamen während dieses Monats circa 12.000 Besucher in das **WALL HOUSE 2**.

L'architecte néerlandais Niek Verdonk, ancien responsable de l'urbanisme de Groningue et l'Allemand Thomas Müller, ancien élève de John Hejduk, ont réalisé ce projet, destiné à l'origine à Ed Bye, un de leurs collègues de Cooper Union, pour être construit à Ridgefield, Connecticut. Comme cette maison a été conçue pour être réellement construite – à la différence de nombreuses autres propositions de hauteur – elle représentait un choix naturel pour ce qui constitue en quelque sorte un hommage au talent de l'architecte. À l'occasion de son déplacement aux Pays-Bas, elle a gagné 20 % en surface pour respecter la réglementation urbanistique locale. On a pu écrire que cette organisation verticale d'objets disparates et colorés est une réponse aux compositions d'objets horizontaux pratiquement monochromes de Le Corbusier, dont la Villa Savoye est le grand exemple. Ou peut-être une manière de les contredire. Comme l'a écrit Hejduk : « La vie est directement concernée par les murs ; nous entrons et nous sortons constamment à travers eux. (…) Le mur est l'élément le plus mince que nous transgressons sans cesse, et le plus rapidement possible. » La **WALL HOUSE 2** a coûté 600 000 dollars et a été vendue à condition d'être ouverte au public un mois par an. En un mois de l'année 2001, 12 000 personnes l'ont visitée.

*The wall is 16 meters high and 23 meters long, the largest concrete pour in The Netherlands. To the right, below, the entrance to the house.*

*Bei der 16 m hohen und 23 m langen Mauer handelt es sich um die größte Gussbetonkonstruktion der Niederlande. Der Hauseingang (rechts unten).*

*Le mur de 16 m de haut et 23 m de long est la plus importante construction en béton coulé des Pays-Bas. À droite, en bas, l'entrée de la maison.*

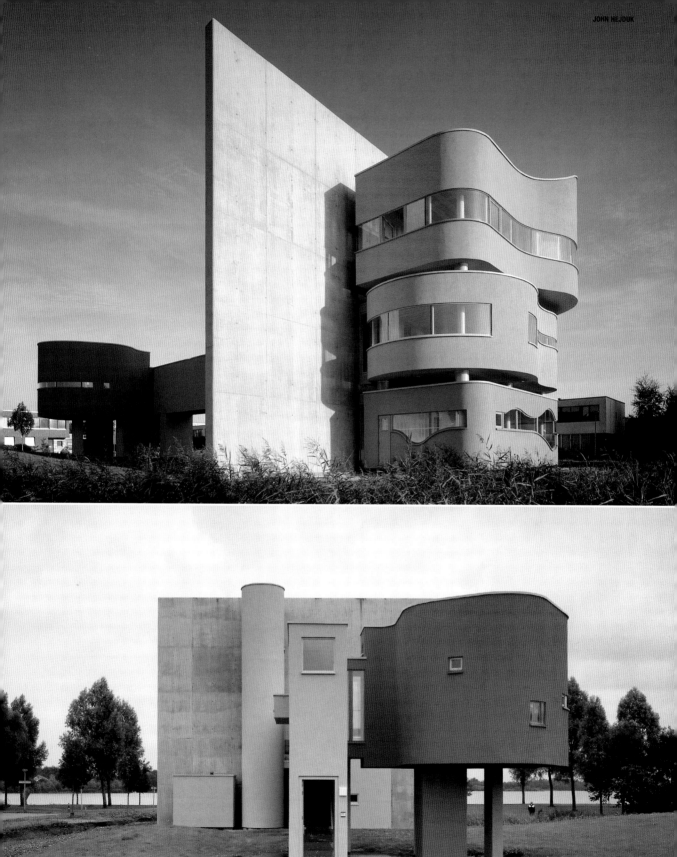

The rounded orange form is a study,
the master bedroom is on the ground
floor, while the dining room and
kitchen are on the second floor.

*Das gerundete orangefarbene Bau-
element enthält einen Arbeitsraum.
Das Hauptschlafzimmer liegt im Erdgeschoss, während sich Esszimmer
und Küche im zweiten Stock befinden.*

*La forme orange abrite le bureau,
la chambre principale se trouve au
rez-de-chaussée, la salle à manger
et la cuisine à l'étage.*

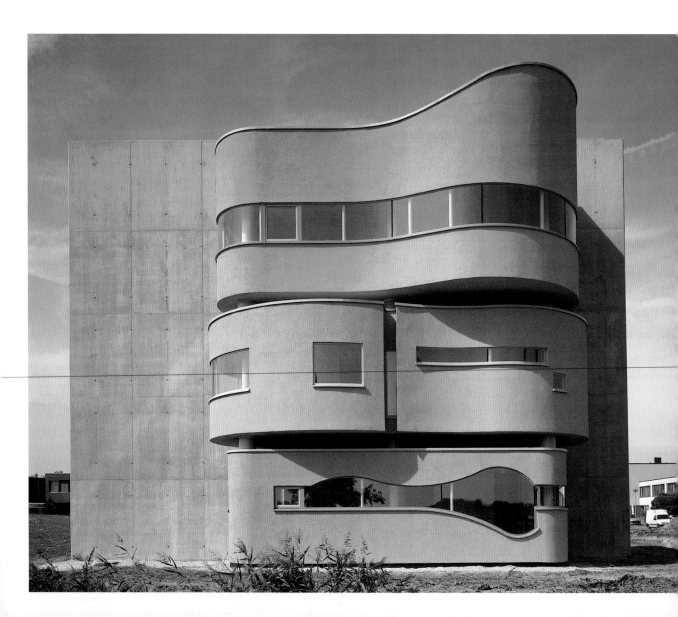

# STEVEN HOLL

*Steven Holl Architects, P. C.*
*450 West 31$^{st}$ street*
*11$^{th}$ floor*
*New York, NY 10001*
*United States*

*Tel: + 1 212 629 7262*
*Fax: + 1 212 629 7312*
*e-mail: mail@stevenholl.com*
*Web: www.stevenholl.com*

Born in 1947 in Bremerton, Washington. Bachelor of Architecture, University of Washington, 1970, in Rome and at the Architectural Association in London (1976). **STEVEN HOLL** began his career in California and opened his own office in New York in 1976. Has taught at the University of Washington, Syracuse University, and, since 1981 at Columbia University. Notable buildings: Hybrid Building, Seaside, Florida (1984–1988); Berlin AGB Library, Berlin, Germany, competition entry (1988); Void Space/Hinged Space, Housing, Nexus World, Fukuoka, Japan (1989–1991); Stretto House, Dallas, Texas (1989–1992); Makuhari Housing, Chiba, Japan (1992–1997); Chapel of St. Ignatius, Seattle University, Seattle, Washington (1994–1997); Kiasma, Museum of Contemporary Art, Helsinki, Finland (1993–1998). Recent work includes the extension to the Cranbrook Institute of Science, Bloomfield Hills, Michigan (1996–1999) published here. Winner of the 1998 Alvar Aalto Medal, Steven Holl recently completed the Bellevue Art Museum, Bellevue, Washington, published here, and is completing an expansion and renovation of the Nelson Atkins Museum of Art (Kansas City, Missouri). Other current work includes the Knut Hamsun Museum (Hamarøy, Norway); an Art and Art History Building for the University of Iowa (Iowa City, Iowa); and the College of Architecture at Cornell University (Ithaca, New York, 2004).

**STEVEN HOLL**, geboren 1947 in Bremerton, Washington, erwarb 1970 den Bachelor of Architecture an der University of Washington in Seattle und studierte anschließend in Rom sowie bis 1976 an der Architectural Association (AA) in London. Er begann seine Karriere als Architekt in Kalifornien und eröffnete 1976 eine eigene Architekturfirma in New York. Holl lehrte an der University of Washington, der Syracuse University und seit 1981 an der Columbia University in New York. Zu seinen bekanntesten Bauten zählen das Hybrid Building in Seaside, Florida (1984–88), der Wettbewerbsbeitrag für die Amerika-Gedenkbibliothek in Berlin (1988), das Wohnungsprojekt Void Space/Hinged Space Nexus World in Fukuoka, Japan (1989–91), das Haus Stretto in Dallas, Texas (1989–92), die Wohnanlage Makuhari in Chiba, Japan (1992–97), die St. Ignatius Kapelle der Seattle University in Seattle, Washington (1994–97) und das Kiasma Museum für Zeitgenössische Kunst in Helsinki, Finnland (1993–98). Zu seinen jüngsten Arbeiten gehört der Erweiterungsbau des Cranbrook Institute of Science in Bloomfield Hills, Michigan (1996–99). Im vergangenen Jahr vollendete Steven Holl, der 1998 mit der Alvar Aalto Medaille ausgezeichnet wurde, das hier vorgestellte Bellevue Art Museum in Bellevue, Washington. Gegenwärtig wird seine Renovierung und Erweiterung des Nelson Atkins Museum of Art in Kansas City, Missouri, abgeschlossen. Ferner arbeitet er am Knut Hamsun Museum in Hamarøy, Norwegen, einem Gebäude für die Abteilung Kunst und Kunstgeschichte der University of Iowa in Iowa City sowie am College of Architecture der Cornell University in Ithaca, New York, das 2004 fertig gestellt werden soll.

Né en 1947 à Bremerton, Washington, B. Arch. de l'Université de Washington, **STEVEN HOLL** étudie à Rome et à l'Architectural Association de Londres en 1976. Il débute sa carrière en Californie et ouvre son agence à New York en 1976. Il a enseigné à l'Université de Washington, à Syracuse University et, depuis 1981, à Columbia University. Parmi ses réalisations les plus notables : Hybrid Building (Seaside, Floride, 1984–88) ; Bibliothèque AGB (Berlin, Allemagne, envoi au concours, 1988) ; Void Space/Hinged Space, logements (Nexus World, Fukuoka, Japon, 1992–97) ; Stretto House (Dallas, Texas, 1989–92) ; logements Makuhari (Chiba, Japon, 1992–97) ; Musée d'art contemporain Kiasma (Helsinki, Finlande, 1993–98). Parmi ses réalisations récentes : extension du Cranbrook Institute of Science (Bloomfield Hills, Michigan, 1996–99) présenté ici. Il a remporté en 1998 la Médaille Alvar Aalto et a récemment achevé le Bellevue Art Museum (Bellevue, Washington) présenté dans ces pages, ainsi que l'extension et la rénovation du Nelson Atkins Museum of Art à Kansas City, Missouri. Il travaille actuellement à divers projets dont le Musée Knut Hamsun (Hamarøy, Norvège) et un bâtiment pour l'art et l'histoire de l'art à l'Université de l'Iowa, Iowa City, ainsi que le College of Architecture de Cornell University (Ithaca, New York, 2004).

# BELLEVUE ART MUSEUM

*Bellevue, Washington, United States, 1999–2001*

*Client: Bellevue Art Museum. Floor area: 3,400 m$^2$.
Cladding: board-formed concrete, marine-aluminum panels, glass.*

*The complex notching and indentations imagined by the architect give the entrance corner a particularly rich appearance (above). Right, the "court of light."*

*Die vom Architekten entworfenen komplexen Stufungen und Einschnitte verleihen dem Eingangsbereich eine beeindruckende Note (oben). Der »Hof des Lichts« (rechts).*

*Le jeu complexe de découpes et d'indentations imaginé par l'architecte donne à l'entrée en angle un aspect particulièrement riche (en haut). À droite, la « cour de lumière. »*

"I grew up in Bellevue waiting to go out," says Washington native Steven Holl. His stunning notched building for the **BELLEVUE ART MUSEUM** goes a long way to relieving the "sameness of its subdivisions and shopping centers" as he says. Indeed, the Bellevue Art Museum began its life on the top floor of the Bellevue Mall. Since the museum described itself with three terms: "see, explore, make art," Holl chose a tripartite composition. Like the fingers of a hand, or the "movement of a negatively-charged particle in a magnetic field," Holl's design makes reference to natural and scientific phenomena or debates such as that over whether light is a wave or a particle ("Court of Light"). Like his Kiasma Museum of Contemporary Art (Helsinki, Finland, 1993–1998) the structure in Bellevue is complex and lyrical, making use of light as a significant element in the design. It is divided into "three main lofts that are each slightly warped and dripped by the end wall structures. The outer walls," says the architect, "in a special 'shot-crete' construction support the inner lightweight steel framework."

»Ich wuchs in Bellevue auf und wartete darauf, dort wegzukommen«, sagt der in Washington geborene Steven Holl. Sein erstaunliches, mit starken Farbflächen strukturiertes Gebäude für das **BELLEVUE ART MUSEUM** gibt sich alle Mühe, Abwechslung in die von ihm beschriebene »Eintönigkeit der Häuserparzellen und Einkaufszentren« dieses Washingtoner Vororts zu bringen. Tatsächlich entstand das Museum auf dem Dachgeschoss der Bellevue Shopping Mall. Da die Institution ein Dreier-Motto hat: »Kunst sehen, erforschen und machen«, wählte Holl eine dreiteilige Entwurfskomposition. Mit Elementen, die aussehen wie die Finger einer Hand oder die »Bewegung eines negativ aufgeladenen Partikels in einem Magnetfeld«, enthält sein Entwurf Bezüge auf natürliche und wissenschaftliche Phänomene. Er verweist auf Debatten, wie die darüber, ob es sich bei Licht um eine Welle oder um ein Partikel handelt (»Court of Light«). Ebenso wie sein Kiasma Museum für Zeitgenössische Kunst in Helsinki (1993–98) zeichnet sich das Bellevue Museum durch ein komplexes und poetisches Design aus, bei dem Licht als wichtiges Gestaltungsmittel genutzt wird. Das Gebäude ist in drei loftartige Hauptbereiche gegliedert, die zu den Schmalseiten hin in einem leicht abfallenden Bogen verlaufen. Die Außenwände, eine Spezialkonstruktion aus Spritzbeton, dienen als Stütze für die innere Stahlrahmenkonstruktion in Leichtbauweise.

« J'ai grandi à Bellevue, en n'espérant qu'une seule chose, en partir », raconte Steven Holl, né dans l'État de Washington. Cette étonnante construction à indentations conçue pour le **BELLEVUE ART MUSEUM** pousse assez loin le désir de faire oublier « la monotonie de ses quartiers (de Bellevue) et de ses centres commerciaux ». En fait le musée avait entamé une première existence au dernier étage du Bellevue Mall. Pour cette institution dont la devise s'écrit en trois propositions : « Voir, explorer, faire de l'art », Holl a déterminé une composition en trois parties. Évoquant les doigts d'une main ou le « mouvement d'une particule à charge négative prise dans un champ magnétique », les plans de Holl font référence aux phénomènes naturels et scientifiques ou à des interrogations comme celles sur la nature de la lumière, onde ou particule (« Cour de lumière »). De même que dans son Kiasma, Museum of Contemporary Art (Helsinki, Finlande (1993–98), la structure complexe et lyrique de Bellevue utilise la lumière comme un élément de composition. Elle se divise en « trois lofts principaux qui sont chacun légèrement gauchis et contraints par les murs d'appui ». Les murs extérieurs, habillés d'un béton projeté spécial, soutiennent une ossature intérieure légère en acier.

The month-long concrete pouring process gave the exterior skin a continuous appearance. While a reddish hue dominates the exterior facades, a gray-white palette dominates the inward facing surfaces.

Der monatelange Prozess des Betongießens lässt die Außenhaut glatt und gleichmäßig aussehen. Während an den Fassaden ein rötlicher Farbton vorherrscht, sind die Innenwände in Grau-Weiß gehalten.

Le processus de coulage du béton qui a duré un mois a permis de donner à la peau extérieure un aspect de continuité. À l'extérieur domine une tonalité rouge, tandis que les surfaces donnant sur l'intérieur obéissent à une palette gris-blanc.

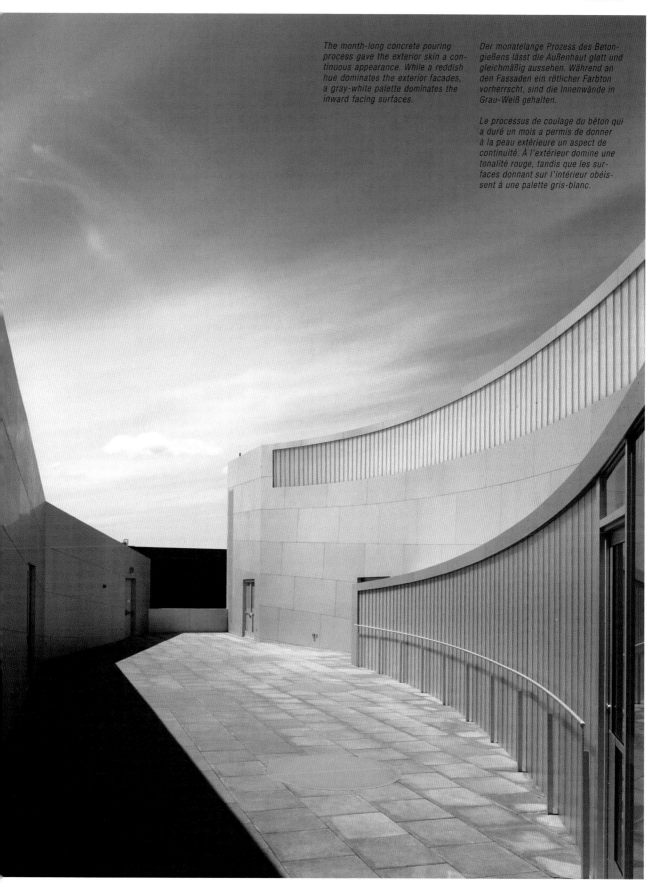

Steven Holl's fascination with light
and unusual forms is evident in these
views of the "Forum" (left) and the
north gallery (this page).

Steven Holls Faszination für Licht und
ungewöhnliche Formen offenbart sich
in diesen Ansichten des »Forums«
(links) und des nördlichen Ausstel-
lungssaals (diese Seite).

La fascination de Steven Holl pour la
lumière et les formes originales est
évidente dans ces vues du « Forum »
(à gauche) et de la galerie nord (cette
page).

Top-lighting and subtle color-effects give an ethereal subtlety to the interior spaces. To the right, the Forum, and on this page a glass-clad stairway leading to the upper galleries.

Oberlichter und dezente Farbeffekte verleihen den Innenräumen eine geradezu ätherische Feinheit. Das Forum (rechts). Eine mit Glas verkleidete Treppe führt in die oberen Ausstellungsräume (diese Seite).

L'éclairage zénithal et de subtils effets de couleurs confèrent une délicatesse aérienne aux volumes intérieurs. À droite, le Forum et, sur cette page, un escalier dans une cage de verre, qui conduit aux galeries des niveaux supérieurs.

# HANS HOLLEIN

*Hans Hollein*
*Argentinierstrasse 36*
*1040 Vienna*
*Austria*

*Tel: + 43 1 505 51 96*
*Fax: + 43 1 505 88 94*
*e-mail: office@hollein.com*

*Interbank Lima*

Born in 1934 in Vienna, **HANS HOLLEIN** studied at the Academy of Fine Arts in Vienna (1956), before attending the Illinois Institute of Technology (1958–1959) and the University of California Institute of Design where he received his Master of Architecture degree in 1960. Some of his significant built works include the Reti Candleshop (Vienna, 1965); the Feigen Gallery (New York, 1967–1974); the Abteiberg Museum (Mönchengladbach, Germany, 1972–1982); Museum of Modern Art (Frankfurt, Germany, 1987–1991); the Haas-Haus (Vienna, 1985–1990); the Interbanktower (Lima, Peru, 1996–2001) published here, and the Vulcania Center (St-Ours-les-Roches, France). Winner of the 1985 Pritzker Prize, Hans Hollein, was cited "as a master of his profession – one who with wit and eclectic gusto draws upon the traditions of the New World as readily as upon those of the old… An architect who is also an artist." Significantly, he is the only architect whose work is represented in both the Museum of Modern Art in New York, and the Centre Pompidou in Paris.

**HANS HOLLEIN**, geboren 1934 in Wien, studierte an der Wiener Akademie der Bildenden Künste (1956), am Illinois Institute of Technology (1958–59) und am Institute of Design der University of California, Los Angeles (UCLA), wo er 1960 den Master of Architecture erwarb. Zu seinen bekanntesten Arbeiten gehören die Kerzenhandlung Retti in Wien (1965), die Feigen Gallery in New York (1967–74), das Museum Abteiberg in Mönchengladbach (1972–82), das Haas-Haus in Wien (1985–90), das Museum für Moderne Kunst in Frankfurt (1987–91) und der hier vorgestellte Interbanktower in Lima, Peru (1996–2001). Über Hans Hollein, der 1985 mit dem Pritzker Prize ausgezeichnet wurde, heißt es, er sei »ein Meister seines Fachs – einer, der mit Esprit und eklektischem Stilvermögen ebenso geschickt aus den Traditionen der Neuen Welt schöpft wie aus denen der Alten … Ein Architekt, der gleichzeitig Künstler ist.« Bezeichnenderweise ist Hans Hollein der einzige Architekt, dessen künstlerische Arbeiten, wie Zeichnungen und Collagen, sowohl in den Sammlungen des Museum of Modern Art in New York als auch in denen des Centre Georges Pompidou in Paris präsent sind.

Né à Vienne en 1934, **HANS HOLLEIN** étudie à l'Académie des Beaux-Arts de Vienne (1956) puis à l'Illinois Institute of Technology (1958–59) et à l'Institute of Design de l'Université de Californie dont il est M. Arch. en 1960. Parmi ses réalisations les plus significatives : la boutique de bougies Reti (Vienne, 1965), la Feigen Gallery (New York, 1967–74) ; le Abteiberg Museum (Mönchengladbach, Allemagne, 1972–82) ; le Musée d'art moderne de Francfort (Allemagne, 1987–91) ; la Haas-Haus (Vienne, 1985–90) et la tour de l'Interbank (Lima, Pérou, 1996–2001) présentée dans ces pages ; le centre Vulcania (Saint-Ours-les-Roches, France, 2002). Titulaire du prix Pritzker (1985), en tant que l'« un des maîtres de sa profession, pour son esprit et son éclectisme qui s'appuient sur les traditions du Nouveau Monde autant que sur celles de l'ancien… un architecte qui est également un artiste. » Il est le seul architecte dont l'œuvre est présentée à la fois au Museum of Modern Art de New York et au Centre Pompidou à Paris.

# INTERBANK LIMA

*Lima, Peru, 1996–2001*

*Site area: 5,000 m². Total area: 45,300 m². Maximum height: 88 meters.*

This building, set on a 5,000 square meter plot on the corner of the Paseo de la Republica and the Avenida Javier Prado in Lima, includes a total built area of 45,300 square meters. The highest point of the complex is at 88 meters above street level. The structure "appears to be fragmented on one side, while on the other it appears smooth; seen from one point of view it looks thin, from another, massive." The facade is overlapped by a grid of titanium tubes illuminated by optic fibers. Intended to be a symbol of the modern development of Peru, the maximum twenty-story height of the **INTERBANK** tower stands out above the mainly low-rise architecture of the Peruvian capital. The developers of the project call attention to the relationship between Hollein's 1968 manifesto *Alles ist Architektur* and the varied approaches to the appearance of this building.

Das neue Bankgebäude steht auf einem 5.000 m² großen Grundstück an der Ecke von Paseo de la República und Avenida Javier Prado in Lima und verfügt über eine Gesamtgeschossfläche von 45.300 m². Sein höchster Punkt liegt 88 m über dem Straßenniveau. Das Bauwerk »wirkt auf der einen Seite wie zersplittert und auf der anderen glatt und geschliffen; aus einem Blickwinkel erscheint es schmal und aus einem anderen massiv.« Die Fassade ist von einem Gitter aus Titanröhren überzogen, die durch Lichtleitfasern illuminiert werden. Mit seiner maximal zulässigen Höhe von 20 Stockwerken ragt der als Symbol für die moderne Entwicklung Perus geplante **INTERBANK**-Hochhausturm über die vorherrschende Flachbauarchitektur der Hauptstadt hinaus. Die an diesem Projekt tätigen Planer lenken die Aufmerksamkeit auf die Beziehung zwischen dem 1968 von Hollein verfassten Manifest *Alles ist Architektur* und den verschiedenartigen Herangehensweisen an das Erscheinungsbild dieses Gebäudes.

De 45 300 m² de surface utile pour 88 m de haut, l'Interbank s'élève sur un terrain de 5000 m² à l'angle du Paseo de la Republica et de l'Avenida Javier Prado à Lima. L'immeuble « semble fragmenté d'un côté et lisse de l'autre ; vu sous un certain angle, il paraît mince, et sous un autre, massif ». La façade est recouverte d'une grille de tubes d'aluminium illuminée par un système de fibres optiques. Symbole du développement économique du Pérou, les vingt niveaux de la tour **INTERBANK** dominent les constructions généralement basses de la capitale péruvienne. Les promoteurs du projet soulignent les relations entre le manifeste de Hollein *Alles ist Architektur*, publié en 1968, et les variations de l'apparence de l'Interbank en fonction de ses approches.

The building is located on the Paseo de la Republica at the Avenida Javier Prado. The screen-like facade takes its curved shape from the street that flanks it.

Das Gebäude liegt an der Kreuzung von Paseo de la República und Avenida Javier Prado. Die Wölbung der gitterförmigen Fassade greift die Krümmung der angrenzenden Straße auf.

Le bâtiment se dresse au carrefour du Paseo de la Republica et de l'Avenida Javier Prado. La façade-écran s'incurve sur la rue qui la longe.

The ground floor has stone walls "imitating the masonry of the Inca civilization," while a fiberglass dome covers the top two floors. The architect strives here for what he calls a "multi-faceted" appearance.

Das Erdgeschoss ist mit Wänden im Stil der Inka-Kultur ausgestattet, während die beiden oberen Stockwerke von einer Kuppel aus Glasfaser überdacht sind. Ziel des Architekten war ein facettenreiches Erscheinungsbild.

Le rez-de-chaussée est en murs de pierre « imitant la maçonnerie de la civilisation inca » et une coupole en fibre de verre recouvre les deux derniers niveaux. L'architecte a voulu cet aspect « multifacettes ».

The muted hues and cutouts in the interiors recall the Viennese work of Hans Hollein. Below and left, the ground floor.

Die gedämpften Farbtöne und Aussparungen der Innenwände erinnern an die Wiener Bauten von Hans Hollein. Das Erdgeschoss (unten und links).

Les tonalités sourdes et les découpes des volumes intérieurs rappellent les réalisations viennoises de Hans Hollein. En bas, à gauche, le rez-de-chaussée.

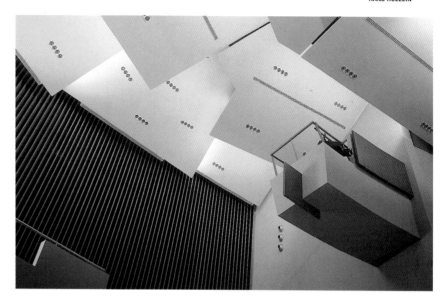

Above the "trading room," and to the left the board room and a spiral interior staircase. The screen like facade on the main tower is covered with a grid of titanium tubes.

Das »Börsenparkett« (oben). Der Sitzungssaal und eine Wendeltreppe (links). Die Fassade des Hauptturms ist mit einem Gitter aus Titanröhren verkleidet.

En haut, la salle des marchés ; à gauche, la salle du conseil et un escalier intérieur en spirale. La façade-écran de la tour principale est recouverte d'une grille en tubes d'aluminium.

# TOYO ITO

*Toyo Ito & Associates, Architects*
*1-19-4 Shibuya, Shibuya-ku*
*Tokyo 150-0002*
*Japan*

*Tel: + 81 3 409 5822*
*Fax: + 81 3 409 5969*

*Mediathequ*

Born in 1941 in Seoul, Korea, **TOYO ITO** graduated from the University of Tokyo in 1965, and worked in the office of Kiyonori Kikutake until 1969. He created his own office in 1971, assuming the name of Toyo Ito Architect & Associates in 1979. His completed work includes the Silver Hut residence (Tokyo, 1984); Tower of the Winds (Yokohama, Kanagawa, 1986); Yatsushiro Municipal Museum (Yatsushiro, Kumamoto, 1989–1991); and the Elderly People's Home (1992–1994) and Fire Station (1992–1995) both located in the same city on the island of Kyushu. He participated in the Shanghai Luijiazui Center Area International Planning and Urban Design Consultation in 1992, and has built a Public Kindergarten (Eckenheim, Frankfurt, Germany, 1988–1991). Recent projects include his Odate Jukai Dome Park (Odate, Japan, 1995–1997); Nagaoka Lyric Hall (Nagaoka, Niigata, Japan, 1995–1997) and Ota-ku Resort Complex (Tobu-cho, Chiisagata-gun, Nagano, 1995–1998).

**TOYO ITO**, 1941 in Seoul geboren, schloss 1965 sein Studium an der Universität Tokio ab und arbeitete bis 1969 im Büro von Kiyonori Kikutake. 1971 gründete er sein eigenes Büro, das 1979 den Namen Toyo Ito & Associates erhielt. Zu seinen Bauten gehören das Wohnhaus Silver Hut in Tokio (1984), der Turm der Winde in Yokohama, Kanagawa (1986), das städtische Museum in Yatsushiro, Kumamoto auf der Insel Kyushu (1989–91) sowie ein Altersheim (1992–94) und eine Feuerwehrstation (1992–95) in derselben Stadt. 1992 nahm Toyo Ito an der internationalen Konferenz für Planung und Entwicklung des Stadtteils Luijiazui in Shanghai teil. Ferner baute er einen städtischen Kindergarten im Frankfurter Stadtteil Eckenheim (1988–91). Zu seinen jüngsten Projekten zählen der Odate Jukai Dome Park in Odate (1995–97), die Nagaoka Lyric Hall in Nagaoka, Niigata (1995–97), sowie der Freizeitkomplex Ota-ku in Nagano (1995–98), alle in Japan.

Né en 1941 à Séoul, Corée, **TOYO ITO** est diplômé de l'Université de Tokyo en 1965 et travaille dans l'agence de Kiyonori Kikutaké jusqu'en 1969. Il crée sa propre agence en 1971, qui prend le nom de Toyo Ito Architect & Associates en 1979. Parmi ses réalisations : la maison Silver Hut (Tokyo, 1984) ; la tour des vents (Yokohama, Kanagawa, 1986) ; le Musée municipal de Yatsushiro (Yatsushiro, Kumamoto, 1989–91) ; une maison de retraite (1992–94) et une caserne de pompiers dans une ville de l'île de Kyushu. Il a participé au concours international d'urbanisme de la zone de Luijiazui à Shanghai, et a construit un jardin d'enfants (Eckenheim, Francfort, Allemagne 1988–91). Parmi ses récents projets : le Odate Jukai Dome Park (Odate, Japon, 1995–97), la salle de concerts lyriques de Nagaoka (Nagaoka, Niigata, Japon, 1995–97), et le complexe touristique Ota-ku (Tobu-Cho, Chiisagata-gun, Nagano, 1995–98).

# MEDIATHEQUE

*Sendai, Miyagi, Japan, 1998–2001*

Site area: 3,949 m². Building area: 2,844 m². Floor area: 21,504 m².

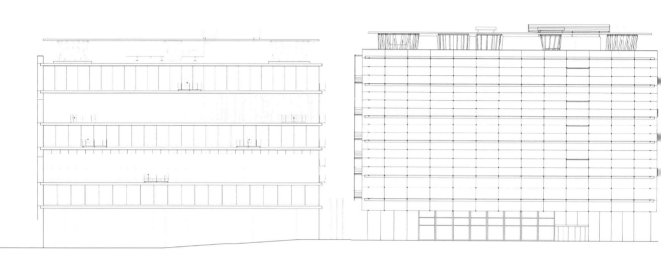

Located on a four thousand square meter lot in the heart of the northern city of Sendai, the 22,000 square meter building is open to the public on all four sides. A seven-story structure, it is one of the most spectacular new buildings to be completed in Japan in recent years. On the ground floor, there is a cafe, bookshop and a 500 square meter "open square" than can be closed off for temporary shows. A second floor contains an information center while there is an open-stack library on the third floor. Professional exhibitions are housed on the sixth floor, and one floor below an assortment of small spaces can be rented out for exhibitions. The top floor contains an audiovisual center. Thirteen structural white steel tubes hold up the building and carry its technical conduits, undulating through the structure like "seaweed." This impression is created by the varying density and angle of the tubes from place to place within the building. The tubes support steel and concrete floor plates, and the whole is enclosed by a very transparent glass and metal skin. Ito describes the whole as a 36 meter high cube in the center of the city, "cut away to expose the volume in cross-section."

Das auf einem 4.000 m² großen Grundstück im Herzen der nordjapanischen Stadt Sendai gelegene, 22.000 m² umfassende Gebäude ist auf allen vier Seiten für die Allgemeinheit zugänglich. Es hat sieben Stockwerke und ist eines der großartigsten neuen Bauwerke, die in den letzten Jahren in Japan entstanden sind. Im Erdgeschoss befinden sich ein Café, eine Buchhandlung und ein 500 m² großer offener Platz, der für besondere Veranstaltungen abgesperrt werden kann. Auf dem zweiten Stock gibt es ein Informationszentrum und auf dem dritten eine öffentliche Bücherei. Im sechsten Stock werden Fachausstellungen präsentiert, während man im darunter liegenden Geschoss eine Auswahl kleiner Räume zu Ausstellungszwecken mieten kann. Im Dachgeschoss ist ein Audiovisionszentrum untergebracht. Das Gebäude und seine technischen Einrichtungen werden von 13 Röhren aus weißem Stahl getragen, die sich wie »Meeresalgen« durch die gesamte Konstruktion winden. Dieser Eindruck entsteht durch die unterschiedliche Dichte und Ausrichtung der Röhren innerhalb des Gebäudes. Dieses Röhrengeflecht trägt die Bodenplatten aus Stahl und Beton, und der gesamte Baukörper ist mit einer transparenten Hülle aus Glas und Metall ummantelt. Toyo Ito beschreibt sein Bauwerk als einen 36 m hohen Kubus im Stadtkern, der aufgeschnitten wurde, um ihn im Querschnitt zu zeigen.

Implanté sur un terrain de 4 000 m² au cœur de la ville septentrionale de Sendaï, ce bâtiment de 22 000 m² sur sept niveaux s'ouvre au public sur ses quatre façades. Il représente l'une des constructions les plus spectaculaires édifiées au cours des années récentes au Japon. Au rez-de-chaussée se trouvent un café, une librairie et un « carré ouvert » de 500 m² qui peut être clos pour des expositions temporaires. Le second niveau est consacré à un centre d'information, le troisième à une bibliothèque en libre service, le cinquième à de petits espaces loués pour des expositions et le septième à un centre audiovisuel. Treize colonnes structurelles cylindriques en acier laqué blanc constituent l'ossature qui soutient les plateaux en acier et béton. Elles dissimulent les conduits techniques, et s'insinuent dans la structure à la manière d'« algues », impression renforcée par leur diamètre et leur inclinaison variables. L'ensemble est recouvert d'une peau très transparente de verre et de métal. Ito voit dans cette médiathèque en plein centre-ville un cube de 36 m de haut « découpé pour exposer son volume en section ».

*In a dense urban environment typical of Japanese cities, the Mediatheque's arborescent structure stands out as an unusually complex, yet calm presence.*

*Durch seine ungewöhnlich komplexe und dennoch ruhige Präsenz hebt sich das verzweigte Gebäude der Mediathek von seinem für japanische Städte typischen dicht besiedelten Umfeld ab.*

*Dans un environnement urbain très dense, typique des villes japonaises, la structure arborescente de la médiathèque affirme sa présence à la fois complexe et sereine.*

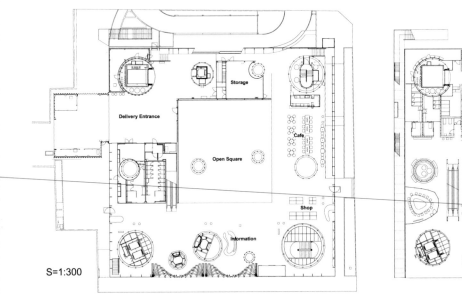

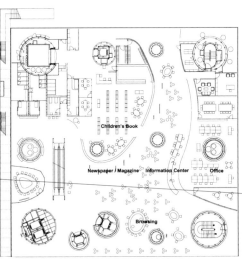

S=1:300

One of the 13 bundled "tube" structures that support the steel-and-concrete floor plates of the building (right). Ross Lovegrove designed furniture in the audiovisual center on the seventh floor. Above, floor plans showing the irregular placement of the tubes.

Eins der 13 Röhrenbündel, die die aus Stahl und Beton bestehenden Bodenplatten des Gebäudes tragen (rechts). Die Möblierung des audiovisuellen Zentrums im 7. Stock wurde von Ross Lovegrove entworfen.

L'une des 13 structures « d'emballage » en tube qui soutiennent les plateaux en béton et acier (à gauche). Ross Lovegrove a conçu le mobilier du centre audiovisuel du septième niveau.

# JAKOB + MACFARLANE

*Jakob + MacFarlane SARL d'Architecture*
*13–15 rue des Petites Écuries*
*75010 Paris*
*France*

*Tel: + 33 1 44 79 05 72*
*Fax: + 33 1 48 00 97 93*
*e-mail: jakmak@club-internet.fr*

**DOMINIQUE JAKOB** received her degree in art history at the Université de Paris 1 (1990) before obtaining her degree in architecture at the École d'Architecture Paris-Villemin (1991). She has taught at the École Spéciale d'Architecture (1998–1999) and the École d'Architecture Paris-Villemin (1994–2000). Born in New Zealand, **BRENDAN MACFARLANE** received his Bachelor of Architecture at SCI-Arc (1984), and his Master of Architecture degree at Harvard, Graduate School of Design (1990). He has taught at the Berlage Institute, Amsterdam (1996), the Bartlett School of Architecture in London (1996–1998) and the École Spéciale d'Architecture in Paris (1998–1999). Their main projects include the T House, La-Garenne-Colombes, France (1994,1998), the Georges Restaurant (Georges Pompidou Center, Paris, France, 1999–2000), and the restructuring of the Maxime Gorki Theater, Le Petit Quevilly, France (1999–2000).

**DOMINIQUE JAKOB**, 1966 in Paris geboren, schloss 1990 ihr Studium der Kunstgeschichte an der Université de Paris I ab und machte 1991 ihren Abschluss in Architektur an der École d'Architecture Paris-Villemin. Von 1998 bis 1999 lehrte sie an der École Spéciale d'Architecture und von 1994 bis 2000 an der École d'Architecture Paris-Villemin. Der in Christ Church in Neuseeland geborene **BRENDAN MACFARLANE** erwarb 1984 seinen Bachelor of Architecture am Southern California Institute of Architecture (SCI-Arc) und 1990 seinen Master of Architecture an der Harvard Graduate School of Design (GSD). Er lehrte am Berlage Institut in Amsterdam (1996), der Bartlett School of Architecture in London (1996–98) und an der École Spéciale d'Architecture in Paris (1998–99). Zu ihren wichtigsten Projekten gehören das T-Haus im französischen La-Garenne-Colombes (1994, 1998), das Restaurant im Pariser Centre Georges Pompidou (1999–2000) und die Neugestaltung des Maxime Gorki Theaters in Le Petit Quevilly in Frankreich (1999–2000).

**DOMINIQUE JAKOB** est diplômée d'histoire de l'art de l'Université de Paris I (1990) et diplômée d'architecture de l'École d'architecture de Paris-Villemin (1991). Elle a enseigné à l'École Spéciale d'Architecture (1988–99) et à l'École d'architecture de Paris-Villemin (1994–2000). Né en Nouvelle-Zélande, **BRENDAN MACFARLANE** est B. Arch. du Southern California Institute of Architecture (1984) et M. Arch. de l'Harvard Graduate School of Design (1990). Il a enseigné à l'Institut Berlage, Amsterdam (1996), à la Bartlett School of Architecture, Londres (1996–98) et à l'École Spéciale d'Architecture de Paris (1998–99). Parmi leurs principaux projets : la Maison T (La Garenne-Colombes, France, 1994–98), le restaurant du Centre Georges Pompidou (1999–2000) et la restructuration du Théâtre Maxime Gorki (Le Petit Quevilly, France, 1999–2000).

# LIBRAIRIE FLORENCE LOEWY

*Paris, France, 2001*

*Area: 45 m². Cost: 26,000 euros for the book shelves.*
*Client: Librairie Florence Loewy Books by Artists.*

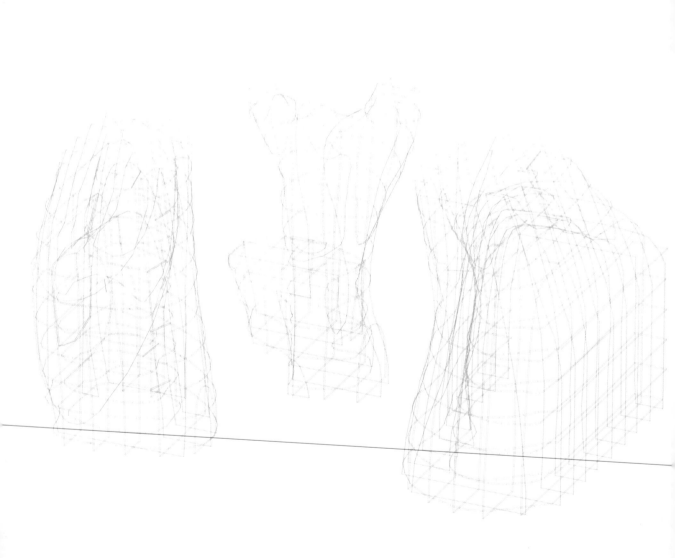

Using sophisticated computer modeling techniques to take on this small project, the architects created irregular wooden display shelves.

Mittels ausgefeilter Computer-Entwurfsprogramme schufen die Architekten für dieses kleinflächige Projekt unregelmäßig geformte Auslageregale aus Holz.

C'est grâce à des techniques sophistiquées de modélisation que les architectes ont créé ces bibliothèques d'exposition.

This **BOOK-SHOP**, located in the Marais district of Paris, is intended largely for books by artists. With an unusual approach, Jakob + MacFarlane said, "Instead of asking ourselves what we could do to display books, it became obvious that we should ask the question in the other sense, if we started with books, could they create the project?" The result of this inquiry was the creation of "one vast solid alveolar block system, filling all of the existing space." Brendan MacFarlane continues, "What results or is left over are three kinds of stacks, or trees of sorts that both become presentation system on the outer side and book storage on the inside." Though the space of the book-shop is small, it is both esthetically interesting and efficient in the presentation of the books.

Diese im Pariser Stadtteil Marais liegende **BUCHHANDLUNG** ist hauptsächlich für den Verkauf von Kunstbüchern bestimmt. Jakob + MacFarlane über ihre ungewöhnliche Herangehensweise: »Statt uns zu fragen, was wir tun könnten, um Bücher zu präsentieren, wurden wir uns darüber klar, dass wir die Frage andersherum stellen sollten: Könnten die Bücher, wenn wir von ihnen ausgingen, das Projekt aus sich selbst hervorbringen?« Das Resultat dieser Fragestellung war die Gestaltung eines »großen, soliden und wabenförmig strukturierten Blocksystems, das den gesamten Verkaufsraum ausfüllt. Daraus entstehen drei Arten von Bücherregalen oder Sortierbäumen, deren Außenseite als Präsentationsfläche und deren Innenseite als Buchlager dienen.« Obgleich der Verkaufsraum der Buchhandlung klein ist, wurde er zu einem sowohl ästhetisch interessanten als auch effizienten Rahmen für die Präsentation von Druckwerken.

Cette **LIBRAIRIE** du quartier du Marais est en grande partie consacrée aux livres d'artistes. Les architectes présentent ainsi leur approche peu classique : « Au lieu de nous demander ce que nous pouvions faire pour présenter des livres, il est devenu de plus en plus évident de nous poser la question à l'envers. Si nous partions des livres, pouvaient-ils créer le projet ? » Le résultat de cette interrogation a été la création d'un « vaste système alvéolaire fixe de blocs remplissant tout l'espace existant ». Brendan MacFarlane poursuit : « Il en résulte, ou il en reste, trois types de présentoirs, sortes d'arbres qui deviennent à la fois le système de présentation des livres vers l'extérieur et un rangement de livres côté intérieur. » Bien que le lieu soit petit, il affiche une esthétique séduisante tout en remplissant ses fonctions avec efficacité.

Located on the street level with almost the entire space visible from the storefront, the shelves are set on a varnished concrete floor. Where possible, the volumes contain interior spaces.

Der im Erdgeschoss liegende Verkaufsraum ist beinahe vollständig von der Straße her einsehbar. Die Regale stehen auf einem gefirnissten Betonboden. Wo möglich, enthalten die Regalelemente Innenräume.

Dans un volume totalement visible de la vitrine, les bibliothèques sont posées sur un sol en béton vernis. Lorsque c'est possible, les volumes intègrent des espaces fonctionnels.

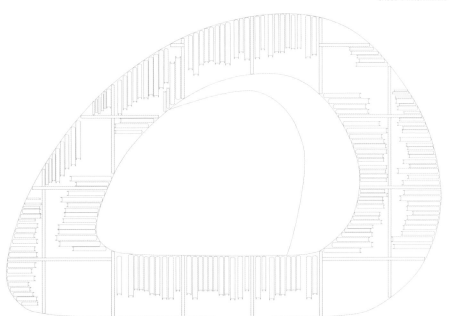

# RENAULT CONFERENCE CENTER

*Boulogne-Billancourt, France, 2002–05*

*Client: Renault/Sicofram. Area: 15,000 m². Cost: 21.2 million euros (2001 estimate).*

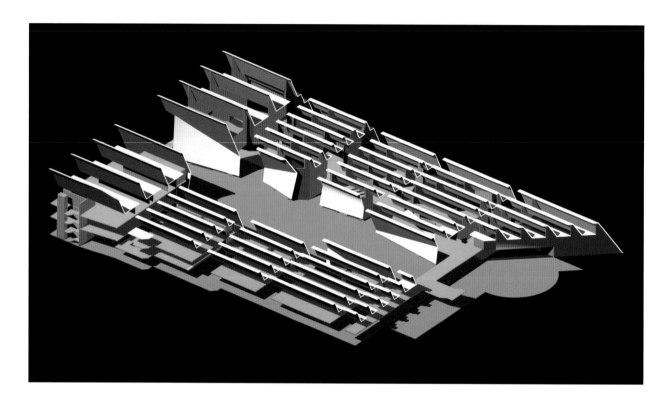

Originally called 57 Métal, this building was built in 1984 by the architect Claude Vasconi as a factory for Renault automobiles. For various reasons, the structure was never used for its original purpose, and the firm decided to organize a competition during the winter of 2000 to renovate it as a place for conventions, receptions and exhibitions, and the public relations of Renault. Designed from the outset as a series of sheds, the 15,000 square meter building will be refurbished by Jakob + MacFarlane with a particular attention to the varied uses planned, ranging from private functions to very large public events. The budget for the project is about 21 million Euros. Since exhibitions and culturally related events are part of the program, this new facility will become part of a newly developed area of Paris to include the Pinault Foundation on the neighboring Ile Seguin (architect: Tadao Ando) and the Hamon Foundation on the Ile Saint Germain (architect: Jean-Michel Wilmotte).

Das ursprünglich 57 Métal genannte Gebäude wurde 1984 von dem Architekten Claude Vasconi als Autofabrik für Renault errichtet, aus verschiedenen Gründen aber nie für diesen Zweck genutzt. Im Winter 2000 entschloss sich das Unternehmen schließlich zur Ausschreibung eines Wettbewerbs, um den Bau für die Unterbringung von Kongress-, Empfangs- und Ausstellungsräumen sowie der PR-Abteilung von Renault umgestalten zu lassen. Der 15.000 m² umfassende Komplex war von Anfang an als Reihe von Hallenbauten konzipiert und wird nun – unter besonderer Berücksichtigung der verschiedenartigen Nutzungspläne, die von privaten Feierlichkeiten zu großen öffentlichen Veranstaltungen reichen – von Jakob + MacFarlane modernisiert. 21 Millionen Euro stehen für dieses Vorhaben zur Verfügung. Mit seinen geplanten Ausstellungen und kulturellen Veranstaltungen wird es zu einem neu erschlossenen Stadtgebiet von Paris gehören, in das auch die Stiftung Pinault auf der benachbarten Île Seguin (Architekt: Tadao Ando) sowie die Stiftung Hamon auf der Île Saint-Germain (Architekt: Jean-Michel Wilmotte) integriert werden sollen.

Appelé à l'origine 57 Métal, ce bâtiment avait été construit en 1984 par l'architecte Claude Vasconi pour servir d'usine. Pour diverses raisons il n'a jamais été utilisé en tant que tel, et Renault a décidé d'organiser à l'hiver 2000 un concours pour en faire un lieu de conventions, de réceptions, d'expositions et son centre de relations publiques. Cette succession de sheds de 15 000 m² sera rénovée par Jakob + MacFarlane pour accueillir les diverses utilisations prévues qui vont de fonctions très privées à de grandes manifestations publiques. Le budget devrait s'élever à 21 millions d'euros environ. Cette partie de la banlieue parisienne en pleine transformation va ainsi bénéficier d'un nouveau lieu d'expositions juste en face de la Fondation Pinault sur l'Île Séguin (architecte : Tadao Ando) et de la Fondation Hamon sur l'Île Saint-Germain (architecte : Jean-Michel Wilmotte).

*Using computer-assisted design Jakob + MacFarlane decompose the vast volume of Renault's 57 Métal building to turn it into a spectacular conference center.*

*Mittels computergestütztem Design verwandeln Jakob + MacFarlane das gewaltige 57 Métal-Gebäude in ein spektakuläres Konferenz- und Veranstaltungszentrum.*

*À l'aide d'un logiciel de CAO, Jakob + MacFarlane ont décomposé le vaste volume du bâtiment 57 Métal pour le transformer en un spectaculaire centre de conférences.*

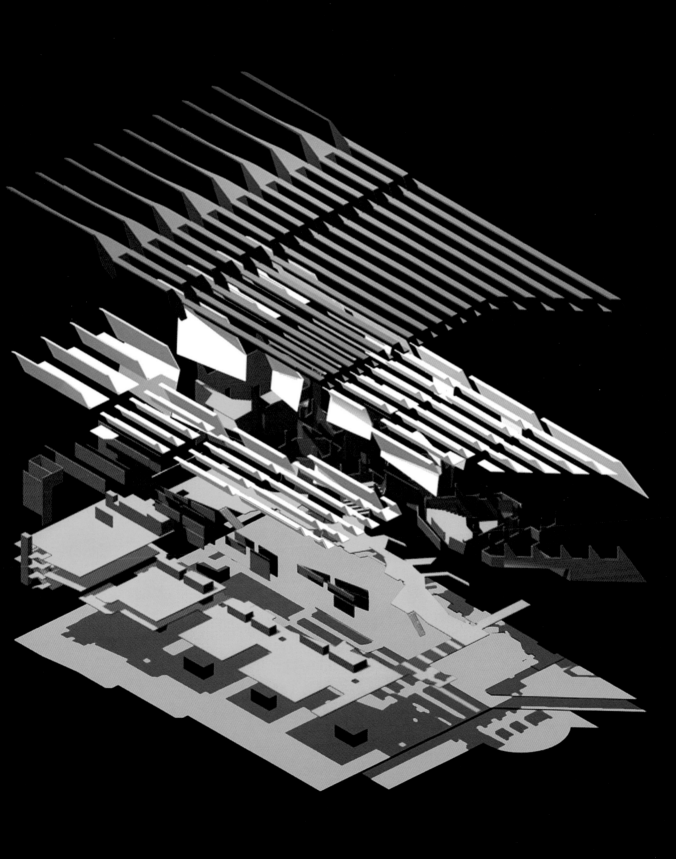

Intent on retaining the vast interior spaces wherever possible, the architects highlight the exceptional nature of the original building and its adaptability to new functions.

Mit der Absicht, die riesigen Innenräume weitgehend zu erhalten, unterstreichen die Architekten den außergewöhnlichen Charakter des Originalgebäudes und heben dessen Eignung für neue Funktionen hervor.

Avec la ferme intention de conserver les immenses espaces intérieurs lorsque c'était possible, les architectes ont souligné la nature exceptionnelle du bâtiment d'origine et son adaptabilité à de nouvelles fonctions.

# MICHAEL JANTZEN

*Michael Jantzen*
*27800 N. McBean Parkway, Suite 319*
*Valencia, California 91354*
*United States*

*Tel: + 1 661 513 9901*
*e-mail: mjantzen@yahoo.com*
*Web: www.humanshelter.org*

In 1971, **MICHAEL JANTZEN** received a Bachelor's degree with a major in fine arts from Southern Illinois University (Edwardsville, Illinois). In 1973, he received an MFA degree with a major in Multi-media from Washington University (St. Louis, Missouri). Jantzen was then hired by Washington University's School of Fine Arts and by the School of Architecture to teach studio courses as a visiting professor. In 1975, one of his first solar houses was featured in numerous national and international magazines. Over the next ten years, he continued to design and build energy-efficient structures with an emphasis on modular high-tech housing systems. In 1997, he was awarded a grant from Art Center College of Design Digital Media Department to develop ideas for an interface between media and architecture. In 1998, Jantzen developed several digital media projects that were published widely. He created a conceptual house called the Malibu Video Beach House, and Elements, an interactive digital media theme park for the next millennium. Early in 1999, he began to design and build the M-House project, a modular, relocatable, environmentally responsive, alternative housing system.

**MICHAEL JANTZEN** erwarb 1971 seinen Bachelor of Fine Arts (BFA) an der Southern Illinois University in Edwardsville, Illinois und 1973 den Master (MFA) im Hauptfach Multimedia an der Washington University in St. Louis, Missouri. Anschließend war Jantzen an der School of Fine Arts und der School of Architecture der Washington University als Gastprofessor tätig. 1975 wurde eins seiner ersten Solarhäuser in etlichen amerikanischen und internationalen Zeitschriften vorgestellt. Während der nächsten zehn Jahre entwarf und gestaltete er Energie sparende Bauten mit dem Schwerpunkt auf modularen Hightech-Wohnbausystemen. 1997 wurde er vom Design Digital Media Department des Art Center College of Design mit einem Stipendium ausgezeichnet, um seine Ideen für ein Interface zwischen elektronischen Medien und Architektur weiterentwickeln zu können. 1998 führte Jantzen mehrere digitale Medienprojekte durch, die große Beachtung fanden. Er entwarf ein Modellhaus namens Malibu Video Beach House sowie einen interaktiven digitalen Medienthemenpark für das neue Jahrtausend namens Elements. Anfang 1999 begann er mit der Planung und Konstruktion des Projekts M-House, bei dem es sich um ein modulares, versetzbares und ökologisch-alternatives Wohnbausystem handelt.

**MICHAEL JANTZEN** est B.A. de la Southern Illinois University (Edwardsville, Illinois) en 1971. En 1973, il est M.A. en Multimédia à Washington University (St. Louis, Missouri) dont il devient immédiatement professeur d'atelier invité par l'École des Beaux-Arts et l'École d'architecture. En 1975, l'une de ses premières maisons solaires est publiée dans de nombreux journaux et magazines internationaux. Au cours des dix années suivantes, il continue à concevoir et réaliser des constructions axées sur les économies d'énergie en étudiant particulièrement des systèmes de logement high-tech modulaires. En 1997, il reçoit une bourse du Art Center College of Design Digital Media Department pour développer ses idées sur une interface médias – architecture. En 1998, il met au point plusieurs projets sur médias numériques amplement publiés. Il a créé une maison conceptuelle, la Malibu Video Beach House, et Elements, un parc thématique en images de synthèse. Dès le début de 1999, il entreprend la conception et la construction de la M-House, un système de logement modulaire, déplaçable et écologique.

# M-HOUSE

*Gorman, California, United States, 2000*

*Area: 90 m². Structure: painted composite concrete panels hinged onto
a steel-tube frame of seven intersecting cubes.*

"It's not just a funny-looking building," says Michael Jantzen, who describes himself more as an artist than an architect. "I'm rethinking the whole notion of living space," he says. What he calls "Relocatable M-vironments" are made of a "wide variety of manipulatable components that can be connected in many different ways to a matrix of modular support frames." He writes that the "**M-HOUSE**, which is made from the M-vironment system, consists of a series of rectangular panels that are attached with hinges to an open space frame grid of seven interlocking cubes. The panels are hinged to the cubes in either a horizontal or a vertical orientation. The hinges allow the panels to fold into, or out of the cube frames to perform various functions." This version of the house was built with nonflammable composite concrete panels hinged to a steel tube frame. Jantzen built this one-bedroom cottage entirely by himself on a site northwest of Los Angeles. The structure is designed to withstand high winds and earthquakes, and can be assembled or disassembled by a crew of four in one week.

»Es ist nicht bloß ein komisch aussehendes Gebäude«, sagt Michael Jantzen, der sich eher als Künstler denn als Architekt sieht, über sein M-House: Vielmehr sei es der Versuch, das Konzept Wohnraum von Grund auf neu zu überdenken. Was der Architekt als »umsiedelbare M-vironments« bezeichnet, besteht aus einer Vielzahl veränderbarer Komponenten, die auf unterschiedliche Weise bausteinartig mit einer Matrix wandelbarer Tragrahmen verbunden werden können. Das aus dem M-vironment-System entstandene **M-HOUSE** besteht aus einer Reihe rechteckiger Paneele, die mittels Scharnieren entweder horizontal oder vertikal an einer offenen Gitterkonstruktion aus sieben ineinander greifenden Kuben befestigt sind. Durch die Scharniere können die einzelnen Paneele in den Rahmen hinein oder aus ihm heraus geklappt werden und auf diese Weise unterschiedliche Funktionen erfüllen. Die hier vorgestellte Ein-Zimmer-Version des Hauses, die der Architekt selbst auf einem Grundstück nordwestlich von Los Angeles aufgebaut hat, wurde aus nichtentflammbaren Verbundbetonplatten und einem Stahlrohrrahmen gefertigt. Dieses Cottage ist so konstruiert, dass es sturmfest und erdbebensicher ist und von einer Gruppe von vier Leuten innerhalb einer Woche auf- oder abgebaut werden kann.

« Ce n'est pas seulement un bâtiment à l'air bizarre », commente Michael Jantzen qui se présente plus comme un artiste qu'un architecte. « Je repense toute la notion d'espace de vie. » Ce qu'il appelle les « Relocatable M-vironments » sont constitués d'une « grande variété de composants manipulables qui peuvent être connectés de multiples façons à une matrice structurelle de soutien modulaire ». « La **M-HOUSE**, qui fait appel au M-vironment System, consiste en série de panneaux rectangulaires attachés par des charnières à une trame structurelle ouverte de sept cubes imbriqués. Les panneaux s'articulent verticalement ou horizontalement sur les cubes par des charnières. Celles-ci permettent aux panneaux de se replier vers l'intérieur ou de s'ouvrir vers l'extérieur pour remplir diverses fonctions. » Cette version de la maison a été construite en panneaux de béton composite non feu articulés à une ossature en tube d'acier. Jantzen a réalisé entièrement lui-même cette maisonnette de deux pièces sur un terrain au nord-ouest de Los Angeles. Elle est conçue pour résister aux vents violents et aux tremblements de terre, et peut être montée ou démontée par quatre personnes en une semaine.

*Although made up here of seven cubes, the structure is infinitely variable and could conceivably be much larger. Its green color, inside and out is intended to "immerse" the resident in the design.*

*Die hier in sieben Kuben ausgeführte Konstruktion ist unendlich variabel und könnte auch sehr viel weiter ausgebaut werden. Die außen und innen angebrachte grüne Farbe soll den Bewohner ganz in das Design hineinziehen.*

*Bien que composée ici de sept cubes, la structure peut varier à l'infini et pourrait être beaucoup plus importante. Sa couleur verte, à l'intérieur comme à l'extérieur, participe à « l'immersion » de l'habitant dans le projet.*

Built-in furniture and a large variety of possible openings make the house both practical and easy to modify.

Einbaumöbel und eine Vielzahl an Öffnungen machen das Haus sowohl praktisch als auch leicht modifizierbar.

Des meubles intégrés et la multiplicité des possibilités d'ouverture rendent la maison à la fois pratique et facile à modifier.

# INTERNET OBSERVATORY

*2001*

*Area: variable. Location: anywhere. Cost: unspecified.*

Michael Jantzen describes this structure as a "kind of a symbolic temple to the computer age, and specifically to the Internet." As he goes on to say, "In this design, the support grid frame represents the matrix of the Internet. The curved space which is contained by the grid, conceptually represents a place where the flow of Internet information is accessed by an individual." Large curved panels are intended to surround the occupant to varying degrees, and conceivably to project images outward. The occupant would be set in an "interactive work station." Jantzen's idea is to create more than one **INTERNET OBSERVATORY**. The Internet Observatory "would have it's own web site, through which people could visit the structure in real time and interact with it in various ways, select images and sounds to be projected, move panels, etc. There could be many of these structures around the world. They could be publicly and or privately owned. The structures could communicate with each other in various ways, as they interact with their occupants." Beyond structures in concrete and steel, designers like Michael Jantzen are pushing the boundaries of architecture outwards, they are expanding its horizons to the realm of the virtual.

Michael Jantzen beschreibt das Observatorium als »eine Art symbolischer Tempel für das Computerzeitalter und speziell für das Internet«. Und er führt weiter aus: »In diesem Entwurf stellt das Gitter des Tragrahmens die Matrix des Internet dar. Der gekrümmte Raum innerhalb des Gitters steht konzeptionell für den Ort, an dem eine Person auf den Informationsfluss des Internet zugreift.« Großflächige gewölbte Wandtafeln in unterschiedlichen Größen sollen den Anwender umgeben und es sollen Bilder nach außen projiziert werden können. Die User würden in einer »interaktiven Workstation« sitzen. Jantzen plant, mehrere **INTERNET OBSERVATORIEN** zu installieren. Jedes hätte seine eigene Website, über die man die Installation in Echtzeit besuchen und auf vielfältige Weise mit ihr interagieren könnte: zum Beispiel indem man sich Bilder und Töne projizieren lässt oder Wandtafeln verschiebt. Die Idee ist, viele solcher Observatorien weltweit zu verteilen, die – in öffentlichem und/oder privatem Besitz – neben der Interaktion mit ihren Anwendern auch miteinander kommunizieren könnten. Gestalter wie Michael Jantzen erweitern die Grenzen von Architektur über Bauten aus Beton und Stahl hinaus bis in den Bereich des Virtuellen.

Michael Jantzen décrit cette structure comme « une sorte de temple symbolique élevé en hommage à l'âge de l'informatique, et spécifiquement à l'Internet ». « Dans ce projet, la trame de soutien représente la matrice de l'Internet. L'espace incurvé qu'elle contient figure conceptuellement un lieu dans lequel un individu peut avoir accès au flux de l'information Internet. » De grands panneaux incurvés entourent l'utilisateur de façons diverses et servent à projeter des images vers l'extérieur. L'occupant se trouve au centre d'un « poste de travail interactif ». L'idée de Jantzen est de créer plusieurs structures de ce type. L'**INTERNET OBSERVATORY** « disposerait de son propre site web, à travers lequel les gens pourraient visiter la structure en temps réel et interagir avec elle de différentes façons, sélectionner les images et les sons à projeter, faire bouger les panneaux, etc. Il pourrait y avoir un grand nombre de ces structures dans le monde. Elles pourraient appartenir à des propriétaires publics ou privés et communiquer entre elles, de même qu'elles communiquent avec leurs occupants. » Au-delà des constructions classiques en verre et en acier, Michael Jantzen et quelques autres déplacent les frontières de l'architecture vers les horizons du virtuel.

*More the fruit of Michael Jantzen's musings as an artist than of a real architectural intention, this Internet Observatory might be reminiscent of H. G. Wells' Time Machine.*

*Eher das Ergebnis von Michael Jantzens künstlerischer Betrachtungen als auf der Basis eines realen architektonischen Plans entstanden, lässt sich das Internet Observatory als eine Referenz an H. G. Wells' Zeitmaschine verstehen.*

*Plus le fruit d'une réflexion de Michael Jantzen que d'intentions architecturales réelles, cet observatoire pourrait évoquer la machine à remonter le temps d'H. G. Wells.*

Like the M-House, the Internet Observatory can either be opened out onto its environment or closed in an almost hermetic way, allowing the visitor to travel in time and space on the Internet.

Ebenso wie das M-House lässt sich das Internet Observatory entweder nach außen öffnen oder fast hermetisch verschließen, was den Besuchern ermöglicht, Reisen in Zeit und Raum durch das Internet zu unternehmen.

Comme la M-House, l'Internet Observatory peut soit s'ouvrir sur son environnement soit se fermer de manière quasi hermétique. Il permet au visiteur de voyager via Internet dans le temps et l'espace.

# JONES, PARTNERS

*Jones, Partners: Architecture*
*141 Nevada Street*
*El Segundo, California 90245*
*United States*

*Tel: + 1 310 414 0761*
*Fax: + 1 310 414 0765*
*e-mail: info@jonespartners.com*
*Web: www.jonespartners.com*

**WES JONES**, born in 1958 in Santa Monica, attended the United States Military Academy at West Point, the University of California at Berkeley (B.A.), and the Harvard Graduate School of Design, where he received a Masters of Architecture Degree. A recipient of the Rome Prize in Architecture, he has served as a visiting Professor at Harvard, Rice, Tulane and Columbia Universities. He worked with Eisenman/Robertson, Architects in New York before becoming Director of Design at Holt & Hinshaw in San Francisco. As Partner in Charge of Design at Holt Hinshaw Pfau and Jones, he completed the Astronauts' Memorial at Kennedy Space Center in Florida and the South Campus Chiller Plant for UCLA. Recent projects include the Brill, Stieglitz, Arias-Tsang, and San Clemente residences, Union Square: Golden Plate, San Francisco, and offices for Andersen Consulting in Kuala Lumpur.

**WES JONES**, 1958 in Santa Monica geboren, studierte an der United States Military Academy in West Point, der University of California in Berkeley (B.A.-Abschluss) und an der Harvard Graduate School of Design (GSD), wo er den Master of Architecture erwarb. Er erhielt den Prix de Rome in Architektur und war als Gastprofessor an den Universitäten Harvard, Rice, Tulane und Columbia tätig. Wes Jones arbeitete im New Yorker Büro Eisenman/Robertson, Architects, bevor er Director of Design bei Holt & Hinshaw in San Francisco wurde. Als Partner und Konstruktionsleiter der Architekturfirma Holt Hinshaw Pfau and Jones führte er das Astronauts' Memorial am Kennedy Space Center in Florida und die Anlage South Campus Chiller Plant für die University of California in Los Angeles (UCLA) aus. Zu seinen jüngsten Bauten gehören die Wohnhäuser Brill, Stieglitz, Arias-Tsang und San Clemente, Union Square: Golden Plate in San Francisco und ein Bürogebäude für Andersen Consulting in Kuala Lumpur, Malaysia.

**WES JONES**, né en 1958 à Santa Monica, étudie à l'école militaire de West Point, à l'Université de Californie à Berkeley (B.A.) et à l'Harvard Graduate School of Design dont il est M. Arch. Titulaire du prix de Rome d'architecture, il a été professeur invité à Harvard, Rice, Tulane et Columbia. Il a travaillé avec Eisenman/Robertson, Architects à New York avant de devenir directeur de la conception chez Holt & Hinshaw à San Francisco. Associé en charge de la conception pour Holt Hinshaw Pfau and Jones, il réalise le Mémorial des astronautes au Kennedy Space Center de Floride, et l'unité de réfrigération du campus sud de UCLA. Parmi ses projets récents : les maisons Brill, Stieglitz, Arias-Tsang et San Clemente, Union Square/Golden Plate à San Francisco et des bureaux pour Andersen Consulting à Kuala Lumpur.

# QUEBRADILLAS HOUSE
## *Quebradillas, Puerto Rico, 2001–2002*

*Client: Eric and Nanette Brill. Structure: cast-in-place reinforced concrete bearing walls and flat slab on concrete footings.
Site area: 1.5 hectares. Area: 190 m².*

Set on a 1.5 hectare site on a volcanic cliff overlooking the sea on the northern coast of Puerto Rico, this house for a couple and their three children is specifically designed to resist frequent hurricane force winds. The house is approached from the roof side. The architect says that the house is to be seen to a certain extent "as an outpost" and as such has "two adjustable wing-mounted, horizontal-axis wind turbine assemblies projecting from the upper deck" to take advantage of the nearly constant wind from the north. Rainwater is stored in cisterns beneath the living spaces and vents provide for natural ventilation. Emphasizing the fortified aspect of the house, the lower walkways and decks "are hinged to rotate up and act as storm shutters, protecting the glazing as well as locking the house up tight." To be made mostly with cast-in-place concrete, the house will have sealed or waxed concrete, local veneer plywoods, stainless steel and plaster for the interior finishes. The floor area of the house is just under 200 square meters.

Das für eine Familie mit drei Kindern gebaute Wohnhaus mit Meerblick liegt an der Nordküste von Puerto Rico auf einem 1,5 ha großen Grundstück am Abhang eines Vulkans. Das Gebäude wurde so konstruiert, dass es den häufig auftretenden Hurrikans standhält; der Zugang liegt auf der Hangseite. Das Haus sei eine Art »Vorposten«, so der Architekt, und habe zwei verstellbare, über das Dach auskragende, flügelartige Windräder mit horizontaler Kippachse, um den fast unablässig von Norden her wehenden Wind zu nutzen. Unterhalb der Wohnräume befinden sich Regenwasserspeicher, Abzugsöffnungen sorgen für eine natürliche Be- und Entlüftung. Die unteren Durchgänge und Dachteile haben eine Kippvorrichtung und lassen sich nach oben drehen, um als Windschutz zu fungieren, was den festungsartigen Charakter des Hauses optisch noch verstärkt und sowohl die Verglasungen schützt als auch das Haus fest verschließt. Der Bau ist hauptsächlich aus vor Ort gegossenem Beton gefertigt. Die Innenräume sind mit versiegeltem oder gewachstem Beton, Furnierplatten aus einheimischem Holz, rostfreiem Stahl und Gipsverputz ausgestattet. Der Grundriss des Hauses umfasst knapp 200 m² Nutzfläche.

Implantée sur un terrain de 1,5 hectare en bordure d'une falaise volcanique qui domine l'océan sur la côte nord de Puerto Rico, cette maison destinée à un couple et ses trois enfants a été conçue pour résister aux ouragans. On y accède par le toit. L'architecte explique qu'elle doit être considérée dans une certaine mesure comme un « avant-poste ». Elle possède « deux turbines éoliennes à axe horizontal montées en ailes réglables qui se projettent du pont supérieur » pour tirer parti du vent qui souffle en permanence du nord. L'eau de pluie est conservée dans des citernes puis la maison et le vent assure la ventilation naturelle. Mettant en valeur l'aspect fortifié de la maison, les ponts et coursives de la partie inférieure « sont articulés pour se refermer et servir de volet de protection en cas de tempête, protéger les baies vitrées et l'étanchéité de la maison ». La maison devrait être essentiellement réalisée en béton coulé sur place, béton lissé ou ciré, contre-plaqués d'origine locale, acier inoxydable et plâtre pour les finitions intérieures. Sa surface totale ne dépassera pas 200 m².

*Located on a cliff, the low-lying house is meant to "break" the force of hurricane winds by facing the ocean at a low angle. This is also the reason that its roof is at the level of the adjacent ground.*

*Das an einem Abhang liegende Haus ist im flachen Winkel zum Ozean hin ausgerichtet, um die Wucht der Hurrikane zu brechen. Aus demselben Grund wurde das Dach nicht über den Hang hinausgebaut.*

*Implantée sur une falaise, cette maison basse veut « briser » la force des vents des ouragans par sa position surbaissée face à l'océan. C'est la raison pour laquelle le toit se trouve au niveau du sol.*

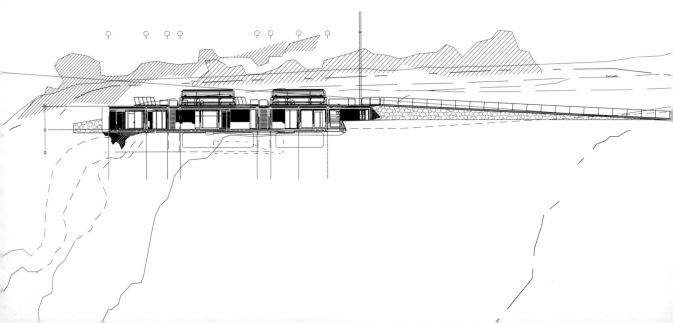

The house is approached from the uphill side, with the visitor coming down toward the roof of the structure. The roof-deck also serves as a platform to observe the ocean.

Der Zugang zum Haus erfolgt von der Hangseite, von wo der Besucher auf das tief liegende Dach zugeht. Die Dachterrasse selbst dient auch als Aussichtsplattform.

Le visiteur accède à la maison par le haut de la colline, et descend donc vers le toit. Celui-ci, qui fait office de terrasse, permet l'observation de l'océan.

P 278.279

As the architect says, "The view is presented directly: as if in deference to its power, the house itself is very simple and straightforward, a linked series of alcoves off the organizing horizon."

Der Architekt über seinen Entwurf: »Der Ausblick präsentiert sich un- mittelbar: Wie in Rücksicht auf seine kraftvolle Wirkung ist das Haus selbst sehr einfach strukturiert – in einer horizontal ausgerichteten Reihe von Nischen.«

Pour l'architecte : « La vue est direc-
te, comme si, par déférence envers
son pouvoir, la maison elle-même se
faisait simple et sans détour, série
d'alcôves reliées entre elles, face à
l'horizon qui lui donne son sens. »

# RICK JOY

*Rick Joy*
*400 South Rubio Ave.*
*Tucson, Arizona 85701*
*United States*

*Tel: + 1 520 624 1442*
*Fax: + 1 520 791 0699*
*e-mail: studio@rickjoy.com*
*Web: www.rickjoy.com*

*Tyler Residence*

**RICK JOY**'s first working experience was not as an architect, but as a musician and a carpenter in Maine. He obtained his degree in architecture in 1990 and spent three years in the office of Will Bruder, working on the design team for the Phoenix Central Library. He then set up his own practice in Tucson. Joy received in 1993 the Young Architects Award from *Progressive Architecture* magazine; the 1994 AIA Honor Award for Arizona Home of the Year; The Architectural League of New York Young Architects Forum Award in 1996; a 1997 *Architectural Record* magazine Record Houses Award; *I. D.* Magazine Award for Environments in both 1997 and 2000; The Architectural League of New York Emerging Voices 2000 Award; the 2000 AIA Honor Award for Arizona Home of the Year, and a high commendation of the AR+D Emerging Architecture Awards program in London. "Bold, modern architecture that is rooted in the context and culture of its place," says Rick Joy, "and that is developed in combination with the basics of proper solar orientation and site protection, and the responsible use of sensible materials and fine craftsmanship, will have the quality to withstand the tests of time."

**RICK JOY** machte seine ersten Berufserfahrungen nicht als Architekt, sondern als Musiker und Zimmermann in Maine. Nachdem er 1990 sein Architekturstudium abgeschlossen hatte, verbrachte er drei Jahre im Büro von Will Bruder, wo er im Planungsteam für die Phoenix Central Library arbeitete. Danach machte er sich mit einem eigenen Büro in Tucson selbständig. Rick Joy erhielt etliche Preise und Auszeichnungen: 1993 den Young Architects Award der Zeitschrift *Progressive Architecture*, 1994 den AIA Honor Award for Arizona Home of the Year, 1996 den Architectural League of New York Young Architects Forum Award, 1997 den Record Houses Award der Zeitschrift *Architectural Record*, 1997 und 2000 den Award for Environments der Zeitschrift *I. D.*, 2000 den Emerging Voices Award der Architectural League of New York, 2000 nochmals den Honor Award for Arizona Home of the Year der AIA sowie eine lobende Erwähnung des AR+D Emerging Architecture Awards Program in London. Rick Joy über die Ziele seiner Arbeit: »Eine kühne, moderne Architektur, die einerseits im Kontext und in der Kultur ihres Standorts verwurzelt ist und sich andererseits auszeichnet durch eine Kombination von optimaler Nutzung der Sonnenenergie, Standortschutz sowie dem verantwortungsvollen Einsatz ökologisch sinnvoller Materialien und der Handwerkskunst, wird immer eine zeitlose Qualität haben.«

**RICK JOY** débute professionnellement comme musicien et charpentier dans le Maine. Diplômé d'architecture en 1990, il passe trois années dans l'agence de Will Bruder où il travaille dans l'équipe projet de la Phoenix Central Library, avant de créer sa propre agence à Tucson. En 1993, il reçoit le Young Architects Award du magazine *Progressive Architecture*; en 1994, le AIA Honor Award pour la maison de l'année en Arizona; en 1996, le Young Architects Forum Award de l'Architectural League of New York; en 1997 le Record Houses Award du magazine *Architectural Record*; en 1997 et 2000, le prix de l'environnement du magazine I. D.; en 2000, l'Emerging Voices Award de l'Architectural League of New York; en 2000 le AIA Honor Award pour la maison de l'année en Arizona. «Une architecture moderne et audacieuse enracinée dans le contexte et la culture du lieu,» commente Rick Joy, «et qui se développe en combinaison avec les fondamentaux de l'orientation solaire et de la protection du site ainsi qu'avec l'usage responsable de matériaux sensibles et un travail d'exécution soigné, résistera au test du temps.»

# TYLER RESIDENCE

*Tubac, Arizona, United States, 1999–2000*

Clients: Warren and Rose Tyler. Area: 230 m² (main house), 140 m² (guest house).
Materials: weathered steel, polished black concrete floors, pale maple, sandblasted glass, stainless steel.

The entrance side of the house seen at nightfall. The use of weathered steel for the exterior cladding gives the geometric forms an appearance not unlike that of some contemporary sculptures.

Die Eingangsseite des Hauses bei Einbruch der Dunkelheit. Der verwitterte Stahl der Außenverkleidung gibt den geometrischen Formen eine gewisse Ähnlichkeit mit modernen Skulpturen.

La façade d'entrée de la maison à la tombée de la nuit. L'habillage externe en acier patiné donne aux formes géométriques un aspect qui n'est pas étranger à celui de certaines sculptures contemporaines.

Set in the Sonoran Desert with views toward the Tumacacori, Santa Rita and San Cayetano mountains, this house is divided into a 240 square meter main structure containing a master bedroom, living, dining and cooking areas as well as two studies, and a 150 square meter guest house, with two bedrooms, a workshop and a garage. The architect chose to give the house a low profile in rapport with the 1.5 hectare site located about twenty kilometers north of the Mexican border. Using a naturally weathered steel for the exterior cladding, the architect placed the openings of the house in specific locations to profit from pre-determined views. In this aspect of the house, both client and architect were influenced by houses in Majorca designed by Jørn Utzon. Polished black concrete floors, pale maple, sand-blasted glass, stainless and matte-gray steel are used for the interiors, completing a Modernist design. Will Bruder, with whom Rick Joy worked for three years, says of his work that it is "of the ages and of our time, reinterpreting simple elements with materials that are responsive to their place."

Das Wohnhaus liegt in der Sonora-Wüste mit Blick auf die Tumacacori, Santa Rita und San Cayetano Berge und setzt sich aus zwei Gebäudeteilen zusammen. Das Haupthaus mit Schlaf-, Wohn- und Essbereich sowie zwei Arbeitsräumen hat 240 m², das Gästehaus mit zwei Zimmern, einem Atelier und einer Garage ist 150 m² groß. Um das circa 20 km nördlich der Grenze zu Mexiko gelegene Gebäude mit dem 1,5 ha großen Grundstück in eine harmonische Beziehung zur Landschaft zu setzen, entschloss sich der Architekt zu einem Flachbau. Für die Fassadenverkleidung wählte Joy einen natürlich verwitterten Stahl und ordnete die Fensteröffnungen des Hauses so an, dass vorher festgelegte Ausblicke optimal zur Geltung kommen. In diesem Gestaltungsaspekt ließen sich sowohl Auftraggeber wie auch Architekt von Wohnhäusern inspirieren, die Jørn Utzon auf Mallorca entworfen hatte. Das modernistische Design wird in den Innenräumen von schwarz geschliffenen Betonböden, hellem Ahornholz, sandgestrahltem Glas, rostfreiem und mattgrauem Stahl ergänzt. Will Bruder, mit dem Rick Joy drei Jahre lang zusammengearbeitet hat, sagt über diese Arbeit, sie sei in ihrer Neuinterpretation schlichter Elemente mit Materialien, die zu ihrer Umgebung in Bezug stehen, ebenso zeitlos wie aktuell.

Implantée dans le désert de Sonora et donnant sur les montagnes de Tumacacori, Santa Rita et San Cayetano, cette maison est divisée en une structure principale de 240 m² contenant la chambre principale, le séjour, les zones de cuisine et de repas, deux bureaux et une maison d'amis de 150 m² à deux chambres, atelier et garage. L'architecte a choisi de donner à l'ensemble habillé d'un acier naturellement vieilli un profil bas adapté au terrain de 1,5 hectare situé à 20 km environ de la frontière mexicaine. Il a disposé les ouvertures de façon à cadrer des vues déterminées. À cet égard, le client et son architecte se sont inspirés des maisons dessinées par Jørn Utzon pour Majorque. Sols en béton noir poli, boiseries d'érable clair, verres sablés, acier inoxydable et acier gris mat sont utilisés à l'intérieur dans un esprit moderniste. Will Bruder, avec lequel Rick Joy a travaillé pendant trois ans, a pu dire de cette maison qu'il s'agissait « [d'une maison] de notre âge, de notre temps, réinterprétant des éléments simples par des matériaux qui répondent au lieu. »

*A shed-like covering used to shade the kitchen, opens toward the southwest where the swimming pool has a spectacular view of the mountains. Above, cast concrete planters in the inner courtyard.*

*Ein hallenartiger Vorbau beschattet die Küche und öffnet sich nach Südwesten, wo man vom Swimmingpool aus eine fantastische Aussicht auf die Berge hat (rechts). Die Pflanztöpfe im Innenhof sind aus Gussbeton (oben).*

*Un toit en sheds abrite la cuisine et s'ouvre vers le sud-ouest et la piscine qui dispose d'une vue spectaculaire sur les montagnes. En haut, les jardinières en béton armé de la cour intérieure.*

# REI KAWAKUBO

*Comme des Garçons*
*5-11-5 Minami Aoyama*
*Minato-ku*
*Tokyo 107*
*Japan*

*Tel: + 81 3 3407 2684*
*Fax: + 81 3 5485 2439*

**REI KAWAKUBO** created the Comme des Garçons label in 1969 and established Comme des Garçons Co. Ltd in Tokyo in 1973. She opened her Paris boutique in 1982, and one in New York two years later. Although she is of course best known as a fashion designer, she has long had an interest in furniture and architecture. Rei Kawakubo introduced the Comme des Garçons furniture line in 1983. The flagship store in Aoyama, Tokyo, which she recently redesigned with the help of Takao Kawasaki (interior designer), Future Systems (architect/facade), Christian Astuguevieille (art director/interior) and Sophie Smallhorn (artist/interior), was first opened in 1989. Rei Kawakubo received an Honorary Doctorate from the Royal College of Art, London, in 1997. The New York boutique, also published here, was designed by Rei Kawakubo with Takao Kawasaki as well as Future Systems.

**REI KAWAKUBO** schuf 1969 das Modelabel Comme des Garçons und gründete 1973 die Firma Comme des Garçons Co. Ltd. in Tokio. 1982 eröffnete sie ihre Boutique in Paris, der zwei Jahre später eine Filiale in New York folgte. Obwohl sie vor allem als Modedesignerin bekannt ist, hat sie seit langem ein großes Interesse an Inneneinrichtung und Architektur. 1983 brachte sie ihre erste Kollektion von Comme des Garçons-Möbeln heraus. 1989 eröffnete sie ihren Flagship Store in Aoyama, Tokio, den sie vor kurzem in Zusammenarbeit mit Takao Kawasaki (Inneneinrichtung), Future Systems (Fassade), Christian Astuguevieille (Artdirector/Interieur) und Sophie Smallhorn (Künstlerin/Interieur) neu gestaltete. 1997 wurde ihr vom Royal College of Art in London die Ehrendoktorwürde verliehen. Ihre im New Yorker Viertel Chelsea gelegene Boutique wurde von Rei Kawakubo zusammen mit Takao Kawasaki und Future Systems entworfen.

**REI KAWAKUBO** a créé la marque Comme des Garçons en 1969 et fondé Comme des Garçons Co. Ltd à Tokyo en 1973. Elle a ouvert sa boutique parisienne en 1982, et celle de New York en 1984. Bien que surtout connue comme styliste de mode, elle s'intéresse depuis longtemps au design de mobilier et à l'architecture. Elle a lancé une ligne de meubles Comme des Garçons en 1983. Son magasin principal d'Aoyama, Tokyo, qu'elle a récemment rénové en collaboration avec Takao Kawasaki (architecte d'intérieur), Future Systems (architecture, façade), Christian Astuguevieille (directeur artistique, aménagements intérieurs) et Sophie Smallhorn (artiste, aménagements intérieurs) avait été inauguré en 1989. Elle est docteur honoris causa du Royal College of Arts de Londres (1997). Sa boutique new-yorkaise a été conçue par elle-même en collaboration avec Takao Kawasaki et Future Systems.

# COMME DES GARÇONS BOUTIQUE

*Paris, France, 2000–2001*

*Client: Comme des Garçons. Location: 54, rue du Faubourg Saint-Honoré.*
*Design: Ab Rogers, Shona Kitchen (KRD), Red Wave, Takao Kawasaki + Architectures Associés, Christian Astuguevieille.*

Located in an interior courtyard at 54, rue du Faubourg Saint-Honoré in Paris, the **COMME DES GARÇONS BOUTIQUE** in Paris is in part the work of the same team Rei Kawakubo recently assembled for her Tokyo and New York shops: the architect Takao Kawasaki and Architectures Associés, teamed with the furniture designer Christian Astuguevieille (for the "Elephant Table"). But whereas the British group Future Systems was responsible for key elements in the other two cases, in Paris Ab Rogers, the son of Richard Rogers and Shona Kitchen his partner at KRD, were called on here to create the so-called "pavilion," a space free of clothes for people to "hang out in." Although from the exterior, the visitor hardly expects anything very unusual since the original facades were preserved, within, almost everything about the boutique is red – from the long acrylic counter to the fiberglass walls designed by Red Wave, an English design duo. Kawakubo in one of her rare quoted remarks says, "Red is as strong as black. And red looks most beautiful in fiberglass. Making a shop is like making clothes: You need to excite and energize people. There has to be the same shock and sense of surprise."

Die im Innenhof eines Hauses in der Rue du Faubourg Saint-Honoré gelegene **COMME DES GARÇONS BOUTIQUE** ist teilweise mit demselben Team entstanden, das Rei Kawakubo kürzlich für ihre Geschäfte in Tokio und in New York zusammengestellt hat: Takao Kawasaki und Architectures Associés als Architekten und Christian Astuguevieille als Möbeldesigner (»Elefantentisch«). Aber während in den anderen beiden Projekten die britische Architektengruppe Future Systems für bauliche Schlüsselelemente wie die Fassadengestaltung verantwortlich war, wurden für die Pariser Niederlassung Ab Rogers, der Sohn von Richard Rogers, und Shona Kitchen, seine Partnerin bei KRD, mit der Ausführung des so genannten »Pavillon« beauftragt. Er stellt keine Modeartikel aus, sondern bietet den Kunden die Gelegenheit zur Entspannung. Obgleich die Außenfassade, deren ursprüngliches Aussehen beibehalten wurde, kaum auf ein besonders ungewöhnliches Interieur schließen lässt, präsentiert sich der Innenraum der Boutique fast gänzlich in Rot – von der lang gestreckten Verkaufstheke aus Acryl bis zu den von Red Wave, einem englischen Designerduo, entworfenen Glasfaserwänden. Wie Kawakubo in einem ihrer seltenen Interviews sagt: »Rot ist ebenso stark wie Schwarz. Und am schönsten wirkt es in Glasfaser. Ein Geschäft zu gestalten ist wie Kleider zu entwerfen: Man muss die Leute in Spannung und Energie versetzen. Es muss ein ebensolcher Schock- und Überraschungsmoment sein.«

Installée dans une cour intérieure 54, rue du Faubourg Saint-Honoré, la **BOUTIQUE COMME DES GARÇONS** est en partie l'œuvre de l'équipe que Rei Kawakubo avait déjà réunie pour ses magasins de Tokyo et de New York : l'architecte Takao Kawasaki, Architectures Associés, et le designer de meubles Christian Astuguevieille (pour la « Elephant Table »). Mais alors que le groupe britannique Future Systems avait signé les principaux éléments des deux points de vente précédents, c'est Ab Rogers, fils de Richard Rogers et son associée Shona Kitchen de KRD qui ont créé à Paris le « pavillon », un espace sans vêtement offert aux visiteurs pour flâner « dedans/dehors ». Si le passant ne peut être surpris par l'extérieur – la façade d'origine a été préservée – l'intérieur est lui intégralement rouge, des longs comptoirs d'acrylique aux murs en fibre de verre conçus par Red Wave, duo de designers anglais. Kawabuko, dans un de ses rares commentaires, a précisé : « Le rouge est aussi fort que le noir. Et le rouge est splendide en fibre de verre. Faire un magasin, c'est comme faire des vêtements. Vous avez besoin d'exciter le visiteur, de donner de l'énergie. Il y faut le même choc, le même sens de la surprise. »

Inserted into an otherwise unremarkable interior courtyard just opposite the Élysée Palace, the Comme des Garçons boutique has a red fiberglass skin that leads on to white-painted walls by the English design duo, Red Wave.

Die in einen eher unauffälligen Innenhof gegenüber dem Élysée-Palast eingefügte Comme des Garçons Boutique wurde von dem englischen Designerduo Red Wave mit einer Hülle aus roten Glasfasern und einzelnen weiß gestrichenen Wänden ausgestattet.

Insérée dans une cour intérieure sans intérêt particulier, face au palais de l'Élysée, la boutique Comme des Garçons est revêtue d'une peau en fibre de verre rouge plaquée sur ses murs blancs par un duo de designers anglais, Red Wave.

The slick red surfaces dominate the interiors, offering a relatively limited exhibition area to the clothes (below), but this kind of unexpected ratio is typical of the boutiques of Rei Kawakubo.

Das Interieur wird von glatten roten Oberflächen beherrscht, wodurch sich für die Modeartikel eine relativ begrenzte Präsentationsfläche ergibt. Diese ungewöhnliche Aufteilung ist jedoch typisch für die Boutiquen von Rei Kawakubo.

Les surfaces rouges et lisses dominent l'aspect intérieur et ne laissent qu'une surface assez réduite aux vêtements (en bas), ratio inattendu mais typique des boutiques de Rei Kawakubo.

Relatively unlike her recent Tokyo and New York boutiques (designed with the assistance of Future Systems for the facades), the Paris shop nonetheless is a strong statement of Kawakubo's own merchandising theories, which have to do with an artistic presence throughout the process from clothing design to sales.

Auch wenn sich die Pariser Boutique ziemlich von den Niederlassungen in Tokio und New York unterscheidet (dort war die Architektengruppe Future Systems für die Fassadengestaltung verantwortlich), ist sie doch ein überzeugendes Beispiel für Rei Kawakubos Marketingkonzept, das den künstlerischen Aspekt der Entstehung von Mode vom Entwurf bis zum Verkauf herausstreicht.

Relativement différent de ses récentes boutiques de New York et de Tokyo (conçues avec l'assistance de Future Systems pour les façades), le magasin de Paris n'en est pas moins une puissante illustration des théories de Kawakubo sur le merchandising, axées sur une forte implication artistique de la conception des vêtements à leur vente.

# WARO KISHI

*Waro Kishi + K. Associates/Architects*
*3F Yamashita Bldg. 10 Nishimotomachi*
*Koyama, Kita-ku*
*Kyoto 6038113*
*Japan*

*Tel: + 81 75 492 5175*
*Fax: + 81 75 492 5185*
*e-mail: warox@ja2.so net.ne.jp*

*House in Kurakuen*

Born in Yokohama in 1950, **WARO KISHI** graduated from the Department of Electronics of Kyoto University in 1973, and from the Department of Architecture of the same institution two years later. He completed his post-graduate studies in Kyoto in 1978, and worked in the office of Masayuki Kurokawa in Tokyo from 1978 to 1981. He created Waro Kishi + K. Associates/Architects in Kyoto in 1993. He completed the Autolab automobile showroom in Kyoto in 1989; Kyoto-Kagaku Research Institute, Kizu-cho, Kyoto in 1990; Yunokabashi Bridge, Ashikita-cho, Kumamoto, 1991; Sonobe SD Office, Sonobe-cho, Funai-gun, Kyoto, 1993; as well as numerous private houses. Recent work includes his Memorial Hall, Ube, Yamaguchi, 1997; and a house in Higashi-nada, Kobe, 1997, and a house in Suzaku (Nara, Japan, 1997–1998).

**WARO KISHI**, geboren 1950 in Yokohama, studierte bis 1973 Elektrotechnik an der Universität Kioto und ebendort bis 1975 Architektur. 1978 schloss er sein Graduiertenstudium an der Universität Kioto ab und arbeitete danach bis 1981 im Büro von Masayuki Kurokawa in Tokio. 1993 gründete Kishi seine eigene Firma, Waro Kishi + K. Associates/Architects in Kioto. Zu Waro Kishis in Japan realisierten Entwürfen zählen der Automobilsalon Autolab in Kioto (1989), das Forschungsinstitut Kioto-Kagaku in Kizu-cho, Kioto (1990), die Yunokabashi-Brücke in Ashikita-cho, Kumamoto (1991), das Bürogebäude Sonobe SD in Sonobe-cho, Funai-gun, Kioto (1993) sowie zahlreiche Wohnhäuser. Zu seinen jüngsten Werken zählen die Memorial Hall in Ube, Yamaguchi (1997), sowie ein Wohnhaus in Higashi-nada, Kobe (1997), und eines in Suzaku, Nara (1997–98).

Né à Yokohama en 1950, **WARO KISHI** est diplômé du Département d'électronique de l'Université de Kyoto en 1973 et du Département d'architecture de la même institution en 1975. Il poursuit des études de spécialisation à Kyoto de 1978 à 1981, puis fonde Waro Kishi + K. Associates/Architects à Kyoto en 1993. Au Japon, il a réalisé, entre autres, le hall d'exposition automobile Autolab (Kyoto, 1989) ; l'Institut de Recherches Kyoto-Kagaku (Kizu-cho, Kyoto, 1990) ; le pont Yunokabashi (Ashikita-cho, Kumamoto, 1991) ; les bureaux de Sonobe SD (Sonobe-cho, Funai-gun, Kyoto, 1993) et de nombreuses résidences privées. Parmi ses récents chantiers : un mémorial (Ube, Yamaguchi, 1997) et une maison à Suzaku (Nara, Japon, 1997–98).

# HOUSE IN KURAKUEN II

*Nishinomiya, Hyogo, Japan, 2000–2001*

*Client: Sogo Jisho Co. Ltd. Site area: 618 m². Building area: 242 m².*
*Floor area: 268 m². Structure: steel frame.*

This 268 square meter house (floor area) was designed in 1996–1997 and built beginning in March 2000. It is a two-story steel frame and reinforced concrete house set on a 618 square meter site. It is located in a sloping residential area facing the sea. There is a view from the house of the suburbs of Osaka and the Bay. Of this exceptional site, Waro Kishi says, "I created two blocks of floating steel reinforced structure. On the left is the private room zone, while on the right are the public living and dining room areas, and both are joined by a sloping ramp. The roof of the topmost floor on the left side individual room block is made to appear as thin as possible," he concludes. The architect chose to frame the view with smaller openings in the living and dining area, while offering a wider, horizontal vista from the private spaces. The metal cladding and dramatic volumes of this house, together with its exceptional site, make it one of Waro Kishi's most exceptional buildings.

Das Wohnhaus mit einer Nutzfläche von 268 m² wurde von 1996–97 geplant und ab März 2000 gebaut. Der zweistöckige Bau aus Stahlrahmen und Stahlbeton wurde auf einem 618 m² großen Grundstück errichtet, das in einer zum Meer hin abfallenden Wohngegend liegt. Vom Haus aus überblickt man die Vororte von Osaka und die Bucht. Waro Kishi über seinen außergewöhnlichen Entwurf: »Ich konstruierte zwei Blöcke mit Stahlarmierung. Im linken liegen die Privaträume, während sich im rechten die öffentlichen Bereiche mit Wohn- und Esszimmer befinden. Beide Gebäudeteile sind durch eine Schrägrampe miteinander verbunden. Das Dach auf dem obersten Geschoss des linken Blocks ist so gestaltet, dass es so dünn wie möglich erscheint.« Während der Architekt den Ausblick im Wohn- und Essbereich durch kleinere Fensteröffnungen begrenzte, gewährte er in den Privaträumen einen weiten Rundblick. Die Metallverkleidung, die interessante Gestaltung der beiden Baukörper und die herausragende Lage machen das Haus zu einem von Waro Kishis außergewöhnlichsten Bauwerken.

Le chantier de cette maison de 268 m² sur deux niveaux conçue en 1996–97 a débuté en mars 2000. Élevée sur un terrain incliné de 618 m² face à la mer, elle est en béton armé sur ossature en acier. Elle donne d'un côté sur la banlieue d'Osaka et la baie. Waro Kishi décrit ainsi son projet : » J'ai créé deux blocs de structure flottante en acier renforcé. À gauche, se trouve la zone privative, et à droite celle du séjour et des repas, reliées par une rampe en pente. Le toit du niveau supérieur au-dessus de la chambre de gauche est réalisé de manière à paraître aussi mince que possible. « L'architecte a cadré la vue par de petites ouvertures dans les zones de séjour et des repas, mais offre une vision élargie et horizontale dans les espaces plus privés. Le bardage en métal et les spectaculaires volumes de cette maison, ainsi que son site exceptionnel, en font une des réalisations les plus remarquables de Waro Kishi.

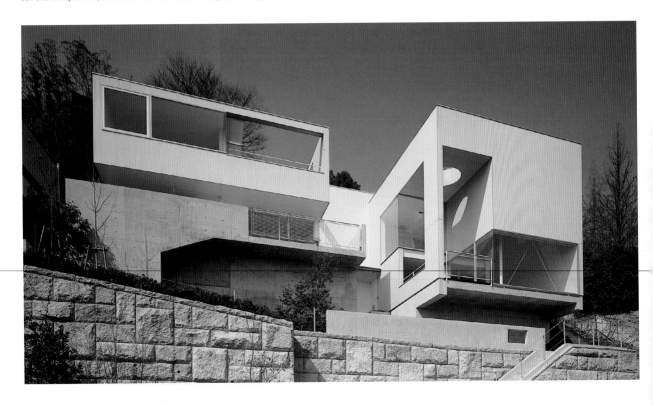

This house is divided into two blocks with a floating steel reinforced structure. On the right in this image (above and right page) the living-dining zone, and on the left the bedroom area.

Das Haus ist in zwei Blöcke aufgeteilt, die aus einer Schwebekonstruktion mit Stahlarmierung bestehen. Wohn- und Essbereich (oben und rechte Seite) sowie Schlafzimmer (oben links).

La maison est divisée en deux blocs à l'intérieur d'une ossature flottante renforcée en acier ; à droite dans cette même image (en haut et page de droite) la zone séjour-repas, et à gauche, la chambre.

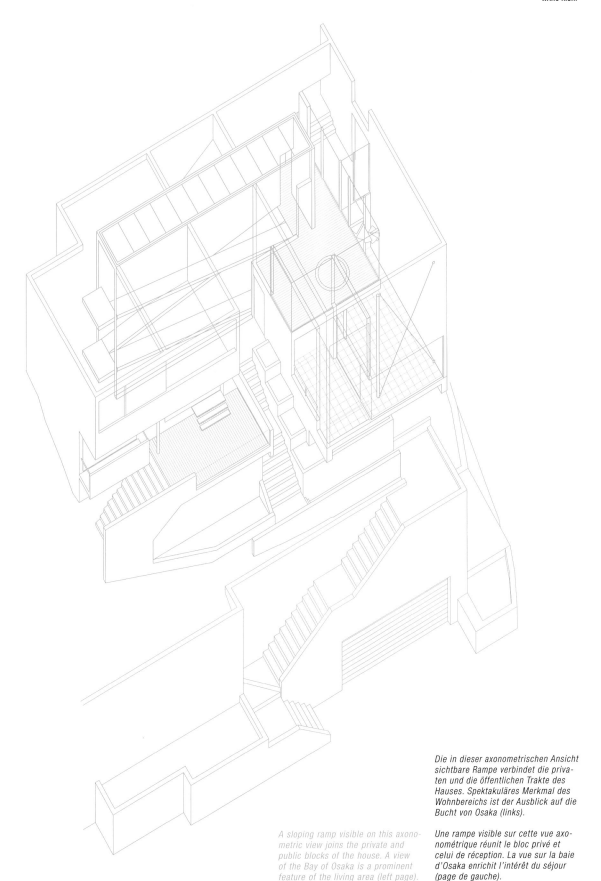

*A sloping ramp visible on this axonometric view joins the private and public blocks of the house. A view of the Bay of Osaka is a prominent feature of the living area (left page).*

*Die in dieser axonometrischen Ansicht sichtbare Rampe verbindet die privaten und die öffentlichen Trakte des Hauses. Spektakuläres Merkmal des Wohnbereichs ist der Ausblick auf die Bucht von Osaka (links).*

*Une rampe visible sur cette vue axonométrique réunit le bloc privé et celui de réception. La vue sur la baie d'Osaka enrichit l'intérêt du séjour (page de gauche).*

The architect's use of opacity and transparency, or heaviness versus lightness is illustrated in these images. Above the ramp connecting the public and private zones.

Kishi wechselt opake und transparente Elemente ab und setzt Kontraste aus Schwere und Leichtigkeit. Die Rampe verbindet öffentliche und private Bereiche (oben).

L'alternance d'opacité et de transparence, ou de poids et de légèreté, se manifeste avec évidence. En haut, la rampe qui connecte les zones privées et de réception de la maison.

# HOUSE IN FUKAYA

*Fukaya, Saitama, Japan, 2000–2001*

*Site area: 343 m². Building area: 172 m². Floor area: 189 m².*
*Structure: steel frame. Materials: galvanized spandrel panel, plaster.*

Designed beginning in August 1999, this steel frame house is set on a 343 square meter site. The building area is 172 square meters and the total floor area is 189 square meters. Located near Tokyo, the site is surrounded by "monotonous, semi-urban" areas. As the architect says, "For this location I proposed a house having a closed attitude towards its surroundings and an interior court." This style is typical of Japanese contemporary architecture in dense urban environments. The plan is rectangular, measuring 9.6 meters on the East-West axis and 23.4 meters in the North-South direction. The southern area of the house contains the garage and bedrooms on two levels, while the northern part, with a 4.5-meter high ceiling, contains the living and dining spaces. A court with a pool separates or connects the northern and southern parts. Waro Kishi chose to use "factory materials and leave visible the stark structural details." "The way to confront the stark surroundings, I felt," says Kishi, "was by presenting not a space replete with the warmth of congenial materials, but rather an aggressive deployment of materials and structures that proliferate in the surroundings."

Das Wohnhaus, mit dessen Planung im August 1999 begonnen wurde, liegt auf einem 343 m² großen Grundstück. Es handelt sich um einen Stahlskelettbau mit einer bebauten Fläche von 172 m² und einer Nutzfläche von 189 m². Der Baugrund liegt in einem monotonen Vorstadtgebiet von Tokio. »Für diese Lage entwarf ich ein Haus mit einem Innenhof, das sich gegenüber seiner Umgebung verschließt«, erklärt der Architekt sein Konzept. Ein Stil, der typisch ist für die zeitgenössische japanische Architektur in dicht besiedelten Stadtgebieten. Der rechtwinklige Grundriss misst 9,6 m in ost-westlicher und 23,4 m in nord-südlicher Richtung. Der südliche Gebäudeteil enthält die Garage und auf zwei Ebenen aufgeteilte Schlafzimmer, während im nördlichen Trakt die 4,5 m hohen Wohn- und Essbereiche angeordnet sind. Zwischen beiden Teilen liegt der mit einem Pool ausgestattete Innenhof. Waro Kishi verwendete industriell gefertigte Materialien und ließ die funktionalen baulichen Details unverkleidet. Kishi dazu: »Ich hatte das Gefühl, man sollte dem vollkommen nüchternen Umfeld nicht mit einem Raum gegenübertreten, der mit warmen Materialien ausgestattet ist, sondern vielmehr mit einem dynamischen Einsatz von Baustoffe und Strukturen, die sich in der Umgebung fortsetzen.«

Conçue en août 1999, cette maison à ossature d'acier s'élève sur un terrain de 343 m² dans les quartiers « monotones, semi-urbains » de la banlieue de Tokyo. Le bâti occupe 172 m² au sol pour une surface totale de 189 m². Comme le note l'architecte : « J'ai proposé pour ce lieu une maison qui se ferme vis-à-vis de son environnement et une cour intérieure. » Ce style est typique de l'architecture japonaise contemporaine en environnement urbain dense. Le plan rectangulaire mesure 9,6 m de long sur l'axe est-ouest et 23,4 m sur l'axe nord-sud. La partie sud de la maison contient le garage et les chambres sur deux niveaux, la partie nord – au plafond de 4,5 m de haut – contient les espaces de séjour et de repas. Une cour occupée par un bassin sépare/relie les deux sections. Waro Kishi a choisi « d'utiliser des matériaux d'usine et de laisser visibles les détails structurels. J'ai pensé que la façon de se confronter à cet environnement brutal était non pas de montrer un espace débordant rendu chaleureux par ses matériaux conviviaux, mais plutôt de déployer avec agressivité les matériaux et structures qui prolifèrent dans les environs. »

*As is frequently the case in Japanese houses, this residence is rather closed on the exterior and open toward the interior. The central pool is however quite unusual in Japan.*

*Wie häufig bei japanischen Häusern der Fall, ist auch dieses nach außen geschlossen und nach innen offen angelegt. Ungewöhnlich für Japan ist jedoch der zentrale Swimmingpool.*

*Comme souvent dans les maisons japonaises, cette résidence est assez fermée vers l'extérieur et ouverte sur l'intérieur. Le principe d'un bassin central est assez rare au Japon.*

Despite its apparently closed exterior nature, the house is filled with light from the central court. The architect chose to "use factory materials and leave visible the stark structural details."

Trotz seines scheinbar geschlossenen Äußeren wird das Haus vom Innenhof her mit Licht erfüllt. Der Architekt entschloss sich hier, industriell gefertigte Baumaterialien zu verwenden und die funktionalen baulichen Details sichtbar zu lassen.

Bien qu'elle soit de nature assez fermée sur l'extérieur, la maison est baignée de lumière grâce à sa cour centrale. L'architecte a choisi « d'utiliser des matériaux d'usine et de laisser visibles les détails structurels bruts. »

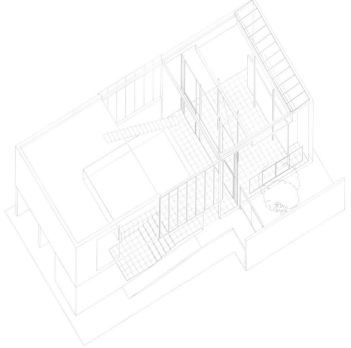

# KOHN SHNIER ARCHITECTS

*Kohn Shnier Architects*
*110 Spadina Avenue, Suite 900*
*Toronto M5V 2K4*
*Canada*

*Tel: + 1 416 504 7508*
*Fax: + 1 416 504 7509*
*e-mail: studio@ksarc.com*
*Web: www.kohnshnierarchitects.com*

*Umbra World Headquarters*

**MARTIN KOHN** and **JOHN SHNIER** opened their office in 1990. Their collaborative work first gained public recognition with their prize-winning entry for the Kitchener City Hall Competition in 1989. The office was awarded the commission to design the new Shore & Moffat Library and The Eric Arthur Gallery at the University of Toronto Faculty of Architecture, Landscape and Design. Kohn Shnier was chosen as design architects, collaborating with Shore Tilbe Irwin Architects on the renovation of the E. J. Pratt Library at Victoria University in Toronto. Most recently, the office has been selected to undertake renovations and additions to the 519 Church Street Community Centre and a new facility for the Claude Watson School for the Arts, both in Toronto. John Shnier is an associate Professor of Design at the University of Toronto Faculty of Architecture, Landscape and Design.

**MARTIN KOHN** und **JOHN SHNIER** gründeten 1990 ihr Architekturbüro. Erste öffentliche Anerkennung fand ihre gemeinsame Arbeit 1989 mit dem preisgekrönten Entwurf für den Kitchener City Hall Wettbewerb. In der Folgezeit erhielt ihr Büro den Auftrag für den Bau der neuen Shore & Moffat Bibliothek und der Eric Arthur Gallery der Fakultät für Architektur, Landschaft und Gestaltung an der Universität Toronto sowie für die Renovierung der E. J. Pratt Bibliothek der Victoria University in Toronto, die in Zusammenarbeit mit Shore Tilbe Irwin Architects ausgeführt wurde. Zu ihren jüngsten Projekten gehören die Modernisierung und Erweiterung des 519 Church Street Community Centre (Gemeindezentrum) sowie ein neues Gebäude für die Claude Watson School for the Arts, beide in Toronto. John Shnier ist außerordentlicher Professor für Gestaltung an der Universität Toronto.

**MARTIN KOHN** et **JOHN SHNIER** ont ouvert leur agence en 1990. Le premier travail en collaboration qui leur a apporté la notoriété est leur participation primée au concours pour le Kitchener City Hall en 1989. L'agence a remporté la commande de la nouvelle Shore & Moffat Library et The Eric Arthur Gallery à la faculté d'architecture, de paysage et de design de l'Université de Toronto. Kohn et Shnier ont été choisis, en collaboration avec Shore Tilbe Irwin Architects pour rénover la E. J. Pratt Library de l'Université Victoria de Toronto. Plus récemment, leur agence a été sélectionnée pour la rénovation et l'extension du 519 Church Street Community Centre et de nouvelles installations pour la Claude Watson School for the Arts, à Toronto. John Shnier est professeur associé de design à l'Université de Toronto.

# UMBRA WORLD HEADQUARTERS

*Toronto, Canada, 1998–1999*

*Client: Les Mandelbaum, Paul Rowan, David Quan. Area: 14 000 m².*
*Cladding: copolyester plastic shaped by resin molds.*

Umbra is a Canadian firm specialized in stylish home furnishings, including the famous "Garbo" garbage can by designer Karim Rashid. In a way it was the success of this ubiquitous object that inspired the architectural solutions set out by Kohn Shnier – turning a basically "ugly and banal" concrete structure into the glamorous symbol of a very trendy company. Set in the east Toronto suburb of Scarborough, the **UMBRA HEADQUARTERS** is located near an eight land highway. The architects simply wrapped the concrete Umbra warehouse building in green plastic. This wrapping is described as "decorative," and was made with identical vacuum-formed modules of copolyester plastic shaped by a resin mold. A heavy steel frame screen wall is thus covered by a light system of pretensioned rods that carry the plastic panels, cantilevered out beyond the underlying standard ten thousand meter concrete structure. This device gives the whole a "designer" feel that is congruous with the image of Umbra while remaining in a very reasonable price range.

Umbra World ist eine kanadische Firma, die sich auf Designermöbel und Einrichtungsgegenstände spezialisiert hat. Hier entstand zum Beispiel die berühmte »Garbo«-Mülltonne des Designers Karim Rashid und in gewisser Weise hat der Erfolg eben dieses Gebrauchsartikels die architektonische Gestaltung von Kohn Shnier inspiriert. So wurde ein im Grunde »hässlicher und banaler« Betonbau in das glanzvolle Symbol eines sehr trendigen Unternehmens verwandelt. Die neue **UMBRA-ZENTRALE** liegt in Scarborough, einem östlichen Vorort von Toronto, nahe einer achtspurigen Autobahn. Die Architekten »verpackten« das Betonlagerhaus einfach mit grünem Kunststoff. Diese dekorative Hülle wurde aus gleichgroßen, in Harzmasse vakuumgeformten Modulen aus grünem Copolyester gefertigt. Sie verdeckt eine massive Schutzmauer aus Stahlrahmen mit einer leichten Konstruktion aus vorgespannten Stabelementen. An diesen Stäben, die über den ursprünglichen, 10.000 m² großen Betonbau hinausragen, sind die Kunststoffplatten befestigt. Ein Kunstgriff, der dem Ganzen einen Designer-Look gibt, ausgezeichnet zum Image von Umbra passt und gleichzeitig die Kosten für den Umbau im Rahmen hielt.

Umbra est une entreprise canadienne spécialisée dans la production de mobilier sophistiqué, dont la fameuse poubelle « Garbo » du designer Karim Rashid. D'une certaine façon, le succès de cet objet très diffusé a inspiré les solutions architecturales mises en œuvre par Kohn Shnier pour transformer une construction de béton « laide et banale » de 10 000 m² en symbole plein de *glamour* d'une société très à la mode. Installé à Scarborough dans la banlieue est de Toronto, le **SIÈGE D'UMBRA** se trouve en bordure d'une autoroute à huit voies. Les architectes ont simplement enveloppé l'entrepôt de plastique vert. Cet emballage décrit comme » décoratif« est réalisé en modules de copolyester formés sous vide dans un moule de résine, tous identiques. Un mur écran lourd à ossature d'acier est recouvert d'un système léger de câbles prétensionnés qui soutiennent les panneaux de plastique, en avancée par rapport au bâtiment de béton. Ce procédé donne à l'ensemble un style « design » en accord avec l'image d'Umbra tout en restant dans une gamme de prix raisonnables.

*The original, unattractive concrete structure is transformed by the addition of a vacuum-formed plastic skin. Acting like a translucid screen around the older building, the skin glows in the dark when the structure is lit.*

*Das ursprünglich unansehnliche Betongebäude wurde durch eine vakuumgeformte Kunststoffhülle verändert. Am Abend geht von der transparenten Hülle um das Gebäude, die wie eine Außenhaut wirkt, ein Leuchten aus.*

*La structure d'origine, peu séduisante, a été transformée par l'addition d'une peau de plastique formée sous vide. Fonctionnant comme un écran translucide autour de l'ancienne construction, la peau irradie lorsque le bâtiment est éclairé pendant la nuit.*

# REM KOOLHAAS

*Office for Metropolitan Architecture*
*Stedebouw BV*
*149 Bokelweg Heer*
*Rotterdam 3032 AD*
*Netherlands*

*Tel: + 31 10 24 38 200*
*Fax: + 31 10 24 38 202*

**REM KOOLHAAS** was born in The Hague in 1944. Before studying at the Architectural Association in London, he tried his hand as a journalist for the Haagse Post and as a screenwriter. He founded the Office for Metropolitan Architecture in London in 1975, and became well known after the 1978 publication of his book *Delirious New York*. His built work includes a group of apartments at Nexus World, Fukuoka (1991) and the Villa dall'Ava, Saint-Cloud (1985–1991). He was named head architect of the Euralille project in Lille in 1988, and has worked on a design for the new Jussieu University Library in Paris. His 1400 page book *S,M,L,XL* (TASCHEN, 1998) has more than fulfilled his promise as an influential writer. Recent work includes a house, Bordeaux, France, movie studios in California and the campus center at the Illinois Institute of Technology, as well as the Guggenheim Las Vegas published here and the recent Prada boutique in the Soho area of New York.

**REM KOOLHAAS**, geboren 1944 in Den Haag, arbeitete vor seinem Studium an der Architectural Association (AA) in London als Journalist bei der *Haagse Post* und als Drehbuchautor. 1975 gründete er in London das Office for Metropolitan Architecture (OMA) und wurde mit seinem 1978 erschienenen Buch *Delirious New York* weithin bekannt. Zu seinen Bauten gehören Wohnungen in Nexus World im japanischen Fukuoka (1991) und die Villa dall'Ava im französischen Saint-Cloud (1985–91). 1988 wurde ihm die Leitung des Euralille-Projekts in Lille übertragen; außerdem arbeitete er an einem Entwurf für die neue Bibliothek der Universität Jussieu in Paris. Mit seinem 1400 Seiten starken Buch *S,M,L,XL* (TASCHEN, 1998) hat er sein Versprechen als einflussreicher Autor mehr als eingelöst. Zu seinen neueren Projekten gehören ein Wohnhaus in Bordeaux, Filmstudios in Kalifornien, das Campus-Zentrum des Illinois Institute of Technology in Chicago sowie die hier vorgestellte Guggenheim-Dependance in Las Vegas und die neue Prada-Boutique im New Yorker Viertel Soho.

**REM KOOLHAAS** naît à La Haye en 1944. Avant d'étudier à l'Architectural Association de Londres, il s'essaye au journalisme pour le *Haagse Post* et à l'écriture de scénarii. Il fonde l'Office for Metropolitan Architecture à Londres en 1975 et devient très connu après la publication en 1978 de son ouvrage *Delirious New York*. Parmi ses réalisations : un ensemble d'appartements à Nexus Next World (Fukuoka, Japon, 1991) ; la Villa dall'Ava (Saint-Cloud, France, 1985–91). Il est nommé architecte en chef du projet Euralille à Lille en 1988 et propose un projet de bibliothèque pour la Faculté de Jussieu à Paris. Son livre de 1400 pages *S,M,L,XL* (TASCHEN, 1998) confirme son influence et son impact de théoricien. Parmi ses réalisations récentes, une maison à Bordeaux, des studios de cinéma en Californie et le Campus Center de l'Illinois Institute of Technology, le Guggenheim Las Vegas présenté ici, et tout récemment, la boutique Prada à Soho, New York.

# GUGGENHEIM LAS VEGAS

*Las Vegas, Nevada, United States, 1999–2001*

*Cost: $30 million (estimate).*
*Area: 710 m² (Guggenheim Hermitage), 5,900 m² (Guggenheim Las Vegas).*

This extravagant project is the latest "folly" of Thomas Krens, the Director of the Guggenheim. Naturally, after the success of the Guggenheim Bilbao, designed by Frank O. Gehry, public tolerance of the innovations of Mr. Krens had reached a high before the attacks of September 11, 2001. The climate of hesitation that ensued made the gamble of the **GUGGENHEIM LAS VEGAS** somewhat less of an obvious success. Ever conscious of the "star quality" of the architects he employs, Krens called on the very fashionable Rem Koolhaas to insert not one but two museum spaces into the heart of a Las Vegas casino, The Venetian. The hotel is nothing less than an imitation of Venice, complete with Saint Mark's tower and the Rialto Bridge. Taking on the image of commercial and gambling excess incarnated by The Venetian, Koolhaas designed the Guggenheim Hermitage with Corten steel walls and the larger Guggenheim Las Vegas in a less restrictive mode to receive large exhibitions like "The Art of the Motorcycle," with its decor designed by Frank O. Gehry. Krens has been one of the few very visible museum figures to bet in a big way on the drawing power of "star" architects. Be it Gehry, Koolhaas, Jean Nouvel, or Zaha Hadid, the architectural profession has benefited from the interest of Thomas Krens in architecture.

Das extravagante Projekt ist der neueste »verrückte Einfall« von Thomas Krens, dem Direktor des Guggenheim Museums. Nach dem Erfolg von Frank O. Gehrys Guggenheim Museum in Bilbao hatte die öffentliche Akzeptanz für Thomas Krens' Innovationen ihren Höhepunkt erreicht. Die Terroranschläge des 11. September 2001 und die darauf folgende Verunsicherung ließen das Wagnis, das mit dem **GUGGENHEIM LAS VEGAS** eingegangen worden war, allerdings etwas weniger erfolgreich ausfallen. Wie stets auf die »Star-Qualität« der von ihm beschäftigten Architekten bedacht, beauftragte Krens den sehr in Mode gekommenen Rem Koolhaas, gleich zwei Museen in das Hotelcasino The Venetian zu integrieren. Das Gebäude, das tatsächlich Elemente der Lagunenstadt inklusive Markusplatz und Rialto-Brücke imitiert, ließ Koolhaas das Image von Kommerz und Glücksspiel aufnehmen. So wählte er für das Guggenheim Hermitage Museum eine Innenraumgestaltung aus Stahlwänden. Das größere Museum Guggenheim Las Vegas, das für umfangreiche Ausstellungen wie die von Gehry eingerichtete »The Art of the Motorcycle« gedacht ist, entwarf er dagegen in einem weniger restriktiven Stil. Krens ist einer der wenigen namhaften Museumsverantwortlichen, der in hohem Maß auf die Anziehungskraft berühmter Architekten setzt. Ob nun Gehry, Koolhaas, Jean Nouvel oder Zaha Hadid die Ausführenden waren, der Berufsstand der Architekten hat ganz allgemein von Thomas Krens' Interesse an der Baukunst enorm profitiert.

Ce projet extravagant est la dernière « folie » de Thomas Krens, le directeur du Guggenheim. Le succès remporté par Krens avec le Guggenheim Bilbao lui avait attiré la faveur enthousiaste du public avant les événements du 11 septembre 2001. Le climat actuel fait du projet d'un **GUGGENHEIM LAS VEGAS** un pari plus difficile. Toujours très conscient de la « qualité de star » des architectes qu'il emploie, Krens a fait appel à Rem Koolhaas, tellement à la mode, pour insérer non pas un mais deux musées dans un casino de Vegas, The Venetian. Cet hôtel est tout simplement une reconstitution de Venise, campanile de Saint-Marc et Rialto compris. Relevant le défi des excès commerciaux incarnés par le Venitian, Koolhaas a conçu un Guggenheim Hermitage à murs en acier Corten et un Guggenheim Las Vegas, plus vaste, de style plus ouvert, pour accueillir de grandes expositions comme « L'art de la moto » et sa mise en scène signée Frank O. Gehry. Thomas Krens est l'un des rares responsables de musée connu à tabler à ce point sur le pouvoir d'attraction des « architectes stars ». Que ce soit Gehry, Koolhaas, Nouvel ou Zaha Hadid, toute la profession architecturale a bénéficié de son intérêt pour l'architecture.

*Above, the Guggenheim Las Vegas is located within the Venetian Resort-Hotel-Casino with its fake Doge's Palace and grand entrance (above). To the right, the installation, by Frank O. Gehry, of the inaugural "The Art of the Motorcycle" exhibition.*

*Das Guggenheim Las Vegas befindet sich im Hotelcasino The Venetian, das mit einer Imitation des Dogenpalastes und einem imposanten Eingang aufwartet (oben). Die von Frank O. Gehry für die Eröffnungsausstellung »The Art of Motorcycle« entworfene Architektur (rechts).*

*En haut, le Guggenheim Las Vegas est situé à l'intérieur du Venitian Resort-Hotel-Casino doté d'un faux palais des Doges et d'une entrée palatiale. À droite, l'installation de l'exposition inaugurale « L'Art de la moto » signée Frank O. Gehry.*

Left and above, within the Guggenheim Hermitage, with its unexpected exhibition walls made of Corten steel, the inaugural exhibition of Modern Masterpieces by such artists as Delaunay or Kandinsky.

Links und oben, die Innenräume der Guggenheim Hermitage mit ihren ungewöhnlichen Stahlwänden; die Eröffnungsausstellung mit Meisterwerken von Künstlern wie Delaunay und Kandinsky.

À gauche et en haute, l'intérieur du Guggenheim Hermitage aux curieux murs d'exposition en acier Corten ; l'exposition d'inauguration avec des chefs-d'œuvre d'artistes comme Delaunay ou Kandinsky.

The Guggenheim Las Vegas space again photographed at the time of the Frank O. Gehry "Motorcycle" exhibition in late 2001. The dynamic interplay of the shed-like space designed by Koolhaas and Gehry's undulating metal surfaces made the presentation of the show a work of art in itself.

Der Ausstellungsraum im Guggenheim Las Vegas, aufgenommen während der »Motorcycle«-Ausstellung Ende 2001. Das dynamische Zusammenspiel von Koolhaas' hallenähnlichem Raum und Gehrys geschwungenen Metallbändern machten aus der Präsentation eine Kunst für sich.

L'espace du Guggenheim Las Vegas photographié lors de l'exposition « Moto » de Frank O. Gehry, fin 2001. Le jeu dynamique de l'espace en forme de shed conçu par Koolhaas et les plans métalliques ondulés de Gehry faisaient de cette mise en scène une œuvre d'art en soi.

# PRADA BOUTIQUE
*New York, New York, United States, 1999–2001*

*Client: Prada. Cost: $40 million. Amphitheater capacity: 200 seats.*

*Koolhaas has made the two levels of the Prada shop (street level + basement) into a continuous whole, so that part of the descent slope is an amphitheater.*

*Koolhaas verband Erdgeschoss und Untergeschoss der Prada Boutique zu einer Einheit, indem er einen Teil der Schräge als eine Art Amphitheater gestaltete.*

*Koolhaas a transformé les deux niveaux de la boutique Prada (rez-de-chaussée + sous-sol) en un continuum, et profité de la pente pour créer une sorte d'amphithéâtre.*

The co-author (with his students from the GSD) of new magnum opus, *The Harvard Design School Guide to Shopping*, Rem Koolhaas has willingly allowed an ambiguity to arise about his own attitude to commercially inspired architecture. Seeking at once to enter the surprisingly vital retail sector with projects such as the new **PRADA BOUTIQUE** in New York, and to question the proliferation of what he calls "junk space," the Dutch architect appears to want to "have his cake and eat it too." Be that as it may, Prada, located on the corner of Broadway and Prince Street in the Soho area of Manhattan, is a highly visible work. Located in the former space of the Guggenheim Soho (originally designed by Arata Isozaki), the shop runs on two levels. As he often has, Koolhaas employs industrial materials such as the metal grating "cages" that serve to present the chic wares. Cleverly turning a sweeping curve leading from the ground floor to the lower level into a ready-made theater and/or shoe sales space, Koolhaas proves his mastery of volumes and materials. At the juncture between retail sales and architecture, between commerce and art, between fashion and serious design, Koolhaas defines a unique place for himself as an arbiter of taste. With the museum boom waning, it may be that fashion boutiques will be the new place for "star" architects to express their talents.

Rem Koolhaas, dessen neues, zusammen mit seinen Studenten von der Harvard Graduate School of Design (GSD) verfasstes Opus *The Harvard Design School Guide to Shopping* heißt, hat zugelassen, dass über seine Haltung gegenüber kommerzieller Architektur eine gewisse Ambiguität entstand. Während er bestrebt ist, den überraschend vitalen Einzelhandelssektor mit Projekten wie der neuen **PRADA BOUTIQUE** in New York für sich zu erobern, kritisiert er gleichzeitig die zunehmende Verbreitung dessen, was er »Junk-Bauten« nennt. Aber trotz dieser scheinbaren Widersprüchlichkeit ist die an der Ecke von Broadway und Prince Street im New Yorker Stadtteil Soho gelegene Prada-Niederlassung eine herausragende Arbeit. Das Geschäft, in dessen ursprünglich von Arata Isozaki entworfenen Räumen vorher das Guggenheim Soho untergebracht war, ist auf zwei Ebenen angelegt. Wie schon so oft hat Koolhaas auch hier industrielle Materialen verwendet, zum Beispiel die »Käfige« aus Metallgitter, in denen die edlen Modeartikel präsentiert werden. Raffiniert führt Koolhaas eine schwungvolle Bogenlinie vom Erdgeschoss zum Untergeschoss und verwandelt sie in eine halbkreisförmig ansteigende Bühne für Konfektionsbekleidung und/oder Schuhe. So beweist er sein Können im Umgang mit Baukörper und Material. An der Grenze zwischen Geschäft und Architektur, zwischen Kommerz und Kunst, zwischen Mode und ernsthaftem Design nimmt Koolhaas eine einzigartige Position als Schiedsrichter in Fragen des Geschmacks ein. Mit dem Abflauen des Museumsbooms kann es durchaus sein, dass Modeboutiquen eine neue Möglichkeit für »Stararchitekten« werden, ihr Talent zum Ausdruck zu bringen.

Auteur, avec ses étudiants, d'un nouveau grand œuvre *The Harvard Design School Guide to Shopping*, Rem Koolhaas laisse volontairement une certaine ambiguïté se développer sur son attitude envers l'architecture d'inspiration commerciale. Cherchant à la fois à pénétrer le secteur de la vente de détail – d'une vitalité étonnante – à travers des projets comme la **BOUTIQUE PRADA** et à mettre en cause la prolifération de ce qu'il appelle les « junk space », espaces-poubelles, l'architecte néerlandais semble courir deux lièvres à la fois. Prada, à l'angle de Broadway et de Prince Street dans le quartier de Soho à Manhattan, n'en est pas moins une réalisation très remarquable. Installé dans l'ancien Guggenheim Soho (conçu à l'origine par Arata Isozaki), le magasin s'étend sur deux niveaux. Comme souvent, Koolhaas emploie des matériaux industriels dont des « cages » en treillis métallique qui servent à présenter les vêtements tellement chics. Transformant avec intelligence la rampe incurvée qui mène du rez-de-chaussée au sous-sol en une sorte de théâtre ready-made ou d'espace de vente pour les chaussures, il prouve sa maîtrise des volumes et des matériaux. A la jonction entre espace de vente et architecture, entre commerce et art, mode et design sérieux, Koolhaas se crée au passage un espace personnel d'arbitre du goût. La vague de construction de musées étant terminée, il se peut que les boutiques de mode soient le nouvel espace d'expression qu'attendent les « stars » de l'architecture.

The Prada designs are often placed in contrast with elements of the architecture such as the track-mounted steel cages where clothes can be displayed.

*Die Modedesigns von Prada kontrastieren mit architektonischen Elementen wie den auf Schienen montierten Stahlkäfigen, die Kleidungsstücke präsentieren.*

*Les modèles de Prada sont placés en contraste avec des éléments d'architecture comme les cages d'acier de présentation des vêtements, accrochées à des rails suspendus.*

# KENGO KUMA

*Kengo Kuma & Associates*
*2-12-12 – 9F Minami Aoyama*
*Minato-ku*
*Tokyo 107-0062*
*Japan*

*Tel: + 81 3 3401 7721*
*Fax: + 81 3 3401 7778*
*e-mail: sugai@kkaa.co.jp*
*Web: www02.so-net.ne.jp/~kuma/*

Born in 1954 in Kanagawa, Japan, **KENGO KUMA** graduated in 1979 from the University of Tokyo with a Masters in Architecture. In 1985–1986, he received an Asian Cultural Council Fellowship Grant and was a Visiting Scholar at Columbia University. In 1987 he established the Spatial Design Studio, and in 1991 he created Kengo Kuma & Associates. His work includes: the Gunma Toyota Car Show Room, Maebashi, 1989; Maiton Resort Complex, Phuket, Thailand; Rustic, office building, Tokyo; Doric, office building, Tokyo; M2, headquarters for Mazda New Design Team, Tokyo, all in 1991; Kinjo Golf Club, Club House, Okayama, 1992: Kiro-san Observatory, Ehime, 1994; Atami Guest House for Bandai Corp, Atami, 1992–1995; Karuizawa Resort Hotel, Karuizawa, 1993; Tomioka Lakewood Golf Club House, Tomioka, 1993–1996; Noh-Theater, Toyoma, Miyagi, 1995–1996; and the Japanese Pavilion for the Venice Biennale, Venice, Italy, 1995. He has recently completed the Stone Museum (Nasu, Tochigi) and a Museum of Ando Hiroshige (Batou, Nasu-gun, Tochigi).

**KENGO KUMA**, geboren 1954 in Kanagawa, Japan, schloss 1979 sein Studium an der Universität Tokio mit dem Master of Architecture ab. Von 1985 bis 1986 arbeitete er mit einem Stipendium des Asian Cultural Council als Gastwissenschaftler an der Columbia University in New York. 1987 gründete Kuma das Spatial Design Studio und 1991 das Büro Kengo Kuma & Associates. Zu seinen Bauten gehören der Gunma Toyota Car Show Room in Maebashi, Japan (1989), die Ferienanlage Maiton in Phuket, Thailand (1991), die Bürogebäude Rustic und Doric sowie M2, die Hauptverwaltung für das neue Designteam von Mazda, alle 1991 in Tokio ausgeführt; ferner das Klubhaus des Kinjo Golf Club in Okayama (1992), das Observatorium Kiro-san in Ehime (1994), das Gästehaus für die Firma Bandai in Atami (1992–95), ein Hotel in Karuizawa (1993), das Klubhaus des Lakewood Golf Club in Tomioka (1993–96), das Noh-Theater in Toyama , Miyagi (1995–96), und der Japanische Pavillon auf der Biennale in Venedig (1995). Seine neuesten Projekte sind das Steinmuseum in Nasu, Tochigi, sowie ein Museum für die Werke von Ando Hiroshige in Batou, Nasu-gun, Tochigi.

Né en 1954 à Kanagawa, Japon, **KENGO KUMA** est M. Arch. de l'Université de Tokyo (1979). En 1984–86, il bénéficie d'une bourse de l'Asian Cultural Council et est chercheur invité à Columbia University. En 1987, il crée le Spatial Design Studio, et en 1991 Kengo Kuma & Associates. Parmi ses réalisations : le show-room Toyota de Gunma (Maebashi, 1989) ; le Maiton Resort Complex (Phuket, Thaïlande, 1991) ; le Rustic Office Building (Tokyo, 1991) ; l'immeuble de bureaux Doric (Tokyo, 1991) ; le siège du département de design de Mazda (Tokyo, 1991) ; le Kinjo Golf Club, Club House, (Okayama, 1992) ; l'Observatoire Kiro-san (Ehime, Japon, 1994) ; l'Atami Guest House pour Bandaï Corp (Atami, 1992–95) ; le Karuizawa Resort Hotel (Karuizawa, 1993) ; le Club House du Tomioka Lakewood Golf (Tomioka, 1993–96) ; le Théâtre Nô (Toyoma, Miyagi, 1995–96), et le pavillon japonais de la Biennale de Venise en 1995. Il vient d'achever le Musée de la pierre (Nasu, Tochigi) et le Musée Ando Hiroshige (Batou, Nasu-gun, Tochigi).

# KITAKAMI CANAL MUSEUM

*Ishinomaki, Miyagi, Japan, 1996–1999*

*Site area: 1,880 m². Building area: 523 m². Total floor area: 613 m².*
*Structure: reinforced concrete, partly steel frame.*

The **KITAKAMI CANAL MUSEUM** is set on an 1,880 square meter site. The building area is 523 square meters and the total floor area is 613 square meters. This is in reinforced concrete. The structure is in good part buried at the juncture between the Kitakami River and the Kitakami Canal. Curiously, this structure recalls funerary mounds without any of the ancient implications of such archeological sites. The building rather gives the impression of a modern, ecologically conscious design, with its metal-louvered canopy and openings out toward the water. Kengo Kuma has distinguished himself by his modern, open approach, unencumbered by a specific style and vocabulary or even a set gamut of materials. Although much of his work does have a relation to Japanese tradition, it is also refreshingly unexpected, particularly in the case of a design such as that of the Kitakami Canal Museum.

Das auf einem 1.880 m² großen Grundstück errichtete **KITAKAMI KANAL MUSEUM** hat eine bebaute Fläche von 523 m² und eine Gesamtgeschossfläche von 613 m². Der zum guten Teil in die Erde verlegte Bau aus Stahlbeton am Zusammenfluss von Kitakami Fluss und Kitakami Kanal erinnert merkwürdigerweise an Grabhügel, ohne jedoch die altertümlichen Bezüge aufzuweisen, die solchen archäologischen Stätten eigen sind. Vielmehr vermittelt das Gebäude mit seinem durch Metalljalousien gerasterten Vordach und den zum Wasser zeigenden Fensteröffnungen den Eindruck von moderner, umweltfreundlicher Architektur. Kengo Kuma hat sich bereits in der Vergangenheit durch seine zeitgemäße, offene Herangehensweise ausgezeichnet, die unbelastet ist von einem speziellen Stil und Vokabular oder gar einem festgelegten Repertoire an Materialien. Obwohl ein großer Teil seines Werkes durchaus Bezüge zur japanischen Tradition aufweist, ist es erfrischend unkonventionell, was auch dieser Entwurf belegt.

Le **KITAKAMI CANAL MUSEUM** est édifié sur un terrain de 1 880 m² et en occupe 523 pour une surface totale utile de 613 m². Au confluent de la rivière Kitakami et du canal du même nom, sa structure en béton armé est en bonne partie enterrée. Elle rappelle curieusement les tumuli funéraires, sans aucune des implications de ces sites archéologiques et donne le sentiment d'une réflexion très actuelle, soucieuse d'écologie, comme le montrent son auvent métallique à persiennes et ses ouvertures donnant sur l'eau. Kengo Kuma s'est fait connaître par une approche moderne et ouverte, libre de tout style ou vocabulaire spécifique, et même de matériaux préférés. Bien qu'une bonne partie de son œuvre soit en relation avec la tradition japonaise, elle revêt parfois, comme c'est ici le cas, des formes heureusement inattendues.

Above, the Museum seen from the northeast, across the Kitakami River. Right, the entrance with its stainless steel louvers and sloping design inserted into the earth.

Das Museum, vom nordöstlich gelegenen Ufer des Kitakami Flusses aus gesehen (oben). Der Eingang mit den Rasterblenden aus rostfreiem Stahl und der schräg abfallenden, in die Erde gebetteten Bauweise (rechts).

En haut, le musée vue du nord-est, de l'autre côté de la rivière de Kitakami. À droite, l'entrée à persiennes d'acier inoxydables et profil en pente creusée dans le sol.

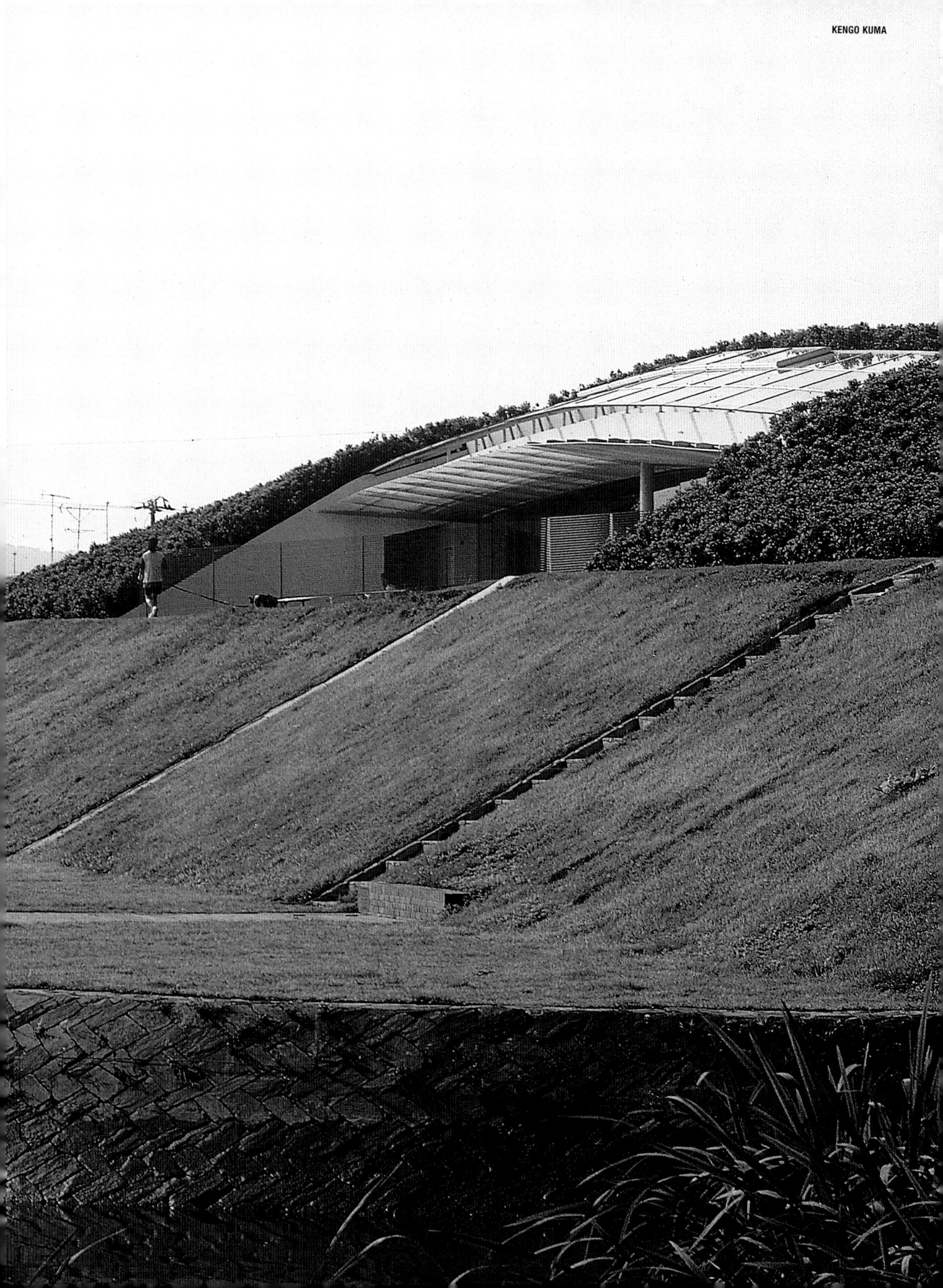

The outer plaza of the Museum (left)
and the view from almost the same
point (above). Below, inside the
museum.

Der Museumsvorplatz (links) und die
Aussicht von dort aus (oben). Das
Museumsinnere (unten).

La place extérieure du musée (à
gauche) et une vue prise pratiquement du même point (en haut).
En bas, l'intérieur du musée.

# LACATON & VASSAL

Lacaton & Vassal
4, place Pey Berland
33000 Bordeaux
France

Tel: + 33 5 56 79 38 10
Fax: + 33 5 56 81 51 91
e-mail: lacaton.vassal@wanadoo.fr

*Palais de Tokyo*

**ANNE LACATON** was born in 1955 in Saint-Pardoux-la-Rivière, France. She received diplomas from the École d'Architecture de Bordeaux (Gironde, 1980) and a DESS degree in Urbanism in Bordeaux in 1984. **JEAN-PHILIPPE VASSAL** was born in 1954 in Casablanca, Morocco. He received his diploma from the École d'Architecture de Bordeaux (Gironde, 1980) and worked as an architect in the Niger from 1980 to 1985. He taught at the École d'Architecture de Bordeaux from 1992 to 1999. Aside from the Palais de Tokyo project published here, the architects have worked on the Café-Restaurant UNA at the Architektur Zentrum in Vienna (2001), and houses in Coutras (2000), Lège-Cap Ferret (1998), and in Dordogne (1997). They won the 1999 Award for Young Architects, given by the French Ministry of Culture.

**ANNE LACATON**, 1955 im französischen Saint-Pardoux-la-Rivière geboren, erwarb 1980 an der École d'Architecture de Bordeaux in Gironde das Diplom und machte 1984 ihren DESS-Abschluss in Urbanistik in Bordeaux. **JEAN-PHILIPPE VASSAL**, geboren 1954 in Casablanca, Marokko, erwarb ebenfalls 1980 sein Diplom an der École d'Architecture de Bordeaux in Gironde und war von 1980 bis 1985 als Architekt in Nigeria tätig. Von 1992 bis 1999 lehrte er an der École d'Architecture de Bordeaux. Zu den gemeinsamen Projekten von Lacaton und Vassal gehören neben dem hier vorgestellten Palais de Tokyo in Paris das Café-Restaurant UNA des Architektur Zentrums in Wien (2001) sowie Wohnhäuser in Coutras (2000), Lège-Cap Ferret (1998) und in der Dordogne (1997). 1999 wurde ihnen vom französischen Kulturministerium der Preis für junge Architekten verliehen.

**ANNE LACATON**, née en 1955 à Saint-Pardoux-la-Rivière (France), est diplômée de l'École d'architecture de Bordeaux (1980) et obtient un DESS d'urbanisme à Bordeaux en 1984. **JEAN-PHILIPPE VASSAL**, né en 1954 à Casablanca, Maroc, est diplômé de l'École d'architecture de Bordeaux (1980) et travaille au Niger de 1980 à 1985. Il enseigne à l'École d'architecture de Bordeaux de 1992 à 1999. En dehors du projet pour le Palais de Tokyo, présenté ici, ils ont réalisé le Café-Restaurant UNA de l'Architektur Zentrum de Vienne (Autriche, 2001), et des maisons à Coutras (2000), Lège-Cap Ferret (1998) et en Dordogne (1997). Ils ont remporté en 1999 le prix des jeunes architectes décerné par le ministère français de la Culture.

# PALAIS DE TOKYO

*Paris, France, 2001–2002*

*Client: Ministère de la Culture – Délégation aux Arts Plastiques.*
*Overall budget: 4.55 million euros. Construction budget: 3.65 million euros. Area: 7,800 m².*

This unusual project concerns the renovation of part of the **PALAIS DE TOKYO** building, erected in Paris in 1937 by the architects Dondel, Aubert, Viart and Dastugue. The eastern wing of the structure has been occupied for sometime by the Paris Museum of Modern Art. The west wing belongs to the French government, and was the home of the National Museum of Modern Art until it was moved to the Pompidou Center in 1974. A plan to convert the space into a Museum of Cinema with the architect Franck Hammoutene was abandoned in 1999. The current project is a use of the space for the display of very contemporary art. Measuring almost 9,000 square meters, the spaces of the Palais de Tokyo have ceiling heights varying between four and eight meters. For budgetary reasons, the architects chose to carry out the work necessary for the space to be in conformity with security codes, and to leave the volumes much as they were when they were built. Rough concrete floors and unpainted walls give a temporary or rough quality to the space which was deemed appropriate to its function as a framework for experimental art.

Das ungewöhnliche Projekt wird im Rahmen der Renovierung eines Teils des 1937 von den Architekten Dondel, Aubert, Viart und Dastugue erbauten **PALAIS DE TOKYO** realisiert. Der Ostflügel des Gebäudes wurde einige Zeit vom Pariser Museum für Moderne Kunst eingenommen, während der Westflügel das Nationalmuseum für Moderne Kunst beheimatete, das 1974 ins Centre Georges Pompidou verlegt wurde. Den ursprünglichen Plan, das Innere von dem Architekten Franck Hammoutene in ein Filmmuseum umwandeln zu lassen, verwarf man 1999, um die Räumlichkeiten nun für die Präsentation avantgardistischer Kunst zu nutzen. Die auf fast 9.000 m² verteilten Räume des Palais haben Wände mit unterschiedlichen Höhen von vier bis acht Metern. Aus finanziellen Gründen beschlossen die Architekten, das Innere weitgehend so zu belassen, wie es ursprünglich gebaut worden war. Es wurde nur soweit umgebaut wie es die Sicherheitsvorschriften erforderten. Ungeschliffene Betonböden und Wände im Rauputz verleihen dem Museum einen provisorischen und spröden Charakter, der seiner Funktion als Rahmen für experimentelle Kunst angemessen erscheint.

Étonnant projet que cette rénovation d'une aile du **PALAIS DE TOKYO**, édifié à Paris en 1937 par les architectes Dondel, Aubert, Viart et Dastugue. L'aile Est abrite le Musée d'art moderne de la ville de Paris, l'aile Ouest, qui appartient à l'État, avait été le siège du Musée national d'art moderne avant qu'il n'emménage au Centre Pompidou en 1974. Son plan de conversion en Cité du cinéma par l'architecte Franck Hammoutène fut abandonné en 1999. Le projet actuel consacre cet espace à la présentation de l'art très contemporain. D'une surface de près de 9 000 m², les volumes du Palais de Tokyo bénéficient de hauteurs de plafond de 4 à 8 m. Pour des raisons budgétaires, les architectes ont décidé de simplement réaliser les travaux de mise en sécurité nécessaires et de laisser les volumes tels qu'ils étaient lors de la construction, avant tout aménagement. Les sols en béton lissé et les murs non peints confèrent un aspect temporaire, ou brut, à cet espace certainement approprié pour accueillir les témoignages de l'art expérimental.

*Above, two views of the interior space of the Palais de Tokyo, before the art was brought in. Stripped down to its bare essentials, the space is ideal for receiving large artworks and a considerable number of visitors (right).*

*Die beiden Ansichten (oben) zeigen das Interieur des Palais de Tokyo, bevor die Kunst Einzug hielt. Der bis auf das Notwendigste reduzierte Ausstellungsraum (rechts unten) ist ein idealer Rahmen für großformatige Kunstwerke und zahlreiche Besucher.*

*En haut : deux vues du nouvel espace intérieur du Palais de Tokyo, avant l'installation des œuvres. Réduit à l'essentiel, le volume convient idéalement aux installations de grandes dimensions et à l'accueil d'un public nombreux (à droite).*

Given the limited budgets and large floor area, the architects opted for an extremely simple, even industrial approach to materials, ranging from simple concrete floors to standard lighting fixtures, used to augment the ample natural overhead lighting.

In Anbetracht des begrenzten Budgets und der großen Nutzfläche entschieden sich die Architekten für den Einsatz äußerst schlichter, industrieller Materialien: ungeschliffene Betonböden und als Ergänzung zur natürlichen Belichtung standardisierte Beleuchtungskörper.

Le budget limité et la surface considérable expliquent en partie l'adoption de matériaux simples, quasi industriels, qui vont des sols en béton aux luminaires basiques qui complètent l'abondant éclairage zénithal naturel.

# GREG LYNN/FORM

Greg Lynn/FORM
1817 Lincoln Boulevard
Venice, CA 90291
United States

Tel: + 1 310 821 2629
Fax: + 1 310 821 9729
e-mail: node@glform.com
Web: www.glform.com

*Embryological House*

**GREG LYNN** was born in 1964. He received his Bachelor of Philosophy and Bachelor of Environmental Design from Miami University of Ohio (1986), and his Master of Architecture from Princeton University (1988). He worked in the offices of Antoine Predock (1987) and Peter Eisenman (1987–1991) before creating his present firm, **FORM**, in 1994. He has worked on the Ark of the World Museum and Interpretive Center, Costa Rica, 1999, the New York Korean Presbyterian Church (Long Island City, New York, 1997–1999) with Garofalo Architects and Michael McInturf Architects, and the Cincinnati Country Day School (also with Michael McInturf, 1997), as well as participating in the last Venice Architecture Biennial.

**GREG LYNN**, 1964 geboren, erwarb 1986 den Bachelor of Philosophy und den Bachelor of Environmental Design an der Miami University of Ohio und 1988 den Master of Architecture an der Princeton University. 1987 arbeitete er im Büro von Antoine Predock und von 1987 bis 1991 bei Peter Eisenman, bevor er 1994 seine Firma **FORM** gründete. Zu seinen Projekten zählen: Ark of the World Museum and Interpretive Center in Costa Rica (1999), die in Zusammenarbeit mit Garofalo Architects und Michael McInturf Architects entstandene koreanische presbyterianische Kirche von New York in Long Island City (1977–99), die Tagesschule Cincinnati Country, ebenfalls zusammen mit Michael McInturf (1997), sowie sein Beitrag für die letzte Architekturbiennale in Venedig.

**GREG LYNN**, né en 1964, est B. Phil. et B. de design environnemental de Miami University of Ohio (1986) et M. Arch de Princeton University (1988). Il travaille dans les agences d'Antoine Predock (1987) et Peter Eisenman (1987–91) avant de créer l'agence **FORM** en 1994. Il est intervenu sur l'Ark of the World Museum and Interpretive Center, Costa Rica (1999) ; la New York Korean Presbyterian Church (Long Island City, New York, 1997–99) avec Garofalo Architects et Michael McInturf Architects, ainsi que sur le Cincinnati Country Day School (également avec M. McInturf, 1997) et il a participé à la dernière Biennale de l'architecture de Venise.

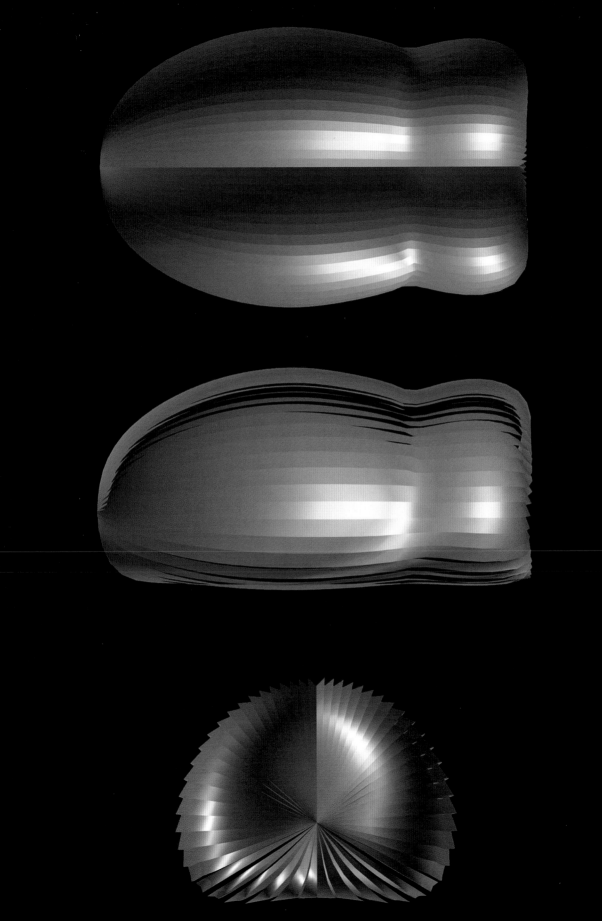

# EMBRYOLOGICAL HOUSE
## *California*

*Structure: 2,048 panels, 9 steel frames,
and 72 aluminum struts networked together to form a monocoque shell.*

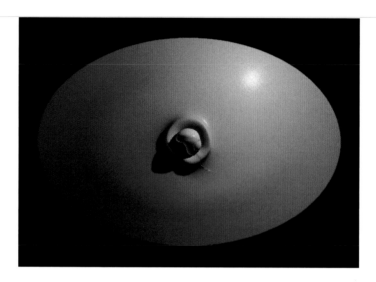

Greg Lynn declares, "The **EMBRYOLOGICAL HOUSE** can be described as a strategy for the invention of domestic space that engages contemporary issues of brand identity and variation, customization and continuity, flexible manufacturing and assembly, and most importantly an unapologetic investment in the contemporary beauty and voluptuous aesthetics of undulating surfaces rendered vividly in iridescent and opalescent colors. The Embryological House employs a rigorous system of geometrical limits that liberate an exfoliation of endless variations." Unlike many architects who work extensively with computer technology, Lynn says, "At this point, I would have to say it is the software making the calls. There is a language of form that comes with the computer, and at first you do what the software does." Lynn has codified the assembly of the Embryological House very strictly: "The domestic envelope of every house is composed of 2,048 panels, 9 steel frames, and 72 aluminum struts are networked together to form a monocoque shell, where each component is unique in its shape and size. Using design techniques of flexible manufacturing borrowed from the industrial, automotive, naval and aeronautical design industries, every house in the line is of a unique shape and size while conforming to a fixed number of components and fabrication operations. The form and space of the houses is modified within the predefined limits of the components."

Der Architekt beschreibt das **EMBRYOLOGICAL HOUSE** »als eine Strategie zur Erfindung von Wohnräumen. Eingebunden in diese Strategie sind aktuelle Kernfragen von Markenidentität und Variationsbreite, Kundenspezifizierung und Kontinuität, flexibler Fertigung und Montage sowie vor allem eine offensive Investition in die zeitgemäße Schönheit und sinnliche Ästhetik geschwungener Oberflächen mit der intensiven Ausdruckskraft bunt schillernder Farben. Das Embryological House setzt ein exaktes System begrenzter geometrischer Elemente ein, die eine Entwicklung endloser Variationsmöglichkeiten bieten.« Im Gegensatz zu vielen anderen Architekten, die in großem Umfang mit Computertechnologie arbeiten, erklärt Lynn: »An diesem Punkt müsste ich ja eingestehen, dass es die Software ist, auf die es ankommt. Der Computer bringt eine gewisse Formensprache mit sich und da macht man zunächst all das, was die Software vorgibt.« Greg Lynn hat die Montage des Embryological House streng kodifiziert: »Die aus 2.084 Tafeln, 9 Stahlrahmen und 72 Aluminiumverstrebungen bestehende Hülle der Häuser wird zu einer selbst tragenden Schalenbaukonstruktion zusammengefügt, in der jedes Bauteil seine individuelle Form und Größe hat. Unter Einsatz von Entwurfstechniken flexibler Fertigungssysteme, wie sie in der Automobil-, Schiffbau- und Luftfahrtindustrie verwendet werden, ist jedes Haus dieser Serie einzigartig in seiner Form und Größe. Gleichzeitig entspricht es einer bestimmten Anzahl von Bauteilen und Fertigungsarbeiten. Innerhalb dieser festgesetzten Grenzen werden Form und Aufteilung der Häuser modifiziert.«

Pour Greg Lynn : « La **MAISON EMBRYOLOGIQUE** peut se décrire comme la stratégie d'invention d'un espace domestique qui met en jeu les problématiques contemporaines d'image de marque et de variation, de ‹customisation› et de continuité, de construction et d'assemblage flexibles. Plus important encore, elle illustre un investissement généreux dans la beauté contemporaine et l'esthétique voluptueuse de surfaces ondulées aux couleurs iridescentes et opalescentes. Elle fait appel à un système rigoureux de contraintes géométriques qui libère une exfoliation de variations infinies. » À la différence de nombreux architectes qui utilisent beaucoup l'informatique, Lynn précise : « Je dois dire que c'est le logiciel qui prend le dessus. Il existe un langage formel qui relève de l'ordinateur, et, au départ, vous faites ce que fait le logiciel. » Lynn a codifié très strictement l'assemblage : « L'enveloppe domestique de chaque maison se compose de 2048 panneaux, 9 cardes d'acier et 72 étais d'aluminium qui constituent une coquille monocoque dans laquelle chaque élément est unique, que ce soit par sa taille ou sa forme. À partir de techniques de conception de fabrication flexible empruntées aux industries de l'automobile, de la construction navale et de l'aéronautique, chaque maison est ainsi originale dans sa forme et ses dimensions tout en se conformant à un nombre déterminé de composants et d'opérations de montage. La forme et l'espace de la maison se modifient dans des limites prédéfinies qui sont celles de ses composants. »

*"This marks a shift from a Modernist mechanical kit-of-parts design and construction technique to a more vital, evolving, biological model of embryological design and construction." G. Lynn*

*»Er markiert eine Wende vom Baukastendesign und einer modernistisch-mechanischen Konstruktionstechnik hin zu einem lebendigeren, sich entwickelnden, biologischen Modell embryologischer Entwurfs- und Konstruktionsart.« G. Lynn*

*« Ce projet marque le passage d'une conception et d'une technique de construction modernistes et mécanique en kit à un modèle biologique, plus vivant, de conception évolutive et de construction embryologique. » G. Lynn*

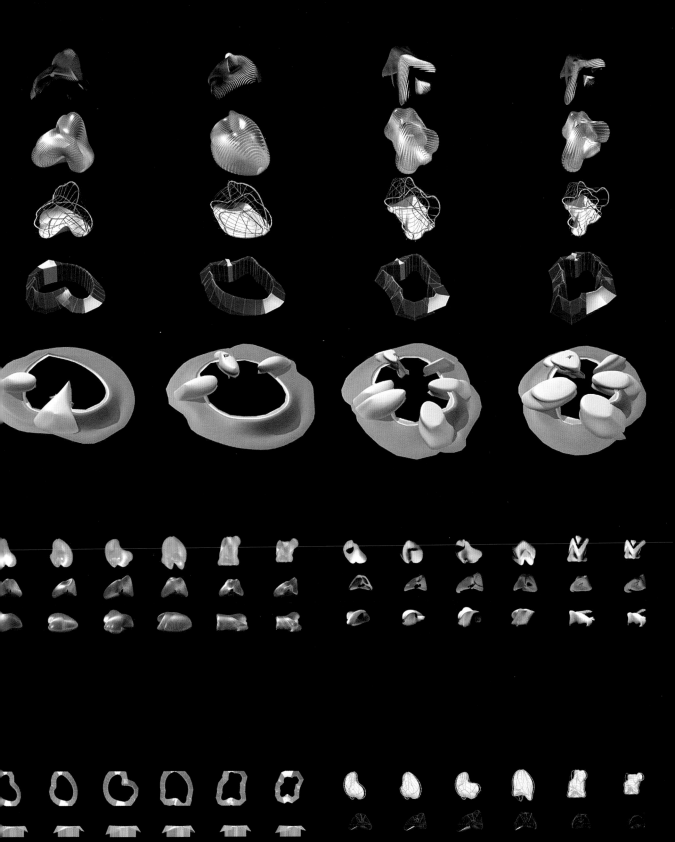

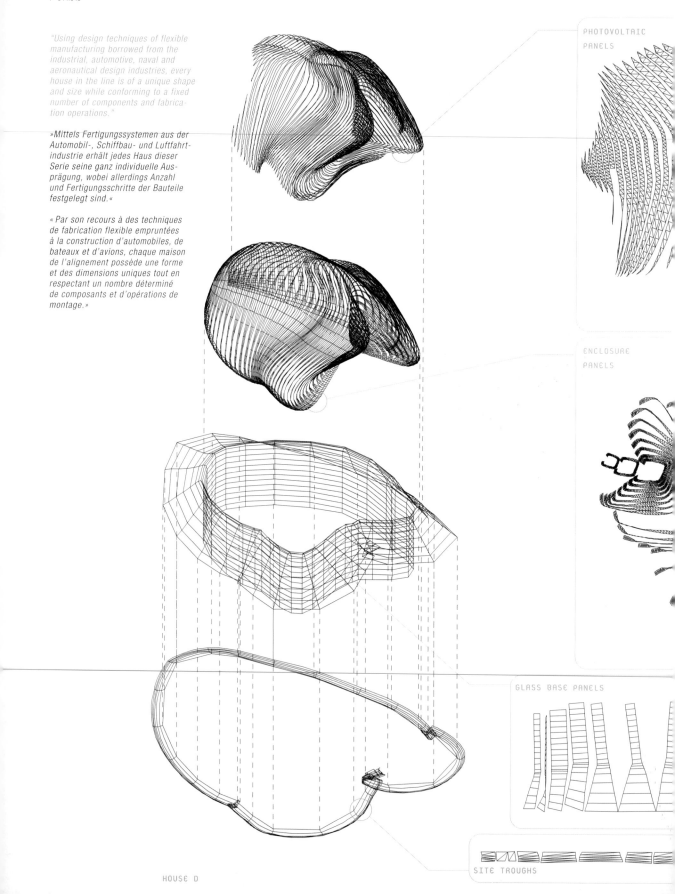

"Using design techniques of flexible manufacturing borrowed from the industrial, automotive, naval and aeronautical design industries, every house in the line is of a unique shape and size while conforming to a fixed number of components and fabrication operations."

»Mittels Fertigungssystemen aus der Automobil-, Schiffbau- und Luftfahrtindustrie erhält jedes Haus dieser Serie seine ganz individuelle Ausprägung, wobei allerdings Anzahl und Fertigungsschritte der Bauteile festgelegt sind.«

« Par son recours à des techniques de fabrication flexible empruntées à la construction d'automobiles, de bateaux et d'avions, chaque maison de l'alignement possède une forme et des dimensions uniques tout en respectant un nombre déterminé de composants et d'opérations de montage.»

PHOTOVOLTAIC PANELS

ENCLOSURE PANELS

GLASS BASE PANELS

SITE TROUGHS

HOUSE D

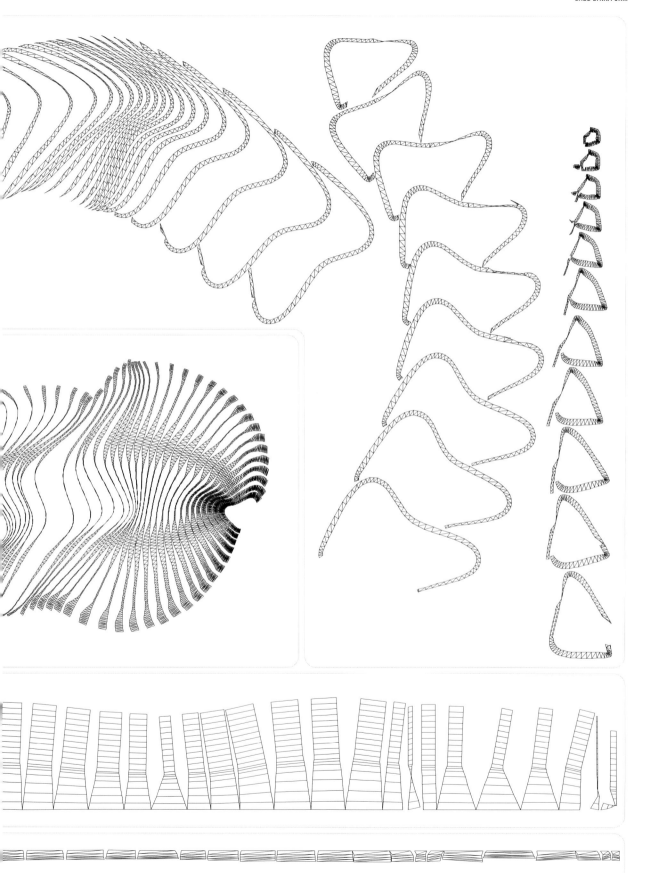

# RICHARD MEIER

*Richard Meier & Partners*
*475 Tenth Avenue*
*New York, New York 10018*
*United States*

*Tel: + 1 212 967 6060*
*Fax: + 1 212 967 3207*

*Federal Building & United States Courthouse*

Born in Newark, New Jersey in 1934. **RICHARD MEIER** received his architectural training at Cornell University, and worked in the office of Marcel Breuer (1960–1963) before establishing his own practice in 1963. He won the 1984 Pritzker Prize and the 1988 Royal Gold Medal. His notable buildings include The Atheneum, (New Harmony, Indiana 1975–1979); Museum of Decorative Arts (Frankfurt, Germany, 1979–1984); High Museum of Art (Atlanta, Georgia, 1980–1983); Canal+ Headquarters (Paris, France, 1988–1992); City Hall and Library (The Hague, Netherlands, 1990–1995); Barcelona Museum of Contemporary Art (Barcelona, Spain, 1988–1995); and the Getty Center (Los Angeles, California, 1984–97). Recent work includes the Federal Building & United States Courthouse, Phoenix, Arizona (1995–2000) published here.

**RICHARD MEIER**, geboren 1934 in Newark, New Jersey, studierte Architektur an der Cornell University und arbeitete von 1960 bis 1963 bei Marcel Breuer, bevor er 1963 sein eigenes Büro eröffnete. Er wurde 1984 mit dem Pritzker Prize und 1988 mit der Royal Gold Medal ausgezeichnet. Zu seinen bedeutendsten Bauten zählen das Atheneum in New Harmony, Indiana (1975–79), das Museum für Kunsthandwerk in Frankfurt am Main (1979–84), das High Museum of Art in Atlanta, Georgia (1980–83), die Hauptverwaltung von Canal+ in Paris (1988–92), Rathaus und Bibliothek in Den Haag (1990–95), das Museum für Zeitgenössische Kunst in Barcelona (1988–95) und das Getty Center in Los Angeles (1984–97). Zu seinen jüngsten Projekten gehört das hier vorgestellte U. S. Courthouse and Federal Building in Phoenix, Arizona (1995–2000).

Né à Newark (New Jersey), en 1934, **RICHARD MEIER** étudie à Cornell University et travaille dans l'agence de Marcel Breuer (1960–63), avant de se mettre à son compte en 1963. Il remporte le prix Pritzker (1984), et la Royal Gold Medal (1988). Ses principales réalisations sont : The Athenaeum, New Harmony, (Indiana, 1975–79) ; Musée des Arts Décoratifs de Francfort-sur-le-Main (1979–84) ; High Museum of Art (Atlanta, Géorgie, 1980–83) ; siège de Canal+ (Paris, 1988–92) ; hôtel de ville et bibliothèque (La Haye, 1990–95) ; Musée d'Art Contemporain de Barcelone (1988–95) ; Getty Center (Los Angeles (Californie, 1984–96). Il achève actuellement le Tribunal fédéral et immeuble de l'administration fédérale de Phoenix (Arizona, 1995–2000), présenté ici.

# FEDERAL BUILDING &
# UNITED STATES COURTHOUSE

*Phoenix, Arizona, United States, 1998–2000*

*Client: General Services Administration (GSA). Cost: $84.7 million. Area: 53,300 m². Atrium area: 5,400 m².*

Richard Meier was awarded this commission in collaboration with the local architect Langdon Wilson in 1994. Although the original design of the building was completed before the 1995 bombing of the Alfred P. Murrah Federal Building in Oklahoma City, Oklahoma, Meier and the client chose not to do away with the central 35 meter high glass atrium that is a centerpiece of the architecture. Rather, laminated glass was used in the first three bands of the eastern and northern exterior walls and in the skylights. The author of another Federal courthouse in Islip, New York, Meier called on his trademark white on white Modernist vocabulary in this $84.7 building. His juxtaposition of the vast atrium space with a rectangular wing containing eighteen courtrooms, offices and space for archives does recall a similar arrangement for the City Hall and Library of The Hague (The Netherlands, 1990–1995). The round, paneled Special Proceedings Courtroom with a glass ceiling designed by James Carpenter Design Associates is another spectacular interior space.

Richard Meier wurde 1994 zusammen mit dem ortsansässigen Architekten Langdon Wilson mit dem Bau des Gerichtsgebäudes beauftragt. Die ursprüngliche Planung war bereits 1995, also vor dem Bombenanschlag auf das Alfred P. Murrah Federal Building in Oklahoma City, abgeschlossen. Dennoch wollten Meier und der Bauherr nicht auf das zentrale Bauelement, das 35 m hohe gläserne Atrium, verzichten, das als Sicherheitsrisiko hätte gelten können. Allerdings wurde für die Außenverkleidung der ersten drei Stockwerke sowie der Oberlichter Verbundsicherheitsglas verwendet. Meier, der auch das Bundesgerichtsgebäude in Islip, New York, entworfen hat, setzt in diesem für 84,7 Millionen Dollar fertig gestellten Gebäude auf sein Markenzeichen: eine ganz auf Weiß basierende, modernistische Formensprache. Die Positionierung des ausladenden Atriums direkt neben einem rechteckigen Gebäudeflügel, in dem 18 Gerichtssäle, Büros und Archivräume untergebracht sind, erinnert an die Gruppierung bei seinem Den Haager Rathaus mit Bibliothek (1990–95). In diesem Gebäude bildet der runde, getäfelte Gerichtssaal für Sondergerichtsverfahren mit einer von James Carpenter Design Associates entworfenen Glasdecke ein weiteres spektakuläres Element der Innenraumgestaltung.

C'est en 1994 que Richard Meier a reçu cette commande réalisée en collaboration avec l'architecte de Phoenix Langdon Wilson. Même si les plans originaux ont été achevés avant l'attentat de 1995 contre l'Alfred P. Murrah Federal Building d'Oklahoma City, Meier et son client ont décidé de conserver l'atrium de verre de 35 m de haut, morceau de bravoure du projet. Un verre laminé a été utilisé pour les trois premiers bandeaux des murs extérieurs est et nord et les verrières. Auteur d'une autre cour fédérale à Islip, New York, Meier marque une fois encore de son vocabulaire moderniste ce bâtiment de 84,7 millions de dollars. La juxtaposition du vaste volume de l'atrium à une aile rectangulaire contenant dix-huit tribunaux, les bureaux et les archives évoque la disposition similaire qu'il avait retenue pour son hôtel de ville-bibliothèque de La Haye (Pays-Bas, 1990–95). La salle des audiences spéciales, ronde et lambrissée à plafond de verre dessiné par James Carpenter Design Associates, est un espace intérieur lui aussi très spectaculaire.

The main entrance to the building is visible above and right. The courthouse is oriented to the east.

Der Haupteingang des nach Osten hin ausgerichteten Gebäudes (oben und rechts).

En haute et à droite, l'entrée principale du bâtiment. Le Palais de Justice est orienté à l'est.

Above, a view into the 35 meter-high atrium. To the right, the Special Proceedings Courtroom paneled in anigre wood, with a glass ceiling by James Carpenter Design Associates.

Blick in das 35 m hohe Atrium (oben). Der mit Anigreholz getäfelte Saal für Sondergerichtsverfahren mit einer von James Carpenter Design Associates ausgeführten Glasdecke (rechts).

En haut, vue de l'atrium de 35 m de haut. À droite, la Cour d'audiences spéciales lambrissée de bois d'anigré. Plafond de verre de James Carpenter Design Associates.

# SAMUEL MOCKBEE AND RURAL STUDIO

*The Rural Studio*
*School of Architecture*
*202 Dudley Commons*
*The College of Architecture, Design and Construction*
*Auburn University, Alabama 36849*
*United States*

*Tel: + 1 334 844 5426*
*Fax: + 1 334 844 5458*
*e-mail: dennemf@auburn.edu*
*Web: www.arch.auburn.edu/ruralstudio/*

**SAMUEL MOCKBEE**, born in 1944, founded Mockbee/Coker Architects, based in Canton, Mississippi and in Memphis, Tennessee, with Coleman Coker in 1984. The firm completed a number of structures including the Barton House and the Cook House, both located in Mississippi. They have had a considerable reputation in the region, established through their contemporary interpretations of local architecture. Samuel Mockbee taught at Yale, at the University of Oklahoma, and was a Professor of Architecture at Auburn University beginning in 1991. He created the **RURAL STUDIO** in 1993 "to extend the study of architecture into a socially responsible context" for fifteen of his students each quarter. He seems to have passed on to the Rural Studio the vocabulary of simple materials and regional inspiration for which Mockbee/Coker is known. Samuel Mockbee died at the end of 2001, but it was immediately decided that the work of the Rural Studio would go on.

**SAMUEL MOCKBEE**, geboren 1944, gründete 1984 zusammen mit Coleman Coker das Büro Mockbee/Coker Architects mit Sitz in Canton, Mississippi, und in Memphis, Tennessee. Die Firma realisierte eine Reihe von Gebäuden, zu denen das Haus Barton und das Haus Cook gehören, beide in Mississippi. Mit ihren modernen Interpretationen lokaler Architekturformen haben sie sich in der Region einen bedeutenden Namen gemacht. Samuel Mockbee lehrte in Yale, an der University of Oklahoma und war seit 1991 Professor für Architektur an der Auburn University im Staat New York. 1993 gründete er **RURAL STUDIO**, nach eigener Aussage um seinen Studenten die Möglichkeit zu geben, ihr Architekturstudium in den Kontext der sozialen Verantwortung zu stellen. Samuel Mockbee hat die auf einfachen Materialien und regionalen Inspirationen beruhende Formensprache, für die Mockbee/Coker bekannt war, auf das Rural Studio übertragen. Als er Ende 2001 starb, wurde beschlossen, die Arbeit des Ateliers in diesem Sinn fortzusetzen.

**SAMUEL MOCKBEE**, né en 1944, a créé l'agence Mockbee/Coker Architects, basée à Canton, Mississippi et à Memphis, Tennessee, en association avec Coleman Coker en 1984. L'agence a réalisé un certain nombre de projets dont la Barton House et la Cook House, toutes deux au Mississippi. Elle est célèbre dans sa région pour ses interprétations contemporaines de l'architecture locale. Samuel Mockbee a enseigné à Yale, à l'Université de l'Oklahoma et a été professeur d'architecture à Auburn University à partir de 1991. Il a créé le **RURAL STUDIO** en 1993 « pour développer l'étude de l'architecture dans un contexte de responsabilité sociale » auprès d'une quinzaine de ses étudiants par trimestre. Il leur a transmis son goût pour un vocabulaire à base de matériaux simples et d'inspiration régionale qui est la marque de son agence. Mockbee est mort fin 2001, mais le fonctionnement du Rural Studio ne devrait pas être remis en question.

# MASONS BEND COMMUNITY CENTER

*Masons Bend, Alabama, United States, 1999–2000*

*Cost: $20,000. Area: 140 m². Materials: rammed earth, aluminum, cypress beams, tube steel, automobile windshields.*

Samuel Mockbee described this structure as a "windshield chapel with mud walls that picks up on the community's vernacular forms and shapes." The **COMMU-NITY CENTER** began its life as a thesis project by four of Mockbee's students at Auburn University. Set on a triangular site belonging to one of the beneficiaries of an earlier Rural Studio design, the "Butterfly House," it is a low profile building with a rammed earth base, "something monumental with thick walls, like a ruin," according to one of the participants, Forrest Fulton. Since the project had to be carried out with an extremely low budget, the roof of the structure was made with eighty Chevy Caprice windshields bought by participant Jon Schumann for $120. A well wisher donated structural steel, permitting the students to complete the job for approximately $20,000. Set in the old Cotton Belt of western Alabama in Hale County, this multi-purpose structure (transportation stop for county-funded mobile projects, outdoor community gathering area and small chapel) is located near other earlier Rural Studio projects.

Samuel Mockbee beschrieb das Gebäude, das im Rahmen einer Abschlussarbeit von vier seiner Studenten an der Auburn University entstanden ist, als eine »Kapelle aus Windschutzscheiben mit Wänden aus Schlamm, die die volkstümlichen Bauformen der Region aufgreift.« Das Butterfly House genannte **GEMEINDEZENTRUM** liegt auf einem dreieckigen Grundstück, das einem Sponsor eines früheren Rural-Studio-Projekts gehört. Der Flachbau mit einem Fundament aus festgestampfter Erde wirkt nach Aussagen von Forrest Fulton, einem der Projektteilnehmer, mit seinen dicken Wänden monumental, fast wie eine Ruine. Da das Projekt mit einem äußerst geringen Budget realisiert werden musste, stellte man das Dach aus 80 Chevy-Caprice-Windschutzscheiben her, die ein anderer Teilnehmer, Jon Schumann, für insgesamt 120 Dollar erstanden hatte. Von einem weiteren Gönner wurde Baustahl gespendet, was den Studenten ermöglichte, das Gebäude für circa 20.000 Dollar zu errichten. Genutzt wird der Mehrzweckbau für öffentlich geförderte Wanderausstellungen, als Versammlungsraum und kleine Kapelle. Er liegt in Hale County, dem ehemaligen Baumwollgebiet von Alabama, in der Nähe früherer Rural-Studio-Projekte.

Samuel Mockbee décrit cette construction comme « une chapelle-pare-brise à murs de boue qui emprunte aux formes vernaculaires de sa communauté ». Le **COMMUNITY CENTER** était à l'origine le projet de thèse de quatre étudiants de Mockbee à Auburn University. Élevé sur un terrain triangulaire qui appartient au propriétaire d'une autre réalisation de Rural Studio, la Butterfly House, il se présente comme un bâtiment bas sur socle de terre compactée, « quelque chose de monumental avec des murs épais, comme une ruine », selon l'un des participants, Forrest Fulton. Le projet étant soumis à un budget extrêmement modeste, le toit a été réalisé grâce à 80 pare-brises de voiture Chevy Caprice achetés pour 120 dollars. Un mécène a offert l'acier de construction, ce qui a permis aux étudiants de terminer le chantier pour 20 000 dollars environ. Au cœur de l'ancienne Cotton Belt de l'Alabama de l'Ouest, dans le comté de Hale, cette structure à fonctions multiples (centre de départ de projets mobiles, réunion en plein air de la communauté, petite chapelle) est située non loin d'un des premiers projets réalisés par Rural Studio.

*Formerly occupied by an abandoned school bus that occupied the site, the Community Center uses the same "footprint." In the foreground above, the type of residence that was typical of the community before the arrival of the Rural Studio.*

*Das Gemeindezentrum nutzt den ehemaligen Abstellplatz eines alten Schulbusses. Im Vordergrund sieht man die Art von Wohnhaus, wie sie für die Gegend typisch war, bevor sich Rural Studio dort niedergelassen hatte (oben).*

*Le Community Center a repris « l'empreinte » laissée par un bus scolaire abandonné. En haut, au premier plan, le style de maison typique de cette communauté avant l'arrivée de Rural Studio.*

Windshields from 1989 GM cars
bought from a salvage lot are used to
form the scaled effect of the glass
facade.

Die schuppenartige Glasverkleidung
der Fassade besteht aus Windschutzscheiben alter Chevrolets vom
Schrottplatz.

Des pare-brise de modèles General
Motors de 1989 trouvés en récupération créent en façade un effet
d'écailles.

# MORPHOSIS

*Morphosis*
*2041 Colorado Avenue*
*Santa Monica, California 90404*
*United States*

*Tel: + 1 310 570 0125*
*Fax: + 1 310 829 3270*
*e-mail: studio@morphosis.net*
*Web: www.morphosis.net*

**MORPHOSIS** principal **THOM MAYNE**, born in Connecticut in 1944, received his Bachelor of Architecture in 1968 at USC, and his Masters of Architecture degree at Harvard in 1978. He created Morphosis in 1979 with Michael Rotondi, who has since left to create his own firm, RoTo. He has taught at UCLA, Harvard, and Yale and SCI-Arc, of which he was a founding Board Member. Based in Santa Monica, California, some of the main buildings of Morphosis are the Lawrence House (1981); Kate Mantilini Restaurant (Beverly Hills, California, 1986), Cedar's Sinai Comprehensive Cancer Care Center (Beverly Hills, California, 1987); Crawford Residence (Montecito, California, 1987–1992); Yuzen Vintage Car Museum (West Hollywood, California project, 1992), as well as the Blades Residence (Santa Barbara, California, 1992–1997) and the International Elementary School (Long Beach, California, 1997–1999). Current work includes the future Children's Museum of Los Angeles, which will be a key factor in the rejuvination of Downtown Los Angeles, and serve as a landmark for the city. In addition, Morphosis is working on several significant public sector projects, including a Federal Courthouse in Eugene, Oregon, the G. S. A. Headquarters building in San Francisco, and the NOAA Satellite Control Center in Washington DC.

Der 1944 in Connecticut geborene Leiter von **MORPHOSIS**, **THOM MAYNE**, erwarb 1968 den Bachelor of Architecture an der University of Southern California (USC) und 1978 den Master of Architecture in Harvard. 1979 gründete er Morphosis in Partnerschaft mit Michael Rotondi, der heute seine eigene Firma namens RoTo besitzt. Mayne lehrte an der University of California, Los Angeles (UCLA), in Harvard und Yale sowie am Southern California Institute of Architecture (SCI-Arc), wo er ein Gründungsmitglied des Vorstands war. Zu den wichtigsten Bauten des im kalifornischen Santa Monica ansässigen Büros Morphosis gehören: das Haus Lawrence (1981), das Restaurant Kate Mantilini (1986) und das Cedar's Sinai Comprehensive Cancer Care Center (1987), beide in Beverly Hills, die Crawford Residence in Montecito (1987–92), das Yuzen Vintage Car Museum in West Hollywood (1992) sowie das Wohnhaus Blades in Santa Barbara (1992–97) und die International Elementary School in Long Beach (1997–99), alle in Kalifornien. Derzeit arbeiten die Morphosis-Architekten am zukünftigen Kindermuseum in Los Angeles, das eine wichtige Position bei der Stadtteilerneuerung von Downtown Los Angeles einnehmen und als Wahrzeichen fungieren wird. Ferner führt Morphosis einige bedeutende Bauprojekte im öffentlichen Sektor aus, wie den Bundesgerichtshof in Eugene, Oregon, die Hauptverwaltung der General Services Administration (G. S. A.) in San Francisco sowie das NOAA Satellite Control Center in Washington DC.

Le dirigeant de **MORPHOSIS**, **THOM MAYNE**, est né en 1944 dans le Connecticut. Il est B. Arch. de USC (1968) et M. Arch. de Harvard (1978). Il crée Morphosis en 1979 avec Michael Rotondi qui est depuis parti créer sa propre agence, RoTo. Il a enseigné à UCLA, Harvard, Yale et SCI-Arc dont il est membre fondateur. Basé à Santa Monica, Californie, Morphosis a réalisé entre autres : la Lawrence House (1981) ; le Kate Mantilini Restaurant (Beverly Hills, Californie, 1986) ; le Cedar's Sinaï Comprehensive Cancer Care Center (Beverly Hills, Californie, 1987) ; la Crawford Residence (Montecito, Californie, 1987–92) ; le Yuzen Vintage Car Museum (West Hollywood, Californie, projet, 1992) ; la Blades Residence (Santa Barbara, Californie, 1992–97) et l'International Elementary School (Long Beach, Californie, 1997–99). Actuellement l'agence travaille au futur Children's Museum de Los Angeles, monument urbain qui devrait jouer un rôle clé dans le rajeunissement du centre de Los Angeles, et sur plusieurs importants projets publics dont un tribunal fédéral à Eugene, Oregon, le siège du G. S. A. à San Francisco, et le NOA Satellite Control Center à Washington DC.

# HYPO ALPE-ADRIA CENTER

*Klagenfurt, Austria, 1998–2000*

Client: Kärntner Landes- und Hypothekenbank AG. Area: 10,200 m². Cost: $1,600/m² (shell and core).
Structure: cast-in-place concrete frame, steel beam and metal deck roofs.

*Above, a view from the southwest. The bank headquarters itself is the five-story mass rising skyward, "declaring itself as a major cultural and civic institution.*

*Ansicht von Südwesten (oben). Die Bankzentrale befindet sich in dem fünfstöckigen Bauteil mit dem himmelwärts strebenden Fassaden-element.*

*En haut, vue prise du sud-ouest. Le siège de la banque se trouve dans le bloc de cinq niveaux qui pointe vers le ciel, « s'affirmant comme une insti-tution culturelle et civique majeure. »*

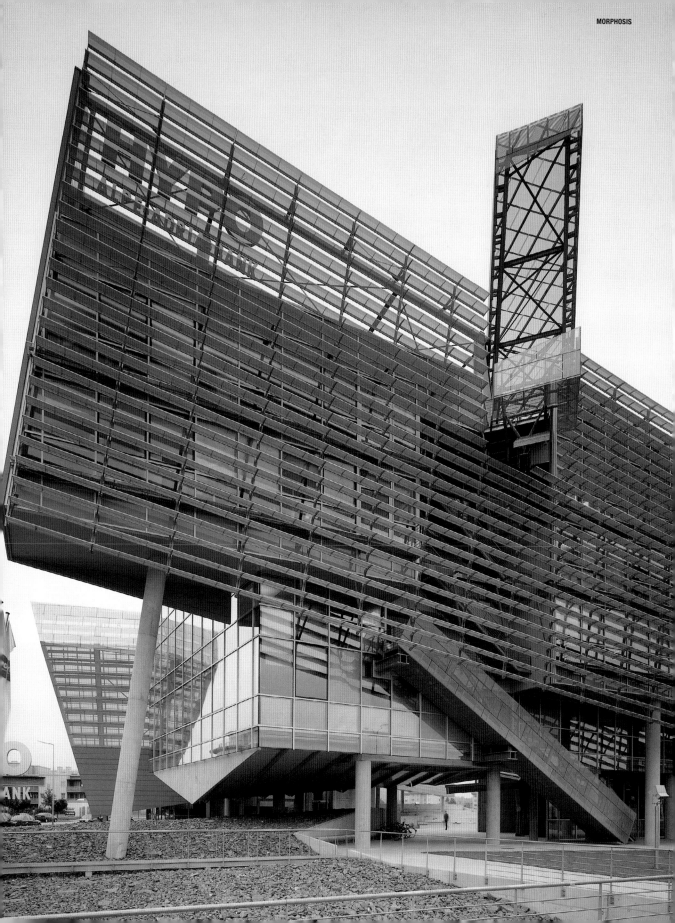

Set in southern Austria near Italy and Slovenia, the **HYPO ALPE-ADRIA CENTER** is also located at the edge of Klagenfurt. The program calls for headquarters space for the Hypo-Bank, office and commercial space, housing and other public facilities. The architects attempted to blend the "typology of the city in one direction, and a typology of the country and landscape, in the other direction." They go on to affirm that "Its dynamic juxtaposition of volumes evokes shifting tectonic plates, yet it strives to establish nodes of stability within turbulence. Colliding and interpenetrating fragments are themselves incomplete, forming a network of referents that extends beyond the limits of the project. The forms are triangulated around an open pedestrian forum, and the entrance is marked by the invitational gesture of a large canopy. Within the central complex, departments are organized around a sky-lit courtyard that allows light to penetrate down to the Branch Bank on the ground floor. Perched upon leaning *pilotis*, a three-story section on the south face seems to surge skyward…" This Phase One structure is made with aluminum curtain wall, perforated aluminum panels, zinc sheet, and a cast-in-place concrete frame, steel beam and metal deck roofs.

Das **HYPO ALPE-ADRIA-ZENTRUM** liegt im Süden Österreichs, an der Grenze zu Italien und Slowenien, und am Stadtrand von Klagenfurt. Der Bauplan sieht die Unterbringung einer Zentrale für die Hypo-Bank, Büro- und Geschäftsräume, Wohnungen und öffentliche Einrichtungen vor. Der Entwurf sollte die Typologie von Stadt, Land und Landschaft miteinander verschmelzen. Die Architekten erläutern: »Die dynamische Anordnung der Bauelemente evoziert das Bild tektonischer Verschiebungen, wobei jedoch Knotenpunkte installiert sind, die innerhalb der Turbulenz für Stabilität sorgen. Sich überschneidende und ineinander geschachtelte Fragmente bilden ein über die Grenzen des Bauwerkes hinausgehendes Referenzsystem. Die einzelnen Bauteile sind in der Form eines Dreiecks um einen offenen Fußgängerbereich angeordnet und der Eingang ist durch die einladende Geste eines ausgedehnten Vordachs markiert. Im Inneren des Hauptgebäudes sind die einzelnen Abteilungen um einen Innenhof gruppiert, durch dessen Oberlicht das Tageslicht bis zu der im Erdgeschoss liegenden Bankfiliale durchdringt. Ein auf geneigten Stützen aufliegendes, dreigeschossiges Teilstück der Südfassade scheint himmelwärts zu streben.« Die Konstruktionsmaterialien des in der ersten Phase fertig gestellten Gebäudes sind: Aluminium für die Vorhangwände und perforierten Tafeln, Zinkblech, ein vor Ort gegossenes Betonskelett sowie Stahlträger und Metallüberdachungen.

Édifié en Autriche méridionale, dans la banlieue de Klagenfurt, le **CENTRE HYPO ALPE-ADRIA** se trouve non loin des frontières avec l'Italie et la Slovénie. Il regroupe le siège social de l'Hypo-Bank, des commerces, des bureaux, des logements et des équipements publics. Les architectes ont voulu fusionner « la typologie de la ville d'un côté, et celle de la campagne et du paysage, de l'autre ». Ils insistent sur « la juxtaposition dynamique de volumes qui évoque le glissement de plaques tectoniques, tout en s'efforçant d'établir des nœuds de stabilité dans une turbulence. Des fragments en collision ou qui s'interpénètrent, incomplets par eux-mêmes, forment un réseau de référents qui dépasse les limites du projet. Les formes sont triangulées autour d'un forum piétonnier ouvert et l'entrée signalée par un vaste auvent, en geste de bienvenue. À l'intérieur, les différentes parties s'organisent autour d'une cour sous verrière qui permet à la lumière naturelle de pénétrer jusqu'à l'agence bancaire du rez-de-chaussée. Au sud, perchée sur pilotis inclinés, une section de trois niveaux semble jaillir vers le ciel. La construction de la Phase I fait appel à un mur rideau d'aluminium, des panneaux d'aluminium perforé, du zinc, une structure en béton coulé sur place, des poutres en acier et des toits-terrasses métalliques.

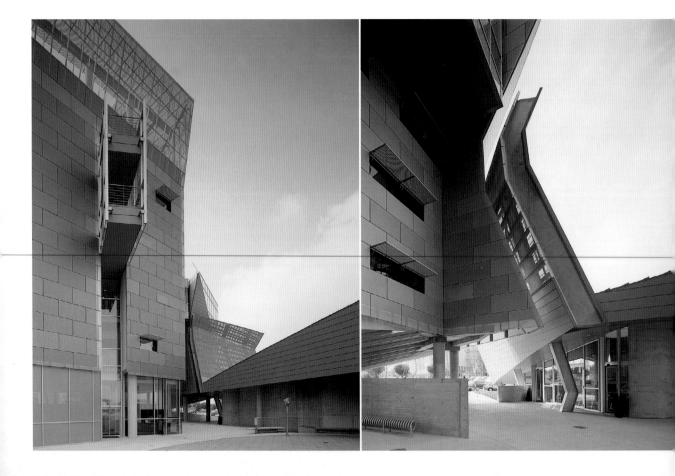

View from the west. According to the architects, the restrained budget and tight time schedule "contributed to the simplicity" of the building, which also includes office, commercial and housing space.

*Ansicht von Westen. Laut Architekten trugen das begrenzte Budget und der straffe Zeitplan zur Schlichtheit des Gebäudes bei, das neben Büros auch Geschäfte und Wohnungen enthält.*

Vue prise de l'ouest. Selon l'architecte, les limites du budget et le planning serré ont « contribué à la simplicité » du bâtiment, qui comprend également des bureaux, des espaces commerciaux et des logements.

The powerful, angular architecture of Morphosis carries through to the interior spaces, here with ample natural light. Concrete columns carry the weight of cantilevered glass and steel forms (left).

Der kraftvolle und kantige Architekturstil von Morphosis setzt sich bis in die hellen Innenräume fort. Betonsäulen tragen das Gewicht der Bauteile aus Glas und Stahl (links).

La puissante et anguleuse vision architecturale de Morphosis se poursuit dans les volumes intérieurs, qui bénéficient d'un généreux éclairage naturel. Des colonnes de béton supportent le poids des volumes de verre et d'acier en porte-à-faux (à gauche).

# JEAN NOUVEL

*Architectures Jean Nouvel*
*10, Cité d'Angoulème*
*75011 Paris*
*France*

*Tel: + 33 1 49 23 83 83*
*Fax: + 33 1 43 14 81 10*

*Barcelona Torre Agbar*

Born in 1945 in Fumel, France, **JEAN NOUVEL** was admitted to the École des Beaux-Arts in Bordeaux in 1964. In 1970, he created his first office with François Seigneur. His first widely-noticed project was the Institut du Monde Arabe in Paris (1981–1987, with Architecture Studio). Other works include his Nemausus housing, Nîmes, (1985–1987); offices for the CLM/BBDO advertising firm, Issy-les Moulineaux (1988–1992); Lyon Opera House, Lyon (1986–1993); Vinci Conference Center, Tours (1989–1993); Euralille Shopping Center, Lille (1991–1994); Fondation Cartier, Paris (1991–1995); Galeries Lafayette, Berlin (1992–1996); and his unbuilt projects for the 400 meter tall "Tours sans fins," La Défense, Paris (1989); Grand Stade for the 1998 World Cup, Paris (1994); and Tenaga Nasional Tower, Kuala Lumpur (1995). His largest recently completed project is the Music and Conference Center in Lucerne, Switzerland (1998–2000). He won both the competition for the Musée du Quai Branly, Paris, and the competition for the refurbishment of the Reina Sofia Center, Madrid, in 1999. Current work includes plans for the Standard Hotel in Soho (New York) and a building for the Dentsu advertising agency in Tokyo.

**JEAN NOUVEL**, geboren 1945 im französischen Fumel, studierte ab 1964 an der École des Beaux-Arts in Bordeaux. 1970 gründete er zusammen mit François Seigneur sein erstes Büro. Weithin bekannt wurde Nouvel durch sein Institut du Monde Arabe in Paris (1981–87), bei dem er mit Architecture Studio zusammenarbeitete. Weitere herausragende Werke sind die Wohnanlage Nemausus in Nîmes (1985–87), die Büros der Werbeagentur CLM/BBDO in Issy-les-Moulineaux (1988–92), das Opernhaus in Lyon (1986–93), das internationale Kongresszentrum Vinci in Tours (1989–93), das Einkaufszentrum Euralille in Lille (1991–94), die Fondation Cartier in Paris (1991–95), die Galeries Lafayette in Berlin (1992–96). Außerdem plante Jean Nouvel den 400 m hohen »Tour sans fin« in La Défense, Paris (1989), das Grand Stade für die Fußball-Weltmeisterschaft von 1998 in Paris (1994) und den Tenaga National Tower in Kuala Lumpur, Malaysia (1995), die aber alle nicht realisiert wurden. Das umfangreichste seiner jüngsten Projekte ist das Kultur- und Kongresszentrum in Luzern (1998–2000). Im Jahr 1999 gewann er sowohl den Wettbewerb für das Musée du Quai Branly in Paris wie den für die Modernisierung des Reina Sofia Zentrums in Madrid. Derzeit plant Jean Nouvel das Hotel Standard im New Yorker Stadtteil Soho und ein Gebäude für die Werbeagentur Dentsu in Tokio.

Né en 1945 à Fumel, France, **JEAN NOUVEL** entre à l'École des Beaux-Arts de Bordeaux en 1964. En 1970, il crée sa première agence en compagnie de François Seigneur. Son premier projet internationalement remarqué est l'Institut du Monde Arabe, à Paris, (1981–87, avec Architecture Studio). Parmi ses autres réalisations : les immeubles d'appartements Nemausus, à Nîmes (1985–87) ; les bureaux de l'agence de publicité CLM/BBDO (Issy-les-Moulineaux, 1988–92) ; l'Opéra de Lyon (1986–93) ; le palais des congrès Vinci (Tours, 1989–93) ; le centre commercial Euralille (Lille, 1991–94) ; la Fondation Cartier (Paris, 1991–95) ; les Galeries Lafayette (Berlin, 1992–96). Parmi ses projets non réalisés : une tour de 400 m, «La tour sans fin» (La Défense, Paris, 1989) ; le Grand Stade de la Coupe du monde de football 1998, (Paris, 1994) ; la Tour nationale Tenaga (Kuala Lumpur, Malaisie, 1995). Son plus récent grand projet est le Centre de Congrès et de Musique de Lucerne (Suisse, 1992–99). En 1999, il a remporté les concours du Musée du Quai Branly (Paris) et celui de la restructuration-extension du Centre Reina Sofia (Madrid). Actuellement, il travaille aux plans du Standard Hotel de Soho (New York), et à ceux d'un immeuble pour l'agence de publicité Dentsu (Tokyo).

# BARCELONA TORRE AGBAR

*Barcelona, Spain, 2001–2003*

*Client: Agbar Water Company. Height: 142 m. Area: 47,500 m². Auditorium size: 350 seats.*

Whether it is seen as an airborne lozenge or a blatant phallic symbol, the **AGBAR TOWER**, set in the heart of the capital of the region of Catalonia in Spain, along the famous Diagonal Avenue, will be a reference point in the Barcelona skyline. "The surface of the building," says Jean Nouvel, "evokes water: smooth, continuous but also vibrant and transparent since its matter can be read as an uncertain depth and color, luminous and with nuances." This reference to water, as elliptical as it may seem translated from French, is a clear evocation of the client's interest since Agbar is the water company of Barcelona. It is to have a height of 142 meters and a total floor area of 47,500 square meters, including a 350-seat auditorium. Though Nouvel speaks of the liquid and thus indeterminate nature of the design, it may also evoke the rougher forms of Antoni Gaudí like the Sagrada Familia. It also bears a partial resemblance to Nouvel's earlier "Tour sans fin" (La Défense, Paris, 1989).

Ob man ihn nun als aufsteigenden Rhombus oder als offenkundiges Phallussymbol betrachtet, der im Herzen der Hauptstadt der spanischen Provinz Katalonien, am berühmten Boulevard Diagonal errichtete **AGBAR-TURM** wird zweifellos zu einem Wahrzeichen der Skyline von Barcelona werden. »Die Gebäudeoberfläche evoziert«, so der Architekt, »das Bild von Wasser: glatt und stetig, aber auch bewegt und transparent, da seine Substanz als farbige und unbestimmte Tiefe voll schimmernder Nuancen interpretiert werden kann.« Auch wenn diese Referenz an das Wasser in der Übersetzung aus dem Französischen vielleicht elliptisch klingt, enthält sie doch einen klaren Verweis auf die unternehmerische Tätigkeit des Bauherrn, da die Firma Agbar für Barcelonas Wasserversorgung zuständig ist. Der Turm wird eine Höhe von 142 m haben und eine Geschossfläche von insgesamt 47.500 m² umfassen, einschließlich eines Veranstaltungssaals mit 350 Sitzen. Obgleich Nouvel von einem fließenden und folglich unbestimmbaren Charakter des Designs spricht, kann seine Gestaltung durchaus an die ungeschliffeneren Formen von Antoni Gaudís »Sagrada Familia« erinnern. Darüber hinaus ähnelt der Turm in gewissen Aspekten Nouvels Entwurf des »Tour sans fin« von 1989 in La Défense, Paris.

Qu'on la considère comme un losange en lévitation ou un symbole phallique évident, la **TOUR AGBAR**, au cœur de la capitale de la Catalogne, le long de la célèbre Avenida Diagonal, sera certainement l'un des nouveaux points de repère du paysage urbain barcelonais. « La surface du bâtiment », explique Jean Nouvel, « évoque l'eau, lisse, continue, mais également vibrante et transparente, dont la matière peut être lue comme une profondeur et une couleur incertaines, lumineuse dans ses nuances ». Cette référence à l'eau évoque les activités d'Agbar, la compagnie des eaux de Barcelone. La tour devrait s'élever à 142 m pour une surface totale de 47 500 m² et comprendra un auditorium de 350 places. Parlant de liquide, Nouvel évoque également une certaine indétermination formelle, mais on peut aussi penser aux formes plus brutales d'Antoni Gaudí, en particulier aux tours de la Sagrada Familia, voire en partie au projet non réalisé de Nouvel pour La Défense (1989), la « Tour sans fin ».

*Situated near a major intersection of the critical Diagonal Avenue, the tower in a sense dominates Barcelona. The Sagrada Familia church by Gaudi is on the right in this computer generated image.*

*Der nahe einer großen Kreuzung am Boulevard Diagonal errichtete Turm ragt aus der Innenstadt von Barcelona empor. Auf der rechten Seite des Computerbilds sieht man die Kirche Sagrada Familia von Antoni Gaudí.*

*Situé auprès d'un grand carrefour de l'avenue Diagonal, la tour domine en quelque sorte Barcelone. Dans cette image de synthèse, l'église de Gaudí, la Sagrada Familia, se trouve sur la droite.*

# TEMPORARY GUGGENHEIM MUSEUM

*Tokyo, Japan, 2001*

*Client: Solomon R. Guggenheim Foundation. Size: 80 m long, 40 m wide, 22 m high (artificial mountain).*
*Total area: 7,640 m². Exhibition area: 4,700 m².*

Modern Japan carefully watches the changing seasons through such events as the cherry blossom season. Seizing on this local fervor, Nouvel makes the Guggenheim into a "natural" event with an artificial mountain.

Auch das moderne Japan schenkt den Jahreszeiten und ihren besonderen Ereignissen wie der Kirschblüte große Aufmerksamkeit. Diese nationale Leidenschaft aufgreifend, macht Nouvel aus dem Guggenheim ein »Naturereignis« mit einem künstlichen Berg.

Le Japon moderne observe toujours avec attention le changement des saisons, par exemple lors de la floraison des cerisiers. S'appuyant sur cette tradition locale, Nouvel fait du Guggenheim un lieu « naturel » au moyen d'une montagne artificielle.

Intended as a location for temporary exhibitions organized by the Solomon R. Guggenheim Foundation, the **TEMPORARY GUGGENHEIM MUSEUM** was the object of a limited competition won by Zaha Hadid. The entry of Jean Nouvel consists of four box-like galleries set under a steel scaffolding that appears to be a hill covered with cherry trees and maples. Nouvel also used the idea of an artificial mountain in an urban setting in his competition entry for the Museum of Human Evolution in Burgos, Spain. Here, Nouvel also plays on the Japanese sensitivity to nature and the change of seasons. The Exhibition Hall of the complex beneath this artificial mountain is designed to be over 80 meters long, forty meters wide and 22 meters high. Exhibition area for the four spaces is 4,700 square meters, with 7,640 square meters as the total gross area of the facility. As sources of inspiration for the design, Jean Nouvel cites, "Mount Fuji, Kapoor, Penone, Koons, Simonds and the pyramid with its buried treasures."

Das **TEMPORARY GUGGENHEIM MUSEUM** Tokyo ist als Standort für Sonderausstellungen der Solomon R. Guggenheim Foundation geplant und war das Resultat eines von Zaha Hadid gewonnenen Wettbewerbs mit beschränkter Teilnehmerzahl. Der Beitrag von Jean Nouvel besteht aus vier schachtelförmigen Ausstellungsräumen unter einem Stahlgerüst, das aussieht wie ein mit Kirsch- und Ahornbäumen bedeckter Hügel. Nouvel hat die Idee eines künstlichen Hügels in einer urbanen Umgebung bereits in seinem Wettbewerbsbeitrag für das Museum der Entwicklungsgeschichte des Menschen im spanischen Burgos verwendet. Hier spielt Nouvel außerdem mit der Empfänglichkeit der Japaner für die Natur und den Wechsel der Jahreszeiten. Der unter diesem künstlichen Berg gelegene Ausstellungssaal ist über 80 m lang, 40 m breit und 22 m hoch. Die vier Räume bieten eine Ausstellungsfläche von 4.700 m², wobei der gesamte Komplex eine Nutzfläche von 7.640 m² umfasst. Als Inspirationsquellen für seinen Entwurf nennt Jean Nouvel »den Berg Fuji, Kapoor, Penone, Koons, Simonds und die Pyramiden mit ihren verborgenen Schätzen«.

Lieu d'expositions temporaires pour la Solomon R. Guggenheim Foundation, le **TEMPORARY GUGGENHEIM MUSEUM** a été l'objet d'un concours restreint remporté par Zaha Hadid. La proposition de Jean Nouvel se composait de six galeries-boîtes sous un échafaudage d'acier formant une colline plantée de cerisiers et d'érables. Nouvel avait déjà utilisé cette idée de montagne artificielle urbaine pour le concours du Musée de l'Évolution Humaine à Burgos, Espagne. Il joue ici sur la sensibilité japonaise à la nature et au changement des saisons. Le hall d'exposition de 80 m de long, 40 de large et 22 de haut s'accompagne de 4 700 m² de surfaces d'exposition réparties dans les quatre volumes, l'ensemble représentant 7 640 m² utiles. Jean Nouvel cite parmi ses sources : « Le Mont Fuji, Kapoor, Penone, Koons, Simonds, les pyramides et leurs trésors enfouis. »

*Beneath the very unexpected artificial mountain, Nouvel has lodged inexpensive sheds intended for the temporary display of contemporary art.*

*Im Inneren des ungewöhnlichen künstlichen Hügels hat Nouvel für Sonderausstellungen zeitgenössischer Kunst schachtelförmige Ausstellungsräume aus preiswerten Materialien installiert.*

*Sous cette curieuse montagne artificielle, Nouvel a logé des sheds de construction économique, adaptés à la présentation temporaire d'œuvres d'art contemporaines.*

The Exhibition Galleries:
*metallic structure of industrial type*
*(sheet pilling)*

The plugging:
*technical logistic in the interface*
*of both structures*
*this system is totally waterproof*

The primary structure
*of vegetalisation*

The vegetalisation

*Restaurant View*

Nouvel's presentation for the Guggenheim competition that he did not
win, includes realistic computer
generated images of the museum
in all seasons, and even a map of
the "topography" of the artificial
mountain.

Zu Nouvels Beitrag für den Guggen-
heim-Wettbewerb gehörten realis-
tische Computerbilder des Museums
zu allen Jahreszeiten und sogar eine
topographische Karte des künstlichen
Hügels.

La présentation de Nouvel pour le
concours du Guggenheim – qu'il
n'a pas remporté – comprenait des
images de synthèse du musée en
toutes saisons, ainsi qu'une carte
« topographique » de la montagne
artificielle.

*Entrance View*

# MARCOS NOVAK

*Marcos Novak*
*510 Venice Way*
*Venice, California 90291*
*United States*

*e-mail: marcos@centrifuge.org*
*Web: www.centrifuge.org/marcos*

*AlloBi*

**MARCOS NOVAK** received a Bachelor of Science in Architecture, a Master of Architecture and a Certificate of Specialization in Computer-Aided Architecture from Ohio State University (Columbus, Ohio). He has worked as a Research Fellow at the Centre for Advanced Inquiry in the Interactive Arts at the University of Wales, as Co-Director of the Transarchitectures Foundation in Paris (with Paul Virilio), and has taught at the University of California (Los Angeles) and at Ohio State University. He has numerous publications to his credit. His work has been essentially virtual, and he is regarded as the "pioneer of the architecture of virtuality" according to the organizers of the 7th International Architecture Exhibition in Venice, in which he participated (Greek Pavilion). He is known for such projects as his "Sensor Space," "From Immersion to Eversion," "Transmitting Architecture," "Liquid Architectures," and "Metadata Visualization."

**MARCOS NOVAK** erwarb den Bachelor of Science in Architecture, den Master of Architecture und ein Spezialisierungszertifikat in computergestützter Architektur an der Ohio State University in Columbus, Ohio. Er war als Research Fellow am Centre for Advanced Inquiry in the Interactive Arts der University of Wales, als Co-Direktor (zusammen mit Paul Virilio) der Stiftung Transarchitectures in Paris tätig, hat an der University of California in Los Angeles und an der Ohio State University in Columbus gelehrt und sich mit zahlreichen Buchpublikationen einen Namen gemacht. Seine bisherigen Architekturprojekte sind größtenteils virtueller Art. Laut den Organisatoren der 7. Architekturbiennale in Venedig, für die er den Griechischen Pavillon gestaltete, gilt Novak allgemein als »Pionier der virtuellen Architektur«. Bekannt wurde er mit Projekten wie Sensor Space, From Immersion to Eversion, Transmitting Architecture, Liquid Architectures und Metadata Visualization.

**MARCOS NOVAK** est titulaire d'un B. Sc. en architecture, d'un M. Arch. et d'un certificat de spécialisation en architecture assistée par ordinateur de l'Ohio State University (Columbus, Ohio). Il a été chercheur au Centre for Advanced Inquiry in the Interactive Arts de l'Université du Pays de Galles, codirecteur de la Fondation transarchitectures (Paris, avec Paul Virilio) et a enseigné à l'Université de Californie (Los Angeles) et Ohio State University. Il a beaucoup publié. Son œuvre est essentiellement virtuelle et il est considéré comme le « pionnier de l'architecture de la virtualité » selon les organisateurs de la 7e Exposition internationale d'architecture de Venise à laquelle il a participé (Pavillon grec). Il est connu pour des projets comme son « Sensor Space », « From Imersion to Eversion », « Transmitting Architecture », « Liquid Architectures » et « Metadata Visualization ».

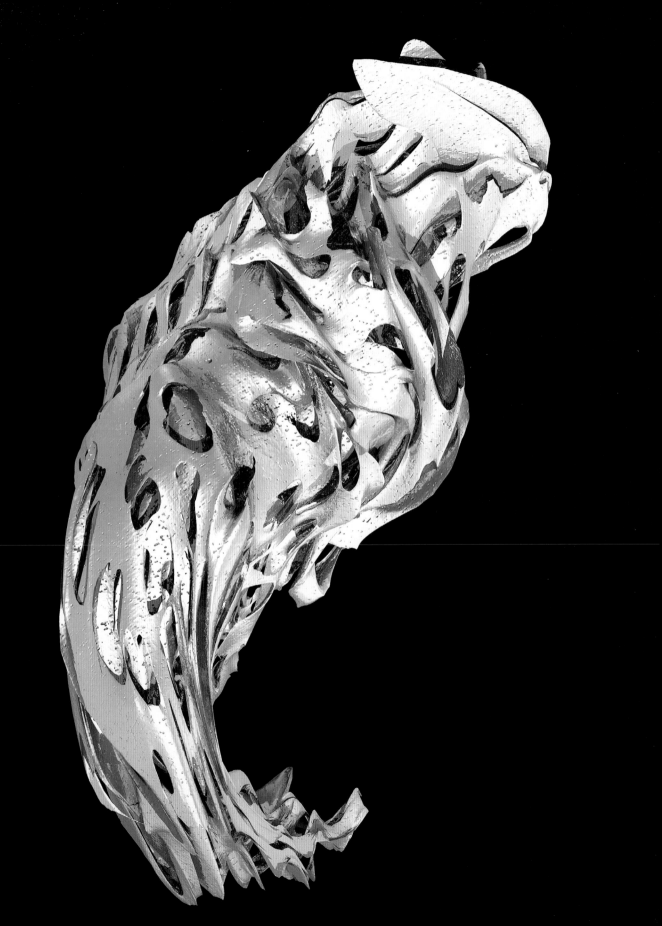

# V4D_TRANSAURA, ECHINODERM, ALIENWITHIN, ECHINODERM_RP, ALLOBIO

*2001*

Marcos Novak is the most visible proponent of cyberspace as an autonomous architectural field of inquiry. He actively uses non-Euclidean spatial concepts with the idea of algorithmic unfolding, the mathematical modeling of data space navigable computer environments to create unexpected forms. He is at the origin of the idea of "liquid architectures" and "transarchitectures" which he sees as part of a larger movement that he terms "transmodernity." Novak can be considered an artist as much as an architect. His liquid architectures are intended to combine opposites – soft and hard, real and virtual, masculine and feminine to create a third or "alien" condition. Novak worked with Kas Oosterhuis on the trans-ports 2001 project (also published in this volume). Novak seeks nothing less than "warpings into alien territory, true transmutations into unpredictable conceptual spaces, phase transitions into completely new states of being."

Marcos Novak ist der bekannteste Verfechter der Idee des Cyberspace als eines autonomen Bereichs der Architektur. Er verwendet nicht-euklidische Raumkonzepte und verknüpft sie mit der Idee algorithmischer Entfaltung, der mathematischen Modellierung von Daten und steuerbaren Computer-Environments, um neue Formen zu kreieren. Die von ihm ausgehende Vorstellung »fließender Architekturen« oder »Transarchitekturen« sieht er als Teil einer größeren Bewegung, für die er den Begriff »Transmodernität« geprägt hat. Novak kann ebenso sehr als Künstler wie als Architekt angesehen werden, der mit seinen fließenden Bauwerken versucht, Gegensätze miteinander zu verbinden — weich und hart, real und virtuell, maskulin und feminin —, um damit einen jeweils dritten oder »fremden« Zustand zu schaffen. Marcos Novak, der zusammen mit Kas Oosterhuis an dem ebenfalls hier vorgestellten Projekt trans-ports 2001 gearbeitet hat, beschreibt seine künstlerischen Ziele als »Verzerrungen, die in fremdes Terrain reichen, als echte Transmutationen in unvorhersehbare konzeptionelle Räume und Phasenumwandlungen in vollkommen neue Seinszustände.«

Marcos Novak est l'un des représentants les plus célèbres du cyberespace, considéré comme un champ de recherches architecturales. Il met en œuvre des concepts spatiaux non-euclidiens, des déploiements algorithmiques et des modélisations mathématiques d'environnements spatiaux numériques navigables pour créer des formes inattendues. Il est à l'origine de l'idée « d'architectures liquides » et de « transarchitectures » dans laquelle il voit les éléments d'un mouvement plus vaste nommé « transmodernité ». Il est autant artiste qu'architecte. Ses architectures liquides combinent des opposés — mou/dur, réel/virtuel, masculin/féminin — pour créer un troisième état « étranger ». Il a travaillé avec Kas Oosterhuis sur le projet trans-ports 2001 (également reproduit dans cet ouvrage). Il ne cherche rien moins que « des gauchissements vers des territoires étrangers, d'authentiques transmutations dans des espaces conceptuels imprévisibles, des phases de transition dans des états entièrement nouveaux ».

*V4D_TransAura: higher dimensional geometries are used to create invisible architectures. Shown above is one of these, presented as a sculpture verging on an architectonic scale.*
*AlloBio: These forms anticipate a radical possibility: that of a literally living architecture, or of an architecture biologically grown of materials that are quasi-alive, while still directly connected to virtual space.*

*V4D_TransAura: Höherdimensionale Geometrie wird zur Gestaltung unsichtbarer Architekturformen eingesetzt, wie die an architektonische Maßstäbe grenzende Skulptur (oben).*
*AlloBio: Diese Formen antizipieren die radikale Möglichkeit einer buchstäblich lebendigen Architektur, beziehungsweise einer Architektur, die biologisch aus quasi-lebendigen und dennoch direkt mit dem virtuellen*

Raum verbundenen Materialien entsteht (rechts).

*V4D_TransAura : Des configurations dimensionnelles plus importantes sont utilisées pour créer des architectures invisibles. En haut, l'une d'elles, présentée comme une sculpture d'une échelle presque architectonique.*
*AlloBio : ces formes anticipent la possibilité radicale d'une architecture*

littéralement vivante, ou d'une architecture d'origine quasi biologique issue de matériaux qui sont à la fois quasi vivants et directement connectés à l'espace virtuel.

AlloBio: Several distinct investigations converge on this project: the overarching question of the theoretical and critical production of the "alien" in our culture; the merging of the technological and the biological; and the continuity between the actual, the virtual, and the invisible.

AlloBio: In diesem Projekt bündeln sich mehrere unterschiedliche Untersuchungsgegenstände: die übergeordnete Frage nach der theoretischen und kritischen Produktion des »Fremden« in unserer Kultur, das Verschmelzen von Technologie und Biologie sowie die Kontinuität zwischen dem Realen, dem Virtuellen und dem Unsichtbaren.

AlloBio : ce projet est l'aboutissement de la convergence de plusieurs recherches distinctes : l'interrogation omniprésente de la production théorique et critique de « l'étranger » dans notre culture ; la fusion du technologique et du biologique ; la continuité entre le réel, le virtuel et l'invisible.

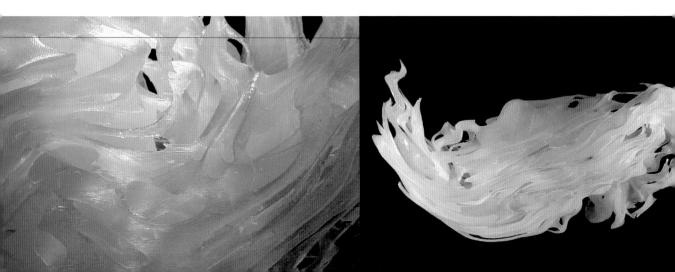

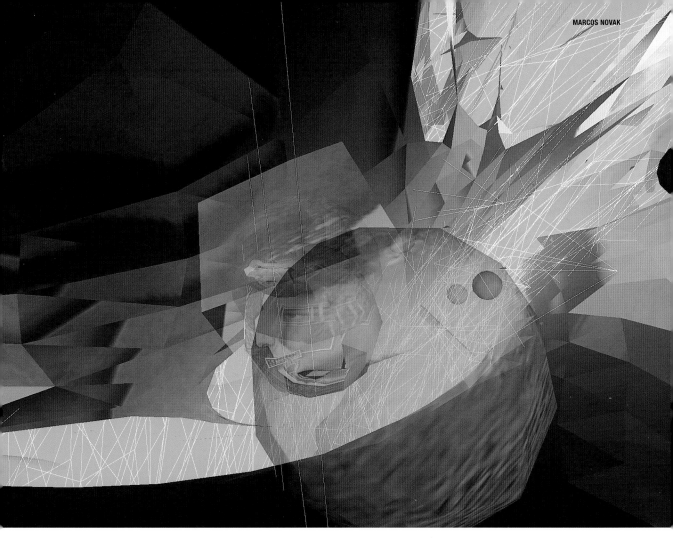

*AlloBio: Viewers and participants in the Allotopes of Venezia, Firenze, and Erice were asked to express their affective state through interactions with sensor-implemented invisible sculptures. These affective data streams were then used to alter and deform the simplified versions of the Echinoderm.*

*AlloBio: Betrachter und Teilnehmer der Allotope in Venedig, Florenz und Erice wurden gebeten, ihre Gefühle in der Interaktion mit den sensorge-führten unsichtbaren Skulpturen aus-zudrücken. Diese affektiven Daten-ströme wurden anschließend dazu verwendet, die vereinfachten Versio-nen des Echinoderms zu verändern und zu verformen.*

*AlloBio : les spectateurs et partici-pants des Allotopes montés à Venise, Florence et Erice étaient conviés à exprimer leur état affectif à travers des interactions avec des sculptures invisibles bardées de capteurs. Ces flux de données affectives servaient ensuite à modifier et déformer les versions simplifiées de l'Echinoderm.*

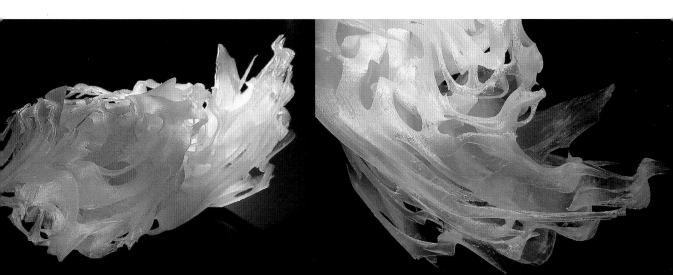

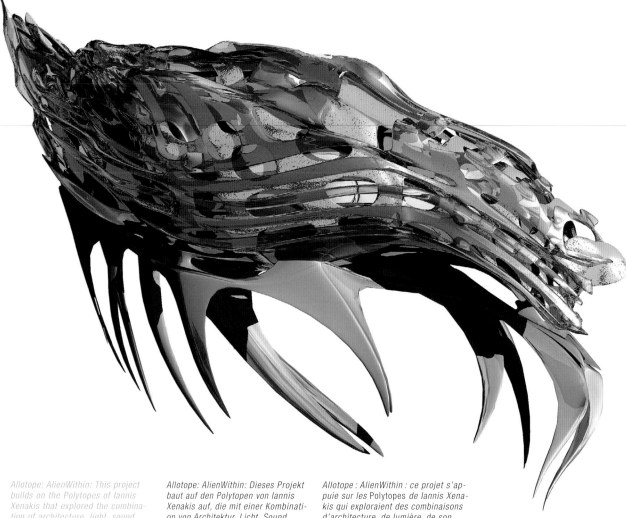

Allotope: AlienWithin: This project builds on the Polytopes of Iannis Xenakis that explored the combination of architecture, light, sound, computation, performance and environmental art. To these, the Allotopes add generativity, transactivity, and virtuality. Shown above are images of navigations through the virtual environments created for this project.

Allotope: AlienWithin: Dieses Projekt baut auf den Polytopen von Iannis Xenakis auf, die mit einer Kombination von Architektur, Licht, Sound, Computeroperation, Performance und Environment-Kunst experimentierten. Die Allotope erweitern diese Elemente um die der Generativität, Transaktivität und Virtualität. Bildliche Darstellung der Navigationen durch die für dieses Projekt erzeugten virtuellen Environments (oben).

Allotope : AlienWithin : ce projet s'appuie sur les Polytopes de Iannis Xenakis qui exploraient des combinaisons d'architecture, de lumière, de son, d'informatique, de performance et d'art environnemental. Les Allotopes y ajoutent reproductivité, transactivité, et virtualité. En haut, images de navigation à travers les environnements virtuels créés pour ce projet.

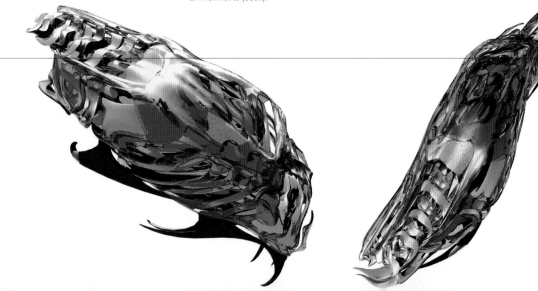

*Echinoderm_RP: Using stereolithography, these were realized as solid objects. In conversations with the artists and scientists of Symbiotica, three possibilities arose: that the forms be replaced with living bone tissue; that these forms be covered with living skin; or both. This led to the idea of a genuinely living architecture, subject of the AlloBio, shown on the previous pages.*

*Echinoderm_RP: Mittels Stereolithographie wurden räumliche Objekte realisiert. In Gesprächen mit den Künstlern und Wissenschaftlern von Symbiotica ergaben sich drei Möglichkeiten: die Formen durch lebendes Knochengewebe zu ersetzen, sie mit lebender Haut zu bedecken oder beides zusammen. Das führte zur Idee einer genuin lebendigen Architektur, Thema des auf den vorigen Seiten abgebildeten AlloBio-Projekts.*

*Echinoderm_RP : ces formes ont été réalisées en objets réels, par le procédé de stéréophotographie. Au cours des conversations avec les artistes et les chercheurs de Symbiotica, trois possibilités sont apparues : que les formes soient remplacées par des tissus osseux vivants ; qu'elle soient recouvertes de peau vivante ; ou les deux. Ceci a conduit à l'idée d'une architecture authentiquement vivante, sujet de AlloBio, montré dans les pages précédentes.*

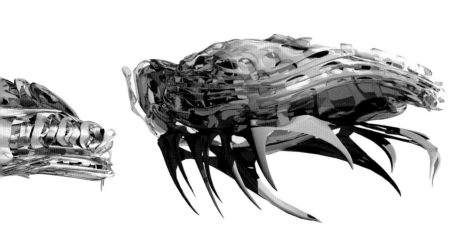

# NOX

*NOX Architekten*
*Mathenesserlaan 443*
*3023 GJ Rotterdam*
*The Netherlands*

*Tel/Fax: + 31 10 477 2853*
*e-mail: nox@luna.nl*

**NOX** is a cooperative venture between **LARS SPUYBROEK**, who was born in 1959 in Rotterdam, and **MAURICE NIO**. Both studied at the Technical University in Delft. Their work has won several prizes (Archiprix 1989, Mart Stam Incentive Prize 1991) and has been supported by various grants (Enterprise Start-up Grants 1989 and 1992, Travel Grants 1992 and 1994, Work Grant 1994). Their work includes the Foam Home, a housing project for the KAN area near Nijmegen, 1997; OffTheRoad/103.8MHz, housing and noise barrier, Eindhoven, 1998–1999, and the V2_Engine, proposed facade for the V2_Organization, Rotterdam, 1997–1999. Simultaneously with the formation of NOX-Architects, they created NOX-Magazine. Other activities include the translation of books into Dutch (Baudrillard: *Fatal Strategies*, and *America*), video productions (Belaagde Landen, Walvisspiegel, NOX' Soft City, Day-Glo LA), and installations (Armed Response, Den Bosch; Heavenly Bodies, Eindhoven). Lars Spuybroek and Maurice Nio regularly give talks and work as lecturers (Rietveld Academy, Amsterdam, Technical University Delft, and the architectural academies at Tilburg, Arnhem and Amsterdam). Lars Spuybroek is also editor of the journal *Forum*.

**NOX** ist der Name des Gemeinschaftsunternehmens von **LARS SPUYBROEK**, geboren 1959 in Rotterdam, und **MAURICE NIO**. Beide studierten an der Technischen Universität in Delft. Für ihre Arbeit erhielten sie etliche Preise und Stipendien, wie den Archiprix von 1989 und den Mart Stam Incentive Prize von 1991. Zu ihren Werken gehören das Foam Home, ein Wohnbauprojekt für das Gebiet KAN bei Nimwegen (1997), OffTheRoad/103,8 Mhz, Wohnungsbau und Schallschutzmauer in Eindhoven (1998–99) sowie V2_Engine, ein Fassadenentwurf für die V2_Organisation in Rotterdam (1997–99). Gleichzeitig mit der Eröffnung des NOX-Büros gründeten Lars Spuybroek und Maurice Nio die Zeitschrift *NOX*. Zu ihren weiteren Aktivitäten gehören Buchübersetzungen (Baudrillard), Videofilmproduktionen (Belaagde Landen, Walvisspiegel, NOX' Soft City, Day-Glo LA) und Installationen (»Armed Response«, Den Bosch; »Heavenly Bodies«, Eindhoven) sowie regelmäßige Vorträge und Diskussionsveranstaltungen an der Rietveld-Akademie in Amsterdam, der Technischen Universität Delft und den Architekturhochschulen in Tilburg, Arnhem und Amsterdam. Lars Spuybroek ist zudem Herausgeber der Zeitschrift *Forum*.

**NOX** est une entreprise coopérative créée par **LARS SPUYBROEK**, né en 1959 à Rotterdam, et **MAURICE NIO**. Tous deux ont étudié à l'Université technique de Delft. Leurs travaux leur ont valu plusieurs prix – Archprix (1989), Mart Stam Incentive Prize (1991) – et ont bénéficié de nombreuses bourses (Enterprise Start-up Grants 1989 et 1992, bourses de voyages 1992 et 1994, bourses de travail 1994). Parmi leurs réalisations : la Foam Home, projet de logement pour le quartier KAN, près de Nimègue, 1997 ; OffTheRoad/103.8 Home, projet de logements et barrière phonique (Eindhoven, 1998–99) et le VR_Engine, façade proposée pour la V2_Organisation (Rotterdam, 1997–99). Parallèlement à NOX-Architects, ils ont lancé *NOX-Magazine*. Parmi leurs autres activités, la traduction de livres en néerlandais (*Stratégies fatales* et *America* de J. Baudrillard), la production de vidéos (Belaagde Landen, Walvisspiegel, NOX'Soft City, Day-Glo LA) et des installations (Armed Response, Den Bosch ; Hevenly Bodies, Eindhoven). Lars Spuybroek et Maurice Nio donnent régulièrement des conférences et sont lecteurs à l'Académie Rietveld, Amsterdam, à l'Université technique de Delft, et aux académies d'architecture de Tilburg, Arnhem et Amsterdam. Lars Spuybroek est également rédacteur en chef du journal *Forum*.

# HOLOSKIN

*Maison Folie, Lille-Wazemmes, France, 2001*

Client: Ville de Lille. Floor area: renovation 3,800 m², Salle de Spectacles 1,100 m².
Materials: concrete, steel and stainless steel mesh. Cost: 5,400,000 euros.

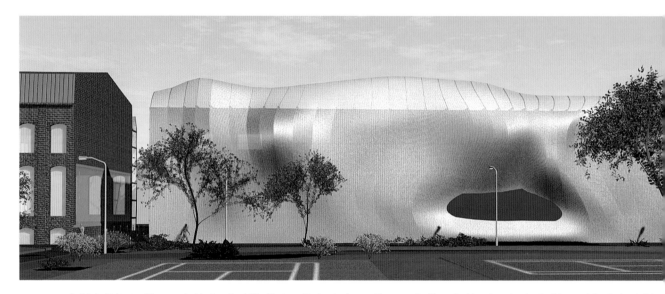

In this invited competition organized by the city of Lille, Nox based their entry for a multi-purpose facility on the idea of a network set within an existing factory building. Their intention was to produce "an ineradicable image, that will be both part of local dreams and memories, the local psychogeography, but also connects to the global layers of art and media." They opted for a "respectful and modest treatment of the existing buildings," including cleaning and repairing of the façades and windows. The Maison Folie's "program needs an architecture that stimulates unexpected encounters," says Lars Spuybroek. An unusual feature is the undulating floor akin to the local "pavés du Nord." "The landscape," another important factor in the design, "makes everything interact more easily," say the architects, "and feeds activity to activity." The strong image is provided by an outside surface they describe in the following manner: "Externally, a beautiful skin, a dress that moves with activities. This glowing, almost holographic dress, not hiding the black box, but shimmering with moiré because of its slight transparency, incorporates all the pulsations of art and life."

Der Entwurf eines Mehrzweckbaus, den NOX für den von der Stadt Lille organisierten Wettbewerb einreichte, basiert auf der Idee, ein Netzwerk in ein bestehendes Fabrikgebäude einzufügen. Ziel der Architekten war es, »ein unauslöschliches Bild« zu kreieren, »das sowohl Teil der Träume und Erinnerungen der ortsansässigen Bewohner, also der lokalen Psychogeografie, werden als auch sich mit den globalen Sphären von Kunst und Medien verbinden sollte«. Sie entschieden sich für eine »respektvolle und bescheidene Bearbeitung der existierenden Gebäudeteile«, einschließlich der Reinigung und Instandsetzung von Außenwänden und Fenstern. »Das Projekt Maison Folie verlangt nach einer Architektur, die zu unerwarteten Begegnungen anregt«, so Lars Spuybroek. Eine Besonderheit der Innenraumgestaltung bilden die gewellten Oberflächen der Böden, die den typischen regionalen Pflastersteinen, den »pavés du Nord«, sehr ähneln. Als weiteren ausschlaggebenden Gestaltungsfaktor nennen die Architekten die Landschaft, »die alles leichter miteinander interagieren lässt und Aktivität mit Aktivität speist.« Der starke Eindruck, den das Gebäude von außen macht, rührt von einer Oberfläche, von der die Gestalter sagen: »Äußerlich ist es eine schöne Haut, ein Kleid, das sich mit den Aktivitäten im Gebäudeinneren bewegt. Dieses glänzende, fast holographische Kleid versteckt nicht die darunter liegende Black Box, sondern wirkt in seiner leichten Transparenz wie ein matt schimmerndes Moiré, ein Stoff, der all die Schwingungen von Kunst und Leben in sich aufnimmt.«

La proposition d'équipement multifonctions de Nox remise pour un concours sur invitation organisé par la ville de Lille repose sur un concept de réseau à l'intérieur d'un bâtiment d'usine existant. L'intention était de produire « une image puissante, qui fera partie à la fois des rêves et de la mémoire locale et de la psychogéographie locale, mais sera également connectée aux strates globales d'art et de médias ». Les architectes ont opté pour « un traitement respectueux et modeste des bâtiments existants comprenant le nettoyage et la réparation des façades et des fenêtres. » Ce programme a besoin d'une architecture qui stimule des rencontres inattendues « a déclaré Lars Spuybroek. Un des éléments les plus étonnants est le sol ondulé qui évoque les pavés du Nord. « Le paysage », autre élément important du projet, « fait que tout interagit plus facilement et que l'activité se nourrit d'activités ». La force de l'image est due à une surface extérieure décrite de la façon suivante : « À l'extérieur, une peau superbe, un vêtement qui bouge avec les activités. Ce vêtement brillant, presque holographique, ne cache pas la boîte noire, mais la fait vibrer d'effets de moire grâce à sa légère transparence, en intégrant toutes les pulsations de l'art et de la vie. »

*Lars Spuybroek sees this unusual, undulating façade as a "beautiful dress," and it fits in well with his own frequent use of non-Euclidean shapes in a largely computer-generated architecture.*

*Lars Spuybroek bezeichnet die ungewöhnlich gewellte Fassade als »schönes Kleid«. Sie passt zu Spuybroeks häufiger Verwendung nicht-euklidischer Formen in einer weitgehend computergenerierten Architektur.*

*Lars Spuybroek voit dans cette curieuse façade ondulée une « robe magnifique. » Elle illustre particulièrement bien son goût pour les formes non-euclidiennes dans ses créations architecturales en grande partie issues de la CAO.*

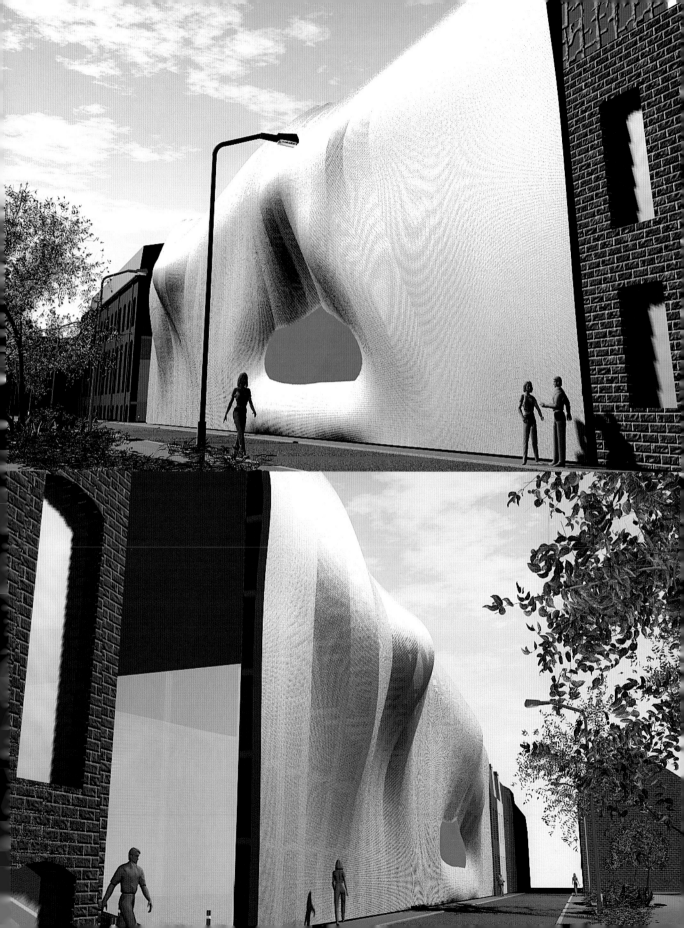

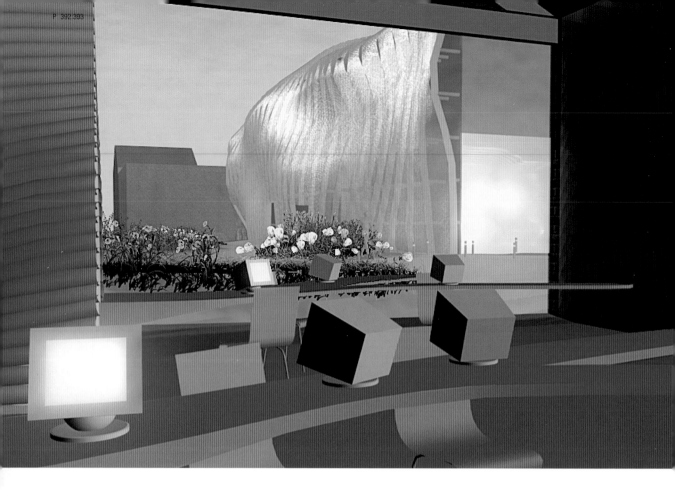

Near the Maison Folie, NOX has been commissioned to create a 5,500 m² mineral garden with concrete, asphalt, grass, and apple trees. Here a "CYBERcafé" across the square from the Maison Folie that NOX is also designing.

NOX erhielt den Auftrag, in der Nähe des Maison Folie einen 5.500 m² großen Mineraliengarten mit Beton, Asphalt, Gras und Apfelbäumen zu gestalten. Das ebenfalls von NOX entworfene CYBERcafé (im Bild) auf der dem Maison Folie gegenüberliegenden Seite des Platzes.

Près de la Maison Folie, NOX a reçu commande d'un jardin minéral de 5 500 m² en béton et asphalte, sans oublier l'herbe et les pommiers. Ici, un « cybercafé » de l'autre côté de la place de la Maison Folie, également conçu par Nox.

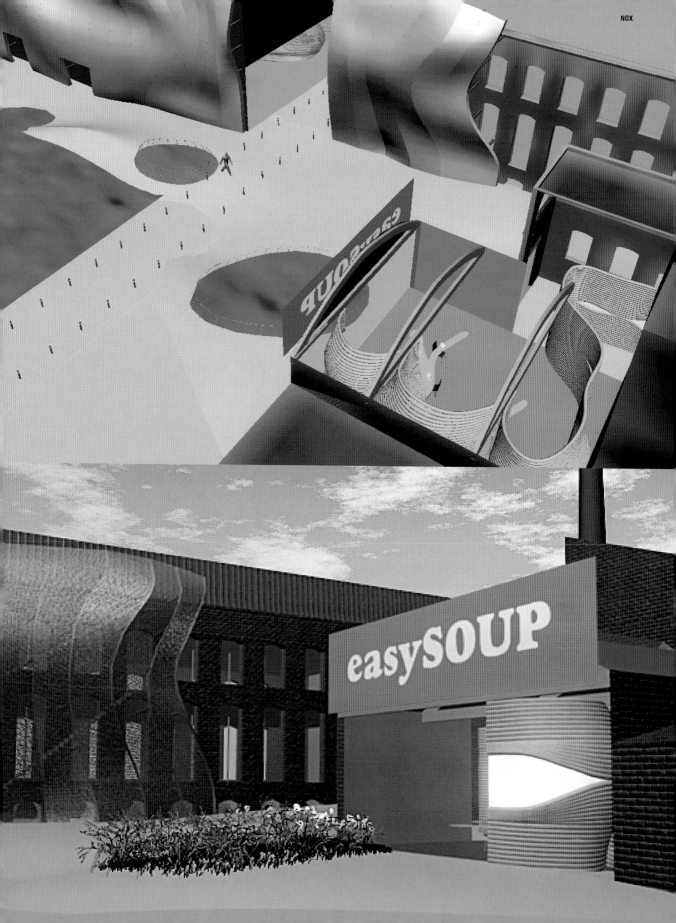

# SOFT OFFICE

*Warwickshire, United Kingdom, 2000–2005*

*Client: TV production company. Floor area: 675 m² (office), 650 m² (children's spaces).*
*Materials: computer-cut wood and polyester. Cost: 2,450,000 euros.*

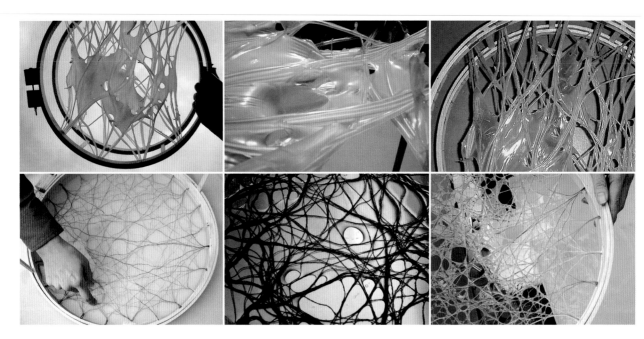

Containing shops, and interactive playground and headquarter offices for a television production company, this project is for an anonymous client in the United Kingdom. The architects have focused carefully on the relationship between work and play in this unusual facility, dividing it into three parts. The first of these they call "The Space," "like a hall, an open flexible space that doesn't have a front elevation at all. This edge splits up in a ceiling going upward and a floor that gently slopes downward into a much higher space. This slope is very well suited for children to sit, even more than in a theatre-like set up, and is always directly connected to the higher part of the hall. We have also developed a part of this area called 'Glob' (the slimy globally networked blob) where the architecture is more present, is connected to the Web and is made interactive with sensors that enable children to make Glob into a living being," says Spuybroek. Another space called "The Sponge" is allocated to office spaces, but also provides for some exchanges between office and Space. Finally, there are "The Fingers." "The building," explains the architect, "splits into four separate fingers that have small gardens in between and glass walls that look out onto these gardens, with sliding doors that will make circulation between the different fingers possible (when the weather allows for it)."

Das Projekt, das Geschäfte, einen interaktiven Kinderspielplatz sowie den Hauptsitz einer Fernsehproduktionsfirma enthalten soll, wurde für einen anonymen Bauherrn in Großbritannien entworfen. Die Architekten haben dieses ungewöhnliche Gebäude in besonderer Beachtung der Beziehung zwischen Arbeit und Spiel in drei Teile aufgegliedert. Der erste, »The Space« genannt, wird von den Architekten als »eine Art Halle, ein offener und flexibler Raum ohne Vorderseitenansicht« beschrieben. »Stattdessen teilt er sich in eine aufwärts strebende Decke und einen sanft abfallenden Boden, der in einen anderen, wesentlich höheren Raum führt. Diese Schräge eignet sich hervorragend als Sitzfläche für Kinder, noch besser als ansteigende Stuhlreihen im Theater, und ist direkt mit dem höheren Teil der Halle verbunden. Ein dem Spielbereich zugeordneter Raum heißt ›Glob‹ (der global vernetzte Schleimball). Hier ist die Architektur präsenter. Der Raum ist an das Internet angeschlossen und mit Sensoren ausgestattet, die es den Kindern ermöglichen, interaktiv aus Glob ein lebendiges Wesen zu machen«, erklärt Spuybroek. Ein zweiter, den Büroräumen zugehöriger Bereich, der auch eine Verbindung zum Spielbereich herstellt, heißt »The Sponge«. Und schließlich gibt es noch »The Fingers«. »Hier teilt sich der Baukörper«, so der Architekt, »in vier einzelne Finger mit kleinen dazwischen liegenden Gärten. Diese Räume haben Glaswände und Schiebetüren, die, falls das Wetter es erlaubt, eine Luftzirkulation zwischen den verschiedenen Bereichen ermöglichen.«

Dans ce projet qui regroupe des commerces, un terrain de jeux interactif et le siège d'une société de production de télévision, les architectes se sont attachés aux relations entre le travail et le jeu. Cette étonnante réalisation se répartit en trois sections. La première, appelée « The Space » est « comme un hall, un espace ouvert et souple sans aucune façade. Il s'ouvre dans un espace beaucoup plus vaste entre un plafond ascendant et un sol en pente douce. La pente est parfaitement adaptée aux enfants qui peuvent s'y asseoir, de façon plus naturelle que dans une organisation classique de théâtre, et reste toujours en connexion avec la partie la plus élevée du hall. Nous avons également développé une partie de cette zone appelée ‹ Glob › dans laquelle l'architecture est davantage présente. Elle est connectée au Web et devient interactive grâce à des capteurs qui permettent aux enfants d'en faire un être quasiment vivant », poursuit Spuybroek. Un autre espace intitulé « The Sponge » est consacré à des bureaux mais facilite certains échanges entre eux et le « Space ». L'ensemble se termine par « The Fingers » (Les doigts). « Le bâtiment », explique l'architecte, « se divise en quatre doigts séparés par de petits jardins et des parois de verre qui donnent sur eux. Des portes coulissantes permettent la circulation entre ces différentes parties lorsque le temps le permet. »

*The web of spaces imagined for the interior of the Soft Office by NOX includes an interactive play area for children (right, below) as well as slightly more traditional offices.*

*Die von NOX entworfenen Innenräume des Soft Office enthalten einen interaktiven Spielbereich für Kinder (rechts unten) sowie etwas traditioneller gestaltete Büros.*

*Les espaces en réseau imaginés pour l'intérieur du Soft Office de NOX comprennent une zone de jeux interactifs pour enfants (en bas à droite) ainsi que des bureaux un peu plus classiques.*

NOX affirms a desire to build completely fluid forms that go beyond the sculptural complexity of Frank O. Gehry's work, for example. Here, both interior and exterior participate in a true reevaluation of the role and nature of architecture.

Ziel von NOX ist es, vollkommen fließende Formen zu konstruieren, die über die skulpturale Komplexität von Arbeiten zum Beispiel eines Frank O. Gehry hinausgehen. Hier findet sowohl mit der Gestaltung des Gebäudeinneren wie der des Äußeren eine Neubewertung der Rolle und des Wesens von Architektur statt.

NOX affiche son désir de construire des formes entièrement fluides qui vont au-delà de la complexité sculpturale des recherches de Frank O. Gehry, par exemple. Ici, l'intérieur comme l'extérieur participent à une authentique réévaluation du rôle et de la nature de l'architecture.

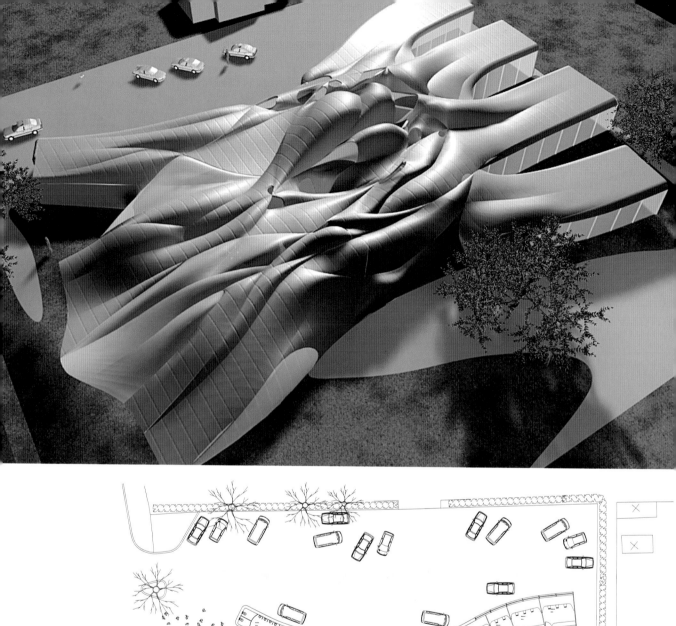

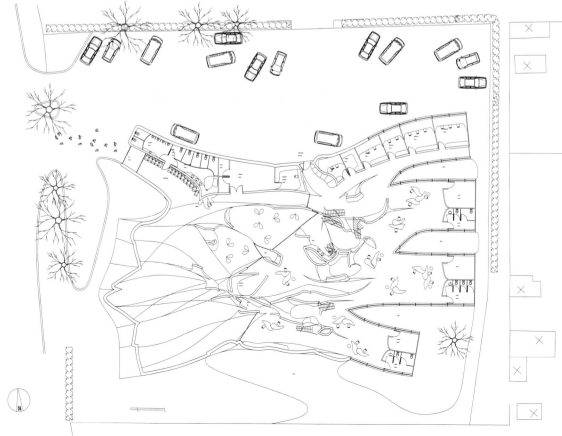

# MANOLO NUÑEZ-YANOWSKY

Manolo Nuñez-Yanowsky
22, Boulevard Flandrin
75116 Paris
France

Tel: +33 1 45 03 03 37
Fax: + 33 1 40 72 80 02

**MANOLO NUÑEZ-YANOWSKY** was born in Samarkand in the Soviet Union and grew up in Odessa before arriving in Spain. From 1962 to 1978, he was involved in the creation and work of the Taller de Arquitectura in Barcelona with Ricardo Bofill. He was involved not only in architecture, but also extensively in stage design at the time. From 1980 to 1991, he worked in Paris as an independent architect. In 1991, he created his present firm, Sade, in association with Miriam Teitelbaum. Between 1975 and 1986, he conceived the Place Pablo Picasso project in Marne la Vallée, a 540 apartment complex. He has built an old age home and housing in Alfortville, near Paris, a Police Headquarters and apartment building in the 12th arrondissement of Paris, and housing in Clermont Ferrand and Dijon (Quartier de Guise). He has also worked extensively in the former Soviet Union, designing a residence for the President of Kazakhstan, and in Korea where he built a hotel, a shoping center and a hotel in Taegu. In Spain after his extensive work with the Taller, he completed the ESADE school in Barcelona and the Lliure Theatre published here.

**MANOLO NUÑEZ-YANOWSKY** wurde in Samarkand in der ehemaligen Sowjetunion geboren und wuchs in Odessa auf, bevor er nach Spanien kam. Von 1962 bis 1978 arbeitete er zusammen mit Ricardo Bofill an der Planung und Konstruktion des Taller de Arquitectura in Barcelona. Zu dieser Zeit war er nicht nur als Architekt, sondern häufig auch als Bühnenbildner tätig. Von 1980 bis 1991 arbeitete er als selbstständiger Architekt in Paris und gründete 1991 zusammen mit Miriam Teitelbaum seine jetzige Firma namens Sade. Zwischen 1975 und 1986 führte Nuñez-Yanowsky das Projekt Place Pablo Picasso in Marne-la-Vallée aus, ein aus 540 Wohnungen bestehender Gebäudekomplex. Ferner baute er ein Seniorenheim und eine Wohnanlage in Alfortville bei Paris, eine Polizeizentrale und ein Apartmentgebäude im 12. Pariser Arrondissement sowie weitere Wohnanlagen in Clermont-Ferrand und in Dijon (Quartier de Guise). Außerdem entwarf er zahlreiche Bauten in der ehemaligen Sowjetunion, wie zum Beispiel die Residenz des Präsidenten von Kasachstan, und baute in Taegu, Korea, zwei Hotels und ein Einkaufszentrum. In Spanien realisierte er nach seiner umfangreichen Arbeit am Taller de Arquitectura die Schule ESADE und das hier vorgestellte Lliure Theater.

**MANOLO NUÑEZ-YANOWSKY** naît à Samarkand, alors en Union soviétique, et grandit à Odessa avant de s'installer en Espagne. De 1962 à 1978, il travaille au Taller de Arquitectura de Ricardo Bofill et intervient non seulement en architecture mais également sur de nombreux décors de scène. De 1980 à 1991, il est architecte indépandant à Paris. En 1991, il fonde son agence actuelle, Sade, en association avec Miriam Teitelbaum. Entre 1975 et 1986, il réalise le projet de la place Pablo Picasso à Marne-la-Vallée, un ensemble de 540 appartements. Il a également construit une maison pour personnes âgées et des logements à Alfortville, près de Paris, un commissariat de police et un immeuble d'appartements dans le XIIe arrondissement de Paris, des logements à Clermont-Ferrand et Dijon (Quartier de Guides). Il a beaucoup travaillé dans l'ex-Union soviétique, concevant la résidence du président du Kazakhstan, et en Corée où il construit un hôtel, un centre commercial et un hôtel à Taegu. En Espagne, après son abondante collaboration avec le Taller, il a achevé l'école ESADE de Barcelone et le théâtre Lliure, présenté ici.

# TEATRE LLIURE FABIÀ PUIGSERVER

*Barcelona, Spain, 1993–2002*

*Client: Fundació Teatro Lliure. Area: 15,000 m². Cost: 30 million euros.*

It was in 1991 that the director of the **TEATRE LLIURE FABIÀ PUIGSERVER** and the architect Manolo Nuñez-Yanowsky made the first plan for a new theatre in the Mercat de les Flors area of Barcelona public. The Barcelona City Council gave the theatre the possibility to renovate an imposing structure that dates from the 1929 International Exhibition, the Palau de l'Agricultura. Work began in March 1996, with funding from the Ministry of Culture, the Generalitat de Catalunya, the Ajuntament de Barcelona and the Diputació de Barcelona. Nuñez-Yanowsky created three spaces within the shell of the existing structure. The Teatre Lliure Fabià Puigserver has a total of 63 platforms that permit a very large number of different configurations and maximum of 750 seats. It is intended for big classical theatre productions. The Espai Lliure, with its Greek cross plan and maximum capacity of 175 seats, is to be used for research into theatrical methods, lectures, dance or musical theatre on a more intimate scale. Finally, the Lliure de Gràcia is to be used for contemporary drama, dance, music and musical theatre. The complex also includes foyers, dressing rooms, rehearsal space, a library and a lecture space.

Der erste Entwurf eines neuen Theaters im Barcelonaer Stadtviertel Mercat de les Flors wurde 1991 vom Direktor des **TEATRE LLIURE FABIÀ PUIGSERVER** und dem Architekten Manolo Nuñez-Yanowsky veröffentlicht. Der Stadtrat von Barcelona stellte dem Theater daraufhin ein imposantes Bauwerk zur Verfügung: den für die Weltausstellung 1929 errichteten Palau de l'Agricultura. Die im März 1996 begonnenen Renovierungsarbeiten wurden vom Kulturministerium und verschiedenen Stellen der Stadt- und Provinzregierung finanziell unterstützt. Nuñez-Yanowsky schuf im Inneren des bestehenden Gebäudes drei Theaterbereiche: Das Teatre Lliure Fabià Puigserver verfügt über insgesamt 63 Podien, die eine große Bandbreite verschiedener Konfigurationen und eine maximale Kapazität von 750 Sitzen bieten. Dieser Bereich ist für große, klassische Theaterproduktionen gedacht. Das zweite Theater, das Espai Lliure, mit seinem Grundriss in Form eines griechischen Kreuzes und einer maximalen Kapazität von 175 Sitzen, ist für kleinere Bühnenarbeiten, Lesungen, Tanz- oder Musikdarbietungen in einem intimeren Rahmen vorgesehen. Und das dritte, das Lliure de Gràcia, soll für die Aufführung zeitgenössischer Theater-, Tanz-, Musik- und Musiktheaterproduktionen dienen. Der Komplex wird durch Wandelgänge, Umkleide- und Proberäume, eine Bibliothek und einen Vortragssaal vervollständigt.

C'est en 1991 que le directeur du **TEATRE LLIURE FABIÀ PUIGSERVER** et l'architecte Manolo Nuñez-Yanowsky ont mis au point les plans de ce nouveau théâtre du quartier du Mercat de les Flores à Barcelone, installé dans un imposant bâtiment de l'Exposition internationale de 1929, le Palau de l'Agricultura. Les travaux entamés en mars 1996 ont été financés par le Ministère de la Culture, la Généralité de Catalogne, la municipalité de Barcelone et la Députation de Barcelone. Nuñez-Yanowsky a créé trois espaces dans l'ancienne structure. Le théâtre est équipé d'un total de 63 plates-formes mobiles qui permettent de très nombreuses configurations pour un maximum de 750 places et de grandes productions théâtrales classiques. L'Espai Lliure de 175 places au plan en croix grecque servira à la recherche scénographique, des conférences, la danse ou les comédies musicales. Le Lliure de Gràcia sera lui affecté aux pièces contemporaines, à la danse, la musique et au théâtre musical. Le complexe comprend également des foyers, des vestiaires, des lieux de répétition, une bibliothèque et un espace de conférence.

*Nuñez-Yanowsky was called on to reuse an existing 1929 building for the theater, which explains its external appearance. The color scheme is echoed inside the theater.*

*Le théâtre occupe un bâtiment de 1929, ce qui explique son apparence extérieure. Une palette chromatique identique se retrouve à l'intérieur.*

*Der Architekt erhielt den Auftrag, ein 1929 entstandenes Bauwerk für das Theater zu nutzen, wodurch sich die Außenansicht des Gebäudes erklärt. Die Farbkombination wiederholt sich in den Innenräumen des Theaters.*

*Nuñez-Yanowsky makes a skillful blend of the existing decor with the new elements he brought in to make the old building into a usable theater.*

*Auf geschickte Weise verbindet Nuñez-Yanowsky das ursprüngliche Dekor mit neuen Elementen, die das alte Gebäude zu einem funktionierenden Theater umgestalten.*

*L'architecte a imaginé un savant mélange de décor existant et d'éléments nouveaux pour transformer le bâtiment ancien en théâtre fonctionnel.*

Entirely new, the theater retains warmth that is not at odds with its external appearance. The project was personally significant for Nuñez-Yanowsky because he was a close friend of Fabià Puigserver.

Auch in der neuen Ausstattung strahlt das Theater eine Wärme aus, die sich gut mit der äußeren Erscheinung des Gebäudes verträgt. Als enger Freund von Fabià Puigserver hatte das Projekt für Nuñez-Yanowsky eine persönliche Bedeutung.

Entièrement nouvelle, la salle de théâtre conserve une chaleur non sans lien avec le style de l'extérieur du bâtiment. Le projet revêtait une signification particulière pour Nuñez-Yanowsky, ami proche de Fabià Puigserver.

# OOSTERHUIS.NL

*oosterhuis.nl*
*Essenburgsingel 94c*
*3022 EG Rotterdam*
*The Netherlands*

*Tel: + 31 10 244 7039*
*Fax: + 31 10 244 7041*
*e-mail oosterhuis@oosterhuis.nl*
*Web: www.oosterhuis.nl*

*trans-ports*

**OOSTERHUIS.NL** is described as a "multi-disciplinary architectural firm where architects, visual artists, web designers and programmers work together and join forces." Kas Oosterhuis was born in Amersfoort in 1951. He studied architecture at the Technical University in Delft (1970–1979) and was a Unit Master at the AA in London in 1987–1989. He has been a Professor at the Technical University in Delft since 2000. He is a member of the board of the Witte de With Museum in Rotterdam. He has built the Multimedia Pavilion (North Holland Floriade, 2000–2001); Headquarters for True Colors (Utrecht, 2000–2001) and the Salt Water Pavilion (Neeltje Jans, Zeeland, 1994–1997). One notable recent project is the WTC 911 project which proposes a "self-executable and programmable hi-rise building which reconfigures its shape, content and character during one year of its life cycle."

**OOSTERHUIS.NL** wird von den Designern beschrieben als »multidisziplinäre Architekturfirma, zu der sich Architekten, bildende Künstler, Webdesigner und Programmierer zusammengeschlossen haben«. Kas Oosterhuis, geboren 1951 in Amersfoort, studierte von 1970 bis 1979 Architektur an der Technischen Universität in Delft und war von 1987 bis 1989 Unit Master an der Architectural Association (AA) in London. Seit 2000 lehrt er an der TU Delft. Außerdem ist er Vorstandsmitglied des Museums Witte de With in Rotterdam. Zu seinen Bauten zählen der Multimedia Pavillon für die North Holland Floriade (2000–01), die Zentrale von True Colors in Utrecht (2000–01) und der Salz-Wasser-Pavillon in Neeltje Jans, Zeeland (1994–97). Zu seinen wichtigsten neueren Arbeiten gehört das WTC-911-Projekt, geplant als »selbstkonstruierbares und programmierbares Wohnhochhaus, das im Laufe eines Jahreszyklus seine Form, seinen Inhalt und seinen Charakter verändert«.

**OOSTERHUIS.NL** est une « agence d'architecture pluridisciplinaire dans laquelle joignent leurs forces et collaborent des architectes, des artistes visuels, des web designers et des programmateurs ». Kas Oosterhuis, né à Amersfoort en 1951, étudie l'architecture à l'Université technique de Delft (1970–79) et est Unit Master à l'Architectural Association de Londres en 1987–89. Il est professeur à l'Université technique de Delft depuis 2000 et membre du conseil d'administration du Witte de With Museum de Rotterdam. Il a construit le Multimedia Pavilion (North Holland Floriade, 2000–01) ; le siège de True Colors (Utrecht, 2000–01) et le Salt Water Pavillon (Neeltje Jans, Zeeland, 1994–97). Une de ses recherches récentes les plus notables est le projet WTC 911 qui propose un « bâtiment auto constructible et programmable haute résistance qui reconfigure sa forme, son contenu et son caractère au cours de son cycle de vie ».

# TRANS-PORTS

*1999–2001*

*Web: www.trans-ports.com. Structure: three-dimensional molded rubber sheet –*
*smaller sheets of rubber are vulcanized together to form a continuous skin.*
*Concept: real and virtual structures experienced as one consistent hyper-body.*

Kas Oosterhuis describes this as a "data-driven pneumatic structure." It was presented at the Venice Architecture Biennial in 2000. The actual shape and content of the design would be modified over time both by visitors and on the basis of incoming information from the Internet, for example. A spaceframe made up of pneumatic bars of adjustable length controlled by structural engineering software would permit this flexibility. The exterior would be made up of molded rubber sheets vulcanized together to form a continuous skin. Presumably there would eventually be a network of such pavilions all over the world. As the architect says, "The interior skin is a giant virtual window to a variety of global information sources like websites or webcams. The public is no longer looking at information, they are immersed inside information." He concludes that "The most important feature of the **TRANS-PORTS** pavilion is that architecture for the first time in its history is no longer fixed and static. Due to its full programmability of both form and information content the construct becomes a lean and flexible vehicle for a variety of usage."

Kas Oosterhuis beschreibt seinen auf der Architekturbiennale 2000 in Venedig präsentierten Entwurf als »datengesteuerte pneumatische Konstruktion«, deren Form und Inhalt mit der Zeit von den Besuchern, sowie den eingehenden Informationen – beispielsweise aus dem Internet – modifiziert werde. Diese Flexibilität werde durch ein Rahmenwerk ermöglicht, das aus pneumatischen, von einer bautechnischen Software gesteuerten Stangen mit verstellbarer Länge besteht. Die Außenhülle werde aus modellierten und durch Vulkanisierung miteinander verbundenen Gummiplatten gefertigt. Ziel des Architekten ist die Installierung eines weltweiten Netzwerkes solcher Pavillons. Oosterhuis über sein Projekt: »Die Innenhaut ist ein gigantisches virtuelles Fenster, das den Blick auf viele verschiedene globale Informationsquellen, wie Websites oder Webcams freigibt. Aber das Publikum sieht diese Informationen nicht nur, sondern wird förmlich in Informationen eingetaucht. Wichtigster Aspekt des **TRANS-PORTS** Pavillons ist, dass die Architektur erstmalig in ihrer Geschichte nicht mehr feststehend und statisch ist. Aufgrund der vollständigen Programmierbarkeit von sowohl Form als auch Informationsgehalt wird die Konstruktion zu einem schlanken und flexiblen Vehikel für vielfältige Anwendungsmöglichkeiten.«

Kas Oosterhuis décrit son projet comme « une structure pneumatique pilotée par données numériques ». Elle a été présentée à la Biennale d'architecture de Venise en 2000. Sa forme et son contenu peuvent être modifiés dans le temps à la fois par les visiteurs et des informations reçues, d'Internet par exemple. Une structure composée de barres pneumatiques de longueur réglable contrôlées par un logiciel spécifique lui assure la souplesse recherchée. L'extérieur devrait être en feuilles de caoutchouc moulé vulcanisées pour former ensemble une peau continue. On pourrait imaginer un réseau de pavillons du même type dans le monde entier. L'architecte précise que « la peau intérieure est une fenêtre virtuelle géante ouverte sur une variété de sources d'information globale comme des sites web ou des webcams par exemple. Le public ne cherche plus une information, il est immergé dans l'information ». Il conclut que « la plus importante caractéristique du pavillon **TRANS-PORTS** est que, pour la première fois dans son histoire, l'architecture n'est plus fixe et statique. Totalement programmable à la fois dans sa forme et son contenu d'information, la structure devient un véhicule actif et souple destiné à une grande variété d'usages. »

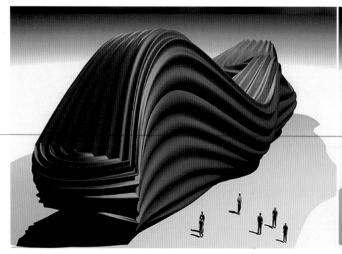

*Kas Oosterhuis – like a number of other Dutch architects – has a vision of a data-driven form of architecture that will be variable and not linked to any one fixed location.*

*Ebenso wie eine Reihe anderer holländischer Architekten hat Kas Oosterhuis die Vision einer datengesteuerten Form von Architektur, die variabel und nicht an einen festen Ort gebunden ist.*

*Comme un certain nombre d'architectes néerlandais, Kas Oosterhuis développe une vision de formes architecturales informatisées variables, non liées à un lieu fixe.*

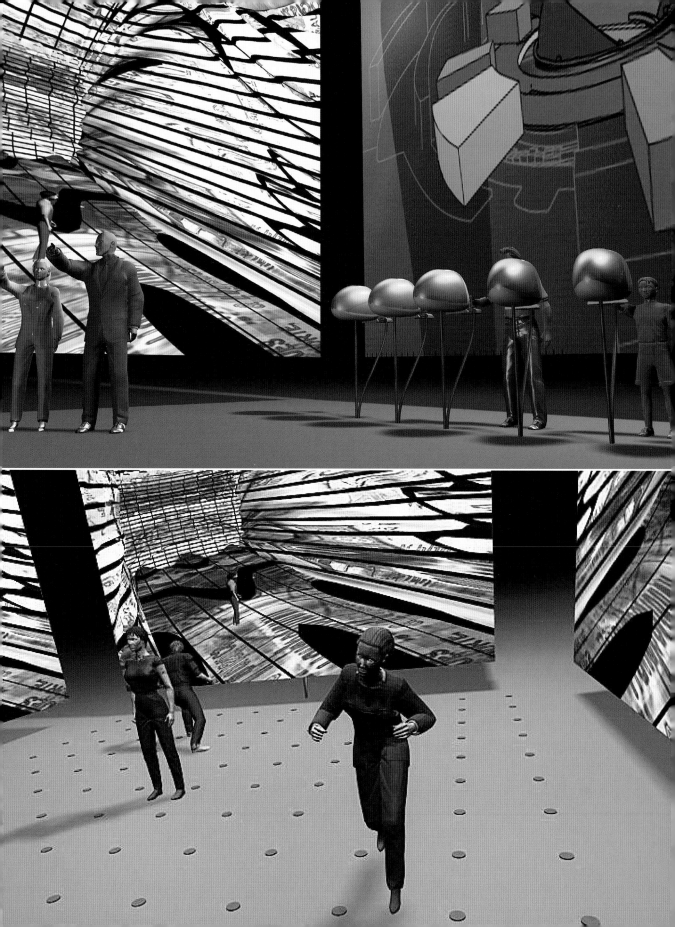

*"The most important feature of the trans-ports pavilion," says Oosterhuis, "is that architecture for the first time in its history is no longer fixed and static."*

*Oosterhuis: »Der wichtigste Aspekt des trans-ports Pavillons ist, dass die Architektur hier nicht mehr feststehend und statisch ist.«*

*« L'aspect le plus important du pavillon trans-ports est que pour la première fois dans l'histoire, l'architecture n'est plus fixe ni statique. » Kas Oosterhuis*

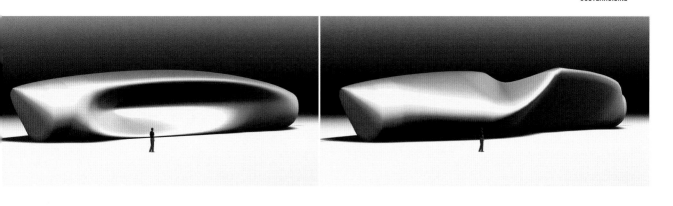

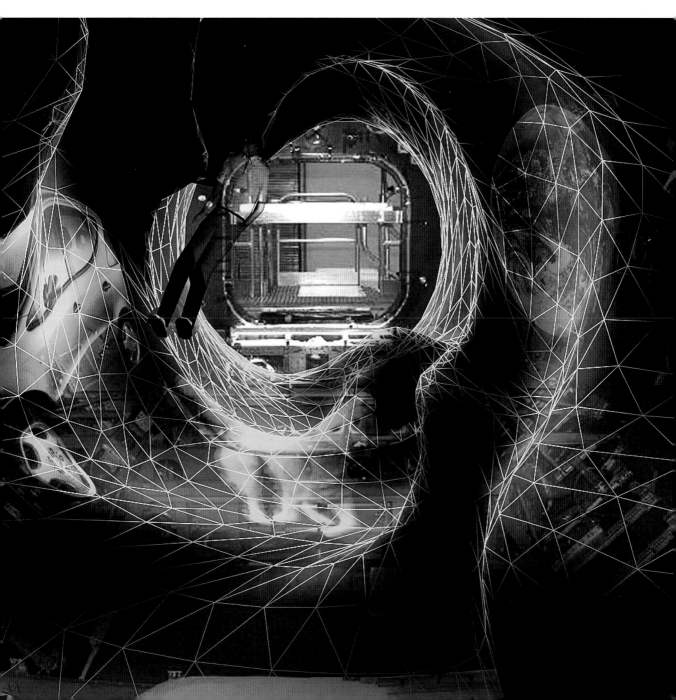

# NORTH HOLLAND PAVILION

*Floriade Terrein Haarlemmermeerpolder, The Netherlands, 2001*

*Client: North Holland Province. Material: a new composite material called hylite.*

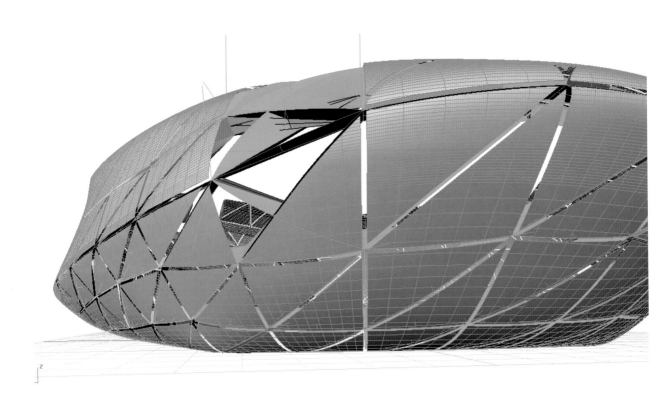

The **WEB OF NORTH HOLLAND** according to the architects is a pavilion "in which visitors, the architecture of the pavilion and the multimedia presentation representing the province of North Holland intertwine into a non-linear interactive game. Visitors play the building, the form and the shape of the presentation by walking around freely in the five brightly colored sectors of the presentation space (the pentagon). Every sector represents a specific aspect of the province of North Holland." The outer skin of the pavilion is designed with the use of triangles made of a new composite material Hylite that are fixed to a spatial triangulated construction. Kas Oosterhuis concludes, "In the space between the inner and outer skin, a dynamic light program reacts to the movements of the flow of visitors. The Web of North Holland is time-based architecture, an experience in real time."

Das **WEB VON NORDHOLLAND** ist laut Beschreibung der Architekten »ein Pavillon, in dem sich die Besucher, die Architektur des Raums und die multimediale Präsentation der holländischen Provinz zu einem nicht-linearen interaktiven Spiel verflechten. Dabei gestalten die Besucher spielerisch das Gebäude, die Form und Erscheinungsweise der Präsentation, indem sie sich frei in den fünf leuchtend bunten Sektoren der Präsentationsfläche, dem so genannten ›Pentagon‹ bewegen. Jeder der Sektoren repräsentiert einen bestimmten Aspekt von Nordholland.« Die Außenhaut des Gebäudes besteht aus Dreiecken, die aus einem neuen Verbundwerkstoff namens Hylite hergestellt und an einer mehrdimensionalen, wiederum aus Dreiecken zusammengesetzten Konstruktion befestigt werden. Kas Oosterhuis abschließend: »In dem Raum zwischen Innen- und Außenhaut reagiert ein dynamisches Lichtprogramm auf den Besucherstrom. Das Web von Nordholland ist eine Architektur auf Zeitbasis, eine Erfahrung in Echtzeit.«

Le **WEB OF NORTH HOLLAND** est un pavillon dans lequel, selon l'architecte, « les visiteurs et les présentations multimédias sur la province de la Hollande du Nord s'intègrent à un jeu interactif non linéaire. Les visiteurs jouent avec la construction, la forme et l'aspect de la présentation en se promenant librement dans les cinq secteurs brillamment colorés (le Pentagone). Chaque secteur représente un aspect spécifique de la province ». La peau externe du pavillon fait appel à des triangles réalisés dans un nouveau matériau, la Hylite, fixée à une structure triangulée dans l'espace. Kas Oosterhuis conclut : « Dans l'espace existant entre la peau interne et externe, un programme lumineux dynamique réagit aux mouvements du flux des visiteurs. Il s'agit d'une architecture basée sur le temps, d'une expérience en temps réel. »

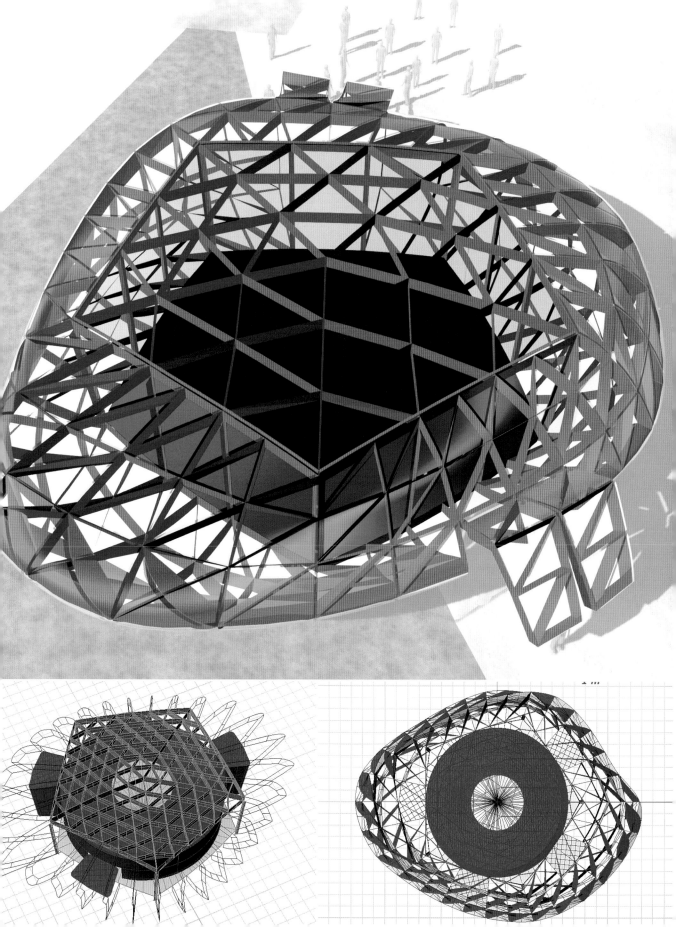

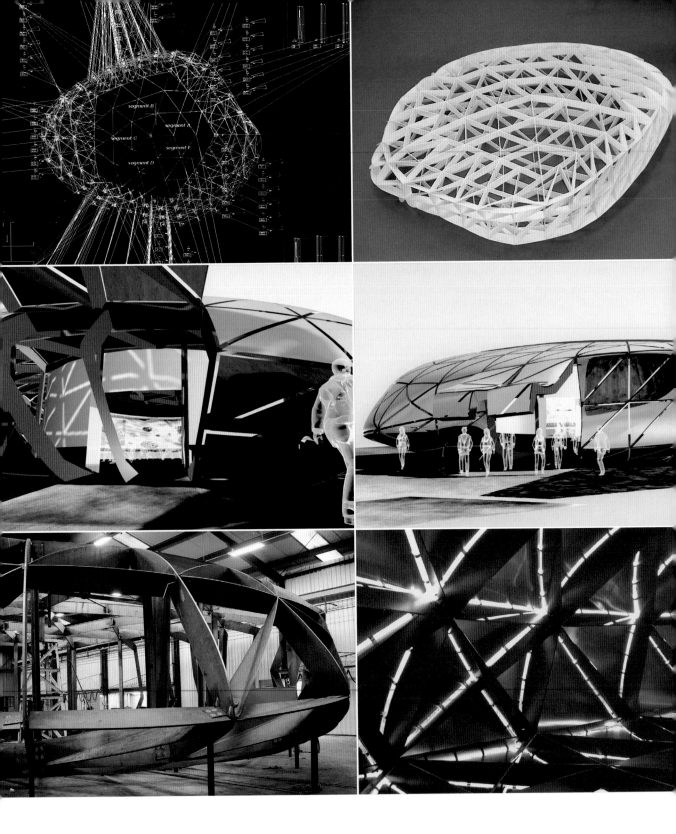

The architect calls this pavilion a "non-linear interactive game." His extensive use of computer technology has clearly given rise to an esthetically unexpected design.

Der Architekt bezeichnet diesen Pavillon als ein »nicht-lineares interaktives Spiel«. Seine umfassende Nutzung der Computertechnologie hat hier ein ästhetisch überraschendes Design hervorgebracht.

L'architecte présente son pavillon comme un « jeu interactif non linéaire. » Le recours important à l'informatique a donné naissance à ce projet d'une esthétique inattendue.

In the space between the inner and outer skin a dynamic light programme reacts to the movements of the continual flow of visitors.

Ein dynamisches, zwischen Innen- und Außenhaut installiertes Lichtprogramm reagiert auf die Bewegungen des stetigen Besucherstroms.

Dans l'espace entre la peau intérieure et la peau extérieure, un programme d'éclairage dynamique réagit aux mouvement du flux continu de visiteurs.

# PEI PARTNERSHIP

*Pei Partnership Architects LLP*
*257 Park Avenue South*
*New York, New York 10010-7304*
*United States*

*Tel: + 1 212 674 9000*
*Fax: + 1 212 674 5900*
*e-mail: leonard@ppa-ny.com*
*Web: www.ppa-ny.com*

**CHIEN CHUNG PEI** was educated at Harvard College (BA, 1968), and the Harvard Graduate School of Design (Master of Architecture 1972). He worked with **I. M. PEI** & Partners (New York, 1971–1989) and Pei Cobb Freed & Partners (New York, 1989–1992) before creating Pei Partnership Architects in 1992. **LI CHUNG PEI** also graduated from Harvard Collage (BA, 1972) and the Harvard Graduate School of Design (Master of Architecture 1976). Like C. C. Pei, he started his career at I. M. Pei & Partners (1976–1989) and at Pei Cobb Freed & Partners (1989–1992) before entering into partnership with his brother in 1992. Their project list includes: Amgen Headquarters (Thousand Oaks, CA); Bank of China Head Office Building (Beijing, China); Cyber City (Shenzhen, China); Chinese Embassy (Washington DC); Everson Museum of Art (Syracuse, NY); Grange Court (Singapore); Kashilri Lakeside Resort Hotel (Yongin Park, Korea); Centro Cultural de Leon (Leon, Guanajuato, Mexico); West Village Townhouse (New York, NY); Vilar Center for the Arts (MIT Arts + Media Building, Cambridge, MA); Palm Beach Opera House (West Palm Beach, FL); Sentra BDNI (Jakarta, Indonesia); Shanghai Commercial Bank Headquarters (Shanghai, China); Tianfu Square (Chengdu, China); UCLA Westwood Replacement Hospital (Los Angeles, CA); Mt. Sinai Medical Center (New York, NY); and work on the Lycée Français de New York (New York, NY).

**CHIEN CHUNG PEI** schloss 1968 sein Studium am Harvard College ab und erwarb 1972 seinen Master of Architecture an der Harvard Graduate School of Design (GSD). Von 1971 bis 1989 arbeitete er bei **I. M. PEI** & Partners in New York und von 1989 bis 1992 bei Pei Cobb Freed & Partners, New York, bevor er 1992 Pei Partnership Architects ins Leben rief. Ebenso wie sein Bruder studierte auch **LI CHUNG PEI** am Harvard College (B. A., 1972) und an der Harvard Graduate School of Design (Master of Architecture 1976). Und auch er begann seine Karriere bei I. M. Pei & Partners (1976–89) und anschließend bei Pei Cobb Freed & Partners (1989–92), bevor er sich 1992 mit seinem Bruder zusammentat. Zu ihren Projekten zählen: die Amgen-Zentrale in Thousand Oaks, Kalifornien, die Cyber City in Shenzhen, China, die Chinesische Botschaft in Washington DC, das Everson Museum of Art in Syracuse, New York, der Grange Court in Singapur, das Kashilri Lakeside Resort Hotel in Yongin Park, Korea, das Centro Cultural de Leon in Guanajuato, Mexiko, das West Village Townhouse in New York, das Vilar Center for the Arts (MIT Arts + Media Building) in Cambridge, Massachusetts, das Palm Beach Opera House in West Palm Beach, Florida, der Hauptsitz der Shanghai Commercial Bank in Shanghai, der Tianfu-Platz in Chengdu, China, das UCLA Westwood Replacement Hospital in Los Angeles, das Mount Sinai Medical Center in New York sowie das Lycée Français de New York in New York.

**CHIEN CHUNG PEI**, B. A. Harvard College (1968) et M. Arch de la Harvard Graduate School of Design (1972) a travaillé avec **I. M. PEI** & Parners (New York, 1971–89), puis Pei Cobb Freed & Partners (New York, 1989–92) avant de créer Pei Partnership Architects en 1992. **LI CHUNG PEI** a suivi le même parcours universitaire que son frère à Harvard (1972, 1976) et a débuté sa carrière chez I. M Pei & Partners (1976–89) puis Pei Cobb Freed & Partners (1989–92), avant de s'associer à lui en 1992. Parmi leurs réalisations : siège social d'Amgen (Thousand Oaks, Californie) ; Cyber City (Shenzhen, Chine) ; ambassade de Chine (Washington DC) ; Everson Museum of Art (Syracuse, New York) ; Grange Court (Singapour) ; Kashilri Lake Resort Hotel (Yongin Park, Corée) ; Centro Cultural de León (León, Guanajuato, Mexique) ; maison de ville à West Village (New York) ; Vilar Center for the Arts (MIT Arts + média building, Cambridge, Massachusetts) ; Palm Beach Opera House (West Palm Beach, Floride) ; siège de la Banque commerciale de Shanghai (Shanghai, Chine) ; UCLA Westwood Replacement Hospital (Los Angeles) ; Mount Sinaï Medical Center (New York). Ils travaillent actuellement à un projet de lycée français à New York.

# BANK OF CHINA HEAD OFFICE BUILDING

*Beijing, China, 1997–2001*

*Office area: 97,250 m². Leasable tenant area: 13,500 m². Atrium area: 3,025 m². Skylight: 45 m from atrium floor.*

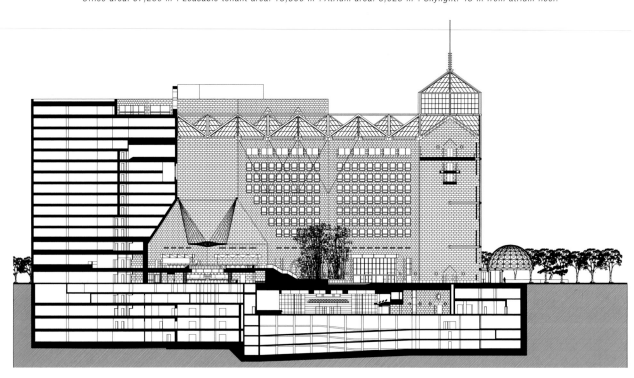

This very large structure (173,000 square meters) is the work of Pei Partnership – the two sons of I. M. Pei, Chien Chung Pei and Li Chung Pei were the Partners in Charge of the project. Rising up to 15 floors above grade, the structure includes a spectacular 45-meter high, 3,025 square meter atrium. The atrium garden is decorated with 40 tons of rock from the Stone Forest in Yunnan Province and bamboo trees from Hangzhou that rise to a height of almost twenty meters. A 2,000 seat auditorium, 97,250 square meters of office space and 13,500 square meters of leasable tenant space, give an idea of the sheer scale of the structure. The materials used are buff-colored Italian travertine with honed finish for the facades, and Chinese gray granites for the exterior paving. In the public interiors and banking halls, Italian travertine, gray granite and marble floors and walls with natural anodized aluminum ceiling panels were used. The very density of the program on the 13,000 square meter site made it difficult to avoid giving a massive profile to the headquarters, but the quality of the design and finishing given by the Pei family, in particular for the atrium and banking halls, manages to reconcile the client's requirements with a true concern for architectural excellence.

Dieser 173.000 m² umfassende Großbau ist das Werk von Pei Partnership, wobei die beiden Söhne von I. M. Pei, Chien Chung Pei und Li Chung Pei die Projektleitung innehatten. Im Inneren des 15-stöckigen Gebäudes wurde ein spektakuläres, 45 m hohes und 3.025 m² großes Atrium angelegt, dessen Garten mit 40 Tonnen Felsgestein aus dem Steinwald der Provinz Yunnan und fast 20 m hohen Bambusbäumen aus Hangzhou dekoriert wurde. Ein Auditorium mit 2.000 Sitzen, eine Bürofläche von 97.250 m² und 13.500 m² für Mietwohnungen vermitteln einen Eindruck von der enormen Größe des Bauwerkes. Für die Fassaden wurde brauner, fein bearbeiteter und geglätteter Travertin und für die Außenpflasterung grauer Granitstein aus China verwendet. Im Inneren wurden die öffentlichen Bereiche und Bankräume mit Travertin, grauem Granit sowie Marmorböden und -wänden ausgestattet, während die Decken mit natürlich eloxierter Aluminiumtäfelung verkleidet sind. Die Dichte des auf einem 13.000 m² großen Grundstück untergebrachten Bauplans bedingt eine gewisse Massivität des Bankgebäudes. Aber durch die Qualität der von der Familie Pei in Entwurf und Ausführung geleisteten Arbeit ist es gelungen, die Anforderungen des Bauherrn mit einem echten Engagement für erstklassige Architektur in Einklang zu bringen.

Ce très grand immeuble de 173 000 m² est l'œuvre de Pei Partnership, l'agence des deux fils d'I. M. Pei, Chien Chung Pei et Li Chung Pei en charge du projet. De quatorze étages, il comprend un atrium spectaculaire de 45 m de haut et de 3 025 m². Le jardin de cet atrium a été aménagé à l'aide de 40 tonnes de rochers de la Forêt de pierre du Yunnan et de bambous de Hangzhou de près de 20 m de haut. Les 2 000 places de l'auditorium, les 97 250 m² de bureaux et les 13 500 m² d'espaces locatifs donnent une idée de l'échelle étonnante de ce projet. Les matériaux choisis sont un travertin italien chamois abrasé pour les façades et divers granits chinois gris pour le pavement extérieur. Dans les espaces publics intérieurs et les halls de la banque, on retrouve du travertin italien, des sols et murs en granit et marbre gris et des plafonds en panneaux d'aluminium anodisé de ton naturel. La densité de ce programme développé sur un terrain de 13 000 m² n'a pas permis d'éviter une certaine massivité du profil, mais la qualité de la conception et de réalisation, en particulier dans l'atrium et les halls de banque ont réussi à concilier les contraintes du client et le souci affirmé d'excellence architecturale.

*The client's very large space requirements compelled the architects to create a dense structure, whose most inventive elements are on the inside.*

*Der große Raumbedarf des Bauherrn bedeutete für die Architekten, dass sie einen dichten Bauplan umsetzen mussten, dessen originellste Elemente im Gebäudeinneren sichtbar werden.*

*Les exigences du client ont obligé les architectes à densifier le projet, dont les éléments les plus inventifs se trouvent à l'intérieur.*

The interior, public spaces of the bank are remarkably generous and undoubtedly bear something of the mark of a Pei style.

Die öffentlichen Innenräume der Bank sind bemerkenswert großzügig angelegt und zweifellos kennzeichnend für den Stil von Pei.

À l'intérieur les espaces de la banque ouverts au public sont remarquablement généreux et portent visiblement la marque du style Pei.

The interior garden contains 40 tons of rocks from the Stone Forest in Yunnan Province. The 15m–18m tall bamboo trees are from Hangzhou.

Der Garten des Atriums ist mit 40 Tonnen Felsgestein aus dem Steinwald in der Provinz Yunnan ausgestattet, während die bis zu 20 m hohen Bambusbäume aus Hangzhou stammen.

Le jardin intérieur contient 40 tonnes de rochers originaires de la Forêt de pierre du Yunnan. Les bambous de 15 à 18 m de haut proviennent de Hangzhou.

# PUGH + SCARPA ARCHITECTURE

*Pugh + Scarpa Architecture*
*Bergamot Station*
*2525 Michigan Avenue*
*Building F1*
*Santa Monica, California 90404*
*United States*

*Tel: + 1 310 828 0226*
*Fax: + 1 310 453 9606*
*Web: www.pugh-scarpa.com*

*Bergamot Station Artist Loft*

**LAWRENCE SCARPA** was educated at the University of Florida and worked in the offices of Paul Rudolph in New York and Holt Hinshaw Pfau Jones in San Francisco before founding his firm with **GWYNNE PUGH** in 1988. Pugh received degrees from Leeds University in Great Britain (1975) and the University of California, Los Angeles (1978), and then worked in several Californian firms before creating Gwynne Pugh Associates (1984–1988). Pugh + Scarpa has offices in Santa Monica, California, and Charlotte, North Carolina. The staff numbers twenty persons. Most recently, the firm has been recognized for their achievements in building Colorado Court, a 44 single room occupancy housing project developed as a model for sustainable living. It is one the first affordable housing projects in the United States to be 100 % energy independent.

**LAWRENCE SCARPA** studierte an der University of Florida und arbeitete in den Büros von Paul Rudolph in New York und Holt Hinshaw Pfau Jones in San Francisco, bevor er 1988 zusammen mit **GWYNNE PUGH** seine eigene Firma gründete. Gwynne Pugh schloss 1975 ihr Studium an der Leeds University in Großbritannien und 1978 das Studium an der University of California Los Angeles (UCLA) ab. Anschließend arbeitete sie zunächst in mehreren kalifornischen Architekturfirmen und war von 1984 bis 1988 in der eigenen Firma, Gwynne Pugh Associates, tätig. Pugh + Scarpa haben Niederlassungen in Santa Monica, Kalifornien sowie in Charlotte, North Carolina, mit insgesamt 20 Angestellten. Kürzlich erhielt die Firma eine lobende Anerkennung für ihre Leistung bei der Planung von Colorado Court, einem aus 44 Einzimmerwohnungen bestehenden Gebäude, das als Modellprojekt für nachhaltiges Wohnen entwickelt wurde. Es stellt eins der ersten Wohnbauprojekte in den Vereinigten Staaten dar, das erschwinglichen Wohnraum mit einer 100-prozentig autarken Energieversorgung bietet.

**LAWRENCE SCARPA** a étudié à l'Université de Floride et travaillé dans les agences de Paul Rudolph (New York) et Holt Hinshaw Pfau Jones (San Francisco) avant de créer sa propre structure en association avec **GWYNNE PUGH** en 1988. Gwynne Pugh est diplômée de Leeds University (Grande-Bretagne, 1975) et de l'Université de Californie, Los Angeles (1978). Elle a travaillé dans plusieurs agences californiennes avant de créer Gwynne Pugh Asociates (1984–88). Pugh + Scarpa possèdent des bureaux à Santa Monica, Californie, et Charlotte, Caroline du Nord et emploient une vingtaine de collaborateurs. Plus récemment, l'agence s'est fait connaître pour Colorado Court, un immeuble de 44 logements pour célibataires sur un modèle de développement durable. C'est l'un des premiers immeubles de logements américains à être 100 % énergétiquement indépendant.

# BERGAMOT STATION ARTIST LOFTS

*Santa Monica, California, United States, 1994–2001*

*Location: 2514 Michigan Avenue, Santa Monica, California.*
*Client/Owner: Bergamot Limited Partners. Total area: 860 m². Cost: $809,000.*

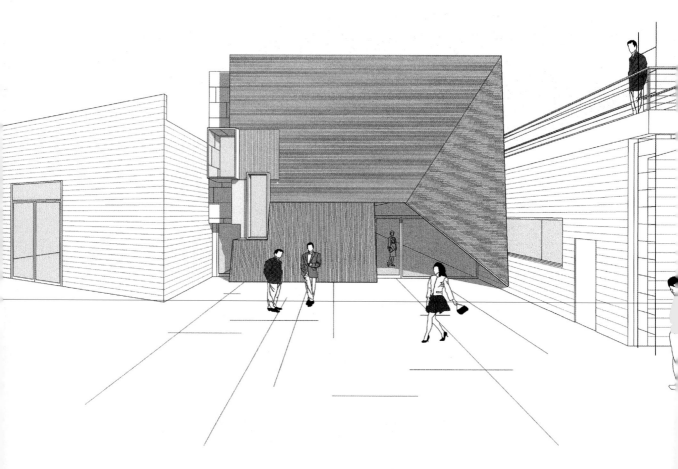

*Flat galvanized and corrugated sheet metal skins on the outside of the Artist Loft Building.*

*Die Außenhülle der Artist Lofts besteht aus flach geriffelten Zinkblechplatten.*

*Peaux en feuilles de métal plat ou ondulé pour l'habillage de l'Artist Loft Building.*

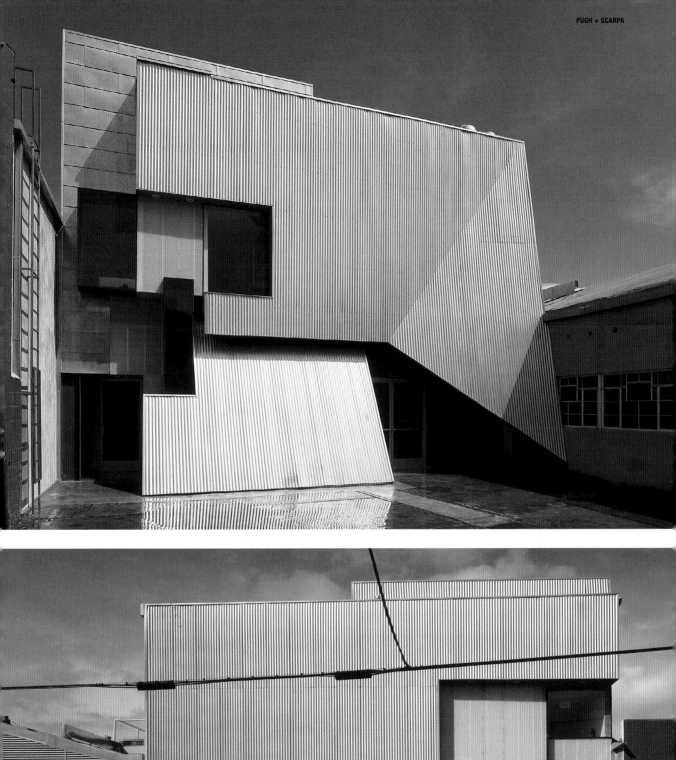

The four-hectare site of the **BERGAMOT STATION ARTS CENTER** is the largest city-owned parcel of land in Santa Monica. A number of corrugated steel and stucco warehouses are set on it. Over thirty art galleries, film studios, design firms and a bookstore occupy much of the space. The Santa Monica Museum of Art, a café and artists lofts make up the rest of the utilization of the area. Working with Fred Fisher, Pugh + Scarpa provided the master plan for the conversion of the former Red Car line station into "creative space" beginning in 1994. Their Bergamot Artist Lofts Building is the only entirely new structure on the site. It is located on the southern most portion of the site, next to the Museum. Flat galvanized and corrugated sheet metal skins were used on the exterior with cold rolled steel, polycarbonite and glass panes inside. A clear effort was made to conserve the "raw, industrial" quality of the other buildings in the vicinity. There are about 400 square meters of gallery space on the ground floor and four artist lofts on the second level of about 110 square meters each.

Das 4 ha große Grundstück des **BERGAMOT STATION ARTS CENTER** ist das größte im Besitz der Stadt Santa Monica befindliche Stück Land. Darauf wurde eine Reihe von Lagerhäusern aus Wellblech und Gipsputz gebaut. Den meisten Raum nehmen über 30 Kunstgalerien, Filmstudios, Designfirmen und eine Buchhandlung ein, den Rest der Nutzfläche machen das Santa Monica Museum of Art, ein Café und Lofts für Künstler aus. In Zusammenarbeit mit Fred Fisher lieferte Pugh + Scarpa den Masterplan für den Umbau der ehemaligen Red Car Line Station zu einem »kreativen Raum«, mit dem 1994 begonnen wurde. Ihr Bergamot Artist Lofts Building ist das einzige neue Gebäude auf dem Gelände. Es befindet sich am südlichsten Ende des Areals, neben dem Museum. Die Außenwände sind mit flachem Zinkwellblech verkleidet und für die Innenwände wurden kalt gewalzter Stahl, Polycarbonat und Glasplatten verwendet. Die Gestaltung lässt eindeutig das Bemühen erkennen, den »rauen, industriellen« Gebäudecharakter der Umgebung beizubehalten. Im Erdgeschoss sind circa 400 m² Ausstellungsfläche und im Obergeschoss vier Künstler-Lofts mit jeweils 110 m² untergebracht.

Les quatre hectares du **BERGAMOT STATION ARTS CENTER** constituent le plus grand terrain municipal de Santa Monica. Un certain nombre d'entrepôts en tôle ondulée et enduit y ont été édifiés. Plus de trente galeries d'art, studios de cinéma, agences de design et une librairie occupent l'essentiel de l'espace tandis que le Santa Monica Museum of Art, un café et des lofts pour artistes se sont vu attribuer le reste. En collaboration avec Fred Fisher, Pugh + Scarpa ont mis au point le plan directeur de la reconversion de l'ancienne gare routière des Red Cars en « espace créatif » à partir de 1994. Dans la partie la plus au sud, près du musée, leur Bergamot Artist Lofts Building est le seul bâtiment entièrement nouveau construit sur le site. Sa construction utilise des « peaux » de métal galvanisé ondulé vers l'extérieur et des panneaux en acier laminé à froid, polycarbonate et verre pour l'intérieur. Le maintien de la qualité « brute, industrielle » des bâtiments du voisinage figurait parmi les objectifs. On y trouve environ 400 m² d'espaces pour galeries d'art au rez-de-chaussée et quatre lofts pour artistes de 110 m² environ chacun à l'étage.

High ceilings give the artists' studios a great sense of spaciousness, while fireplaces give added warmth to a space where concrete floors and exposed ceiling ducts are more "industrial" in their appearance.

Die hohen Wände lassen die Künstlerateliers offen und geräumig wirken, während die Kamine den Räumen, die durch ihre Betonböden und freiliegenden Deckenrohre einen eher industriellen Charakter haben, mehr Wärme verleihen.

La hauteur des plafonds donne un fort sentiment d'espace dans les ateliers d'artistes. Les cheminées apportent une certaine chaleur à un volume dans lequel les sols en béton et la tuyauterie apparente donnent un aspect plutôt « industriel. »

# MICHELE SAEE

*Michele Saee*
*5366 Wilshire Boulevard Suite B*
*Los Angeles, California 90036*
*United States*

*Tel: + 1 323 932 1793*
*Fax: + 1 323 932 0293*
*e-mail: saeestudio@aol.com*

**MICHELE SAEE** believes that "architecture is a part of everyday life, and that the work of architecture evolves around our needs, our desires, and our ability to improve the quality of our relationships towards the spirit of creativity and adventure." His work has received numerous awards and he has exhibited and lectured throughout the world. His work and writings on architecture have appeared in numerous national and international publications, and is the subject of a monograph published by Rizzoli International, *Michele Saee: Buildings + Projects.* Michele Saee graduated from the University of Florence with a Master of Art in Architecture degree, and received a Post-graduate degree in Technical Urban Planning from the Politecnico di Milano, Italy. He has been a member of the faculty of the Southern California Institute of (SciArc), RWTH, Aachen, Germany, Otis Parsons School of Design in Los Angeles, and L'Universita' degli Studi di Firenze. He and his partner, Brant Gordon, are currently principals of BUILDING, inc., with offices in Los Angeles and Paris. His work includes the International Center for Comparative Cultural Studies Sardinia, Italy, 1999–2003; the Los Angeles Department of Parks & Recreation, Eagle Rock Childcare Center (with Kanner Architects), Eagle Rock, CA, 2001; the Drugstore Publicis Restaurants, shops, and movie theaters along the Champs Élysées, Paris, France, 2000–2002; as well as the Café Nescafe projects published here.

**MICHELE SAEE** ist davon überzeugt, dass »Architektur ein Teil des Alltagslebens ist und dass sich die Arbeit von Architekten um unsere Bedürfnisse, unsere Wünsche und unsere Fähigkeit dreht, die Qualität unserer Beziehungen in Richtung Kreativität und Abenteuerlust zu verbessern.« Er erhielt zahlreiche Auszeichnungen und war in der ganzen Welt mit Ausstellungen und Vorträgen aktiv. Seine Schriften über Architektur wurden in zahlreichen nationalen und internationalen Zeitschriften publiziert, und bei Rizzoli International erschien eine Monografie über ihn mit dem Titel: *Michele Saee: Buildings + Projects.* Saee schloss sein Studium an der Universität in Florenz mit einem Master of Arts in Architektur ab und erwarb seinen Graduiertenabschluss in technischer Stadtplanung am Polytechnikum in Mailand. Seither lehrte er am Southern California Institute of Architecture (SciArc), an der RWTH in Aachen, der Otis Parsons School of Design in Los Angeles und an der Università degli Studi di Firenze. Er und sein Partner Brant Gordon sind derzeit als Leiter bei BUILDING, Inc. tätig, einer Firma mit Niederlassungen in Los Angeles und Paris. Zu seinen Projekten zählen: das Internationale Zentrum für Vergleichende Kulturstudien auf Sardinien (1999–2003), die Los Angeles Dependance von Parks & Recreation, Eagle Rock Childcare Center (in Zusammenarbeit mit Kanner Architects) im kalifornischen Eagle Rock (2001), die Drugstore Publicis Restaurants, Geschäfte und Kinos auf den Pariser Champs-Élysées (2000–02) sowie das hier vorgestellte Projekt Café Nescafé.

**MICHELE SAEE** pense que « l'architecture fait partie de la vie quotidienne, et que le travail d'architecture se fait autour de nos besoins, de nos désirs et de notre capacité à améliorer la qualité de nos relations envers l'esprit de créativité et d'aventure. » Il expose et donne des conférences dans le monde entier et son travail a souvent été primé. Ses réalisations et ses écrits sur l'architecture ont été publiés aux Etats-Unis et dans de nombreux pays. Il a été le sujet d'une monographie publiée par Rizzoli : *Michele Saee: Building = Projects.* Il est M. Arch. de l'université de Florence, et diplômé d'études supérieures des techniques d'urbanisme du Politecnico de Milan, Italie. Il a enseigné au Southern California Institute of Architecture (SciArc), au RWTH de Aix-la-Chapelle, Allemagne, à l'Otis Parsons School of Design à Los Angeles et à l'Universita degli Studi de Florence. Avec son associé, Brant Gordon, il dirige l'agence BUILDING, Inc. qui possède des bureaux à Los Angeles et Paris. Parmi ses réalisations : l'International Center for Comparative Cultural Studies, Sardaigne, 1999–2003 ; le Los Angeles Department of Parks and Recreation, Eagle Rock Childcare Center (avec Kanner Architects), Eagle Rock, Californie, 2001 ; les Drugstore Publicis Restaurants, boutiques, cinéma aux Champs-Élysées, Paris, France, 2000–2002 ; le projet Nescafé, présenté ici.

# CAFÉ NESCAFÉ

*Paris, France and other locations, 2002*

As a reaction to the spreading presence of Starbucks Coffee Shops, Nestlé has actively envisaged the creation of Nescafé Coffee Shops around the world. The first prototype is already open on the Avenue de Wagram in Paris, with others scheduled to be completed in the near future. As the architect has written, "This project addresses the question of creating architecture for corporate identity. Commercial chain operations are best known for their 'rubber stamp' architecture… To address the need for adaptability without resorting to rubberstamping, we began by developing a flexible system composed of three variables: the wrapping skin, the coffee bar interface, and the graphic ribbon." The "graphic ribbon" here is a "main graphic interface containing the required branding images of the product." Although the original test area for these shops is Paris, sites around the world ranging "from historic and civic buildings to train stations, airports, and shopping malls" are planned. As Michele Saee concludes, "The clients themselves wanted to break out of the food chain mold: they were looking for something dynamic and distinctive, but they still wanted to maintain affordability and create a clear identity for their stores."

Als Reaktion auf die zunehmende Verbreitung von Starbucks Coffee Shops plant der Nestlé Konzern, auf der ganzen Welt Nescafé Coffee Shops einzurichten. Das erste, als Prototyp gedachte Geschäft wurde bereits auf der Avenue de Wagram in Paris eröffnet und in nächster Zukunft sind weitere Filialen geplant. Der Architekt Michele Saee schreibt über seine Herangehensweise: »Bei diesem Projekt geht es um die Frage, wie Architektur zur Corporate Identity beitragen kann. Ladenketten sind vor allem für ihre einfallslose Architektur bekannt. Um das Bedürfnis nach Funktionalität zu erfüllen, ohne auf das Routinemäßige zurückzugreifen, entwickelten wir ein flexibles System aus drei Variablen: die äußere Hülle, die Kaffeebar und das Grafikband.« Bei dem Grafikband handelt es sich um ein grafisches Interface mit den wichtigsten Markenzeichen des Produkts. Neben den Läden im ursprünglichen Testgebiet Paris sind Niederlassungen in der ganzen Welt geplant, deren Standorte »von historischen und öffentlichen Gebäuden bis zu Bahnhöfen, Flughäfen und Einkaufszentren« reichen. Dazu noch einmal Michele Saee: »Die Auftraggeber selbst wollten aus den typischen Einheitsmustern der Imbissketten ausbrechen. Sie suchten nach einem Konzept, das dynamisch und eigenständig ist; gleichzeitig sollte es finanzierbar bleiben und den Geschäften eine eigene Identität verleihen.«

C'est en réaction devant le développement des Starbucks Coffee Shops que le groupe Nestlé a activement étudié la création de Nescafé Coffee Shops au niveau international. Le premier prototype a ouvert ses portes avenue de Wagram à Paris, d'autres étant d'ores et déjà prévus. Comme l'écrit l'architecte : « Ce projet traite de la création d'une architecture d'identité institutionnelle. Les points de vente des chaînes de distribution sont surtout réputés pour leur architecture ‹ copié-collé ›. (…) Pour répondre au besoin d'adaptabilité, sans tomber dans le ‹ copié-collé ›, nous avons commencé par mettre au point un système flexible composé de trois variables : la peau d'habillage, l'interface du café lui-même, et le bandeau graphique. » Le « bandeau graphique » est aussi « une interface graphique principale qui contient les éléments d'image de marque du produit. » « Bien que la première zone test de ce concept soit Paris, les sites prévus vont » de bâtiments historiques et publics, à des gares, des aéroports et des centres commerciaux. Michele Saee conclut : « les clients eux-mêmes voulaient une rupture avec le moule de la chaîne de restauration classique : ils recherchaient quelque chose de dynamique et d'original, mais voulaient en faire un lieu accessible et créer une identité claire pour ces nouveaux points de ventre. »

The first Café Nescafé opened in 2002 on the Avenue de Wagram in Paris not far from the Place Charles de Gaulle.

Das erste Café Nescafé wurde 2002 auf der Pariser Avenue de Wagram, unweit des Place Charles de Gaulle, eröffnet.

Le premier Café Nescafé a ouvert en 2002, avenue de Wagram à Paris, près de la place Charles de Gaulle.

The limited space of the shop on the Avenue de Wagram nonetheless offers conviviality and a sense of design quality.

Trotz seiner relativ geringen Größe macht das Geschäft auf der Avenue de Wagram einen einladenden und gastlichen Eindruck und lässt eine Qualität im Design erkennen.

Limité, le volume de l'avenue de Wagram n'en offre pas moins une convivialité et un sentiment de qualité de conception.

*Another location envisaged in Paris is the historic Rue de Rivoli, where Michele Saee's design shows that the architecture can be adapted to the constraint of the street's covered arcades.*

*Autre lieu envisagé à Paris, la rue de Rivoli qui demontre que le projet de Michele Saee peut s'adapter aux contraintes d'une rue à arcades.*

*Eine weitere in Paris geplante Filiale befindet sich in der Rue de Rivoli. Michele Saees Entwurf zeigt, wie sich die Architektur an die von den historischen Arkaden vorgegebenen Einschränkungen anpassen lässt.*

*cafe* RIVOLI

a-graphic ribbon
b-coffee counter
c-skin wraps

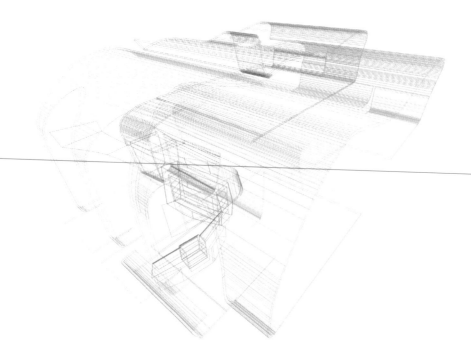

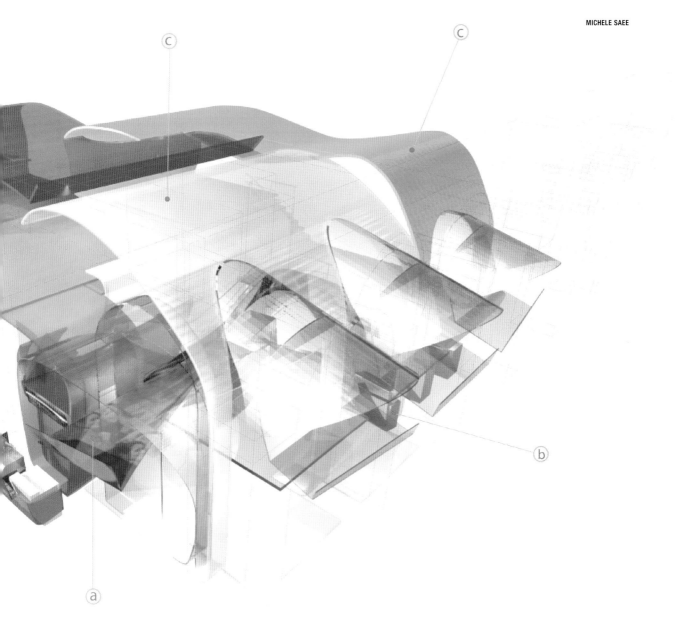

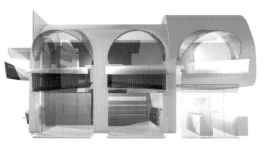

This project addresses the question of creating architecture for corporate identity. Commercial chain operations are best known for their "rubber stamp" architecture (faux-terra cotta roofs, colored formica counters, and plastic booths). Cut and paste fast food culture provides little room for inventiveness resulting in the proliferation of generic experiences. While participating in a competition for a series of cafés for Nestle, we began to ask:

*Nestlé gave an unprecedented challenge to Michele Saee, seeking to create a generic shop type adaptable to very different locations all around the world.*

*Nestlé stellte Michele Saee vor die große Herausforderung, den Prototyp eines Geschäfts zu entwerfen, der für die unterschiedlichsten Standorte in der ganzen Welt adaptierbar sein soll.*

*Nestlé a posé un défi sans précédent à Michele Saee : créer un type de point de vente générique, adaptable à toutes sortes d'implantations partout dans le monde.*

How do we break out of a system where architecture plays second to logos on nap

# HARRY SEIDLER

*Harry Seidler and Associates*
*2 Glen Street*
*Milsons Point NSW 2061*
*Australia*

*Tel: + 61 2 9922 1388*
*Fax: + 61 2 9957 2947*
*e-mail: hseidler@seidler.net.au*
*Web: www.seidler.net.au*

Born in Vienna, Austria, **HARRY SEIDLER** studied architecture at the University of Manitoba in Winnipeg (B. Arch., 1944) before winning a scholarship to Harvard, where he participated in the Masters Class of Walter Gropius (M.Arch., 1946). He also studied design under Josef Albers at Black Mountain College in North Carolina and was the chief assistant of Marcel Breuer in New York from 1946 to 1948. He worked with Oscar Niemeyer in Rio de Janeiro before opening his own practice in Sydney in 1949. He has taught at the Harvard Graduate School of Design (1976–77), and at the ETH in Zurich (1993) as well as at the University of Sydney. Winner of the RIBA Gold Medal in 1996, he is the author of the Australian Embassy in Paris (1973–77), of the Horizon apartment towers in Sydney, the Shell Headquarters in Melbourne and a social housing complex for 2,500 people along the Danube in Vienna.

Der in Wien geborene **HARRY SEIDLER** schloss 1944 sein Architekturstudium an der University of Manitoba in Winnipeg, Kanada, ab, bevor er ein Stipendium für Harvard erhielt, wo er die Meisterklasse von Walter Gropius besuchte und 1946 seinen Master of Architecture erwarb. Er studierte außerdem Entwerfen bei Josef Albers am Black Mountain College in North Carolina und war von 1946 bis 1948 leitender Assistent bei Marcel Breuer in New York. Bevor er 1949 sein eigenes Büro in Sydney gründete, arbeitete er bei Oscar Niemeyer in Rio de Janeiro. Er lehrte an der Harvard Graduate School of Design (1976–77), an der Eidgenössischen Technischen Hochschule (ETH) in Zürich (1993) sowie an der University of Sydney. 1996 erhielt er die RIBA-Goldmedaille. Zu seinen Bauten gehören die Australische Botschaft in Paris (1973–77), die Wohnhaustürme Horizon in Sydney, die Shell-Zentrale in Melbourne und ein Wohnkomplex für 2.500 Menschen an der Wiener Donau.

Né à Vienne, Autriche, **HARRY SEIDLER** étudie l'architecture à l'Université du Manitoba à Winnipeg (B. Arch., 1944) avant de recevoir une bourse pour Harvard où il participe au cours de maîtrise de Walter Gropius (M. Arch., 1946). Il étudie également la conception avec Josef Albers au Black Mountain College de Caroline du Nord et devient premier assistant de Josef Albers à New York de 1946 à 1948. Il travaille auprès d'Oscar Niemeyer à Rio de Janeiro avant d'ouvrir son agence à Sydney en 1949. Il a enseigné à l'Harvard Graduate School of Design (1976–77), et à l'ETH de Zurich (1993) ainsi qu'à l'Université de Sydney. Titulaire de la Médaille d'or du RIBA en 1996, il est l'auteur de l'ambassade d'Australie à Paris (1973–77), des tours d'appartements Horizon à Sydney, du siège social de Shell à Melbourne et d'un ensemble de logements pour 2 500 personnes à Vienne.

# BERMAN HOUSE

*Joadja, New South Wales, Australia, 1996–1999*

Client: Mr. and Mrs. Berman. Site area: 91 hectares. Floor area: 570 m². Cost: $ 1.6 million

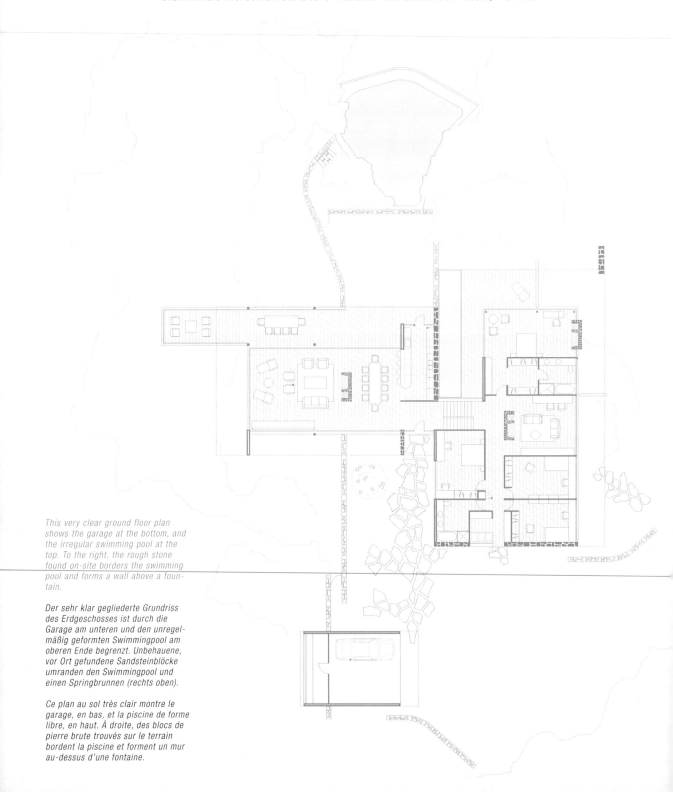

*This very clear ground floor plan shows the garage at the bottom, and the irregular swimming pool at the top. To the right, the rough stone found on-site borders the swimming pool and forms a wall above a fountain.*

*Der sehr klar gegliederte Grundriss des Erdgeschosses ist durch die Garage am unteren und den unregelmäßig geformten Swimmingpool am oberen Ende begrenzt. Unbehauene, vor Ort gefundene Sandsteinblöcke umranden den Swimmingpool und einen Springbrunnen (rechts oben).*

*Ce plan au sol très clair montre le garage, en bas, et la piscine de forme libre, en haut. À droite, des blocs de pierre brute trouvés sur le terrain bordent la piscine et forment un mur au-dessus d'une fontaine.*

Set on a cliff edge on a one hundred-hectare property overlooking a river and a vast wilderness area, this house has a suspended living zone and a projecting balcony hung from the roof's steel columns. Using new technologies, the architect has framed the roofs of the living area, bedroom wing and garage with curved steel beams. The floors are made of concrete with Altasite stone paving. Sandstone boulders found on the site form the rough retaining walls that "anchor" the house to its natural setting and surround the irregular-shaped swimming pool. These harsh stone walls contrast dramatically with the sophisticated white curves of the house itself. A lack of municipal water dictates the collection of rainwater from the roofs and the design of the swimming pool to serve as a reservoir in case of bush fires. Inside, stone fireplaces and radiant floor heating are intended to increase energy self-sufficiency. The fireplaces "define specific areas within the most open-planned space."

Das Haus liegt am Rand eines Felsens auf einem 100 ha großen Grundstück mit Blick auf einen Fluss und ein riesiges Wüstengebiet. Zu seinen Besonderheiten gehören der abgehängte Wohnbereich und ein vorspringender, an den Stahlstützen des Daches befestigter Balkon. Unter Einsatz neuer Technologien verwendete der Architekt für die Überdachungen von Wohnbereich, Schlafzimmertrakt und Garage gebogene Stahlrahmenträger. Die Fußböden bestehen aus Beton- und Steinplatten. Im Gelände vorgefundene Sandsteine dienten als Baumaterial für die unbearbeiteten Stützmauern, die das Haus in seiner natürlichen Umgebung »verankern«, sowie für die Umgrenzungsmauer des unregelmäßig geformten Swimmingpools. Diese rauen Steinwände bilden einen scharfen Kontrast zu den eleganten weißen Bogenlinien des Hauses selbst. Die fehlende städtische Wasserversorgung machte es notwendig, dass ein Auffangbecken für die Sammlung von Regenwasser installiert wurde und der Swimmingpool auch als Wasservorrat für den Fall eines Buschfeuers dient. Im Inneren des Hauses tragen offene Kamine zur Selbstversorgung mit Energie bei. Die steinernen Kamine dienen zudem zur räumlichen Abgrenzung der einzelnen Wohnbereiche innerhalb des sehr offen angelegten Grundrisses.

Implantée sur l'arrête d'une falaise dans un domaine de 100 ha dominant un fleuve et une vaste étendue sauvage, cette maison possède une zone de séjour suspendue et un balcon projeté accroché aux colonnes d'acier du toit. Faisant appel à de nouvelles technologies, l'architecte a structuré les toits de la zone de séjour, l'aile de la chambre et le garage à l'aide de poutres d'acier incurvées. Les sols sont en béton recouvert d'un dallage de pierre d'Altasite. Des rochers de grès trouvés sur place ont été utilisés dans les murs de soutènement qui « ancrent » la maison dans son cadre naturel et entourent la piscine de forme irrégulière. Ces murs de pierre brute contrastent spectaculairement avec les courbes blanches sophistiquées de la maison. L'absence de branchement au réseau d'eau public, explique la récupération d'eau de pluie des toits et le dessin de la piscine qui sert de réservoir en cas de feux naturels. À l'intérieur, les cheminées en pierre et le chauffage central au sol participent à l'autarcie énergétique de la maison ; les cheminées « définissent des zones spécifiques dans l'espace de plan en grande partie ouvert.»

*The spectacular wave-like roof lifts above the living space, offering views onto the neighboring countryside. In contrast to the hard surfaces of the house, lighting, a fireplace, and the site itself provide a natural counterpoint.*

*Das spektakuläre, sich wellenförmig über dem Wohnbereich erhebende Dach mit Ausblicken auf die Umgebung. Im Gegensatz zu den harten Oberflächen des Hauses setzen die Beleuchtung, ein offener Kamin und die Lage selbst einen natürlichen Kontrapunkt.*

*Le spectaculaire toit en vague se soulève au dessus du séjour, en dégageant des perspectives sur le paysage environnant. L'éclairage, la cheminée et le site lui-même fournissent un contrepoint naturel aux surfaces « dures » de la maison.*

A terrace cantilevers out over the abrupt cliff visible on page 441. Like many earlier Modernist houses, the Berman residence sits easily on its rugged site, not visually disturbing the natural rock formations.

Die Terrasse ragt über den auf Seite 441 abgebildeten steil abfallenden Hang hinaus. Das Haus Berman fügt sich natürlich in seine zerklüftete Umgebung mit ihren Felsformationen ein.

Une terrasse s'élève en porte-à-faux au dessus de la falaise abrupte. Comme beaucoup de maisons modernistes antérieures, la résidence des Berman a aisément trouvé sa place dans un site sauvage, sans apparemment déranger le cadre naturel des rochers.

From every vantage point, the
house opens out in a spectacular
fashion onto the wilderness. The
walls and cladding offer varying
degrees of roughness, from smooth
glass to rough sandstone.

Aus allen Blickwinkeln öffnet sich
das Haus auf spektakuläre Weise
gegenüber der Wildnis ringsum. Die
Oberflächen der Wände und Verklei-
dungen reichen von glattem Glas bis
zu unbearbeitetem Sandstein.

De tous les côtés, la maison s'ouvre
de manière spectaculaire sur la nature. Les murs et l'habillage présentent
divers degrés de finition de surface,
du verre lisse à la pierre calcaire
brute.

# SNØHETTA

*Snøhetta as*
*Christian Krohgsgata 32 B*
*0186 Oslo*
*Norway*

*Tel: + 47 22 98 8230*
*Fax: +47 22 98 8231*
*e-mail: post@snoarc.no*
*Web: www.snoarc.no*

**SNØHETTA** is a mountain in central Norway. It is a central theme in early Viking sagas and is the mythical home of Valhalla. Henrik Ibsen developed the story of Peer Gynt around Snøhetta, which gave its name to the architectural practice founded in 1987 in Oslo. Directed by Craig Dykers, Christoph Kapeller, and Kjetil Trædal Thorsen, Snøhetta has a staff of twentynine architects, nine landscape architects and four interior designers. Aside from the Alexandria Library published here, Snøhetta has recently won an anonymous, open international competition for the New National Opera house in Oslo scheduled to be completed in 2008. Other recent work of the firm includes the Hamar Town Hall (Hamar, Norway, 2000); the Karmøy Fishing Museum, (Karmøy, Norway, 1999); and the Skistua School (Skistua, Narvik, Norway, 1998). They also took the second prize in the 1997 open international competition for the Kansai-Kan Library in Japan, and built the Lillehammer Art Museum, the centerpiece cultural building for the 1993 Winter Olympics.

**SNØHETTA**, der Namensgeber für das 1987 in Oslo gegründete Architekturbüro, ist ein Berg in Zentralnorwegen. Er spielt als die mythische Heimstatt von Walhalla eine wichtige Rolle in alten Wikingersagen, und auch in Henrik Ibsens Geschichte von Peer Gynt. Unter der Leitung von Craig Dykers, Christoph Kapeller und Kjetil Trædal Thorsen beschäftigt Snøhetta 29 Architekten, neun Landschaftsarchitekten und vier Innenarchitekten. Neben der hier vorgestellten Bibliothek von Alexandria gewann Snøhetta kürzlich den anonymen, internationalen Wettbewerb für den Bau der Neuen National Oper in Oslo, dessen Fertigstellung für 2008 geplant ist. Ferner gehören zu den neueren Bauprojekten der Firma das Rathaus in Hamar (2000), das Fischereimuseum in Karmøy (1999) und die Skistua-Schule in Skistua, Narvik (1998), alle in Norwegen. 1997 gewannen sie den zweiten Preis im offenen internationalen Wettbewerb für die Kansai Kan Bibliothek in Japan und stellten 1993 mit dem Kunstmuseum in Lillehammer das wichtigste Kulturgebäude für die Winterolympiade fertig.

**SNØHETTA**, cette montagne du centre de la Norvège qui donne donc son nom à l'agence d'architecture fondée en 1987 à Oslo, figure dans les anciennes sagas des Vikings. Elle y est le siège mythique du Valhalla, et Henrik Ibsen y a situé *Peer Gynt*. Dirigée par Craig Dykers, Christoph Kapeller et Kjetil Trædal Thorsen, elle compte vingt-neuf architectes, neuf architectes paysagistes et quatre architectes d'intérieur. En dehors de la bibliothèque d'Alexandrie présentée ici, Snøhetta a récemment remporté le concours international pour le nouvel opéra national d'Oslo, qui devrait être achevé en 2008. Parmi ses autres travaux récents : l'hôtel de ville de Hamar (Hamar, Norvège, 2000), le musée de la pêche de Karmøy (Karmøy, Norvège, 1999) et l'école de Skistua (Skistua, Narvik, Norvège, 1998). Il ont également remporté le second prix du concours international de 1997 pour la bibliothèque de Kansaï-Kan au Japon et édifié le musée d'art de Lillehammer, à l'occasion des J. O. d'hiver de 1993.

# BIBLIOTHECA ALEXANDRINA

*Alexandria, Egypt, 1995–2001*

*Client: Arab Republic of Egypt. Area: 70 000 m². Cost: $150 million.*

Winners of a 1989 open international competition that drew 524 entries from 52 countries, Snøhetta devised a circular, tilting form for the structure, rising from the ground to reveal rough stone walls heavily carved with inscriptions. Subsequent to the original competition, they were also awarded contracts for the landscape and interior design of this project sponsored by Unesco and the Arab Republic of Egypt. This massive 70,000 square meter structure had a budget of $150 million. Founded shortly after the creation of the city by Alexander the Great in 331 BC, the **GREAT LIBRARY** was a center of learning in the ancient world. Parts of it burned during the civil war between Cesar and Mark Anthony, and the rest was destroyed in the third and fourth centuries after Christ. The intention of Unesco in sponsoring the project was to resurrect a symbol, but also to create a new center in this major Egyptian city. A great reading room, typical of many of the world's major libraries but organized in this case in a cascade of descending terraces, is one of the main interior features. The facility is designed to receive 3,500 readers per day.

Der 1989 als Sieger aus einem offenen, internationalen Wettbewerb mit 524 Beiträgen aus 52 Ländern hervorgegangene Entwurf von Snøhetta Architects besteht aus einem kreisförmigen, geneigten Bau. Die vom Erdgeschoss aufsteigenden Wände aus unbearbeitetem Stein sind reich mit gemeißelten Inschriften geschmückt. Im Anschluss an den eigentlichen Wettbewerb erhielten Snøhetta Architects auch die Folgeaufträge für Landschaftsarchitektur und Innenraumgestaltung dieses von der UNESCO und der Arabischen Republik Ägypten unterstützten Projekts. Das massive, 70.000 m² umfassende Gebäude wurde für 150 Millionen US Dollar realisiert. Die **ALEXANDRINISCHE BIBLIOTHEK**, die einige Jahre nach der Gründung Alexandrias durch Alexander den Großen (331 v. Chr.) erbaut wurde, war in der Antike ein Zentrum der Kunst und Wissenschaft. Während des Krieges zwischen Cäsar und Marcus Antonius fiel sie teilweise den Flammen zum Opfer, Ende des 4. Jahrhunderts n. Chr. wurde sie dann vollständig zerstört. Die UNESCO beabsichtigte mit ihrer finanziellen Unterstützung sowohl die Wiedererrichtung eines symbolischen Bauwerkes als auch die Initiation eines neuen Zentrums des Geisteslebens in dieser ägyptischen Großstadt. Eines der Hauptmerkmale der Innenraumgestaltung ist ein ausgedehnter Lesesaal, der in einer Kaskade abfallender Terrassen angelegt wurde. Der Komplex ist für eine Nutzungskapazität von täglich 3.500 Lesern konzipiert.

Vainqueurs en 1989 du concours international qui a attiré 524 participants de 52 pays, l'agence Snøhetta a conçu une structure circulaire inclinée qui se soulève du sol pour découvrir des murs de pierre brute sur lesquels sont gravées des inscriptions. Elle a également été chargée des aménagements paysagers et intérieurs de ce projet financé par l'Unesco et l'Égypte. Cette massive construction de 70 000 m² aura coûté 150 millions de dollars. Fondée peu après la création de la ville par Alexandre le Grand en 331 av. J.-C., la **GRANDE BIBLIOTHÈQUE D'ALEXANDRIE** fut l'un des centres du savoir de l'Antiquité. Une partie brûla lors du conflit entre César et Marc-Antoine, et le reste fut détruit aux IIIe et IVe siècles. L'intention de l'Unesco est de redonner vie à ce symbole, mais également de créer un nouveau pôle de développement pour la grande ville égyptienne. Une vaste salle de lecture, organisée en une cascade de terrasses est l'une des principales caractéristiques intérieures du bâtiment qui devrait recevoir 3 500 lecteurs par jour.

The design is a tilted torus with a slanted roof. The footbridge here connects the Library to the campus of the University of Alexandria.

Der Entwurf besteht aus einem geneigten Torus mit schräg gestellter Bedachung. Der hier abgebildete Steg (links) verbindet die Bibliothek mit dem Campus der Universität von Alexandria.

Le projet consiste en un tore basculé et un toit incliné. La passerelle connecte la bibliothèque au campus de l'Université d'Alexandrie.

*Left the footbridge to the Library.
Above, the roof, and below, a triangular curtain wall faces southwest and
opens onto the lobby of the structure.*

*Mündung des Stegs in die Bibliothek
(links). Das Dach (oben). Eine drei-
seitige, nach Südwesten ausgerichtete Vorhangwand öffnet sich zur
Eingangshalle hin (unten).*

*À gauche, la pénétration de la passe-
relle dans la bibliothèque. En haut,
le toit, et en bas, un mur-rideau triangulaire orienté sud-ouest qui ouvre
sur l'atrium du bâtiment.*

The concrete columns in the main reading room are a variant of the lotus-topped pharaonic designs. Above, a wedge-shaped observation deck is set above the reading room.

Die Betonpfeiler im Hauptlesesaal sind eine Variation der altägyptischen, mit Lotos bekrönten Säulen. Über dem Lesesaal erhebt sich eine keilförmige Aussichtsplattform (oben).

Les colonnes de béton de la salle de lecture principale représentent une variante des colonnes égyptiennes à chapiteau en fleur de lotus. En haut, une terrasse d'observation, au-dessus de la salle de lecture.

# JULIE SNOW ARCHITECTS

*Julie Snow Architects, Inc.*
*2400 Rand Tower*
*527 Marquette Avenue*
*Minneapolis, Minnesota 55402*
*United States*

*Tel: + 1 612 359 9430*
*Fax: + 1 612 359 9530*
*Web: www.juliesnowarchitects.com*

*Koehler House*

**JULIE SNOW** created her own firm in 1988 after working since 1974 with the firm of Hammel, Green and Abrahamson. She prides herself on a "certain fascination with the technical aspects of building assembly." Recent work includes the Vista Building for Microsoft/Great Plains Software in Fargo, North Dakota (2001); Light Rail Transit Stations for Minneapolis (completion in 2004); the New School of Business, University of South Dakota (Vermillion, South Dakota, 2001 competition); and the Koehler Residence, published here. Another ongoing project is the Jackson Street Roundhouse (St. Paul, Minnesota, 1995–2005). The firm's earlier Origen Center for the Philips Plastics Corporation (Menomonie, Wisconsin, 1994) won several awards, including an AIA MN Honor Award in 1995.

**JULIE SNOW** gründete 1988 ihre eigene Firma, nachdem sie seit 1974 im Büro von Hammel, Green and Abrahamson gearbeitet hatte. Laut eigener Aussage faszinieren sie besonders die technischen Aspekte an einem Bauprojekt. Zu ihren jüngsten Werken zählen das Vista Building für Microsoft/Great Plains Software in Fargo, North Dakota (2001), die Transitbahnhöfe von Light Rail in Minneapolis (Fertigstellung: 2004), die New School of Business der University of South Dakota in Vermillion (Wettbewerb: 2001) sowie die hier vorgestellte Koehler Residence. Ein weiteres zur Zeit in Arbeit befindliches Projekt ist das Jackson Street Roundhouse in St. Paul, Minnesota (1995–2005). Für das von ihrer Firma 1994 fertig gestellte Origen Center der Firma Philips Plastics Corporation in Menomonie, Wisconsin, gewann sie mehrere Preise, so 1995 den AIA MN Honor Award.

**JULIE SNOW** crée son agence en 1988 après avoir travaillé depuis 1974 chez Hammel, Green and Abrahamson. Elle avoue une « certaine fascination pour les aspects techniques de la construction ». Parmi ses travaux récents : le Vista Building pour Microsoft/Great Plains Software à Fargo, Dakota du Nord (2001) ; les stations d'un système de transport léger pour Minneapolis (achevé en 2004) ; la Koehler Residence, présentée dans ces pages. Elle travaille actuellement au projet de la Jackson Street Roundhouse (St. Paul, Minnesota, 1995–2005). Son Origen Centre pour la Philips Plastics Corporation (Menomonie, Wisconsin, 1994) a remporté plusieurs prix, y compris un AIA MN Honor Award en 1995.

# KOEHLER HOUSE

*New Brunswick, Canada, 2000*

*Client: David and Mary Beth Koehler. Floor area: 150 m².*
*Structure: wood frame, Douglas fir columns, and concrete foundations.*

Set on the edge of the Bay of Fundy, this 150 square meter house is intended as a family retreat. The Minneapolis residents David and Mary Beth Koehler chose this rugged twenty-hectare site located about 40 kilometers from the Maine border for their open, rectangular, two-level house. Piled like two boxes, one on top of the other, the lower floor is cantilevered over the rock, no more than 30 meters from the average high tide line of the ocean. The owners of the house were apparently inspired by Mies van der Rohe's Farnsworth House, a still-simpler one story structure. The living room, dining room and kitchen are a continuous space on the lower floor, while the master bedroom, porch and sitting room and on the upper level. Poured-in-place concrete foundations with steel pins anchor the house to the rocks while the roof and floors are designed with plywood membranes and wooden trusses – all of this with the intention of protecting the house against the weather conditions that occur frequently in the area.

Das an der Spitze der Bay of Fundy gelegene, 150 m² große Haus ist als Zufluchtsort der in Minneapolis lebenden Familie David und Mary Beth Koehler gedacht. Als Bauplatz für ihr rechteckiges, offen gestaltetes und auf zwei Ebenen angelegtes Haus wählten sie ein 20 ha großes, zerklüftetes Stück Land, circa 40 km von der Grenze zu Maine entfernt. Das Gebäude erweckt den Eindruck von zwei aufeinander gestapelten Kisten, von denen die untere über die Felskante hinausragt, und zwar nur 30 m oberhalb des durchschnittlichen Flutpegels des Atlantik. Offenbar ließen sich die Bauherren von Mies van der Rohes Farnsworth House inspirieren, einem noch schlichteren 1-stöckigen Gebäude. Wohnzimmer, Esszimmer und Küche befinden sich in einem offenen Raum im Erdgeschoss, während das Hauptschlafzimmer, eine Veranda und ein kleinerer Wohnraum im Obergeschoss liegen. Durch ein Fundament aus Gussbeton mit Stahlbolzen wird das Haus auf den Felsen verankert, während Dach und Böden aus Sperrholzmembranen und Holzbalken gefertigt sind. All diese bautechnischen Maßnahmen dienen dazu, das Haus gegen die in dieser Region häufig auftretenden Unwetter zu schützen.

Implantée au bord de la baie de Fundy, cette maison de 150 m² est une résidence familiale de loisirs. Ce sont David et Mary Beth Koehler, de Minneapolis, qui ont choisi ce terrain de 20 hectares à 40 km environ de la frontière du Maine pour y créer cette maison ouverte, rectangulaire, de deux niveaux empilés l'un sur l'autre à la manière de boîtes. Le niveau du rez-de-chaussée en porte-à-faux au-dessus du rocher se trouve à 30 m de la ligne des grandes marées. Les propriétaires ont sans doute été sensibles à la Farnsworth House de Mies van der Rohe, également à deux niveaux, mais encore plus épurée. Au rez-de-chaussée, le séjour, la salle à manger et la zone de préparation des repas sont traités en espace continu tandis que la chambre principale, un salon et une véranda occupent le niveau supérieur. Des fondations en béton coulé sur place et broches en acier ancrent la maison au rocher, le toit et les sols sont en poutres de bois et panneaux-membranes de contre-plaqué, le tout calculé pour protéger la maison du mauvais temps fréquent dans cette région.

Although it appears to be very light and transparent, the house is designed to withstand high winds and very cold conditions.

Obgleich es sehr leicht und transparent wirkt, ist das Haus so konstruiert, dass es Stürmen und äußerst kalten Temperaturen standhält.

Bien qu'elle paraisse particulièrement légère et transparente, la maison a été conçue pour résister aux vents et au climat très froid.

The owner comments that the site
of this house is much as it must
have been when the French explorer
Champlain saw the shore for the
first time 400 years ago.

*Laut Eigentümer sieht die Umgebung
des Hauses nicht viel anders aus als
vor 400 Jahren, als die Küste von
dem Franzosen Samuel de Champlain
entdeckt wurde.*

*Pour les propriétaires, ce site est
resté tel qu'il était lorsque l'explora-
teur Champlain aborda cette côte
pour la première fois, il y a 400 ans.*

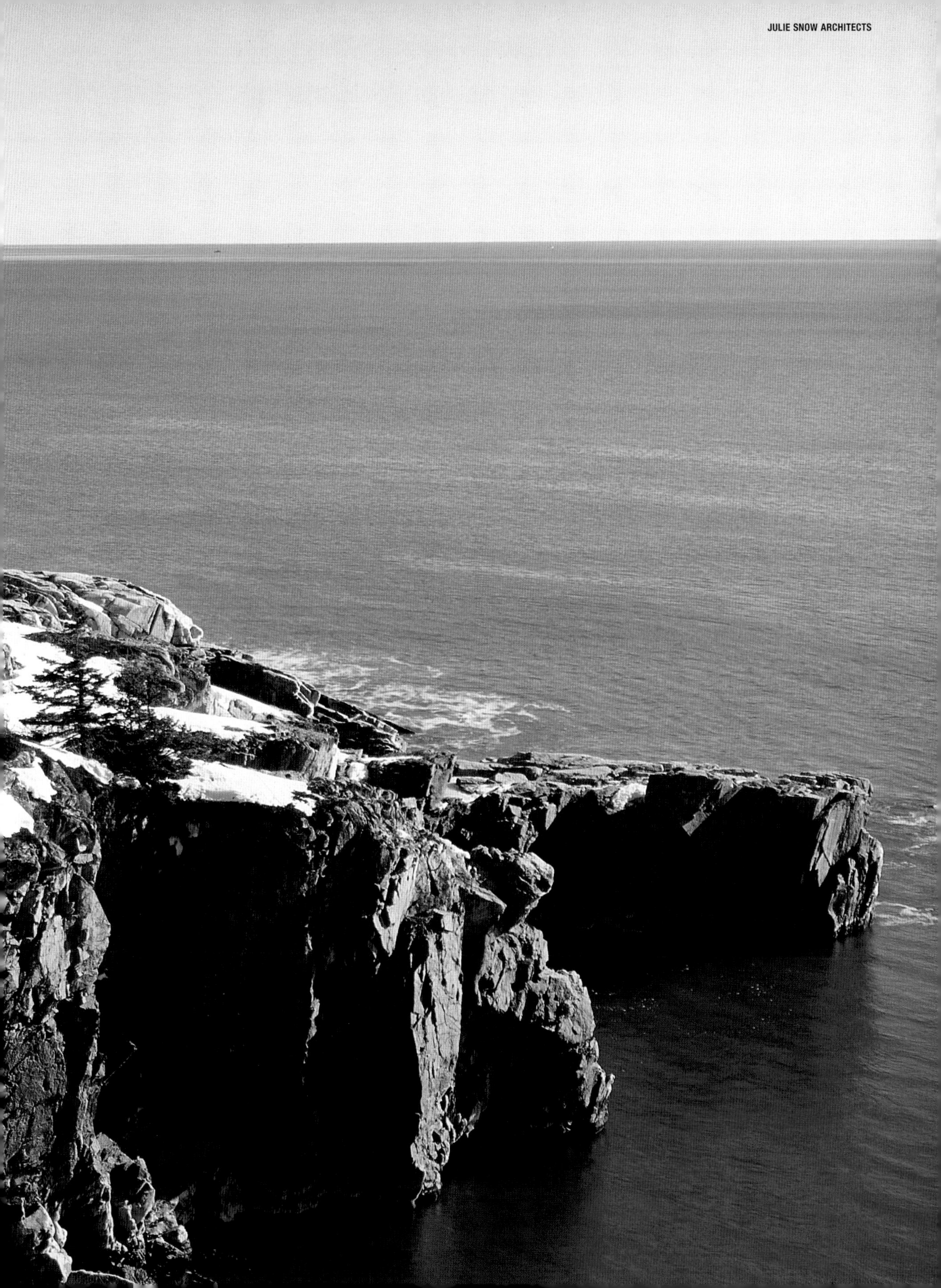

The situation of the house above the ocean gives it something of the feeling of a boat. Furniture selected by the owners is mostly by Le Corbusier or Mies.

Durch seine Lage direkt über dem Ozean hat das Haus etwas von einem Schiff. Die von den Besitzern ausgewählten Möbel sind größtenteils von Le Corbusier oder Mies van der Rohe entworfen.

La situation de la maison au-dessus de l'océan donne parfois le sentiment d'être dans un bateau. Le mobilier choisi par les propriétaires est généralement signé Le Corbusier ou Mies van der Rohe.

# PHILIPPE STARCK

*Philippe Starck*
*27, rue Pierre Poli*
*92130 Issy-les-Moulineaux*
*France*

*Tel: + 33 1 41 08 82 82*
*Fax: + 33 1 41 08 96 65*
*e-mail: starck@sky.fr*
*Web: www.philippe-starck.com*

**PHILIPPE STARCK** was born in 1949 and attended the École Nissim de Camondo in Paris. Though he is of course best known as a furniture and object designer, his projects as an architect include the Café Costes, Paris, 1984; Royalton Hotel, New York, 1988; Laguiole Knife Factory, Laguiole (1987); Paramount Hotel, New York, 1990; Nani Nani Building, Tokyo, 1989; Asahi Beer Building, Tokyo, 1990; the Teatriz Restaurant, Madrid, 1990; and his Baron Vert building in Osaka, 1992. He has also designed a number of private houses and apartment blocks, for example Le Moult in Paris (1985–1987), The Angle in Antwerp (1991), apartment buildings in Los Angeles (1991) and a private house in Madrid (1996). More recently, he completed the interior design of the Saint Martin's Lane and Sanderson Hotels in London.

**PHILIPPE STARCK**, geboren 1949 in Paris, studierte an der École Nissim de Camondo in Paris. Obwohl er vor allem als Designer von Möbeln und Objekten bekannt wurde, hat er auch Architekturprojekte ausgeführt. Zu diesen zählen das Café Costes in Paris (1984), das Royalton Hotel (1988) und das Paramount Hotel (1990), beide in New York, die Messerfabrik Laguiole in Laguiole, Frankreich (1987), das Nani Nani Gebäude (1989) und das Gebäude der Asahi-Brauerei (1990), beide in Tokio, das Restaurant Teatriz in Madrid (1990) sowie das Baron Vert Gebäude in Osaka (1992). Darüber hinaus hat Starck auch eine Reihe von Privathäusern und Apartmentgebäuden geplant, wie etwa das Haus Le Moult in Paris (1985–87), das Haus »The Angle« in Antwerpen (1991), Wohnbauten in Los Angeles (1991) und ein Privathaus in Madrid (1996). Zu seinen jüngsten Arbeiten gehört die Innenraumgestaltung der Londoner Hotels Saint Martin's Lane und Sanderson.

Né en 1949, **PHILIPPE STARCK** a été élève à l'École Camondo à Paris. Bien qu'il soit surtout connu comme designer d'objets et de mobilier, il est l'auteur de plusieurs réalisations architecturales dont le Café Costes, Paris, 1984 ; le Royalton Hotel, New York, 1988 ; une usine de coutellerie à Laguiole (1987) ; le Paramount Hotel, New York, 1990 ; le Nani Nani Building, Tokyo, 1989 ; l'Asahi Beer Building, Tokyo, 1990 ; le Teatriz restaurant, Madrid, 1990 ; le Baron Vert Building, Osaka, 1992. Il a également conçu un certain nombre de maisons particulières et d'immeubles d'habitation, comme la maison Le Moult à Paris, 1985–87 ; The Angle à Anvers, 1991 ; des immeubles d'appartements à Los Angeles, 1991 ; une résidence privée à Madrid, 1996. Plus récemment, il a achevé l'aménagement des hôtels Saint Martin's Lane et Sanderson à Londres.

# TASCHEN SHOP

*Paris, France, 2001*

Located near the heart of historic Paris in the Saint-Germain-des-Prés area, the new **TASCHEN SHOP** occupies a deep, relatively narrow space on the rue de Buci. When weather permits, the shop's counters extend out onto the sidewalks of the busy pedestrian street. Called "a stage setting for books," the interior design contrasts an undeniable modernity with bronze surfaces and dark rare wood enveloped in shadows. Affordable books are thus given a prestigious setting where it is quite easy for visitors to browse and choose. A large video screen fills the back wall of the boutique. An identical deep space on the second floor is occupied by the offices of TASCHEN France, with furniture by Jean Nouvel and 28 meter long computer-generated murals by the artist Albert Oehlen.

Die neue, nahe dem historischen Zentrum von Paris im Viertel Saint-Germain-des-Prés gelegene **TASCHEN-BUCHHANDLUNG** ist in einem langen und relativ schmalen Ladenlokal auf der Rue de Buci untergebracht. Wenn es das Wetter erlaubt, lassen sich die Verkaufstische bis auf den Bürgersteig der belebten Fußgängerzone verlängern. Das »Bühnenbild für Bücher« genannte Design setzt eine unleugbare Modernität in Kontrast zu bronzefarbenen Oberflächen und seltenen, dunklen Hölzern. Dadurch erhalten die preisgünstigen Bücher einen kostbaren Rahmen, in dem die Besucher in Ruhe stöbern und auswählen können. Die Rückwand des Geschäfts wird von einer großen Videoleinwand eingenommen. In einem identisch geschnittenen Raum im Obergeschoss befinden sich die Büros von TASCHEN France, die mit Möbeln von Jean Nouvel und einem 28 m langen, computergenerierten Wandgemälde des Künstlers Albert Oehlen ausgestattet sind.

Située en plein quartier de Saint-Germain-des-Prés, la **BOUTIQUE TASCHEN** occupe un local profond mais assez étroit, rue de Buci. Lorsque le temps le permet, les comptoirs sont installés sur le trottoir de cette rue très fréquentée. «Mise-en-scène pour les livres», l'aménagement intérieur fait contraster dans un esprit indéniablement contemporain des bois exotiques rares, des éléments de bronze et de miroir. Des ouvrages de grande diffusion bénéficient ainsi d'un cadre prestigieux et peuvent être facilement feuilletés par les visiteurs. Un grand écran de télévision remplit le mur du fond. Au premier étage, un espace identique est occupé par les bureaux de TASCHEN France. Son mobilier est de Jean Nouvel et une grande peinture murale à base d'images numériques est signée par l'artiste Albert Oehlen.

The almost unadorned facade of the building was modified several times in the course of design work, due to the rigid attitude of France's historic monuments authorities. Above, the rear of the boutique with its large-scale video screen.

Die fast schmucklose Fassade des Gebäudes wurde aufgrund der strengen Vorschriften des französischen Denkmalamts im Verlauf der Bauarbeiten mehrmals verändert. Der rückwärtige Teil der Buchhandlung mit der großformatigen Videoleinwand (oben).

La façade presque sans ornement a été modifiée à plusieurs reprises pour se plier aux règles strictes de la protection des sites classés. En haut : le fond de la boutique et son grand écran vidéo.

Warm wood tones and subtle lighting together with selected pieces of old furniture give the boutique a luxurious aspect that contrasts with the up-to-date nature of the books themselves.

Die warmen Farbtöne der Hölzer und eine dezente Beleuchtung verleihen dem Geschäft zusammen mit einigen erlesenen Antiquitäten eine exquisite Note, die mit dem modernen Charakter der Bücher selbst kontrastiert.

Les tonalités chaleureuses du bois et l'éclairage subtil se combinent à des meubles de style ancien pour donner à cette boutique une atmosphère luxueuse qui contraste avec la nature très actuelle des livres présentés.

# JYRKI TASA

Jyrki Tasa
Architectural Office
Nurmela-Raimoranta-Tasa Ltd.
Kalevankatu 31
00100 Helsinki
Finland

Tel: + 358 9 686 6780
Fax: + 358 9 685 7588
e-mail: tasa@n-r-t.fi
Web: www.n-r-t.fi

*Into House*

Born in Turku, Finland in 1944, **JYRKI TASA** graduated from the Helsinki University of Technology in 1972. He set up an architectural office with Matti Nurmela and Kari Raimoranta in Helsinki the next year. He has been a professor at the Helsinki University of Technology since 1988. He has won 17 first prizes in architectural competitions. He won the Finnish State Prize in Architecture and Planning in 1987. His most significant work includes the Malmi Post Office, the Kuhmo Library, the Paavo Nurmi Stadium in Turku, the Into House in Espoo published here and the BE Pop Shopping Center in Pori. All of these projects are located in Finland.

**JYRKI TASA**, geboren 1944 im finnischen Turku, schloss 1972 sein Studium an der Technischen Universität Helsinki ab. Im darauffolgenden Jahr gründete er zusammen mit Matti Nurmela und Kari Raimoranta eine Architekturfirma in Helsinki. Seit 1988 lehrt er außerdem an der Technischen Universität Helsinki. Jyrki Tasa hat im Laufe seiner Karriere 17 Mal den ersten Preis bei Architekturwettbewerben gewonnen und 1987 wurde ihm der finnische Staatspreis für Architektur und Bauplanung verliehen. Zu seinen bedeutendsten, alle in Finnland entstandenen Bauten gehören das Postamt in Malmi, die Bibliothek in Kuhmo, das Paavo Nurmi Stadion in Turku, das hier vorgestellte Haus Into in Espoo sowie das BE Pop Einkaufszentrum in Pori.

Né à Tuku, Finlande, en 1944, **JYRKI TASA** sort diplômé de l'Université de Technologie d'Helsinki en 1972. Il crée son agence d'architecture avec Matti Nurmela et Kari Raimoranta à Helsinki l'annéé suivante. Il enseigne à l'Université de Technologie d'Helsinki depuis 1988 et a remporté 17 premiers prix de concours architecturaux. Il a remporté le Prix de Finlande d'architecture et d'urbanisme en 1987. Parmi ses réalisations les plus marquantes, toutes en Finlande : la poste de Malmi, la bibliothèque de Kuhmo, le Stade Paavo Nurmi de Turku, la maison Into à Espoo présentée ici, et le centre commercial BE Pop à Pori.

# INTO HOUSE

*Espoo, Finland, 1997–1998*

*Client: Into Tasa. Floor area: 187 m². Structure: steel tubes and wood. Cost: 400,000 euros.*

This three-level family house is accessible via a walkway at the rear of the house. The relatively closed rear facade contrasts with the open glazed front of the house. Wood paneling and a spectacular suspended spiral staircase animate the interior spaces. With its tilted metal exterior columns, slanted roof and cantilevered main body, this house is dramatic and unexpected. Though it is clearly rooted in modern Finnish architecture, it does not appear to be firmly tied to its own site. The angling of the columns and the cantilevering almost give the impression that the house has just moved from its original location. This kind of imbalance and unexpected design has been seen throughout Tasa's career, as buildings such as the Commercial Center in Pori, Finland (1987–1989) show. With a design such as that of the Into House, Tasa shows his ability to step back from the Post-Modern tendencies shown in buildings like the Library in Kuhmo (1982–84) while still retaining a degree of fantasy or constructive imbalance.

Der Zugang zu dem auf drei Ebenen angelegten Einfamilienhaus erfolgt über einen Gehweg an der Rückseite des Gebäudes. Die relativ geschlossene rückwärtige Fassade des Hauses bildet einen Kontrast zur offenen, verglasten Vorderfront. Das Interieur beleben die Holztäfelungen und eine auffallende abgehängte Wendeltreppe. Mit den geneigten Außenträgern aus Metall, dem Schrägdach und dem vorspringenden Hauptteil handelt es sich um ein spektakuläres und verblüffendes Gebäude. Wenngleich eindeutig in der modernen finnischen Architektur verwurzelt, scheint es mit seinem eigenen Grund nicht fest verbunden zu sein. Vielmehr entsteht durch die Schräge der Träger und den frei schwebenden Rumpf der Eindruck, als sei das Haus soeben von seinem ursprünglichen Standort hierher gerückt worden. Das Ungleichgewicht und die überraschenden Gestaltungselementen ziehen sich durch die gesamte Karriere von Tasa, so findet man sie auch an Gebäuden wie dem Einkaufszentrum im finnischen Pori (1987–89). In diesem Entwurf des Hauses Into spiegelt sich die Fähigkeit des Architekten, die postmodernen Vorlieben, wie er sie etwa in seiner Bibliothek in Kuhmo (1982–84) umgesetzt hat, fallen zu lassen und sich dabei dennoch ein hohes Maß an Fantasie und konstruktiver Unausgewogenheit zu bewahren.

On accède à cette maison familiale de trois niveaux par une allée située à l'arrière dont la façade relativement fermée contraste avec la façade avant, ouverte et vitrée. Des lambris de bois et un spectaculaire escalier suspendu en spirale animent les espaces intérieurs. Les colonnes extérieures penchées, le toit incliné et la partie principale en porte-à-faux lui donnent un aspect spectaculaire et inattendu. Bien que nettement enracinée dans l'architecture finlandaise actuelle, elle ne semble pas vraiment liée à son terrain. L'inclinaison des colonnes et le porte-à-faux donnent presque l'impression qu'elle vient de quitter son implantation d'origine. Cette sorte de déséquilibre et de dessin étrange est récurrente dans le travail de Tasa, comme on l'observe déjà dans le Centre commercial de Pori (Finlande, 1987–89). Dans ce projet, Tasa montre sa capacité à évoluer par rapport à ses tendances postmodernes illustrées dans des réalisations comme la bibliothèque de Kuhmo (1982–84), tout en conservant un certain degré de fantaisie ou de déséquilibre constructif.

Left page, the front facade of the house and this page a side view showing the tilted columns and the large glazed surfaces.

*Vorderseite des Hauses (links). Seitenansicht mit den geneigten Stützen und den großflächigen Verglasungen (diese Seite).*

*A gauche, la façade principale de la maison et, en bas, une vue latérale des colonnes inclinées et des vastes surfaces vitrées.*

*Below, an exploded axonometric drawing of the Into House, and to the right, the interior and sundeck.*

*Axonometrische Darstellung des Hauses (unten). Interieur und Sonnenterrasse (rechts).*

*En bas, un dessin axonométrique de la maison et, à droite, l'intérieur et le solarium.*

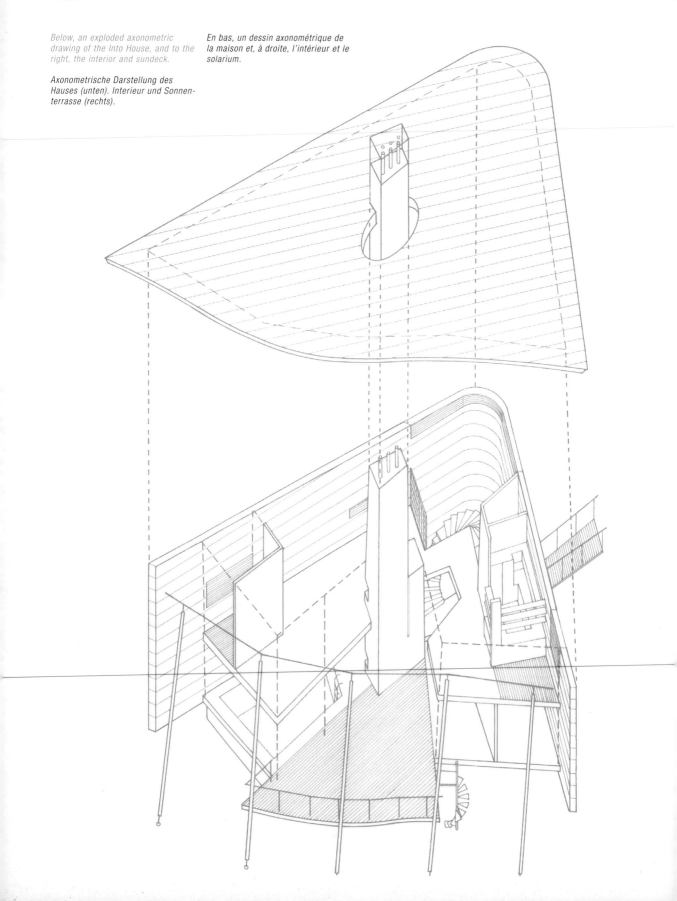

# BERNARD TSCHUMI

*Bernard Tschumi Architects*
*227 West 17th Street*
*New York, New York 10011*
*United States*

*Tel: + 1 212 807 6340*
*Fax: + 1 212 242 3693*
*e-mail: nyc@tschumi.com*
*Web: www.tschumi.com*

**BERNARD TSCHUMI** was born in Lausanne, Switzerland, in 1944. He studied in Paris and at the Federal Institute of Technology (ETH), Zurich. He taught at the Architectural Association, London (1970–1979), and at Princeton (1976–80). He has been Dean of the Graduate School of Architecture, Planning and Preservation of Columbia University in New York since 1984. He opened his own office, Bernard Tschumi Architects (Paris, New York), in 1981. Major projects include: Parc de la Villette (Paris, France, 1982–95); Second Prize in the Kansai International Airport Competition, 1988; Video Gallery (Groningen, The Netherlands, 1990); Le Fresnoy National Studio for Contemporary Arts (Tourcoing, France, 1991–97); Lerner Student Center, Columbia University (New York, 1994–99); School of Architecture (Marne-la-Vallée, France, 1994–98); and the Interface Flon railroad station in Lausanne, Switzerland.

**BERNARD TSCHUMI**, geboren 1944 in schweizerischen Lausanne, studierte in Paris und an der Eidgenössischen Technischen Hochschule (ETH) in Zürich. Von 1970 bis 1979 lehrte er an der Architectural Association (AA) in London und von 1976 bis 1980 in Princeton. Seit 1984 ist er Dekan der Graduate School of Architecture, Planning and Preservation der Columbia University in New York. 1981 gründete Tschumi sein eigenes Büro, Bernard Tschumi Architects, mit Niederlassungen in Paris und New York. Zu seinen wichtigsten Projekten gehören: der Parc de la Villette in Paris (1982–95), sein Wettbewerbsbeitrag für den internationalen Flughafen Kansai (1988), für den er den zweiten Preis erhielt, die Videogalerie im niederländischen Groningen (1990), das staatliche Zentrum für zeitgenössische Kunst Le Fresnoy in Tourcoing, Frankreich (1991–97), das Lerner Hall Student Center der Columbia University in New York (1994–99), die Architekturschule im französischen Marne-la-Vallée (1994–98) sowie der Bahnhof Interface Flon in Lausanne.

Né à Lausanne, Suisse, en 1944, **BERNARD TSCHUMI** étudie à Paris et à l'Institut Fédéral de technologie de Zurich (ETH). Il enseigne à l'Architectural Associa-tion, (Londres, 1970–79), et à Princeton (1976 et 1980). Il est doyen de la Graduate School of Architecture, Planning and Preservation de Columbia University, New York, depuis 1988. Il ouvre son agence, Bernard Tschumi Architects, en 1981 (New York et Paris). Parmi ses principaux projets : le Parc de la Villette (Paris, 1982–95) ; le second prix du concours pour l'aéroport international de Kansaï (1988) ; la Glass Video Gallery (Groningue, Pays-Bas, 1990, récemment intégrée au Musée de Groningue) ; le Centre National pour les Arts contemporains du Fresnoy (Tourcoing, France, 1991–97) ; le Lerner Hall Student Center (Columbia University, New York, 1994–99) et l'École d'Architecture de Marne-la-Vallée, (1994–98) ainsi que la gare d'interconnections du quartier de Flon à Lausanne (Suisse).

# ZÉNITH

*Rouen, France, 1999–2001*

*Cost: $21 million (Concert Hall), $9 million (Exhibition Hall). Area: 6,500 m² (Exhibition Hall).*
*Concert Hall: 7,000 seats. Site area: 30 hectares.*

This 7,000-seat **ZÉNITH** hall for rock concerts, political meetings and other gatherings cost $21 million to build. It has a 107-meter diameter, and is set on a 30-hectare site with a $9 million 6,500 meter Exhibtion Hall. The Exhibition Hall is 213 meters long. The architect has placed a double envelope around the Concert Hall to provide sound insulation, forming a "broken torus" of insulated corrugated steel. Tschumi describes the space between the interior structural envelope and the exterior (weather, security) envelope as an "in-between" space, one of his favorite concepts that he also describes as a "place of movement." Three masts with tension cables permit a lightened truss system for the Zenith. The form of the torus, which he calls a "geometric, tectonic solution" as opposed to a computer-generated solution, is made to appear to hover off the ground because the first 2.5 meters of the structure from the ground up are glazed. Acrylic plastic seats continue the impression of lightness imparted by the exterior, whose billowing forms have been likened to those of sails in the wind.

Die **ZÉNITH** genannte Halle mit 7.000 Plätzen wurde für Rockkonzerte, politische und andere Veranstaltungen konzipiert. Die Baukosten des Gebäudes, das einen Durchmesser von 107 m hat, betrugen 21 Millionen US Dollar. Es liegt auf einem 30 ha großen Gelände, auf dem sich außerdem eine für 9 Millionen US-Dollar gebaute, 6.500 m² umfassende Ausstellungshalle mit einer Längsseite von 213 m befindet. Der Architekt hat die Halle zum Zweck der Schalldämmung mit einer doppelten Hülle versehen, die einen »gebrochenen Ringwulst« aus isoliertem, geschweißtem Stahl bildet. Tschumi bezeichnet den Abstand zwischen innerer und äußerer Hülle als einen »Zwischen-Raum«, eine seiner bevorzugten Gestaltungsideen, die er auch als einen »Ort der Bewegung« definiert. Drei mit Spannseilen versehene Masten bilden das Hängewerk für die Halle. Der »Ringwulst«, den Tschumi als »geometrische, tektonische Lösung« im Gegensatz zu einer computergenerierten bezeichnet, ist so konstruiert, dass er über dem Erdboden zu schweben scheint, da der untere 2,5 m hohe Bereich des Gebäudes verglast ist. Der Eindruck von Leichtigkeit, den die Außenfassaden vermitteln, deren wogende Formen mit Segeln im Wind verglichen wurden, entsteht durch eine Bestuhlung aus Acryl auch im Inneren.

Ce **ZÉNITH** de 7000 places, salle de concerts, de réunions politiques et autres rencontres a été réalisé pour un budget de 21 millions de dollars. Construit sur un terrain de 30 ha, il mesure 107 m de diamètre et a été complété par un palais d'expositions de 213 m de long et 6500 m² (budget : 9 millions de dollars). L'architecte a imaginé une double enveloppe en forme de « tore brisé » en acier ondulé qui entoure la salle de concert pour assurer son isolation phonique. Il parle d'un « entre-deux », l'un de ses concepts favoris, et de « lieu de mouvement » pour l'espace entre l'enveloppe interne structurelle et l'extérieur (protection contre les éléments). Trois mâts d'où partent des câbles en tension constituent l'ossature légère de l'ensemble. La forme de tore, « solution géométrique, tectonique » et non solution générée par ordinateur, semble flotter légèrement au-dessus du sol car la base de la structure a été vitrée sur 2,5 mètres. Les sièges en plastique acrylique renforcent l'impression générale de légèreté de ce vaste bâtiment dont les formes enflées ont été comparées à des voiles gonflées par le vent.

*The space between the structural/*
*acoustical envelope and the weather/*
*security envelope can be described*
*as an "in-between" – a place of*
*movement, according to the architect.*

*Der »Zwischen-Raum« zwischen äuße-*
*rer und innerer Hülle ist laut Architekt*
*ein Ort der Bewegung.*

*L'espace entre l'enveloppe structurel-*
*le et acoustique et celle de sécurité*
*et de protection peut être considérée*
*comme un « entre-deux », lieu propice*
*au mouvement, selon l'architecte.*

The sweeping curves of the inner
envelope of the structure give a
dynamic movement to the spaces.
Below, the Concert Hall is visible
at right, and to the left, the long
Exhibition Hall.

Die geschwungenen Linien der inneren Hülle verleihen den Räumen einen
dynamischen Aspekt. Der Konzertsaal
und die lang gestreckte Ausstellungshalle, links im Bild (unten).

Les courbes de l'enveloppe intérieure
de la structure créent un mouvement
dynamique à l'intérieur des volumes.
En bas à droite, l'auditorium ; à
gauche, le long hall d'exposition.

The 7,000-seat Concert Hall with its
transparent acrylic seats, is designed
so that different parts can be closed
off, according to the capacity desired
for different events.

Der mit 7.000 Sitzplätzen aus trans-
parentem Acryl ausgestattete Konzertsaal ist so konzipiert, dass je nach
erforderlicher Kapazität für verschiedene Veranstaltungen unterschiedliche Raumteile abgeteilt werden
können.

L'auditorium de 7 000 places doté de
sièges en acrylique transparent peut
être modulé en fonction de l'affluence
prévue.

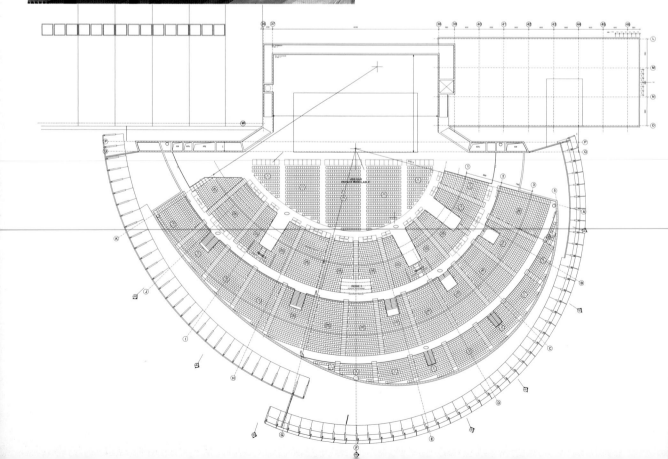

# JAMES TURRELL

*web: www.rodencrater.org*

*Roden Crater Projec*

**JAMES TURRELL** was born in Los Angeles in 1943. He received a diploma in psychology from Pomona College (1965) and in art from the University of California, Irvine, in 1966. Since that time, he has been responsible for a very large number of exhibitions and installations all over the world. He completed an installation with the architect Tadao Ando on the island of Naoshima in the Inland Sea of Japan in 1999. His interest is in the perception of light in various forms. Although he does not claim to be an architect, he has shown a consistent interest in the use of space in his work, and in particular in the case of the Roden Crater, which he purchased in 1977, of which images are published here. He recently conceived the lighting of the Pont du Gard near Nîmes in France, and participated in the exhibition "La beauté" in Avignon (2000).

**JAMES TURRELL**, geboren 1943 in Los Angeles, erwarb 1965 sein Diplom in Psychologie am Pomona College und 1966 sein Kunstdiplom an der University of California in Irvine. Seither gestaltete er zahlreiche Ausstellungen und Installationen in der ganzen Welt. 1999 führte er zusammen mit dem Architekten Tadao Ando eine Installation auf der Insel Naoshima im japanischen Binnenmeer aus. Sein besonderes Interesse gilt der Wahrnehmung von Licht in seinen verschiedenen Erscheinungsformen. Obwohl er sich nicht als Architekt definiert, zeugen seine Arbeiten von einer konsequenten Auseinandersetzung mit dem Thema Raum, was sich besonders im Fall des von ihm 1977 erworbenen Geländes Roden Crater und des gleichnamigen Projekts zeigt, das hier vorgestellt wird. Seine neuesten Arbeiten sind das Lichtdesign für die Pont du Gard nahe der französischen Stadt Nîmes sowie ein Beitrag für die Ausstellung »La Beauté« in Avignon (2000).

Né à Los Angeles en 1943, **JAMES TURRELL** est diplômé en psychologie de Pomona College (1965) et en art de l'Université de Californie, Irvine, en 1966. Depuis cette époque, il a beaucoup exposé et monté des expositions dans le monde entier. Il a, entre autres, créé une installation avec l'architecte Tadao Ando sur l'île de Naoshima (Mer intérieure du Japon, 1999). Il s'intéresse à la perception de la lumière sous des formes variées. Bien qu'il ne se prétende pas architecte, il montre un intérêt permanent pour l'utilisation de l'espace, en particulier dans le projet du Roden Crater, volcan acquis en 1977, présenté ici. Il a récemment conçu l'éclairage du Pont du Gard (Nîmes, France) et participé à l'exposition « La Beauté » en Avignon (2000).

# RODEN CRATER PROJECT

*near Flagstaff, Arizona, United States, 1977–2006*

*Date of purchase: 1977. Site area: 50,000 hectares.*

Roden Crater is located about forty miles from Flagstaff Arizona. The volcano, which has been extinct for 390,000 years, was bought by James Turrell in 1977, and is surrounded by fifty thousand hectares of land that also belongs to the artist. The remnants of some six hundred volcanoes surround the site of Roden Crater. The first phase of the project will be completed and opened to the public (14 persons per day) in the fall of 2003. The **RODEN CRATER PROJECT** is funded partially by the Dia and Lannan Foundations, as well as a ranch owned by the artist on the site. Turrell has engaged in extensive earthmoving work (several hundred thousand cubic meters of earth have been displaced) to turn the crater into an observatory of celestial phenomena, be they frequent, or rare, such as the Lunar Solstice that occurs every 18 years (the next time in 2006). The tunnels and rooms within the crater are all intended to bring the visitor into contact with light. "I am trying to make light a physical experience, so when you see light it is no longer illuminating other things, it is *the* thing," says the artist.

Roden Crater liegt circa 65 km von Flagstaff, Arizona, entfernt. 1977 erwarb James Turrell den seit 390.000 Jahren erloschenen Vulkan zusammen mit dem angrenzenden 50.000 ha großen Gelände, auf dem sich die Überreste von etwa 600 weiteren Vulkanen befinden. Die erste Phase des Projekts wird im Herbst 2003 abgeschlossen sein. Ab diesem Zeitpunkt ist das **RODEN CRATER PROJEKT** für Besucher – begrenzt auf 14 Personen täglich – geöffnet. Es wird teilweise von der Dia Art Foundation und der Lannan Foundation unterstützt, ebenso wie eine auf dem Grundstück liegende Ranch des Künstlers. Turrell ließ umfangreiche Erdarbeiten ausführen, bei denen mehrere Hunderttausend Kubikmeter Erde verschoben wurden, um den Krater in ein Observatorium für Himmelserscheinungen zu verwandeln, seien sie häufig oder selten auftretend, wie die Mondwende, die alle 18 Jahre eintritt (das nächste Mal 2006). Die im Kraterinneren angelegten Tunnel und Räume sollen die Besucher mit Licht in Kontakt bringen. »Ich versuche, das Licht zu einer physischen Erfahrung zu machen, sodass es nicht mehr dazu dient, etwas anderes zu beleuchten, sondern selbst die Hauptsache ist«, so der Künstler.

Roden Crater se trouve à environ 65 km de Flagstaff, en Arizona. Ce volcan, éteint depuis 390 000 ans, a été acheté par James Turrell en 1977 ainsi que les 50 000 hectares de terres qui l'entourent. Le site est marqué par les restes de quelque six cents volcans. La première phase du projet sera achevée et ouverte au public (14 personnes par jour) à l'automne 2003. Le **PROJET RODEN CRATER** est financé en partie par les fondations Dia et Lannan, ainsi que le ranch propriété de l'artiste sur le site. Turrell s'est engagé dans d'énormes travaux de terrassement (plusieurs centaines de milliers de m³ ont été déplacés) pour transformer le cratère en un observatoire des phénomènes célestes, fréquents ou rares comme le solstice lunaire qui ne se produit que tous les 18 ans (le prochain aura lieu en 2006). Les tunnels et salles creusés dans le cratère mettent le visiteur en situation de contact avec la lumière. « J'essaye de faire de la lumière une expérience physique. Lorsque vous voyez la lumière, ce n'est plus seulement un phénomène d'éclairage d'autres choses, c'est la chose même », explique l'artiste.

*The visible profile of the volcano has not changed (above, seen from the west), but Turrell has dug profoundly into the mountain to create spaces with openings to the sky (right), one of which is the eye of the crater.*

*Während das sichtbare Profil des Vulkans unverändert blieb (oben von Westen aus gesehen), hat Turrell tief in den Berg hineingegraben, um Räume zu schaffen, die sich nach oben öffnen (rechte Seite), wobei es sich bei einem dieser Räume um das Zentrum des Kraters handelt.*

*Le profil visible du volcan n'a pas été modifié (en haut, vue de l'ouest), mais Turrell a fait creuser la montagne en profondeur pour créer des espaces ouverts vers le ciel (à droite), dont l'un est le centre du cratère.*

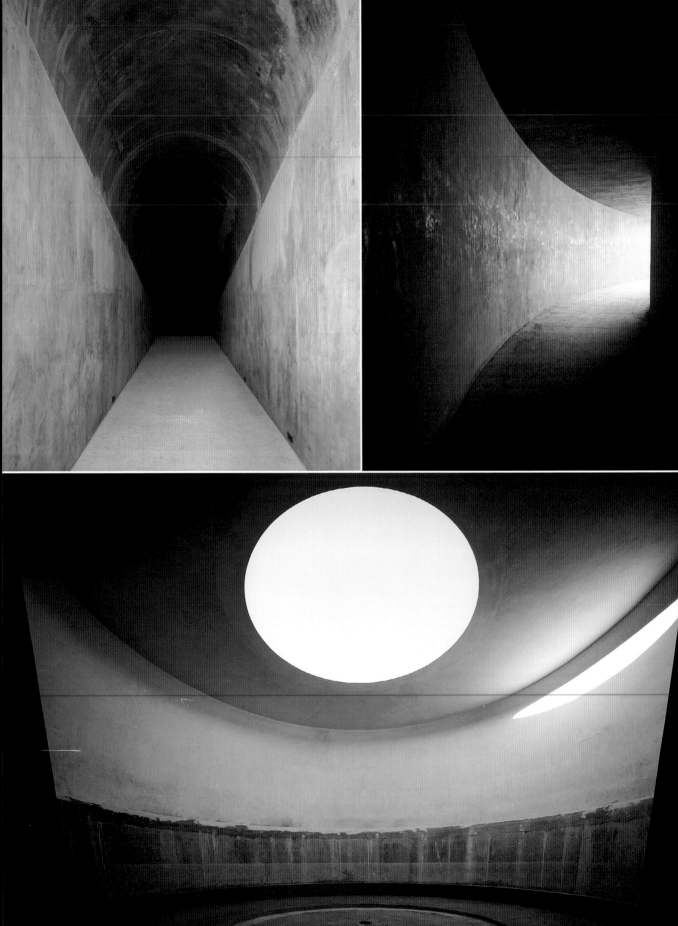

Above left the "Alpha Tunnel" that leads to the East Portal. Below left, the room below the eye of the crater. Above, an access ramp leading to the bowl of the crater.

Der zum Ostportal führende »Alpha Tunnel« (links oben). Der unterhalb des Kraterzentrums liegende Raum (links unten). Eine in den Kraterkessel führende Rampe (oben).

En haut, l'Alpha Tunnel, qui mène à la porte d'entrée Est. En bas, à gauche, la salle sous le centre du cratère. En haut, une rampe d'accès conduit au fond du cratère.

# UN STUDIO

*UN Studio*
*Stadhouderskade 113*
*1073 AX Amsterdam*
*The Netherlands*

*Tel: + 31 20 570 2040*
*Fax: + 31 20 570 2041*
*e-mail: info@unstudio.com*
*Web: www.unstudio.com*

**BEN VAN BERKEL** was born in Utrecht in 1957 and studied at the Rietveld Academie in Amsterdam and at the Architectural Association (AA) in London, receiving the AA Diploma with honors in 1987. After working briefly in the office of Santiago Calatrava, in 1988 he set up his practice in Amsterdam with **CAROLINE BOS**. In 1998, they created **UN STUDIO**, a subsidary which is a network of specialists in architecture, urban development and infrastructure. Van Berkel has been a Visiting professor at Columbia, New York, and Visiting Critic at Harvard, 1994. He was a Diploma Unit Master at the AA, London, 1994–95. As well as the Erasmus Bridge in Rotterdam (inaugurated in 1996), Van Berkel & Bos Architectural Bureau has built the Karbouw and ACOM (1989–93) office buildings, and the REMU electricity station (1989–93), all in Amersfoort, housing projects and the Aedes East Gallery for Kristin Feireiss in Berlin. More recent projects include the Möbius House, 't Gooi (1993–98); Het Valkhof Museum, Nijmegen, and an extension for the Rijksmuseum Twente, Enschede (1992–1996); a Music Facility, Graz, Austria (1998–2002); and a Switching Station, Innsbruck, Austria (1997–2000). Ben van Berkel and Caroline Bos recently won the competition to expand and renovate the Wadsworth Atheneum Museum of Art.

**BEN VAN BERKEL**, geboren 1957 in Utrecht, studierte an der Rietveld Academie in Amsterdam und an der Architectural Association (AA) in London, wo er 1987 sein Diplom mit Auszeichnung erwarb. Nach kurzer Tätigkeit bei Santiago Calatrava gründete er 1988 zusammen mit **CAROLINE BOS** ein eigenes Büro in Amsterdam. 1998 eröffneten van Berkel und Bos die Tochtergesellschaft **UN STUDIO**, ein Netzwerk von Spezialisten aus den Bereichen Architektur, Stadtplanung und Infrastruktur. 1994 war van Berkel als Gastprofessor an der Columbia University in New York sowie als Gastkritiker in Harvard und von 1994 bis 1995 als Diploma Unit Master an der AA in London tätig. Neben der 1996 eröffneten Erasmus-Brücke in Rotterdam hat das Architekturbüro Van Berkel & Bos die Bürogebäude Karbouw und ACOM sowie das Elektrizitätswerk REMU ausgeführt, die alle in den Jahren zwischen 1989 und 1993 im niederländischen Amersfoort entstanden. In Berlin gestalteten sie Wohnbauten und die Galerie Aedes East für Kristin Feireiss. Ferner gehören zu ihren neueren Projekten das Möbius-Haus in Naarden (1993–98), das Museum Het Valkhof in Nimwegen, ein Erweiterungsbau für das Rijksmuseum Twente in Enschede (1992–96), ein Musiktheater in Graz (1998–2002) sowie ein Umspannwerk in Innsbruck (1997–2000). Im Anschluss eines kürzlich ausgetragenen Wettbewerbs erhielten Ben van Berkel und Caroline Bos dem Auftrag für die Renovierung und Erweiterung des Wadsworth Atheneum Museum of Art.

**BEN VAN BERKEL** naît à Utrecht en 1957 et étudie à la Rietveld Academie d'Amsterdam ainsi qu'à l'Architectural Association de Londres dont il sort diplômé avec honneurs en 1987. Après avoir brièvement travaillé pour Santiago Calatrava en 1988, il ouvre son agence à Amsterdam, en association avec **CAROLINE BOS**. En 1998, ils créent une filiale, **UN STUDIO**, qui réunit un réseau de spécialistes en architecture, développement urbain et infrastructures. Van Berkel a été professeur invité à Columbia University, New York, critique invité à Harvard en 1994 et Unit Master pour le diplôme à l'AA en 1994–95. En dehors du pont Erasme à Rotterdam (inauguré en 1996), Van Berkel & Bos Architectural Bureau ont construit les immeubles de bureaux Karbouw et ACOM (1989–93), le poste d'électricité REMU (1989–93), le tout à Amersfoort, ainsi que des logements et l'Aedes East Gallery de Kristin Feireiss à Berlin. Parmi leurs projets plus récents, la maison Moebius ('t Gooi, 1993–98), le musée Het Valkhof (Nimègue), l'extension du Rijksmuseum Twente (Enschede, Pays-Bas, 1992–96), un complexe consacré à la musique (Graz, Autriche, 1998–2002), et une gare d'interconnexion (Innsbruck, Autriche, 1997–2000). Ben van Berkel et Caroline Bos ont récemment remporté le concours pour l'extension et la rénovation du Wadsworth Atheneum Museum of Art.

# NEUTRON MAGNETIC RESONANCE FACILITIES

*Bijvoet University Campus, Utrecht, The Netherlands, 1997–2000*

Client: University of Utrecht. Area: 1,650 m². Cost: 3,267,000 euros (excluding installations).

This laboratory building was designed for the analysis of the structure and behavior of proteins using high-frequency magnetic pulses. The program required the installation of eight spectrometers, a console and a control facility. The presence of high-energy magnetic fields posed specific problems, not only for the machines themselves, which had to be protected against irregularities in their immediate environment, but also for the users of the building. The magnetic fields also disturb computers, credit cards or pacemakers for example. As the architects said, "The magnetic radius shapes structure and surface, directs the program and equipment and affects internal circulation." As it did in the case of the Erasmus Bridge, the philosophy of the firm leads them naturally to projects like this one, that require intensive collaboration with specialists from fields very different from architecture.

Das Laborgebäude wurde für die Analyse der Struktur und des Verhaltens von Proteinen mittels Hochfrequenz-Magnetimpulsen entworfen. Dazu war die Installation von acht Spektralapparaten, einem Bedienungspult und einer Kontrollvorrichtung erforderlich. Das Vorhandensein hoch energetischer Magnetfelder warf besondere Probleme auf, da nicht nur die Maschinen und Geräte vor Störungen geschützt werden mussten, sondern auch die Benutzer des Gebäudes. Können durch Magnetfelder doch beispielsweise die Funktion von Computern, Kreditkarten oder Herzschrittmachern beeinträchtigt werden. »Der Magnetradius bestimmt Form und Oberfläche des Gebäudes, das Raumprogramm und die Ausstattung und wirkt sich auf die interne Zirkulation aus«, so die Erläuterung der Architekten. Wie bereits bei der Erasmus-Brücke in Rotterdam führt die Philosophie von UN Studio zu Projekten wie diesem, welche die intensive Zusammenarbeit mit Spezialisten aus weit von der Architektur entfernten Bereichen erfordert.

Ce laboratoire se consacre à l'analyse de la structure et du comportement des protéines à partir des résonances magnétiques. Le programme comprenait l'installation de huit spectromètres et d'équipements de contrôle. La présence de champs magnétiques de haute énergie posait des problèmes spécifiques non seulement pour les utilisateurs, qui devaient être protégés, mais également pour les appareillages et les machines aisément perturbés. « Le rayon des ondes magnétiques a joué un rôle dans la détermination des structures et des surfaces, a orienté le programme et les équipements, ainsi que les circulations internes », explique l'architecte. Comme dans le cas du pont Érasme, la philosophie de l'agence s'adapte naturellement à des projets de ce type qui requièrent une collaboration très étroite avec des spécialistes de domaines très particuliers et très éloignés de l'architecture.

*The wrapped, interconnected volumes of the NMR-facilities are unexpected and yet dictated by the functional requirements of this very particular structure.*

*Die Gestaltung der miteinander verbundenen, ummantelten Bauteile des Laborgebäudes ist überraschend unkonventionell und dennoch von den funktionalen Erfordernissen dieser speziellen Einrichtung bestimmt.*

*Les volumes enveloppés et interconnectés du NMR surprennent mais sont dictés par les exigences fonctionnelles de ce bâtiment très particulier.*

A thin concrete shell wraps around a steel and glass envelope, enclosing the equipment in an appropriate manner but also creating a contrast between a certain heaviness and a sense of movement. The thin wrappers contain the installations and routing system of the laboratory.

Die innere Hülle aus Stahl und Glas ist von einer dünnen Betonummantelung umgeben, in der die technischen Installationen des Labors untergebracht sind. Diese Konstruktion dient zum einen der Sicherheit und schafft darüber hinaus einen optischen Kontrast zwischen Schwere und Bewegung.

Une fine coque de béton se drape autour d'une enveloppe de verre et d'acier pour enfermer l'outil de recherche tout en générant un contraste entre une certaine pesanteur et un sentiment de mouvement. Les fins enveloppements contiennent les installations et le système de transmission du laboratoire.

An unexpected planar inclination, a glass envelope sitting on top of another one, each feature of the NMR facility attracts attention and alleviates any sense of monotony that might normally arise with such a building. Above, a factory-like interior.

Ungewöhnliche schräge Flächen und zwei aufeinander gesetzte Glashüllen – jedes Gestaltungsmerkmal des NMR-Gebäudes weckt Aufmerksamkeit und verhindert, dass der Eindruck von Monotonie entsteht, der sich häufig bei solchen Zweckbauten einstellt. Ein fabrikähnlicher Innenraum (oben).

Inclinaison surprenante, enveloppes de verre superposées : chaque caractéristique du NMR attire l'attention et allège la monotonie dont ce type de construction est généralement victime. En haut, un style intérieur de type industriel.

# VARIOUS ARCHITECTS

*Jorge Vergara Cabrera,*
*Zaha Hadid, Daniel Libeskind, Thom Mayne, Carme Pinós,*
*Tod Williams and Billie Tsien, Jean Nouvel, Wolf D. Prix and Helmut Swiczinsky,*
*Philip Johnson, Toyo Ito, Teodoro González de Léon, Enrique Norton*

On this page, the 300-room hotel designed by Zaha Hadid for the complex. The construction area for this project is 35,400 m$^2$.

Das von Zaha Hadid für den Komplex entworfene Hotel mit 300 Betten. Die für dieses Projekt vorgesehene Baufläche beträgt 35.400 m$^2$.

Sur cette page, l'hôtel de 300 chambres conçu par Zaha Hadid pour le complexe. Sa surface représente 35 400 m$^2$.

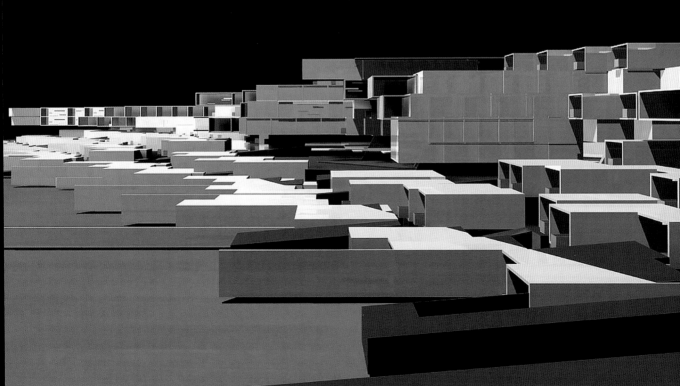

# JVC CONVENTION AND EXHIBITION CENTER

*Guadalajara, Mexico, 2001–*

This very ambitious Culture, Convention and Business Center inclues the work of eleven international architects: Daniel Libeskind, Zaha Hadid, Thom Mayne, Carme Pinós, Jean Nouvel, Wolf D. Prix and Helmut Swiczinsky (Coop Himmelb(l)au), Tod Williams and Billie Tsien, Toyo Ito, Philip Johnson, Teodoro González de Léon and Enrique Norton (TEN Arquitectos). Conceived by Jorge Vergara Cabrera CEO of Omnilife, the complex is to include his own offices, an entertainment and shopping complex, museums, a hotel, an amphitheater, a university and even, most unexpectedly, a palenque, which is to say cockfighting ring (designed by Thom Mayne of Morphosis). 80 % financed by Omnilife, the project is intended as a "city and not as a museum of architecture" according to Vergara. Highlights of the program include the 117,000 square meter convention center by Enrique Norton, the Omnilife offices by Jean Nouvel, the shopping center by Coop Himmelb(l)au, a Museum of Contemporary Art by Toyo Ito and a University of Sciences by Daniel Libeskind.

Das äußerst ambitiöse Kultur-, Kongress- und Geschäftszentrum umfasst die Arbeit von elf internationalen Architekten: Daniel Libeskind, Zaha Hadid, Thom Mayne, Carme Pinós, Jean Nouvel, Wolf D. Prix und Helmut Swiczinsky (Coop Himmelb(l)au), Tod Williams & Billie Tsien, Toyo Ito, Philip Johnson, Teodoro Gonzáles de Léon und Enrique Norton (TEN Arquitectos). Der von Jorge Vergara Cabrera, dem CEO von Omnilife, in Auftrag gegebene Komplex umfasst seine eigene Firma, ein Freizeit- und Einkaufszentrum, Museen, ein Hotel, ein Amphitheater, eine Universität und sogar – höchst ungewöhnlich – eine Palenque, also einen Ring für Hahnenkämpfe (von Morphosis-Architekt Thom Mayne entworfen). Das zu 80 Prozent von Omnilife finanzierte Projekt ist »als Stadt und nicht als ein Museum der Architektur« gedacht, so Vergara Cabrera. Zu den Glanzpunkten des JVC Center gehören das 117.000 m² umfassende Kongresszentrum von Enrique Norton, die Omnilife-Büros von Jean Nouvel, das Einkaufszentrum von Coop Himmelb(l)au, ein Museum für zeitgenössische Kunst von Toyo Ito sowie die naturwissenschaftliche Universität von Daniel Libeskind.

Ce très ambitieux centre culturel, de congrès et d'affaires regroupe les interventions de onze architectes de réputation internationale : Daniel Libeskind, Zaha Hadid, Thom Mayne, Carme Pinós, Jean Nouvel, Wolf D. Prix et Helmut Swiczinsky (Coop Himmelb(l)au), Tod Williams & Billie Tsien, Toyo Ito, Philip Johnson, Teodoro González de Léon et Enrique Norton (TEN Arquitectos). Conçu par Jorge Vergara Cabrera, directeur général d'Omnilife, ce complexe comprendra les bureaux de sa société, un centre commercial et de spectacles, des musées, un hôtel, un amphithéâtre, une université et même, plus inattendu, une palanque, c'est-à-dire une arène pour combats de coq conçue par Thom Mayne, de Morphosis. Financé à 80 % par Omnilife, le projet se veut « une ville et non un musée d'architecture », selon Vergara. Les points forts du programme comprennent le centre de congrès de 117 000 m² d'Enrique Norton, les bureaux d'Omnilife par Jean Nouvel, le centre commercial de Coop Himmelb(l)au, un Musée d'art contemporain par Toyo Ito et une Université des Sciences par Daniel Libeskind.

*Above and right, Coop Himmelb(l)au's Shopping and Entertainment Center is a 44,000 m² facility inserted into a site measuring 73,500 m². Capacity is over 21,000 people per day.*

*Das Einkaufs- und Vergnügungszentrum von Coop Himmelb(l)au (oben und rechts) ist ein 44.000 m² umfassender Komplex auf einem 73.500 m² großen Gelände. Die geplante Kapazität liegt bei über 21.000 Besuchern täglich.*

*En haut et à droite, le Centre commercial et de divertissement de Coop Himmelb(l)au de 44 000 m² occupe un terrain de 73 500 m². Sa capacité d'accueil est de 21 000 visiteurs/jour.*

The Museum of Art by Toyo Ito,
covering a total area of 14,400 m²
on a 15,900 m² site, has a capacity
of 2,000 persons, and is intended to
exhibit works in an "informal" way.

Das von Toyo Ito geplante Kunstmuseum liegt auf einem 15.900 m² großen
Gelände, hat eine Nutzfläche von
14.400 m² und fasst 2.000 Besucher.
Die Kunstwerke sollen dem Betrachter
auf eine eher zwanglose Weise nahe-
gebracht werden.

Le Musée d'art, par Toyo Ito compte
14 400 m² sur un terrain de 15 900 m²
pour une capacité quotidienne de
2 000 visiteurs. Il devrait présenter les
œuvres d'une manière « informelle. »

Jean Nouvel's offices for the Omnilife Group cover an area of 20,100 m² and are intended to house 600 people.

In Jean Nouvels Bürogebäude für die Omnilife Gruppe mit einer Nutzfläche von 20.100 m² sollen 600 Mitarbeiter untergebracht werden.

Destinés à accueillir 600 personnes, les bureaux conçus par Jean Nouvel pour l'Omnilife Groupe couvrent une surface de 20 100 m².

The Fair Grounds and bridges by Carme Pinós spread over 360,000 m², 45,700 m² covered, for a capacity of over 350,000 persons per day.

The Palenque stadium, seating 6,250, designed by Morphosis, Los Angeles. The total area is 16,800 m².

Teodoro González de Léon is responsible for the Omnilife Staff Club House (below) with a total area of 14,200 m² and a capacity of 600 persons.

Der von Carme Pinós geplante Vergnügungspark mit seinen Brücken erstreckt sich über die riesige Fläche von 360.000 m², 45.700 m² überdacht. Das Projekt ist für über 350.000 Besuchern täglich konzipiert.

Die Palenque-Arena wurde von Morphosis, Los Angeles, entworfen. Sie bietet Platz für 6.250 Zuschauer und umfasst 16.800 m².

Teodoro González de Léons Beitrag ist das 14.200 m² große und 600 Personen fassende Clubhaus für die Angestellten von Omnilife (unten).

Le parc d'attraction et les ponts conçus par Carme Pinós se répartissent sur 360 000 m² dont 45 700 m² couverts ; capacité théorique est de 350 000 visiteurs/jour.

Le stade de Palenque – 6 250 spectateurs – conçu par Morphosis, Los Angeles. La surface totale de ce projet est de 16 800 m².

Teodoro González de Léon est responsable de l'Omnilife Staff Club House (en bas) de 14 200 m² pour une capacité de 600 personnes.

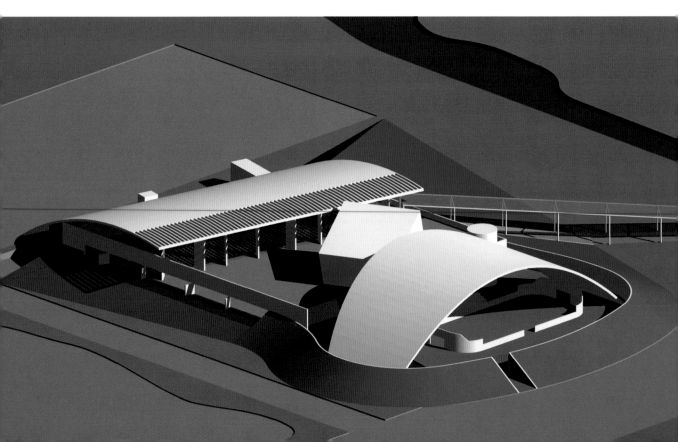

*Architects Philip Johnson and Alan Ritchie designed the Children's World Complex, measuring 1,550 m² with 366 m² roofed and a capacity of a thousand children.*

*Below, the University of Success, a 35,000 m² facility for 3,800 students designed by Daniel Libeskind. This project and the others published here are presently halted.*

*Der Komplex »Children's World« wurde von den Architekten Philip Johnson und Alan Ritchie entworfen. Er umfasst 1.550 m², davon 366 m² überdacht, und bietet Raum für 1.000 Kinder.*

*Das von Daniel Libeskind geplante Universitätsgebäude (unten) umfasst 35.000 m² und ist für 3.800 Studenten konzipiert. Die Arbeiten an allen hier vorgestellten Projekten wurden bis auf weiteres eingestellt.*

*Les architectes Philip Johnson et Alan Ritchie ont conçu le complexe du Monde des Enfants qui mesure 1 550 m² dont 366 m² couverts pour une capacité de 1 000 enfants.*

*En bas, l'Université du Succès, un équipement de 35 000 m² pour 3 800 étudiants, conçu par Daniel Libeskind. Ce projet et les autres présentés ici sont actuellement arrêtés.*

TEN Arquitectos designed the
Convention Center whose capacity
of 50,000 persons includes an
exhibition area of 33,250 m² and
a convention area of 54,800 m².

Der Entwurf des Kongresszentrums
stammt von TEN Arquitectos. Es
umfasst eine Fläche von 54.800 m²
für Kongresse und Veranstaltungen
sowie 33.250 m² für Ausstellungen
und hat ein Fassungsvermögen
von 50.000 Personen.

TEN Arquitectos a conçu le Centre de
congrès d'une capacité de 5 000 personnes. Il comprend une surface
d'exposition de 32 500 m² et une
zone de congrès de 54 800 m².

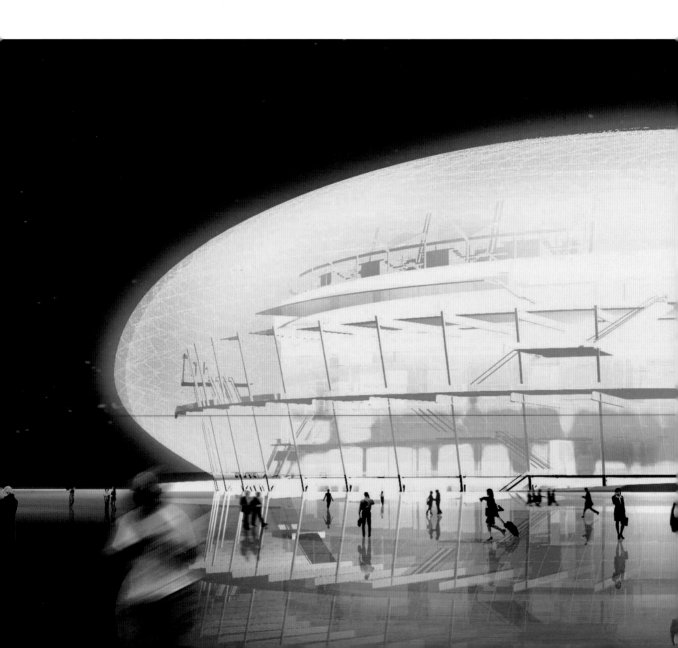

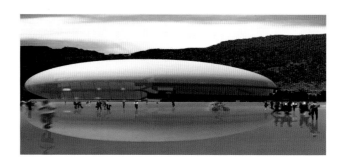

# KOEN VAN VELSEN

Koen J.van Velsen
Spoorstraat 69a
1211 GA Hilversum
The Netherlands

Tel: + 31 35 622 2000
Fax: + 31 35 6288 8991
e-mail: kvv@architecten.A2000.nl

*Hous*

Born in Hilversum in 1952, **KOEN VAN VELSEN** graduated from the Academy of Architecture in Amsterdam in 1983. He started his own firm in Hilversum in 1977. His major works include the Discotheque Slinger (Hilversum, 1978–1979); the van Velsen shop and house (Hlversum, 1980–1981); a public library in Zeewolde (1985–1989); the Rijksakademie van Beeldende Kunsten (Amsterdam, 1985–1992); a multiplex cinema on Schouwburgplein in Rotterdam (1992–1996); the Town Hall of Terneuzen (extension of the 1972 building by Van den Broek & Bakema, 1994–1997); and the Film Academy in Amsterdam (1995–1999). He also worked on alterations of the Armamentarium (Delft, 1982–1989); the Ministry of Welfare, Public Health and Culture (Rijswijk, 1985–1986); and the Hotel Gooiland (Hilversum, 1989–1990). Van Velsen attempts to avoid a personal esthetic, preferring to analyze each new project in its contextual, programmatic and other specific features in order to propose his designs.

**KOEN VAN VELSEN**, geboren 1952 in Hilversum, schloss 1983 sein Studium an der Akademie für Architektur in Amsterdam ab. Seine eigene Firma hatte er bereits 1977 in Hilversum gegründet. Zu seinen wichtigsten Bauten zählen: die Diskothek Slinger in Hilversum (1978–79), Geschäft und Wohnhaus van Velsen in Hilversum (1980–81), eine öffentliche Bibliothek in Zeewolde (1985–89), die Rijksakademie van Beeldende Kunsten in Amsterdam (1985–92), ein Multiplexkino am Schouwburgplein in Rotterdam (1992–96), die Erweiterung des 1972 von Van den Broek & Bakema geplanten Rathauses von Terneuzen (1994–97) sowie die Filmakademie in Amsterdam (1995–99). Weitere Projekte van Velsens sind: die Umbauten am Zeughaus Armamentarium in Delft (1982–89), am Ministerium für Wohlfahrt, öffentliche Gesundheit und Kultur in Rijswijk (1985–86) und am Hotel Gooiland in Hilversum (1989–90). Van Velsen geht es in seinen Entwürfen nicht um eine persönliche Ästhetik. Vielmehr entwickelt er seine Konzepte aus der Analyse jedes neuen Projekts mit seinen jeweiligen kontextuellen und programmatischen Merkmalen.

Né à Hilversum en 1952, **KOEN VAN VELSEN** est diplômé de l'Académie d'architecture d'Amsterdam (1983). Il ouvre son agence à Hilversum en 1977. Parmi ses principales réalisations : la discothèque Slinger (Hilversum, 1978–79) ; la maison et le magasin van Velsen (Hilversum, 1980–81) ; une bibliothèque publique à Zeewolde (1985–89) ; la Rijksakademie van Beeldende Kunsten (Amsterdam, 1985–92) ; un cinéma multisalles sur Schouwburgplein à Rotterdam (1992–96) ; l'Hôtel de ville de Terneuzen (extension d'un bâtiment de 1972 de Van den Broek et Bakema, 1994–97) ; et l'Académie du film (Amsterdam, 1995–99). Il est également intervenu sur les transformations de l'Armamentarium (Delft, 1982–89) ; le ministère des affaires sociales, de la santé publique et de la culture (Rijswijk, 1985–86) ; l'Hotel Gooiland (Hilversum, 1989–90). Van Velsen s'efforce d'éviter une esthétique trop personnelle, lui préférant une analyse approfondie de chaque nouveau projet dans son contexte, ses contraintes de programmation.

# HOUSE

*Scheepstimmermanstraat, Zeeburg, Amsterdam, 1999*

*Location: Borneo Island, Amsterdam. Building cost: 550,000 guilders.
Furnishing cost: 150,000 guilders. Area: 140 m². Client: B. Vos.*

Borneo and Sporenburg are peninsulas in the eastern harbor area of Amsterdam. It was decided to create 1,550 flats and houses, with a maximum height of three stories. Each house has its own front door on the street and its own garden or patio. In addition to this low-rise housing, Borneo and Sporenburg have three large blocks of flats, with a total of some 600 housing units designed by Koen van Velsen (Pacman), Erick van Egeraat and Steven Holl. The Amsterdam Department of Physical Planning, working with West 8 landscape architects & urban planners and Rudy Uytenhaak, developed the urban planning design for Borneo and Sporenburg. This small house by Koen van Velsen with its black beam structure creates a pleasant living space on the Scheepstimmermanstraat. This house has an almost Japanese quality in the alternating effects of transparency and opacity together with the single tree in the patio to the rear of the residence.

Auf den Amsterdamer Halbinseln Borneo und Sporenburg, die im östlichen Hafengebiet liegen, sollen im Auftrag der Stadt 1.550 Wohnungen und Häuser mit maximal drei Stockwerken entstehen. Jedes der Wohnhäuser verfügt über einen individuellen Zugang von der Straße und einen eigenen Garten oder Innenhof. Zusätzlich zu diesen niedrigen Bauten werden auf Borneo und Sporenburg drei große Wohnbauten mit insgesamt über 600 Wohnungen errichtet, die von Koen van Velsen (Pacman), Erick van Egeraat und Steven Holl geplant werden. Das städtebauliche Konzept wurde von der Amsterdamer Baubehörde in Zusammenarbeit mit dem Planungsbüro West 8 landscape architects & urban planners und Rudy Uytenhaak entwickelt. Das kleine, hier vorgestellte Wohnhaus von Koen van Velsen liegt in der Scheepstimmermanstraat. Seine Bauweise aus einer dunklen Trägerkonstruktion in Verbindung mit den abwechselnd transparenten und opaken Elementen und dem im Innenhof stehenden einzelnen Baum verleihen ihm eine angenehme, fast japanisch anmutende Atmosphäre.

Borneo et Sporenburg sont d'anciens docks en forme de péninsule dans la partie est du port d'Amsterdam. Le département d'urbanisme de la ville d'Amsterdam, en collaboration avec West 8 landscape architects & urban planners et Rudy Uytenhaak, a planifié la construction de 1550 appartements et maisons individuelles d'une hauteur maximum de deux étages. Chaque maison possède sa propre porte sur la rue, son jardin ou un patio. Trois importantes barres de 600 appartements ont été construites par Koen van Velsen (Pacman), Erick van Egeraat et Steven Holl. La petite maison de Koen van Velsen à l'intéressante ossature de poutres noires offre un cadre de vie agréable. Elle est presque japonaise d'esprit dans son alternance d'effets de transparence et d'opacité ou dans l'arbre solitaire du patio à l'arrière de la maison.

Aligned with other similar houses on the former dock peninsula of Borneo in Amsterdam, the house stands out through its vertical bays, defined by regularly spaced black beams.

Obwohl das Haus auf der ehemaligen Hafenmole von Borneo in einem Ensemble ähnlicher Gebäude steht, hebt es sich durch seine vertikalen Nischen, die in regelmäßigen Abständen zwischen dunklen Trägern angeordnet sind, von seiner Umgebung ab.

Dans un alignement de maisons similaires édifiées dans les anciens docks de Borneo à Amsterdam, la maison se distingue par ses travées verticales et régulières définies par un jeu de poutres noires.

The interiors are luminous and offer numerous views toward the wide basins that separate Borneo from Sporenburg.

Die Innenräume sind von Licht durchflutet und bieten zahlreiche Ausblicke auf die breiten Hafenbecken, die Borneo von Sporenburg trennen.

L'intérieur lumineux offre de nombreuses perspectives vers les bassins qui séparent Borneo de Sporenburg.

A rather strict simplicity, recalling
the recent Dutch taste for neo-mini-
malist modernism, is contrasted with
a single tree rising through metal
grating to the rear of the house.

Eine eher strenge Schlichtheit, die an
eine noch nicht lange zurückliegende
Vorliebe der Niederländer für neo-
minimalistische Designs erinnert,
kontrastiert mit einem auf der Rückseite des Hauses stehenden Baum,
der durch ein Metallgitter wächst.

Un arbre solitaire, qui pousse à travers une grille de métal à l'arrière
de la maison, rappelle le goût récent
de l'architecture néerlandaise pour
un néo-minimalisme moderniste.

# HENDRIK VERMOORTEL

*Buro II*
*Hoogleedsesteenweg 415*
*8800 Roeselare*
*Belgium*

*Tel: + 32 51 21 11 05*
*Fax: + 32 51 22 46 74*
*e-mail info@buro2.be*
*Web: www.buro2.be*

*Buro Interior*
*Tel: + 32 51 22 33 00*
*Fax: + 32 51 24 55 86*
*e-mail info@buro-interior.be*
*Web: www.buro-interior.be*

*Studio*

Buro II was founded in 1978 by the architect **HENDRIK VERMOORTEL**. In 1983 Buro Interior was founded by the interior architect **RITA HUYS**. Buro Interior often works together with Buro II, collaborating on architectural matters of both theory and practice. Hendrik Vermoortel was born in 1950, and received his Diploma in Architecture from the Saint Lucas Institute in Ghent (1974). He created the architectural office 'Vermoortel Hendrik' in Hooglede in 1977 in co-operation with Ms. Huys. Since then, Buro II – headed by Hendrik Vermoortel – has developed into a multidisciplinary office with about sixty employees. Buro II has designed several public commissions, service flats and old people's homes, banks, industrial buildings, schools, sports facilities, multifunctional houses, apartments, and residences. Rita Huys was also born in 1950 and obtained her degree in Interior Architecture from the Saint Lucas Institute in Ghent in 1973.

Der Architekt **HENDRIK VERMOORTEL** gründete 1978 die Firma Buro II. 1983 wurde Buro Interior von der Innenarchitektin **RITA HUYS** eröffnet. Beide Firmen arbeiten häufig zusammen, und zwar sowohl in theoretischen als auch praktischen Fragen der Architektur. Hendrik Vermoortel, geboren 1950, erwarb 1974 sein Diplom in Architektur am Saint Lucas Institut in Gent. 1977 gründete er zusammen mit Rita Huys die Architekturfirma Vermoortel Hendrik in Hooglede. Seither hat sich Buro II – unter der Leitung von Hendrik Vermoortel – zu einem multidisziplinären Unternehmen mit circa 60 Mitarbeitern entwickelt. Die Architekturfirma realisierte mehrere öffentliche Bauaufträge wie Seniorenheime, Schulen und Sportanlagen, aber auch Banken, Industriegebäude, multifunktionale Bauten und Wohnhäuser. Rita Huys, ebenfalls 1950 geboren, schloss 1973 ihr Studium der Innenarchitektur am Saint Lucas Institut in Gent ab.

L'agence Buro II a été fondée en 1978 par l'architecte **HENDRIK VERMOORTEL**, et Buro Interior par l'architecte d'intérieur **RITA HUYS**. Les deux agences collaborent souvent, tant dans le domaine théorique que celui de la réalisation. Hendrik Vermoortel est né en 1950 et est diplômé d'architecture de l'Institut St. Lucas de Gand (1974). Il a ouvert sa première agence « Vermoortel Hendrik » à Hooglede en 1977 en association avec Rita Huys. Buro II est une agence pluridisciplinaire qui compte une soixantaine de collaborateurs. Elle a conçu des logements, des maisons de retraite, des banques, des bâtiments industriels, des écoles, des équipements sportifs, des maisons multifonctions, des appartements et des résidences privées. Rita Huys, née en 1950 a été diplômée en architecture intérieure de l'Institut St Lucas de Gand en 1973.

# STUDIO

*Roeselare, Belgium, 1993–*

*Site area: 19,897 m². Total floor area: 2,380 m². Cost: 1,500,000 euros.*

Contrary to appearances, the offices of Buro II and Buro Interior in Roeselare, Belgium, are located in an extension of an old farmhouse. The architects first converted renovated barns to house their offices, but the requirements of the expanding practice soon outgrew the available space, and the decision was made to enlarge the existing building in an unexpected way. They decided to place the historic barn structure within a new building. The result was a tension between old and new, interior and exterior. An artificial lake surrounds the complex with something of the feeling of a drawbridge in the approach path. The facilities involved with client relations are housed on the ground floor. The second floor provides space for design studios and differs in its working environment from the other spaces, as reflected for example in the fenestration. As the architects say, "The new building is regarded as the conveyor of multiple elements, that can be added to, removed, or replaced with the course of time. Encapsulated with this project can be seen the vision of Buro II." The architect considers this to be an ongoing project, with no specific completion date.

Dem äußeren Anschein zum Trotz sind die Firmenräume von Buro II und Buro Interior im Anbau eines alten Bauernhauses untergebracht, das im belgischen Roeselare liegt. Zunächst hatten die Architekten Hendrik Vermoortel und Rita Huys die ursprünglichen Scheunen renoviert und in Büroräume umgewandelt. Diese wurden für die Anforderungen ihrer expandierenden Firma aber bald zu klein und so beschlossen sie, das bestehende Gebäude auf ungewöhnliche Weise zu vergrößern, indem sie den historischen Bauteil in eine neu errichtete Konstruktion einfügten. Daraus entstand eine Spannung zwischen Alt und Neu, zwischen Innen und Außen. Der Komplex wird von einem künstlichen See umgeben, der wie eine Art Burggraben mit Zugbrücke wirkt, wenn man sich auf dem Zugangsweg nähert. Im Erdgeschoss sind die für den Kundenverkehr vorgesehenen Räume untergebracht, während das Obergeschoss Raum für Designstudios bietet. Die Arbeitsplatzgestaltung im ersten Stock unterscheidet sich von der übrigen Innenarchitektur, was sich zum Beispiel in der unterschiedlichen Fensterung zeigt. »Das neue Gebäude ist als Medium multipler Elemente gedacht, die im Lauf der Zeit hinzugefügt, entfernt oder ausgetauscht werden können. Hierin drückt sich die Vision von Buro II aus«, so die Architekten. Sie betrachten das Projekt als fortlaufenden Prozess, für das kein bestimmtes Fertigstellungsdatum vorgesehen ist.

Contrairement aux apparences, les bureaux Buro II et Buro Interior de Roeselare sont installés dans l'extension d'une ferme ancienne. Les architectes ont commencé par transformer deux granges pour abriter leurs bureaux, mais le développement rapide de leur agence a bientôt nécessité l'agrandissement du bâtiment existant de cette manière inattendue. Ils ont décidé d'intégrer la structure ancienne dans un bâtiment nouveau, pour produire une tension entre le neuf et l'ancien, l'intérieur et l'extérieur. Un lac artificiel entoure l'ensemble et crée une sorte d'impression de pont-levis sur l'allée d'accès. L'accueil et les réunions avec les clients se déroulent au rez-de-chaussée. L'étage est réservé aux ateliers de dessin et à divers autres espaces, comme le montre le fenêtrage. Ainsi que le déclare l'architecte : « Le nouveau bâtiment est le convoyeur de multiples éléments qui peuvent être ajoutés, supprimés ou remplacés dans le temps. Dans ce projet se perçoit déjà, comme encapsulée, la version de Buro II. » Aucune date spécifique d'achèvement n'a été fixée à ce projet en développement permanent.

*Above, the back of the building.*
*Right page, top, the front with the*
*"encapsulated" older structure.*

*Die Rückseite des Gebäudes (oben).*
*Die Fassade mit dem »eingekapsel-*
*ten« älteren Bauteil (rechte Seite,*
*oben).*

*En haut, l'arrière du bâtiment.*
*Page de droite, en haut, la façade*
*et l'ancien bâtiment « encapsulé. »*

*Above, an aerial view of the farm before the work began. Right, the rear bridge leading to the service structure.*

*Luftaufnahme des Bauernhauses vor Beginn der Bauarbeiten (oben). Die Brücke an der Rückseite des Hauses (rechts), in die für den Kundenverkehr vorgesehenen Räume führt.*

*En haut, vue aérienne de la ferme avant le début des travaux. À droite, la passerelle arrière qui mène au bâtiment de service.*

Die Rückseite mit dem integrierten
Bauernhaus (oben). Rückseitige
Terrasse und Brücke (rechte Seite).

En haut, l'arrière du bâtiment des
bureaux et la ferme « encapsulée ».
À droite, la terrasse arrière et la
passerelle.

The exhibition space and meeting room, with a work by Panamarenko on the ceiling. To the right, the same room, with the library visible above.

Der Besprechungs- und Ausstellungsraum mit einer Arbeit von Panamarenko an der Decke (oben). Derselbe Raum mit der Bibliothek im oberen Bereich (rechte Seite).

L'espace d'exposition et la salle de réunion. Au plafond, œuvre de Panamarenko. À droite, la même pièce, avec en haut, la bibliothèque.

Left, the stairs that lead to the terrace and exhibition space, showing the outside part of a work by Panamarenko (left). This page, the view from the hallway near the exhibition room toward the lake.

Die zur Terrasse und zum Ausstellungsraum führende Treppe mit einer weiteren Arbeit von Panamarenko (links). Blick vom Korridor beim Ausstellungsraum auf den See (unten).

À gauche, les escaliers qui conduisent à la terrasse et à l'espace d'exposition, montrant la partie extérieure de l'œuvre de Panamarenko (à gauche). Sur cette page, la vue du hall, près de la salle d'exposition vers le lac.

# MAKOTO SEI WATANABE

*Makoto Sei Watanabe, Architects' Office*
*#2806 Azumabashi 1–23–30*
*Sumida-ku, Tokyo, 130*
*Japan*

*Tel: + 81 3 3829 3221*
*Fax: + 81 3 3829 3837*
*Web: www.makoto-architect.com*

*Iidabashi Subway Station*

Born in 1952 in Yokohama, **MAKOTO SEI WATANABE** attended Yokohama National University from which he graduated with a Master's Degree in Architecture in 1976. In 1979, he went to work for Arata Isozaki & Associates, and in 1984, he established Makoto Sei Watanabe/Architects' Office. His first work, the Aoyama Technical College built in the Shibuya-ku area of Tokyo in 1989, brought him international attention because of its spectacular forms influenced by cartoon graphics. His other work includes: Chronospace, Minato-ku, Tokyo, 1991; Mura-no-Terrace gallery, information office and cafe, Sakauchi Village, Ibi-gun, Gifu, 1995; Fiber Wave, environmental art, Gifu and Tokyo, 1995–1996; Atlas, housing, Suginami-ku, Tokyo, 1996; K-Museum, Koto-ku, Tokyo, 1996; Fiber Wave, environmental art, The Chicago Athenaeum, Chicago, 1998; and the Iidabashi Subway Station published here.

**MAKOTO SEI WATANABE**, geboren 1952 in Yokohama, studierte an der Staatlichen Universität Yokohama, wo er 1976 seinen Master of Architecture erwarb. 1979 begann er seine Tätigkeit bei Arata Isozaki & Associates und gründete 1984 Makoto Sei Watanabe/Architects' Office. Sein erster Bau, das Aoyama Technical College in Shibuya-ku, Tokio (1989), fand mit seinen von Cartoonzeichnungen beeinflussten, spektakulären Formen internationale Beachtung. Zu Watanabes weiteren Arbeiten zählen Chronospace in Minato-ku, Tokio (1991), Mura-no-Terrace, eine Galerie mit Informationszentrum und Café in Sakauchi Village, Ibi-gun, Gifu (1995), das Environment-Projekt Fiber Wave in Gifu und Tokio (1995–96), die Wohnanlage Atlas in Suginami-ku, das K-Museum in Koto-ku, beide 1996 in Tokio fertig gestellt, das Fiber Wave-Environment für das Chicago Athenaeum (1998) sowie die hier vorgestellte Iidabashi-U-Bahn-Station in Tokio.

Né en 1952 à Yokohama, **MAKOTO SEI WATANABÉ** a étudié à l'Université nationale de Yokohama dont il sort diplômé en 1976. En 1979, il travaille pour Arata Isozaki & Associates, et en 1984 crée l'agence Makoto Sei Watanabé/Architects' Office. Sa première réalisation est le Collège technique d'Aoyama construit dans le quartier Shibuya-ku de Tokyo en 1989, qui attire sur lui l'attention internationale par ses formes spectaculaires inspirées de la bande dessinée. Parmi ses autres réalisations : Chronospace (Minato-ku, Tokyo, 1991) ; la galerie Mura-no-Terrace, bureau d'information et café à Sakauchi Village (Ibi-gun, Gifu, 1995) ; Fiber Wave, art environnemental (Gifu et Tokyo, 1995–96) ; Atlas, ensemble de logements à Suginami-ku (Tokyo, 1996) ; le K Museum (Koto-ku, Tokyo, 1996 ; Fiber Wave, art environnemental, Chicago Athenaeum (Chicago, 1998), et la station de métro d'Iidabashi, publiée ici.

# IIDABASHI SUBWAY STATION

*Tokyo, Japan, 1999–2000*

As the architect says, "This is one of the first attempts at deciding the actual form of construction at the will of the computer." For the **IIDABASHI SUBWAY STATION** on Tokyo's new Oedo line (opened December 12, 2000), Watanabe installed a computer-generated structure made of green steel pipes, 7.6 centimeters in diameter, forming an interlaced three-dimensional network over the stairs, escalators and platforms of the station. Actually the result of a "dialogue" between Watanabe and the computer program, the design was inspired by the architect's image of the subway network as an overlapping system of tubes, or a "jungle of steel structures," as he says. His intention is to "make visible what is invisible" in the dense urban environment of Tokyo. The "Web Frame" computer programme used is based on engineering data and enabled to automatically generate code within the established framework.

»Es handelt sich hier um einen der ersten Versuche, den Computer die eigentliche Form der Konstruktion bestimmen zu lassen«, so der Architekt über sein Projekt. Für die Tokioter **U-BAHNSTATION IIDABASHI** der neuen Oedo-Linie, die am 12. Dezember 2000 eröffnet wurde, installierte Watanabe eine computergenerierte Struktur aus grünen Stahlröhren. Mit einem Durchmesser von 7,6 cm erstrecken sie sich als dreidimensionales, miteinander verflochtenes Netzwerk über die Treppen, Rolltreppen und Bahnsteige. Dieses Design war gewissermaßen das Resultat eines »Dialogs« zwischen dem Architekten und dem Computerprogramm und wurde von Watanabes Vorstellung vom U-Bahnnetz als einem überlappenden System von Röhren, oder, wie er es nennt, einem »Dschungel aus Stahlkonstruktionen« inspiriert. Seine Absicht ist, im dicht bebauten Stadtgefüge von Tokio »das Unsichtbare sichtbar zu machen«. Das von ihm verwendete Computerprogramm »Web Frame« basiert auf bautechnischen Daten und kann innerhalb einer festgelegten Grundstruktur eine automatische Programmierung vornehmen.

Dans la présentation de son projet, l'architecte précise qu'« il s'agit d'une des premières tentatives de laisser la décision de la forme réelle d'une construction à la bonne volonté d'un ordinateur ». Pour la **STATION DE MÉTRO IIDABASHI** située sur la nouvelle ligne d'Oedo à Tokyo (ouverte en décembre 2000), Watanabé a réalisé une structure générée par informatique constituée de tuyaux d'acier vert de 7,6 cm de diamètre, formant un réseau tridimensionnel d'entrelacs au-dessus des escaliers, des escalators et des quais. Résultat d'un « dialogue » entre l'architecte et l'ordinateur, le projet lui a été inspiré par sa vision du réseau de métro, système de tubes se chevauchant, ou « jungle de structures d'acier ». Son intention est de « rendre visible ce qui est invisible » dans l'environnement urbain particulièrement dense de Tokyo. Le logiciel d'« ossature de réseau » utilisé fonctionne à partir de données d'ingénierie et génère automatiquement des codes à l'intérieur d'une structure établie.

YŪRAKUCHŌ-LINE

NANBOKU-LINE

TŌZAI-LINE

ŌEDO-LINE

SUBWAY STATION : IIDABASHI

*Above, a map of the region of Tokyo where the station is located. To the right, the structures designed by Makoto Watanabe visible from the street. This "Wing" houses the ventilation and air-conditioning equipment for the subway station.*

*Plan des Tokioter Stadtviertels (oben), in dem die Station liegt. Die von der Straße aus sichtbaren, von Makoto Watanabe entworfenen Bauteile (rechte Seite): Hier sind die Belüftungs- und Klimatisierungsvorrichtungen der U-Bahnstation untergebracht.*

*En haut, carte de la partie de Tokyo où se trouve la station de métro. À droite, les bâtiments de Makoto Watanabé, tels qu'on les voit de la rue. Cette « aile » abrite les installations de ventilation et de climatisation de la station.*

Watanabe's theory about this station is even more elaborate than its appearance might lead the visitor to believe. He speaks of the invisible and interconnected web usually unseen by to the travelling public. Here tunnels within the station.

Watanabes im Zusammenhang mit diesem Projekt entwickelte Gestaltungstheorie ist noch sorgfältiger durchdacht, als es das äußere Erscheinungsbild der Station verrät. So spricht er etwa von dem dicht geknüpften Netz, das für die Passagiere normalerweise unsichtbar bleibt, wie beispielsweise die hier abgebildeten Tunnel.

La théorisation de cette station par Watanabé est encore plus élaborée que son apparence ne pourrait le faire croire. Il parle ainsi de réseaux cachés et interconnectés, habituellement invisibles des voyageurs. Ici, des tunnels de la station.

An architect with a solid reputation for doing the unexpected in his designs, Makoto Sei Watanabe was called on here to deal with the rigorous demands of a system that handles millions of passengers every day. Theory meets reality.

Als Architekt, der den Ruf hat, mit seinen Entwürfen für Überraschung zu sorgen, wurde Makoto Sei Watanabe beauftragt, sich mit den hohen Anforderungen eines Systems auseinander zu setzen, das täglich Millionen von Passagieren befördert.

Quand la théorie rencontre la réalité : architecte réputé pour l'originalité de ses réalisations, Makoto Sei Watanabé a été appelé pour répondre aux exigences rigoureuses d'un système qui traite des millions de passagers chaque jour.

# Generating Program / WEB FRAME 2000

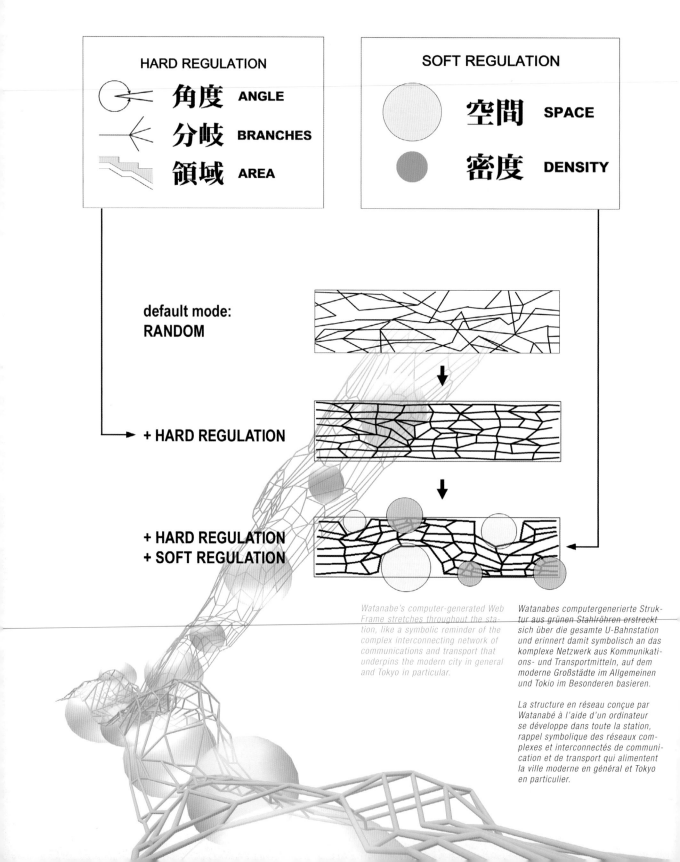

**HARD REGULATION**

角度 ANGLE
分岐 BRANCHES
領域 AREA

**SOFT REGULATION**

空間 SPACE
密度 DENSITY

default mode:
**RANDOM**

**+ HARD REGULATION**

**+ HARD REGULATION
+ SOFT REGULATION**

*Watanabe's computer-generated Web
Frame stretches throughout the station, like a symbolic reminder of the
complex interconnecting network of
communications and transport that
underpins the modern city in general
and Tokyo in particular.*

*Watanabes computergenerierte Struk-
tur aus grünen Stahlröhren erstreckt
sich über die gesamte U-Bahnstation
und erinnert damit symbolisch an das
komplexe Netzwerk aus Kommunikati-
ons- und Transportmitteln, auf dem
moderne Großstädte im Allgemeinen
und Tokio im Besonderen basieren.*

*La structure en réseau conçue par
Watanabé à l'aide d'un ordinateur
se développe dans toute la station,
rappel symbolique des réseaux complexes et interconnectés de communi-
cation et de transport qui alimentent
la ville moderne en général et Tokyo
en particulier.*

# WESLEY WEI

*Wesley Wei Architects*
*307 Cherry Street*
*Philadelphia, Pennsylvania 19106*
*United States*

*Tel: + 1 215 592 8118*
*Fax: + 1 215 922 5019*
*e-mail: wwei@wweiarchitects.com*
*Web: www.wweiarchitects.com*

*Maryland House*

Educated at Pennsylvania State University (Bachelor of Architecture, 1976) and at the University of Pennsylvania (Masters in Architecture, 1977), **WESLEY WEI** created his own firm in 1981 after having worked at Mitchell and Giurgola (1976), and Venturi Scott Brown (1977). He has been a Thesis Advisor at the University of Pennsylvania Graduate Design Studios since 1992. His office has a staff of five persons and he has received several Philadelphia AIA Awards, including Honor Awards for the two projects published here. His work includes the Woodrock Youth Center in Philadelphia, the Philadelphia Chinatown Community Center, and a number of private residences.

**WESLEY WEI** erwarb 1976 den Bachelor of Architecture an der Pennsylvania State University und 1977 den Master of Architecture an der University of Pennsylvania. Nachdem er von 1976 bis 1977 bei Mitchell and Giurgola und bei Venturi Scott Brown gearbeitet hatte, gründete er 1981 sein eigenes Büro, das mittlerweile fünf Angestellte beschäftigt. Seit 1992 ist er außerdem als Dissertationsbetreuer am Graduate Design Studio der University of Pennsylvania tätig. Wesley Wei hat etliche Preise des AIA Philadelphia erhalten, zu denen auch die Honor Awards gehören, die ihm für die beiden hier vorgestellten Projekte verliehen wurden. Zu seinen Bauten zählen das Woodrock Youth Center und das Gemeindezentrum von Chinatown, beide in Philadelphia, sowie einige Privathäuser.

Après des études à Pennsylvania State University (B. Arch. 1976) et University of Pennsylvania (M. Arch. 1977), **WESLEY WEI** crée son agence en 1981 après avoir travaillé chez Mitchell and Giurgola (1976) et Venturi Scott Brown (1977). Il est conseiller de thèse à l'Université de Pennsylvanie Graduate Design Studios depuis 1992. Son agence – cinq collaborateurs – a reçu plusieurs prix de l'Architectural Association de Philadelphie, dont le prix d'honneur pour les deux projets présentés ici. Il a réalisé le Woodrock Youth Center à Philadelphie, le Philadelphia Chinatown Community Center et un certain nombre de résidences privées.

# MARYLAND HOUSE

*Easton, Maryland, United States, 1995–1996*

*Client: Names withheld upon request. Area: 233 m². Cost: Withheld at owner's request.*

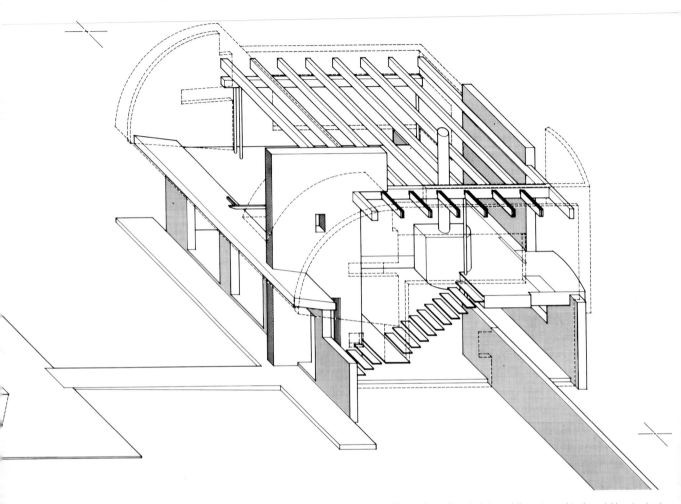

Set on a wooded site on Maryland's eastern shore, near the town of Oxford, this residence allows views both toward the water and to the neighbouring landscape. The ground floor includes a kitchen, bath and bedrooms. Brick, a common local material, is used to "define and extend the space of the rooms into the landscape." The second floor has a large, open living room with views of the gardens and Tred Avon River. The maple floor continues to curve up toward the roof whose exterior is in lead-coated copper. The architect insists on the fact that numerous elements of the house "float and slide" like the hanging fireplace or powder room wall, an effect that "is achieved through the use of contrasting materials to the brick and cedar main walls – lead-coated copper, aluminum, stainless steel, painted ash and steel are amongst the materials used.

Das auf einem bewaldeten Grundstück an der Ostküste von Maryland, unweit der Stadt Oxford gelegene Wohnhaus gewährt Ausblicke sowohl auf das Meer als auch auf die umliegende Landschaft. Im Erdgeschoss befinden sich die Küche, Bad und Schlafzimmer. »Um den Wohnraum zu definieren und in die Landschaft hinein auszudehnen«, wurde für die Mauern hauptsächlich der in dieser Gegend übliche Backstein verwendet. Das Obergeschoss nimmt ein großer, offener Wohnraum ein, von dem aus man den Garten und den Fluss Tred Avon überblickt. Hier setzt sich der Ahornboden in der Krümmung des Dachs fort, dessen Außenverkleidung aus feuerverbleitem Kupfer besteht. Der Architekt hebt hervor, dass etliche Elemente des Hauses »schweben und gleiten«, wie etwa der Kamin oder die Badezimmerwand. Dieser Effekt sei durch die Verwendung von Materialien erzielt worden, die mit dem Backstein und Zedernholz der tragenden Wände kontrastieren: feuerverbleites Kupfer, Aluminium, rostfreier und gewöhnlicher Stahl sowie gestrichenes Eschenholz.

Construite sur un terrain boisé de la côte est du Maryland, près d'Oxford, cette résidence bénéficie de vues sur l'océan et le paysage environnant. Le rez-de-chaussée comprend la cuisine, les chambres et les salles de bains. La brique, matériau local, sert à « définir et dilater l'espace des pièces dans le paysage ». L'étage possède un grand séjour ouvert donnant sur le jardin et la Tred Avon River. Le sol en érable se poursuit jusqu'à remonter vers le toit recouvert à l'extérieur de cuivre enduit de plomb. L'architecte insiste sur le fait que de nombreux éléments de la maison « flottent et glissent » comme la cheminée suspendue, ou le mur du cabinet de toilette, effet « atteint grâce au recours à des matériaux qui contrastent avec la brique et le cèdre des murs principaux, comme le cuivre, l'enduit de plomb, l'aluminium, l'acier inoxydable, le hêtre peint et l'acier.

Above, left page, an axonometric view of the house, and on this page a photograph from the garden with the curved roof visible.

Axonometrische Ansicht des Hauses (linke Seite). In der Aufnahme vom Garten aus (oben) zeigt sich auch die Krümmung des Dachs.

En haut, page de gauche, vue axonométrique de la maison, et sur cette page, une photographie prise du jardin qui montre la courbe du toit.

Stained maple flooring continues up the inside curve of the main roof in the living room, above. According to the architect, the "brick walls define and extend the space of the rooms into the landscape."

Oben: Im Wohnzimmer setzt sich der Ahornboden bis in die Krümmung des Hauptdaches fort. Laut Architekt werden die Innenräume durch die Backsteinmauern abgegrenzt und gleichzeitig in die Landschaft hinein ausgedehnt.

En haut, le sol en érable teinté remonte sur la courbe intérieur du toit principal dans le séjour. Selon l'architecte, « les murs de brique définissent l'espace des pièces et le dilatent dans le paysage. »

# LOFT HOUSE

*Philadelphia, Pennsylvania, United States, 1998–99*

Client: Rae Lea. Area: 280 m². Cost: $750,000.

Located in a five story brick building erected in 1876, this **LOFT** renovation makes use of the history of the space to define a new identity. Thus, new walls are seen by the architect as "figured planes grafted onto the existing walls." Since the space had had no less than eight owners and twenty-two documented uses before this intervention, the assumed wealth of experiences accumulated in the space was considerable, leading Wesley Wei to conceive that new elements could be imagined as "parasites" added to the existing volume or "host." This, together with the owners' desire for a "deliberate and sculptured home," formed the basic design format and requirements of the residence.

Bei der Renovierung des **LOFT**s, das sich in einem 1876 erbauten fünfstöckigen Backsteingebäude befindet, nutzte der Architekt die Geschichte der ehemaligen Fabriketage, um ihr eine neue Identität zu geben. So sieht er die neuen Wände als »designte Flächen, die auf die bestehenden Wände aufgepfropft wurden«. Da die Räume vor ihrer Umgestaltung nicht weniger als acht Vorbesitzer hatten und zu 22 verschiedenen Zwecken genutzt wurden, hatte sich in ihnen eine beträchtliche Fülle von Erfahrungen angesammelt. Dies brachte Wesley Wei auf die Idee, die von ihm entworfenen neuen Elemente als »Parasiten« zu definieren, die dem ursprünglichen Baukörper oder »Wirt« hinzugefügt werden. Dieser Gedanke bildete zusammen mit dem Wunsch des neuen Besitzers nach einem »überlegt und bildhauerisch gestalteten Zuhause« das Grundkonzept für das Design und die funktionale Ausstattung der Wohnung.

Cette rénovation de **LOFT** dans un immeuble de brique de cinq niveaux datant de 1876, s'appuie sur l'histoire du lieu pour définir une nouvelle identité. Pour l'architecte, par exemple, les murs sont « des plans figurés greffés sur les existants ». Le loft n'ayant pas compté moins de huit propriétaires précédents et vingt-deux utilisations répertoriées, la richesse d'expériences accumulée était considérable, ce qui a conduit Wesley Wei à penser pouvoir ajouter de nouveaux éléments « parasites » à « l'hôte ». Cette approche et le désir des propriétaires d'un » foyer sculptural témoignant d'une volonté «constituent le concept de base et les contraintes de réalisation de cette résidence.

*A perspective view of the exterior, and right, a detail of a bathroom within this 1876 renovated building.*

*Eine perspektivische Außenansicht und eine Detailaufnahme eines Badezimmers (rechts) in dem 1876 entstandenen, umgebauten Gebäude.*

*Vue perspective de l'extérieur. À droite, détail de salle de bains dans cette construction rénovée datant de 1876.*

To the left below, the kitchen, music and living room. Above, left, the articulation of plaster walls with a built-in desk. Above, the generous, modern spaces of the residence hardly betray the period of the building's origin.

Küche, Musik- und Wohnzimmer (links unten). Die Anordnung der Gipswände mit integriertem Schreibtisch (links oben). Die großzügigen, modernen Wohnräume lassen die Entstehungszeit des Gebäudes kaum erkennen (oben).

À gauche, en bas, la cuisine, la salle de séjour et de musique. En haut, à gauche, l'articulation des murs enduits et d'un bureau intégré. En haut, les généreux espaces modernes de la résidence masquent la date de la construction de l'immeuble.

# WILKINSON EYRE ARCHITECTS

*Wilkinson Eyre Architects*
*Transworld House*
*100 City Road*
*London EC1Y 2BP*
*Great Britain*

*Tel: + 44 20 7608 7900*
*Fax: + 44 20 7608 7901*
*e-mail: info@wilkinsoneyre.com*
*Web: www.wilkinsoneyre.com*

**CHRIS WILKINSON** founded the practice in 1983. He has directed a large number of their key projects, including Stratford Market Depot in London, the Dyson Headquarters in Wiltshire, the Bristol 2000 Science World Building and The Magna Project. He has over thirty years experience in architectural practice, including work with Foster Associates, Michael Hopkins Architects and Richard Rogers & Partners. **JAMES EYRE** has been a Partner/Director of Wilkinson Eyre Architects since 1987 and has been responsible for managing the practice's transportation, bridge and infrastructure projects. He has over 18 years experience in architectural practice, including working with Michael Hopkins Architects for six years prior to joining Wilkinson Eyre in 1986. Amongst the projects of Wilkinson Eyre: The South Quay Footbridge (London, 1998) a 180m span cable-stayed 'S' shaped bridge, winner of a competition for the design of an opening landmark footbridge from Canary Wharf to South Quay held by the London Docklands Development Corporation, winner of the American Institute of Architects Excellence in Design Award, 1999; the Wellcome Wing, Science Museum London. A masterplan and fit-out of the new ground floor exhibition space at the Science Museum, London. Conceived as a "Theatre of Science" within which "performance" occur, the Wellcome Wing gallery explores themes in contemporary science and technology; and the Fenchurch Street City Tower, a 56,900 m², 34 story, 144 m high structure submitted for planning consent in July 2000.

**CHRIS WILKINSON** gründete seine Firma 1983 und hat seither viele bedeutende Aufträge ausgeführt, wie etwa das Stratford Market Depot in London, die Dyson-Zentrale in Wiltshire, das Bristol 2000 Science World Building sowie das Magna-Projekt. Er verfügt über mehr als 30 Jahre praktische Erfahrung in verschiedenen Architekturbereichen, einschließlich seiner Tätigkeiten bei Foster Associates, Michael Hopkins Architects sowie Richard Rogers & Partners. **JAMES EYRE** ist seit 1987 Partner und Direktor bei Wilkinson Eyre Architects und verantwortlich für die Projekte aus den Bereichen Transport, Brückenbau und Infrastruktur. Bevor er sich 1986 mit Chris Wilkinson zusammentat, hatte er über 18 Jahre als Architekt gearbeitet, darunter sechs Jahre lang bei Michael Hopkins Architects. Wilkinson und Eyre entwarfen die Fußgängerbrücke South Quay in London (1998), eine 180 m überspannende, S-förmige Schrägseilbrücke, mit der sie den von der London Docklands Development Corporation ausgeschriebenen Wettbewerb für die Gestaltung einer charakteristischen Fußgängerbrücke zwischen Canary Wharf und South Quay sowie 1999 den vom American Institute of Architects verliehenen Excellence in Design Award gewannen. Zu ihren Projekten zählt auch der Wellcome Wing des Science Museum in London, das aus einem Gesamtplan sowie der Ausstattung neuer Ausstellungsflächen im Erdgeschoss besteht. Der Wellcome Wing ist als ein »Theater der Naturwissenschaften« konzipiert, in dem aktuelle naturwissenschaftliche und technologische Themen didaktisch aufbereitet werden. Zu ihren jüngsten Planungen gehört der Londoner Fenchurch Street City Tower, ein 144 m hoher und 56.900 m² umfassender Hochhausturm mit 34 Stockwerken, dessen Entwurf im Juli 2000 eingereicht wurde.

**CHRIS WILKINSON**, auteur d'un grand nombre de réalisations majeures, dont le Stratford Market Depot à Londres, l'usine et le siège social Dyson dans le Wiltshire, le Bristol 2000 Science World Building et le Magna Project, a fondé son agence en 1983. Au cours de ses 30 ans de carrière, il a été amené à travailler avec Foster Associates, Michael Hopkins Architects et Richard Rogers & Partners. **JAMES EYRE** est associé et directeur de Wilkinson Eyre depuis 1987, responsable des projets dans le domaine des transports, des ponts et des infrastructures. Architecte depuis 18 ans, il a travaillé pour Michael Hopkins Architects pendant six ans avant de rejoindre Wilkinson en 1986. Parmi les projets récents de Wilkinson Eyre : le South Quay Footbridge (Londres, 1998), passerelle à entretoises en S qui a remporté le concours de passerelle monumentale entre Canary Wharf et South Quay organisé par la London Docklands Development Corporation ainsi que l'«Excellence in Design Award» de l'American Institute of Architects en 1999 ; la Wellcome Wing du Science Museum, Londres. Conçue comme un «théâtre de la science» à l'intérieur duquel se déroule un «spectacle», cette galerie explore les thèmes de la science et de la technologie contemporaines ; la Fenchurch Street City Tower, tour de 34 niveaux, 144 m de haut et 56 900 m², qui attend son permis de construire depuis juillet 2000.

# MAGNA

*Rotherham, South Yorkshire, England, 1999–2001*

*Site area: 12 hectares. Funding: Millennium Commission, English Partnerships, ERDF.*
*Cost: £35 million (£17 million for construction).*

A former steelworks was reused to create a landmark building to house the UK's first Science Adventure Centre. The design makes use of the two massive 350-meter long bays that form the main cathedral-like shed that houses the attraction. The architects used computer perspectives, some of which are published here to give an idea of the spectacular interior spaces before they were built. These views recall the illustrations of science fiction cartoons to some extent. As for the actual building, only the old scrap bay and delivery bay on the north side were demolished. The interior of the shed is an awe-inspiring space with a scale and grandeur only hinted at by the exterior. Chris Wilkinson, who headed this project, is the author of "Supersheds," a text on the architecture of long-span, large volume buildings. The design maximizes this quality and retains the extraordinary atmosphere of the building, while creating space for the attractions. Special effects, using the latest technology, are used to explore the elements of earth, air, fire and water – the basic components of the steel making process. The project opened to the public in April 2001, and has proved a popular success with over 100,000 visitors in the first six weeks.

Um das erste Science Adventure Centre Großbritanniens in einem herausragenden Bauwerk unterzubringen, wurde ein ehemaliges Stahlwerk umfunktioniert. Der Entwurf macht sich die beiden massiven, 350 m langen Mauerabschnitte zunutze, die zusammen die kathedralenartige Hauptausstellungshalle bilden. Dazu verwendeten die Architekten Computeransichten, von denen einige hier abgebildet sind, um einen Eindruck von den spektakulären Innenräumen vor ihrer Fertigstellung zu vermitteln. In gewisser Weise erinnern diese Bilder an Sciencefiction-Comics. Außer den alten Schrott- und Anlieferungsplätzen an der Nordseite blieb von dem ursprünglichen Gebäude alles erhalten. Das Innere besteht aus einem gewaltigen Raum, dessen Ausmaß und Großartigkeit von der Fassade nur angedeutet werden. Chris Wilkinson, der Leiter dieses Projekts, ist auch Verfasser eines Textes mit dem Titel »Supersheds«, in dem er über die Architektur von Bauten mit riesiger Spannweite und großen Volumen schreibt. Der hier vorgestellte Entwurf hebt diese besondere Qualität hervor, bewahrt seine besondere Atmosphäre und schafft gleichzeitig Raum für die Besucherattraktionen. Mittels Spezialeffekten und unter Einsatz von neuesten Technologien lassen sich hier die für die Stahlverarbeitung grundlegenden Elemente Erde, Luft, Feuer und Wasser erkunden. Das Wissenschaftsmuseum wurde im April 2001 eröffnet und hat sich mit einer Besucherzahl von über 100.000 in den ersten sechs Wochen bereits als voller Erfolg erwiesen.

C'est une ancienne aciérie qui a servi de base à ce bâtiment monumental qui abrite le premier « Centre de l'aventure de la Science » britannique. Le projet a réutilisé deux massives travées de 350 m de long qui constituent un hall aux dimensions de cathédrale. Les architectes ont réalisé des images de synthèse pour mieux faire comprendre le caractère spectaculaire des volumes à créer, dont le rendu n'est pas éloigné de certaines bandes dessinées de science-fiction. Seules les anciennes sections réservées à la récupération et aux livraisons ont été démolies. Le volume du hall est aussi impressionnant de l'intérieur que de l'extérieur. Chris Wilkinson, responsable du projet, est l'auteur de *Supersheds*, un texte sur l'architecture des hypervolumes sous couverture de longue portée. La conception a joué au maximum sur l'effet de gigantisme et préservé l'atmosphère extraordinaire de l'ancien bâtiment, tout en laissant la place nécessaire aux présentations. Des effets spéciaux à base de lasers permettent d'explorer les quatre éléments fondamentaux – air, eau, terre, feu – qui sont aussi à la base de la fabrication de l'acier. Magna réussit mieux que d'autres installations de ce type à attirer le grand public.

While much of the exterior of the industrial building has remained intact, within, its spectacular spaces have been ably converted to their new use. On the following double-page, a computer perspective shows the interior facility devoted to "air."

Während ein Großteil der Außenfassade dieses Industriegebäudes erhalten blieb, wurden seine spektakulären Innenräume geschickt für ihre neue Nutzung umfunktioniert. Auf der folgenden Doppelseite zeigt eine Computeransicht die dem Thema »Luft« gewidmete Abteilung.

Si, vu de l'extérieur, l'essentiel du bâtiment industriel est resté intact, les volumes intérieurs ont été entièrement convertis à leur nouvel usage. Double page suivante : une perspective en image numérique montre la partie consacrée à l'air.

Interior lighting contributes to
the awe-inspiring aspect of the
cavernous spaces. To the right,
the "air" exhibit, seen in the form
of a computer perspective in the
previous double-page.

Die Innenbeleuchtung trägt zu der
beeindruckenden Wirkung der höhlenartigen Räume bei. Der auf der
vorhergehenden Doppelseite als Com-
puterbild dargestellte Ausstellungs-
bereich »Luft« (rechts).

L'éclairage intérieur renforce l'aspect
impressionnant de ces espaces caverneux. À droite : « l'air » présenté dans
la double page précédente en image
de synthèse.

# TOD WILLIAMS, BILLIE TSIEN & ASSOCIATES

*Tod Williams, Billie Tsien & Associates*
*222 Central Park South*
*New York, NY 10019*
*United States*

*Tel: + 1 212 582 2385*
*Fax: + 1 212 245 1984*
*e-mail: mail@twbta.com*
*Web: www.twbta.com*

**TOD WILLIAMS**, born in Detroit in 1943, Bachelor of Arts, 1965, Master of Fine Arts, 1967 Princeton University. After six years as Associate Architect in the office of Richard Meier in New York, he began his own practice in New York in 1974. He taught at the Cooper Union for more than 15 years and has also taught at Harvard, Yale, the University of Virginia, and Southern California Institute of Architecture. Tod Williams received a mid-career Prix de Rome in 1983. **BILLIE TSIEN** was born in Ithaca, New York, in 1949. She received her Bachelor of Arts at Yale, and her Masters of Architecture from UCLA (1977). She has been a painter, and a graphic designer (1971–1975). She has taught at Parsons School of Design, Southern California Institute of Architecture (SCI-ARC), Harvard and Yale. Their built work includes: Feinberg Hall (Princeton, New Jersey, 1986); New College, University of Virginia (Charlottesville, Virginia, 1992); as well as the renovation and extension of the Museum of Fine Arts in Phoenix, Arizona (1996). Recent projects include the Williams Natatorium – phase 1 for the Cranbrook Academy (Bloomfield Michigan); the Museum of American Folk Art in New York published here, and the John Hopkins University Student Arts Center (Baltimore, Maryland).

**TOD WILLIAMS**, geboren 1943 in Detroit, erwarb 1965 den Bachelor of Arts und 1967 den Master of Fine Arts an der Princeton University. Nach sechsjähriger Mitarbeit im New Yorker Büro von Richard Meier machte er sich 1974 mit einem eigenen Architekturbüro in New York selbständig. Er lehrte mehr als 15 Jahre an der Cooper Union, in Harvard und Yale, der University of Virginia und am Southern California Institute of Architecture (SCI-Arc). 1983 wurde Tod Williams der Prix de Rome verliehen. **BILLIE TSIEN**, geboren 1949 in Ithaca, New York, erwarb den Bachelor of Arts an der Yale University und 1977 den Master of Architecture an der University of California, Los Angeles (UCLA). Von 1971 bis 1975 arbeitete sie als Malerin und Grafikerin. Außerdem lehrte sie an der Parsons School of Design, am SCI-Arc, in Harvard und Yale. Zu den wichtigsten Bauten von Williams und Tsien gehören die Feinberg Hall in Princeton, New Jersey (1986), das New College der University of Virginia in Charlottesville (1992) sowie der Umbau des Museums of Fine Arts in Phoenix, Arizona (1996). Zu ihren jüngsten Projekten zählen das Williams Natatorium – Phase 1 für die Cranbrook Academy in Bloomfield, Michigan, das hier vorgestellte Museum of American Folk Art in New York und das Student Arts Center der John Hopkins University in Baltimore, Maryland.

**TOD WILLIAMS** est né à Detroit en 1943. B. A. en 1965, M. F. A. en 1967, Princeton University. Après avoir été pendant six ans architecte associé auprès de Richard Meier (1967–73), il crée son agence à New York en 1974. Il enseigne pendant plus de 15 ans à Harvard, Yale, l'Université de Virginie, et au Southern California Institute of Architecture (SCI-Arc). Prix de Rome en 1983. **BILLIE TSIEN**, née à Ithaca, New York, en 1949, B. Arch., Yale, M. Arch., UCLA, 1977, a été peintre et graphiste de 1971 à 1975, et a enseigné à la Parsons School of Design, SCI-Arc, Harvard et Yale. Parmi leurs réalisations : Feinberg Hall (Princeton, New Jersey, 1986) ; New College, University of Virginia (Charlottesville, Virginie, 1992) ; restauration complète et extension du Museum of Fine Arts de Phoenix (Phoenix, Arizona,1996). Parmi leurs projets récents : le Williams Natatorium – phase I, pour Cranbrook Academy (Bloomfield, Michigan), le Museum of American Folk Art (New York) et le John Hopkins University Student Arts Center (Baltimore, Maryland).

# MUSEUM OF AMERICAN FOLK ART

*New York, New York, United States, 1999–2001*

*Cost: $25 million. Gallery area: 1,170 m². Collection: 3,500 objects.*

Set just next to the Museum of Modern Art on 53rd Street, the **MUSEUM OF AMERICAN FOLK ART** is an entirely new eight level 3,000 square meter building with about 1,400 square meters of exhibition space. It contains a library, store, cafe and offices as well as the galleries. Although the architects did not design the specific displays for the museum, many of the larger, more significant objects were placed by them. This is in particular true of the public spaces such as the entrance hall and stairwell. As they have in other cases, the architects engaged in a series of rich confrontations of different materials ranging from a green fiberglass screen running along the main stair to the surprising metal facade on 53rd Street. Daylight is brought into the building from the topmost levels, filtering down along slit openings through each floor. Alternating rough finish and polished concrete, they obtain a sensuality in the materials that is unusual in such a building in the heart of Manhattan.

Das **MUSEUM OF AMERICAN FOLK ART** liegt direkt neben dem Museum of Modern Art an der 53rd Street. Das komplett neu errichtete Gebäude hat acht Stockwerke und 3.000 m² Nutzfläche, von denen circa 1.400 m² für Ausstellungsräume vorgesehen sind. Außerdem enthält es eine Bibliothek, einen Museumsshop, ein Café und Büros. Auch wenn die eigentlichen Ausstellungsräume nicht von den beiden Architekten ausgestaltet wurden, stammen etliche der größeren und signifikanteren Einrichtungsobjekte von ihnen, insbesondere in den öffentlichen Bereichen wie Eingangshalle und Treppenhaus. Wie schon in anderen Bauten haben Williams und Tsien auch hier eine Fülle verschiedener, miteinander kontrastierender Materialien eingesetzt, von einer grünen Glasfaserblende, die entlang der Haupttreppe verläuft, bis zu der auffallenden Metallfassade an der 53rd Street. Das vom Dachgeschoss einfallende Tageslicht dringt durch Fensterschlitze in alle Stockwerke vor. Im Wechsel von roh bearbeiteten Oberflächen und geschliffenem Beton erzielen die Architekten eine Sinnlichkeit in den Materialien, die für ein Gebäude im Herzen Manhattans ungewöhnlich ist.

Juste à côté du Museum of Modern Art sur 53th Street, le **MUSEUM OF AMERICAN FOLK ART** est un bâtiment entièrement nouveau de huit niveaux et 3 000 m², qui comprend des espaces d'expositions de 1 400 m², une bibliothèque, une boutique, un café et des bureaux. Si les architectes n'ont pas conçu la présentation des collections, la plupart des œuvres significatives ont été implantées par eux. C'est en particulier le cas dans les espaces publics comme le hall d'entrée et la cage d'escalier. Comme dans leurs autres réalisations, ils ont organisé une série de confrontations entre divers matériaux allant de l'écran de fibre de verre vert le long de l'escalier principal à la surprenante façade métallique sur la rue. La lumière naturelle est canalisée à partir des niveaux supérieurs et se fraye son chemin par des fentes aménagées à chaque niveau. L'alternance de béton poli ou brut crée une sensualité de matériaux inhabituelle dans ce type de bâtiment au cœur de Manhattan.

*Adjoining a lot presently under construction for the Museum of Modern Art, the eight-story Museum of American Folk Art is just 12 meters wide. Its irregular metal facade gives the building a distinct presence in the street.*

*Das achtstöckige und nur 12 m breite American Museum of Folk Art grenzt an das Grundstück des Museum of Modern Art, an dem derzeit gebaut wird. Durch seine unregelmäßig geformte Metallfassade tritt das Gebäude im Straßenbild deutlich hervor.*

*Adjacent à une parcelle en construction pour le Museum of Modern Art, le Museum of Folk Art et ses six niveaux ne mesure que 12 m de large. Ses façades métalliques irrégulières lui confèrent une présence urbaine particulière.*

Certain works were placed by the architects including the large weather vane in the form of an American Indian (left page, upper left). The architects' subtle use of surfaces and materials gives a richness to the relatively modest-sized space.

Mehrere Exponate, wie etwa die Wetterfahne in Gestalt eines Indianers (linke Seite, oben links), wurden von den Architekten platziert. Der raffinierte Einsatz von Oberflächen und Materialien bereichert den relativ kleinen Innenraum.

Certaines œuvres ont été mises en place par les architectes dont la girouette en forme d'Indien américain (page de gauche, en haut à gauche). Le recours subtil des architectes au traitement des surfaces et des matériaux confère une certaine richesse aux espaces de petites dimensions.

# JEAN-MICHEL WILMOTTE

Jean-Michel Wilmotte
Wilmotte & Associés SA
68, rue du Faubourg Saint-Antoine
75012 Paris
France

Tel: + 33 1 53 02 22 22
Fax: + 33 1 43 44 17 11
e-mail: wilmotte@wanadoo.fr

Born in 1948, a graduate of the Camondo School in Paris, **JEAN-MICHEL WILMOTTE** created his own firm, Governor, in 1975. Although he is best known for his work in interior design, including private apartments for François Mitterrand in the Élysée Palace, Wilmotte joined the Order of Architects in France in 1993. With approximately 60 employees, his office works on industrial and furniture design, such as the new lighting fixtures and benches installed on the Champs-Élysées, but he also participated in the competition for the British Museum, making use of the experience he gathered as architect of the Decorative Arts Department of the Louvre for the Richelieu Wing, completed in 1993. As an architect, Jean-Michel Wilmotte completed two buildings in Tokyo, the International Executive Offices Building in the Shinjuku area, and the New N°3 Arai Building, while he also carried out the furniture design for the Bank of Luxembourg building, completed by Arquitectonica in 1994. He recently completed the Gana Art Center, Seoul (South Korea, 1996–1998) and a museum for the presents given to French President Jacques Chirac in Sarran, France. Current work includes the design of a new boutique concept for Cartier (Paris, Milan, New York, Los Angeles, Tokyo), the MK2 Cinema complex in Paris, and the construction of offices, hotels and residences near the station in Antwerp, Belgium.

**JEAN-MICHEL WILMOTTE**, geboren 1948, studierte an der École Nissim de Camondo in Paris und gründete 1975 seine eigene Firma namens Governor. Obwohl er vor allem als Innenarchitekt bekannt wurde – so gestaltete er zum Beispiel die Privatwohnung des damaligen Staatspräsidenten François Mitterand im Élysée-Palast –, trat er 1993 dem französischen Ordre des Architectes bei. Mit seinen circa 60 Mitarbeitern ist das Büro hauptsächlich in den Bereichen Industrie- und Möbeldesign tätig und hat zum Beispiel die neuen Beleuchtungskörper und Sitzbänke auf den Champs-Élysées entworfen. Außerdem hat Jean-Michel Wilmotte auch am Wettbewerb für die Ausstattung des British Museum teilgenommen, wobei er die Erfahrungen nutzen konnte, die er als Architekt der 1993 fertig gestellten Abteilung für Angewandte Kunst im Richelieu-Flügel des Louvre erworben hatte. Zu seinen Bauprojekten gehören das International Executive Offices Building und das New N°3 Arai-Gebäude, beide in Tokio, das Gana Art Center in Seoul, Südkorea (1996–98), sowie ein Museum für Geschenke, die der französische Präsident Jacques Chirac auf seinen Staatsbesuchen erhalten hatte, in Sarran, Frankreich. Er entwarf auch die Möbel für das 1994 von Arquitectonica realisierte Gebäude der Bank von Luxemburg. Zu seinen jüngsten Arbeiten zählen ein neues Einrichtungskonzept für die Cartier-Niederlassungen in Paris, Mailand, New York, Los Angeles und Tokio, der Kinokomplex MK2 in Paris sowie eine Anlage von Büros, Hotels und Wohnhäusern in Antwerpen.

Né en 1948, diplômé de l'École Camondo à Paris, **JEAN-MICHEL WILMOTTE** crée l'agence Governor, en 1975. Surtout connu pour ses travaux d'architecture intérieure – dont une partie des appartements privés du président Mitterrand à l'Élysée –, il s'inscrit à l'ordre des architectes en 1993. Comptant environ 60 collaborateurs, son agence qui intervient également sur le design de mobilier public comme les nouveaux bancs et lampadaires des Champs-Élysées, ou le mobilier de la Banque du Luxembourg d'Arquitectonica, a également participé au concours du British Museum, mettant à profit son expérience de l'architecture du département des arts décoratifs du Louvre (1993). Jean-Michel Wilmotte a réalisé deux immeubles à Tokyo, l'International Executive Offices Building dans le quartier de Shinjuku, et le New N°3 Arai Building ; le Gana Art Center (Séoul, Corée du Sud, 1996–98), le Musée des cadeaux reçus par le président Chirac (Sarran, France, 2000). Parmi ses interventions récentes : un nouveau concept de boutique pour Cartier (Paris, Milan, New York, Los Angeles, Tokyo), le complexe de cinémas MK2 à Paris et la construction de bureaux, hôtels, et résidences près de la gare d'Anvers (Belgique).

# CONTEMPORARY ART CENTER

*Hamon Donation, Issy-les-Moulineaux, France, 2002–04*

*Client: Syndicat Mixte de l'Ile St Germain. Area: 6,434 m², 150 hectares (site area).
Cost: 11,717,632 euros (planned budget).*

This **CONTEMPORARY ART CENTER** will be located in a park (on the Île Saint-Germain) on the banks of the Seine not far from the planned Pinault Foundation, to be designed by Tadao Ando. The concept is to place a low horizontal volume between two old existing walls. With sculptures placed inside and outside, there will be a sense of continuity between the garden and the interior. Natural overhead lighting and frequent openings toward the exterior will permit visitors to orient themselves and to appreciate the works of art in excellent conditions. The areas around the building, including the gardens, are intended as a natural prolongation of the architecture itself. Lifted up off the ground 80 centimeters in case of flooding from the Seine, a basic exhibition space 62 meters long by 26 meters wide and 7 meters high on the ground level can be subdivided to create more intimate spaces. Built in reinforced concrete with a metal frame, the building will have a concrete and white stone cladding. Oak floors are planned for most interior spaces with an Hainault type stone for the entrance area.

Das **ZENTRUM FÜR ZEITGENÖSSISCHE KUNST** wird in einem Park auf der Île Saint-Germain, am Ufer der Seine unweit der Fondation Pinault liegen, die Tadao Ando entwerfen wird. Das Konzept sieht einen horizontalen Flachbau zwischen zwei alten, bereits bestehenden Mauern vor. Durch die sowohl innen als auch außen aufgestellten Skulpturen wird ein Gefühl der Kontinuität zwischen Garten und Innenraum hergestellt. Oberlichter und zahlreiche Fensteröffnungen ermöglichen den Besuchern, sich zu orientieren und die Kunstwerke unter optimalen Bedingungen zu betrachten. Die das Gebäude umgebenden Bereiche wie Park und Garten sind so konzipiert, dass sie wie eine natürliche Erweiterung der Architektur wirken. Im Untergeschoss, das für den Fall, dass die Seine über die Ufer tritt, um 80 cm erhöht ist, befindet sich ein Ausstellungsraum mit 62 m Länge, 26 m Breite und 7 m Wandhöhe, der in mehrere kleinere und überschaubarere Räume unterteilt werden kann. Das aus Stahlbeton mit einer Metallrahmenkonstruktion errichtete Gebäude wird mit Beton und weißem Stein verkleidet. Für den größten Teil der Innenräume sind Eichenböden geplant, während die Eingangshalle mit einem Hainault-artigen Stein ausgestattet wird.

Ce **CENTRE D'ART CONTEMPORAIN** s'élèvera dans un parc de l'île Saint-Germain au milieu de la Seine, non loin de la Fondation Pinault que va réaliser Tadao Ando. Le concept est celui d'un volume horizontal bas pris entre deux murs anciens existants. Le placement des sculptures à l'intérieur et à l'extérieur assurera un sentiment de continuité entre le jardin et l'intérieur. L'éclairage naturel zénithal et les nombreuses ouvertures sur l'extérieur permettront aux visiteurs de s'orienter et d'apprécier les œuvres dans d'excellentes conditions. Les zones autour du bâtiment, y compris les jardins, se veulent un prolongement naturel de l'architecture. Surélevé du sol de 80 cm pour se protéger des débordements de la Seine, l'espace principal de 62 m de long par 26 de large et 7 de haut peut être divisé pour créer des espaces plus intimes. Construit en béton armé sur ossature d'acier, le bâtiment sera habillé de béton et de pierre blanche. La plupart des sols devraient être en chêne à l'exception de celui de l'entrée, en pierre du Hainault.

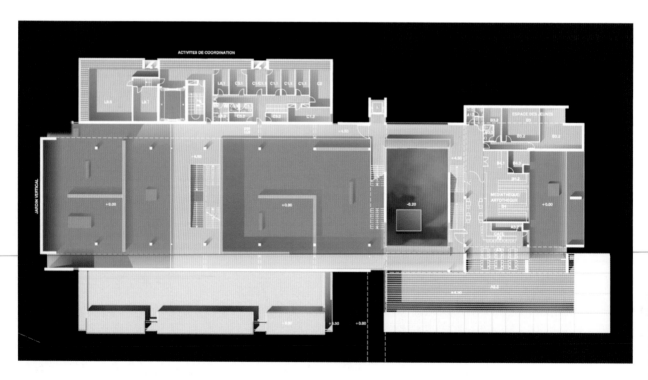

Wilmotte's drawings give a sense of the space of the future center, whose layout is simple, and takes into account the most rigorous standards for the exhibition of art.

Wilmottes Zeichnungen vermitteln einen Eindruck von der räumlichen Gestaltung des zukünftigen Kunstzentrums. Das Gebäude hat einen schlichten Grundriss und entspricht höchsten Anforderungen für die Präsentation von Kunst.

Les dessins de Wilmotte précisent le sentiment d'espace que donnera ce futur centre artistique. De plan simple, il obéit aux standards d'exposition les plus rigoureux.

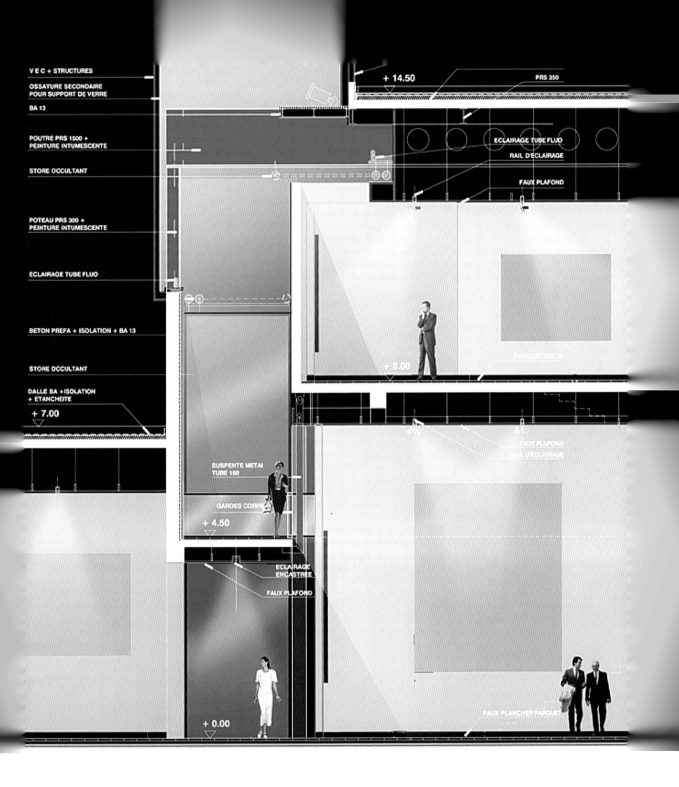

V E C + STRUCTURES

OSSATURE SECONDAIRE
POUR SUPPORT DE VERRE

BA 13

POUTRE PRS 1500 +
PEINTURE INTUMESCENTE

STORE OCCULTANT

POTEAU PRS 300 +
PEINTURE INTUMESCENTE

ECLAIRAGE TUBE FLUO

BETON PREFA + ISOLATION + BA 13

STORE OCCULTANT

DALLE BA +ISOLATION
+ ETANCHEITE

+ 7.00

SUSPENTE METAL
TUBE 150

GARDES CORPS

+ 4.50

ECLAIRAGE
ENCASTREE

FAUX PLAFOND

+ 0.00

+ 14.50

PRS 350

ECLAIRAGE TUBE FLUO

RAIL D'ECLAIRAGE

FAUX PLAFOND

+ 8.00

PARQUET COLLE

FAUX PLAFOND
RAIL D'ECLAIRAGE

FAUX PLANCHER PARQUET

Public spaces around the building will extend its area in the summer months, rendering its proximity along the Seine to other future museums like the Pinault Foundation all the more palpable.

Um das Gebäude herum angelegte öffentliche Räume werden das Museum in den Sommermonaten nach außen erweitern und damit seine Nähe zu anderen am Seine-Ufer geplanten Institutionen wie der Fondation Pinault umso stärker sichtbar werden lassen.

Les espaces publics qui entourent le bâtiment permettront d'accroître sa surface en été et rendront la proximité d'un autre futur grand musée voisin, la Fondation Pinault, encore plus palpable.

# INDEX OF PLACES

# CREDITS

## PHOTO CREDITS

**CREDITS PLANS / DRAWINGS / CAD DOCUMENTS**

# *"Case Study Houses*: once you hold it in your hands, you immediately want to get a martini and sit by one of the pools."

—*Literaturen*, Berlin

**Case Study Houses** Elizabeth A.T. Smith / Ed. Peter Gössel
English/German/French / Hardcover, format: 40 x 31 cm (15.7 x 12.2 in.),
464 pp. / US$ 150 / £ 100 / € 150 / ¥ 20.000

"You need a California workout to lift [it], but the book, an exhaustive homage to the houses, is worth the effort."
—*The New York Times*, New York

The Case Study House program (1945–1966) was an exceptional, innovative event in the history of American architecture and remains to this day unequalled in its uniqueness. The program, which concentrated on the Los Angeles area and oversaw the design of 36 prototype homes, sought to make available plans for modern residences that could be easily and cheaply constructed during the postwar building boom. The program's chief motivating force was *Arts & Architecture* editor John Entenza, a champion of modernism who had all the right connections to attract some of architecture's greatest talents, such as Richard Neutra, Charles and Ray Eames, and Eero Saarinen.

Highly experimental, the program generated houses that were designed to redefine the modern home, and thus had a pro-nounced influence on architecture—American and international—both during its existence and even to this day. TASCHEN brings you a monumental retrospective of the entire program with comprehensive documentation, brilliant photographs from the period and, for the houses still in existence, contemporary photos, as well as extensive floor plans and sketches.

*"Lavishly produced, handsomely illustrated.... Five of the program's surviving architects met at the Museum of Contemporary Art in downtown Los Angeles, [where] TASCHEN hosted a reception and book-signing... a rare and timely reunion. Audience members bought copies of the book and waited patiently in line for half an hour to get them signed." —*L.A. Times

The author: **Elizabeth A.T. Smith**, Chief Curator at the Museum of Contemporary Art in Chicago since 1999, was formerly Curator at The Museum of Contemporary Art, Los Angeles. She was Adjunct Professor in the School of Fine Arts' Public Art Studies Program at the University of Southern California in Los Angeles and has published and lectured widely on a variety of topics in contemporary art and architecture.

The editor: **Peter Gössel** runs a practice for museum and exhibition design. He previously edited numerous volumes on architecture for TASCHEN, such as *Neutra, Architecture in the Twentieth Century, Julius Shulman*, and *John Lautner*.